S/O
£70.40

THE UNIVERSITY OF BOLTON
365474

*Advances in*

# COMPUTERS

## VOLUME 72

# Advances in COMPUTERS

## High Performance Computing

*EDITED BY*


MARVIN V. ZELKOWITZ

Department of Computer Science
University of Maryland
College Park, Maryland



VOLUME 72

AMSTERDAM • BOSTON • HEIDELBERG • LONDON • NEW YORK • OXFORD
PARIS • SAN DIEGO • SAN FRANCISCO • SINGAPORE • SYDNEY • TOKYO
Academic Press is an imprint of Elsevier

BIB 144320

Academic Press is an imprint of Elsevier
84 Theobald's Road, London WC1X 8RR, UK
Radarweg 29, PO Box 211, 1000 AE Amsterdam, The Netherlands
30 Corporate Drive, Suite 400, Burlington, MA 01803, USA
525 B Street, Suite 1900, San Diego, CA 92101-4495, USA

First edition 2008

Copyright © 2008 Elsevier Inc. All rights reserved.

No part of this publication may be reproduced, stored in a retrieval system or transmitted in any form or by any means electronic, mechanical, photocopying, recording or otherwise without the prior written permission of the publisher.

Permissions may be sought directly from Elsevier's Science & Technology Rights Department in Oxford, UK: phone (+44) (0) 1865 843830; fax (+44) (0) 1865 853333; email: permissions@elsevier.com. Alternatively you can submit your request online by visiting the Elsevier web site at http://elsevier.com/locate/permissions, and selecting *Obtaining permission to use Elsevier material*.

Notice
No responsibility is assumed by the publisher for any injury and/or damage to persons or property as a matter of products liability, negligence or otherwise, or from any use or operation of any methods, products, instructions or ideas contained in the material herein.

ISBN: 978-0-12-374411-1

ISSN: 0065-2458

For information on all Academic Press publications visit our website at elsevierdirect.com

Printed and bound in USA

08 09 10 11 12 10 9 8 7 6 5 4 3 2 1

Working together to grow libraries in developing countries

www.elsevier.com | www.bookaid.org | www.sabre.org

ELSEVIER BOOK AID International Sabre Foundation

# Contents



## DARPA's HPCS Program: History, Models, Tools, Languages

**Jack Dongarra, Robert Graybill, William Harrod, Robert Lucas, Ewing Lusk, Piotr Luszczek, Janice McMahon, Allan Snavely, Jeffrey Vetter, Katherine Yelick, Sadaf Alam, Roy Campbell, Laura Carrington, Tzu-Yi Chen, Omid Khalili, Jeremy Meredith and Mustafa Tikir**



## Productivity in High-Performance Computing

**Thomas Sterling and Chirag Dekate**

## Performance Prediction and Ranking of Supercomputers

**Tzu-Yi Chen, Omid Khalili, Roy L. Campbell, Jr., Laura Carrington, Mustafa M. Tikir and Allan Snavely**



## Sampled Processor Simulation: A Survey

**Lieven Eeckhout**

## Distributed Sparse Matrices for Very High Level Languages

**John R. Gilbert, Steve Reinhardt and Viral B. Shah**



## Bibliographic Snapshots of High-Performance/High-Productivity Computing

**Myron Ginsberg**

# Contributors

**Sadaf R. Alam** is a research staff member in the Future Technologies Group at Oak Ridge National Laboratory's Computer Science and Mathematics Division. Her research interests include scientific high-performance computing and architecture for high-end computing platforms. She received her PhD in Computer Science from the University of Edinburgh.

**Roy L. Campbell**, Jr., received his Ph.D. from Mississippi State University. He is currently employed by the Army Research Laboratory as a computer engineer and is a technical advisor to the Deputy Director of the DoD HPC Modernisation Program.

**Laura Nett Carrington** received her Ph.D. degree in Chemical Engineering from the University of California, San Diego, and has experience in high-performance computing benchmarking, programming and linear algebra software. Her engineering background is in the numerical and experimental investigation of the detailed kinetics of catalytic reactions through porous medium. She is currently working in the PMaC lab at SDSC in the areas of performance prediction and benchmarking of HPC systems.

**Tzu-Yi Chen** received her Ph.D. in Computer Science from the University of California at Berkeley. She is currently an Assistant Professor in the Computer Science Department at Pomona College. Her research interests include sparse matrix computations and performance modelling.

**Chirag Dekate** is a Ph.D. candidate at the Department of Computer Science at Louisiana State University. He received his Masters in System Science and Bachelors in Computer Science from Louisiana State university in 2004 and 2002, respectively. His research interests include parallel symbolic computing, parallel algorithms for solving dynamic graph problems, run-time scheduling and machine intelligence.

**Jack Dongarra** holds an appointment as University Distinguished Professor of Computer Science in the Electrical Engineering and Computer Science Department at the University of Tennessee and holds the title of Distinguished Research Staff in the Computer Science and Mathematics Division at Oak Ridge National Laboratory (ORNL), Turing Fellow in the Computer Science and Mathematics Schools at the University of Manchester, and an Adjunct Professor in the Computer Science Department at Rice University. He specialises in numerical algorithms in linear algebra, parallel computing, use of advanced-computer architectures, programming methodology and tools for parallel computers. His research includes the development, testing and documentation of high-quality mathematical software. He has contributed to the design and implementation of the following open source software packages and systems: EISPACK, LINPACK, the BLAS, LAPACK, ScaLAPACK, Netlib, PVM, MPI, NetSolve, Top500, ATLAS, Open-MPI, and PAPI. He has published approximately 200 articles, papers, reports and technical memoranda and is the co-author of several books. He is a Fellow of the AAAS, ACM and the IEEE and a member of the National Academy of Engineering.

**Lieven Eeckhout** is an Assistant Professor in the Department of Electronics and Information Systems (ELIS) at Ghent University, Belgium, and a Postdoctoral Fellow of the Fund for Scientific Research – Flanders (Belgium) (F.W.O. Vlaanderen). His research interests include computer architecture, virtual machines, performance analysis and modelling, and workload characterisation. He obtained his PhD in Computer Science and Engineering from Ghent University in December 2002. He can be contacted at leeckhou@elis.UGent.be.

**John R. Gilbert** received his Ph.D. in Computer Science at Stanford University in 1981. From 1981 to 1988, he was a Computer Science faculty at Cornell University. In 1988, he moved to Xerox PARC, where he performed and directed research in parallel computing, computational geometry, languages and compilers for high-performance computing and mathematical algorithms and software. In 1997, he founded the Computation and Matter Area at PARC, the projects of which included distributed data analysis for collaborating sensors, meso-scale MEMS for active surfaces and modular robotics. In 2002, Dr. Gilbert joined the Computer Science Department and the Computational Science and Engineering program at the University of California, Santa Barbara, where he leads research in high-performance computing, interactive supercomputing and combinatorial and sparse matrix algorithms for scientific computation. Dr. Gilbert has served in the Council of the Society for Industrial and Applied Mathematics, has chaired the SIAM Activity Group on Supercomputing and the ACM Special Interest Group on Numerical Mathematics, and has served as the editor for several journals in computational science and applied mathematics.

**Myron Ginsberg** is an independent HPC consultant with scientific and engineering computing expertise in private industry and government research labs as well as extensive faculty experience in academia. He has focused his research and development efforts on evaluating hardware and software performance for large-scale scientific and engineering applications in industrial environments. He was significantly involved in General Motors' initial and continuing supercomputer efforts and was instrumental in initiating the first in-house installation of a supercomputer in the world automotive community at General Motors Research. He was so recognized by the Association for Computing Machinery (ACM) that honored him as an ACM Fellow. He has served as a distinguished national lecturer in HPC and computational science for six professional societies. Myron has a BA and MA in Math and a Ph.D. in Computer Science. He is a member of The Councils of Advisors in HPC for the Gerson Lehrman Group which provides collaborative research and consulting to the financial community.

**Robert Graybill**, representing University of Southern California Information Sciences Institute (ISI) at the Council of Competitiveness, is leading the formation of an advanced national high-performance computing (HPC) collaborative system that will link companies, universities and national laboratories together to share high-performance computing systems and computational science expertise. Mr. Graybill has an extensive background in embedded and high-performance computing, with over 30 years of experience in the defense, government and commercial industry. Before joining ISI, he spent six years at DARPA, where he designed, developed and implemented six new transformational programs in high-end computing architectures and responsive embedded computing hardware, software and network systems. These programs were coordinated with other government agencies, laboratories, federally funded research and development centers and non-profit organisations. He was a member of the Senior Science Team, leading a number of government-sponsored studies in high-end computing, including the Defense Science Board task force on DoD Supercomputing Needs and the High-End Computing Revitalisation Task Force.

Before joining DARPA, Mr. Graybill worked in advanced research, development, flight testing, and production for radar, sonar, electronic warfare, space surveillance systems and commercial products in organisations such as Westinghouse, Motorola, Martin Marietta Naval Systems, Martin Marietta Corporate Laboratories, Sanders and Lockheed Martin Government Electronic Systems.

**William Harrod** joined DARPA IPTO in December 2005. His area of interest is extreme computing, including a current focus on advanced computer architectures and system productivity. This includes self-monitoring and self-healing processing,

ExaScale computing systems, highly productive development environments and high-performance, advanced compilers.

Building on over 20 years of algorithmic, application, and high-performance processing computing experience in industry, academics and government, Dr. Harrod has a broad background in computing challenges. Before he was employed at DARPA, he was awarded a technical fellowship for the intelligence community while employed at Silicon Graphics Incorporated (SGI). Before this, at SGI, Dr. Harrod led technical teams developing specialised processors and advanced algorithms and high-performance software. Dr. Harrod holds a B.S. in Mathematics from Emory University and a M.S. and a Ph.D. in Mathematics from the University of Tennessee.

**Omid Khalili** received his BA in Mathematics–Computer Science from the University of California at San Diego in 2005 followed by his MS in Computer Science in 2007. His interests lie in parallel computing and large-scale systems.

**Robert F. Lucas** is the Director of the Computational Sciences Division of the University of Southern California's Information Sciences Institute (ISI). There he manages research in computer architecture, VLSI, compilers and other software tools. Before joining ISI, he was the Head of the High-Performance Computing Research Department in the National Energy Research Scientific Computing Center (NERSC) at Lawrence Berkeley National Laboratory. There he oversaw work in scientific data management, visualisation, numerical algorithms and scientific applications. Before joining NERSC, Dr. Lucas was the Deputy Director of DARPA's Information Technology Office. He also served as DARPA's Program Manager for Scalable Computing Systems and Data-Intensive Computing. From 1988 to 1998, he was a member of the research staff of the Institute for Defense Analyses, Center for Computing Sciences. From 1979 to 1984, he was a member of the Technical Staff of the Hughes Aircraft Company. Dr. Lucas received his BS, MS and PhD degrees in Electrical Engineering from Stanford University in 1980, 1983 and 1988, respectively.

**Ewing 'Rusty' Lusk** is director of the Mathematics and Computer Science Division at Argonne National Laboratory and an Argonne Distinguished Fellow. He received his B.A. in mathematics from the University of Notre Dame in 1965 and his Ph.D. in mathematics from the University of Maryland in 1970. He was a professor of computer science at Northern Illinois University before joining Argonne in 1982. His current research interests include programming models for scalable parallel computing, implementation issues for the MPI Message-Passing Interface standard, parallel performance analysis tools and system software for large-scale machines. He is the author of five books and more than a hundred research articles in mathematics, automated deduction and parallel computing.

**Piotr Luszczek** received his MSc degree from the University of Mining and Metallurgy in Krakow, Poland, for work on parallel out-of-core libraries. He earned his doctorate degree for the innovative use of dense matrix computational kernels in sparse direct and iterative numerical linear algebra algorithms at the University of Tennessee. He applied this experience to develop fault-tolerant libraries that used out-of-core techniques. Currently, he is a Research Professor at the University of Tennessee, Knoxville. His work involves standardisation of benchmarking of large supercomputer installations. He is an author of self-adapting software libraries that automatically choose the best algorithm to efficiently utilise available hardware and can optimally process the input data. He is also involved in high-performance programming language design and implementation.

**Janice Onanian McMahon** received B.S. and M.S. degrees in Computer Science from MIT in 1989. She has many years of experience in the radar, sonar and high-performance computing industries. Her specific expertise includes application mapping and software development for massively parallel processors. She was among the first to implement radar processing on large-scale SIMD architectures for Raytheon Company. She has worked as a system engineer for MasPar Computer Corporation where she ran high-performance benchmarks in the areas of computational holography, computational biology and database processing as well as signal processing. She spent 9 years at MIT Lincoln Laboratory, where she contributed to system implementations involving a first-of-its-kind massively parallel processor for space-time adaptive processing and was also a principal investigator for DARPA architecture research programs. She is currently a project leader at USC Information Sciences Institute, where she is overseeing projects that involve cognitive and multi-core architectures and is specifically interested in issues pertaining to run-time resource allocation and dynamic code generation for those architectures.

**Jeremy Meredith** is a computer scientist in the Future Technologies Group at the Oak Ridge National Laboratory's Computer Science and Mathematics Division. His research interests include high-performance computation on emerging architectures and scientific visualisation and analysis. He received his MS in computer science from Stanford University.

**Allan Snavely** received his Ph.D. from the University of California, San Diego. He has worked at SDSC in various capacities since 1995. Allan founded the PMaC laboratory in 2001 and is currently the PMaC group leader and the UCSD Primary Investigator for the DoE PERC project and the DoD HPC Performance Modelling project. He is an Assistant Adjunct Professor in the Department of Computer Science and

Engineering at UCSD. His research interests include hardware multi-threading and operations research, as well as performance modelling.

**Steve Reinhardt** leads Interactive Supercomputing's funded research efforts. He helped develop the first UNIX-based supercomputers at Cray Research Inc. in the mid 1980s. Steve has worked on parallel system designs for a number of notable projects, including as project director for the T3E project – considered by many to be one of the best parallel systems ever developed. He also played a significant role in the development of SGI's Altix systems, which were the first strongly scalable supercomputers to be built from mass-market components (industry-standard Intel processors with the Linux operating system) and thereby affordable by a wider range of customers. Steve's major interests are in the integration of hardware, software and application abilities to provide high system performance and in providing easier software means to exploit the performance of highly parallel systems.

**Viral B. Shah** received his Ph.D. in Computer Science, with an emphasis on computational sciences and engineering at the University of California, Santa Barbara, in 2007. He developed the parallel sparse matrix infrastructure in Star-P before it was commercialised. His research interests include combinatorial and sparse matrix algorithms and language design for high-productivity parallel computing. He is currently a senior research engineer at Interactive Supercomputing.

**Thomas Sterling** is the Arnaud & Edwards Professor of Computer Science at Louisiana State University, a Faculty Associate at California Institute of Technology, and a Distinguished Visiting Scientist at Oak Ridge National Laboratory. He received his Ph.D. as a Hertz Fellow from MIT in 1984. He is probably best known as the *father* of Beowulf clusters and for his research on Petaflops computing architecture. His current research is on the *ParalleX* execution model and its practical implementation in computer architecture and programming methods. Professor Sterling is the co-author of six books and holds six patents. He was awarded the Gordon Bell Prize with collaborators in 1997.

**Mustafa M. Tikir** received his Ph.D. degree from the University of Maryland, College Park. He received his BS degree from the Middle East Technical University, Ankara, and MS degree from the University of Maryland, College Park. His research interests are in the areas of High-Performance Computing, Programming Languages and Operating Systems. He is primarily interested in performance prediction and tuning of HPC applications.

**Jeffrey Vetter** is a computer scientist in the Computer Science and Mathematics Division (CSM) of Oak Ridge National Laboratory (ORNL), where he leads the Future Technologies Group and directs the Experimental Computing Laboratory. Dr. Vetter is also a Joint Professor in the College of Computing at the Georgia Institute of Technology, where he earlier earned his PhD. He joined ORNL in 2003, after four years at Lawrence Livermore National Laboratory. Vetter's interests span several areas of high-end computing (HEC) – encompassing architectures, system software, and tools for performance and correctness analysis of applications.

**Katherine Yelick** is the Director of the National Energy Research Scientific Computing Center (NERSC) at Lawrence Berkeley National Laboratory and a Professor of Electrical Engineering and Computer Sciences at the University of California at Berkeley. She has received a number of research and teaching awards and is the author or co-author of two books and more than 85 refereed technical papers on parallel languages, compilers, algorithms, libraries, architecture and storage. She co-invented the UPC and Titanium languages and demonstrated their applicability across architectures. She developed techniques for self-tuning numerical libraries, which automatically adapt the code to machine properties. Her work includes performance analysis and modelling as well as optimisation techniques for memory hierarchies, multi-core processors, communication libraries and processor accelerators. She has worked with interdisciplinary teams on application scaling and her own applications work includes parallelisation of a model for blood flow in the heart. She earned her Ph.D. in Electrical Engineering and Computer Science from MIT and has been a professor of Electrical Engineering and Computer Sciences at UC Berkeley since 1991, with a joint research appointment at Berkeley Lab since 1996.

# Preface

This book is volume 72 of the **Advances in Computers**, a series that began back in 1960, which is the oldest continuing series, chronicaling the ever-changing landscape of information technology. Each year three volumes are produced, which present approximately 20 chapters that describe the latest technology in the use of computers today. In this volume 72, we present the current status in the development of a new generation of high-performance computers (HPC).

The computer today has become ubiquitous with millions of machines being sold (and discarded) annually. Powerful machines are produced for only a few hundred U.S. dollars, and one of the problems faced by vendors of these machines is that, due to the continuing adherence to Moore's law, where the speed of such machines doubles about every 18 months, we typically have more than enough computer power for our needs for word processing, surfing the web or playing video games. However, the same cannot be said for applications that require large powerful machines. Applications involving weather and climate prediction, fluid flow for designing new airplanes or automobiles, or nuclear plasma flow require as much computer power as we can provide, and even that is not enough. Today's machines operate at the teraflop level (Trillions of Floating-Point Operations per Second) and this book describes research into the petaflop region ($10^{15}$ FLOPS). The six chapters provide an overview of current activities that will provide the introduction of these machines in the years 2011 through 2015.

The first chapter, by Jack Dongarra and 16 co-authors, 'DARPA's HPCS Program: History, Models, Tools, Languages', describes the approximately 10 years of effort by the U.S. Defense Advanced Research Projects Agency (DARPA) to design and build a petascale computing machine. The chapter gives an overview of the activities to date in developing the High-Productivity Computing System (HPCS) program and describes some of the research that is being conducted to build these machines. Issues discussed include productivity modelling of these new systems, what architecture is needed to reach petascale levels, what programming languages can be used to program these machines, how do we measure programmer performance in producing programs for these machines and how will we eventually measure the actual performance of these machines, once they are built.

The next three chapters describe efforts to measure how well these machines should perform and how well they actually perform. These methods include performance modelling and performance evaluation using simulation and benchmarking. In Chapter 2, 'Productivity in High-Performance Computing' by Thomas Sterling and Chirag Dekate, the authors describe various methods to measure the productivity in the high-performance domain. For manufactured products such as pencils or computer (hardware), productivity is a relatively well-understood concept. It is usually defined as the amount of output per unit of input, as in the case of a factory that can produce so many objects per year at a total cost of so much money. But for computer software, the situation is more complex. Is productivity the lines of code a programmer can produce per day, the number of lines of code a computer can execute per unit of time or the time it takes to solve a particular problem? When we go to the HPC domain, where we have thousands of processors working cooperatively to solve a given problem, the situation is considerably more complex. In this chapter, Sterling and Dekate present various formal models using which one can measure such productivity.

In Chapter 3, 'Performance Prediction and Ranking of Supercomputers' by Tzu-Yi Chen, Omid Khalili, Roy L. Campbell, Jr., Laura Carrington, Mustafa M. Tikir, and Allan Snavely, the authors continue with the theme presented in the previous chapter on productivity. In this case, they look at various ways to benchmark programs in order to determine their expected performance on other non-benchmarked programs. Their goal is to address trade-offs in the following two conflicting goals in benchmarking an HPC machine: (1) Performance prediction asks how much time executing an application is likely to take on a particular machine. (2) Machine ranking asks which of a set of machines is likely to execute an application most quickly.

Lieven Eeckhout in Chapter 4, 'Sampled Processor Simulation: A Survey', explores the other main aspect of performance prediction – that of computer simulation. As he explains it: 'Simulating industry-standard benchmarks is extremely time-consuming. Sampled processor simulation speeds up the simulation by several orders of magnitude by simulating a limited number of sampling units rather than the entire program execution'. In this chapter, he explores this approach towards simulating computers and gives examples of this approach applied to the various architectural components of modern HPC machines.

In Chapter 5, 'Distributed Sparse Matrices for Very High-Level Languages' by John R. Gilbert, Steve Reinhardt and Viral B. Shah, the authors discuss an important application that generally requires the use of HPC machines; that is, how to solve problems that require large space matrices, i.e., matrices where most of the entries are zero. In this chapter, the authors describe an infrastructure for implementing languages effective in the solution of these problems. They demonstrate the versatility of their infrastructure by using it to implement a benchmark that creates and manipulates large graphs.

In case this volume does not provide enough information that you desire on HPC systems, the final chapter by Myron Ginsberg, 'Bibliographic Snapshots of High-Performance/High-Productivity Computing', provides a comprehensive summary of the various aspects of HPC systems and a detailed bibliography of hundreds of additional sources of such information. He covers HPC application domains, architectures, benchmarking and performance issues, as well as additional comments on the DARPA HPCS program described by Dongarra in Chapter 1.

I hope this volume meets your needs in the area of high-performance computing. I am always looking for new and different chapters and volume themes to use for future volumes. If you know of a topic that has not been covered recently or are interested in writing such a chapter, please let me know. I am always looking for qualified authors. I can be contacted at mvz@cs.umd.edu. I hope you like these volumes and look forward to producing the next one in this long-running series.

Marvin Zelkowitz
University of Maryland
College Park, Maryland

# DARPA's HPCS Program: History, Models, Tools, Languages

JACK DONGARRA
*University of Tennessee and Oak Ridge National Lab, Tennessee, USA*

ROBERT GRAYBILL
*USC Information Sciences Institute*

WILLIAM HARROD
*DARPA*

ROBERT LUCAS
*USC Information Sciences Institute*

EWING LUSK
*Argonne National Laboratory*

PIOTR LUSZCZEK
*MathWorks Inc.*

JANICE MCMAHON
*USC Information Sciences Institute*

ALLAN SNAVELY
*University of California – San Diego*

JEFFREY VETTER
*Oak Ridge National Laboratory*

KATHERINE YELICK
*Lawrence Berkeley National Laboratory*

SADAF ALAM
*Oak Ridge National Laboratory*

ROY CAMPBELL
*Army Research Laboratory*

LAURA CARRINGTON
*University of California – San Diego*

TZU-YI CHEN
*Pomona College*

ADVANCES IN COMPUTERS, VOL. 72
ISSN: 0065-2458/DOI: 10.1016/S0065-2458(08)00001-6



Copyright © 2008 Elsevier Inc.
All rights reserved.

OMID KHALILI
*University of California – San Diego*

JEREMY MEREDITH
*Oak Ridge National Laboratory*

MUSTAFA TIKIR
*University of California – San Diego*

**Abstract**

The historical context with regard to the origin of the DARPA High Productivity Computing Systems (HPCS) program is important for understanding why federal government agencies launched this new, long-term high-performance computing program and renewed their commitment to leadership computing in support of national security, large science and space requirements at the start of the 21st century. In this chapter, we provide an overview of the context for this work as well as various procedures being undertaken for evaluating the effectiveness of this activity including such topics as modelling the proposed performance of the new machines, evaluating the proposed architectures, understanding the languages used to program these machines as well as understanding programmer productivity issues in order to better prepare for the introduction of these machines in the 2011–2015 timeframe.

## 1. Historical Background

The historical context with regard to the origin of the High Productivity Computing Systems (HPCS) program is important for understanding why federal government agencies launched this new, long-term high-performance computing program and renewed their commitment to leadership computing in support of national security, large science and space requirements at the start of the 21st century.

The lead agency for this important endeavour, not surprisingly, was DARPA, the Defense Advance Research Projects Agency. DARPA's original mission was to prevent technological surprises like the launch of Sputnik, which in 1957 signalled that the Soviets had beaten the U.S. in space research. Still, DARPA's mission is to prevent technological surprises, but over the years it has expanded to include the creation of technological surprises for America's adversaries. DARPA conducts its mission by sponsoring revolutionary, high-payoff research that bridges the gap between fundamental discoveries and their military use. DARPA is the federal government's designated 'technological engine' for transformation, supplying advanced capabilities, based on revolutionary technological options.

Back in the 1980s, a number of agencies made major investments in developing and using supercomputers. The High Performance Computing and Communications Initiative (HPCCI), conceived in that decade, built on these agency activities and in the 1990s evolved into a broad, loosely coupled program of computer science research. Key investments under the HPCCI and other programs have enabled major advances in computing technology and helped maintain U.S. leadership in the world computer market in the recent decades.

In the late 1990s and early 2000s, U.S. government and industry leaders realized that the trends in high-performance computing were creating technology gaps. If left unchecked, these trends would threaten continued U.S superiority for important national security applications and could also erode the nation's industrial competitiveness. The most alarming trend was the rapid growth of less-innovative, commodity-based clustered computing systems ('clusters'), often at the expense of the leading-edge, capability-class supercomputers with key characteristics supportive of an important set of applications. As a result of this strong market trend, the entire ecosystem that needed to maintain leadership in high-end, capability-class supercomputers was at risk: the few companies producing high-end supercomputers had less money to invest in innovative hardware research and development, and firms that created high-performance versions of software applications, environments and tools for high-end supercomputers had a more difficult time making a business case for this specialized activity. The seemingly inexorable increase in of commodity microprocessor speeds following Moore's Law propelled the growth of clusters with hundreds and then thousands of processors (although this same increasing parallelism also gave rise to the programming challenge that continues to plague the high-performance computing industry today).

*1.0.0.1 Chronology.* The goal of this section is to provide the first comprehensive chronology of events related to the HPCS program. The chronology is based on reports, documents and summaries that have been accumulated over time by more people than I can mention here. Special credit is due to Charles Holland, Richard Games and John Grosh for their contributions, especially in the early years leading up to the HPCS program. In the chronology, events that were part of the HPCS program, or sponsored by the program, are highlighted in italics.

**1992:** DARPA funding support focuses on companies developing massively parallel processing (MPP) systems based on commodity microprocessors (e.g., Thinking Machines' Connection Machine CM5, Intel's Paragon system).

**1995:** The Department of Energy establishes the Accelerated Strategic Computing Initiative (ASCI) to ensure the safety and reliability of the nation's nuclear weapons stockpile through the use of computer simulation rather than nuclear testing. ASCI adopts commodity HPC strategy.

**25 February 1996:** Silicon Graphics acquires Cray Research, which becomes a subsidiary of SGI.

**17 May 1996:** The University Corporation for Atmospheric Research (UCAR), a federally funded agency in Boulder, Colorado, awards a $35 million contract for a supercomputer purchase to a subsidiary of NEC of Japan. The U.S.-based subsidiary of NEC outbids two other finalists for the contract – Fujitsu U.S. and Cray Research of Eagan, Minnesota – to supply a supercomputer to UCAR's National Center for Atmospheric Research (NCAR) for modelling weather patterns.

**29 July 1996:** Cray (now an SGI subsidiary) petitions the International Trade Administration (ITA), a division of the U.S. Commerce Department, claiming that it had been the victim of 'dumping'. The ITA upholds the dumping charge and the NCAR purchase of the NEC supercomputer is cancelled.

**19 June 1997:** Sandia National Laboratories' 'ASCI Red' massive parallel processing system uses 9,216 Intel Pentium Pro microprocessors to achieve 1.1 trillion floating-point operations per second on the Linpack benchmark test, making it the top supercomputer in the world and the first to break the teraflop/s barrier.

**26 September 1997:** The International Trade Commission (ITC) determines that Cray Research has suffered 'material injury' and imposes punitive tariffs of between 173% and 454% on all supercomputers imported from Japan, a barrier so high that it effectively bars them from the U.S. market.

**22 September 1999:** SGI announces that it will be receiving significant financial aid from several U.S. government agencies to support the development of the company's Cray SV2 vector supercomputer system.

**15 November 1999:** Jacques S. Gansler tasks the Defense Science Board (DSB) to address DoD supercomputing needs, especially in the field of cryptanalysis.

**2 March 2000:** Tera Computer Company acquires the Cray vector supercomputer business unit and the Cray brand name from SGI. Tera renames itself as Cray Inc.

**11 October 2000:** The DSB Task Force on DoD Supercomputing Needs publishes its report. The Task Force concludes that current commodity-based HPCs are not meeting the computing requirements of the cryptanalysis mission. The Task Force recommends that the government:

1. Continue to support the development of the Cray SV2 in the short term.
2. In the mid term, develop an integrated system that combines commodity microprocessors with a new, high-bandwidth memory system.
3. Invest in research on critical technologies for the long term.

***Fall 2000:*** *DARPA Information Technology Office (ITO) sponsors high-performance computing technology workshops led by Candy Culhane and Robert Graybill (ITO).*

**23 March 2001:** Dave Oliver and Linton Wells, both from the DoD, request a survey and analysis of national security high-performance computing requirements to respond to concerns raised by U.S. Representative Martin Sabo (D-Minn.) that eliminating the tariffs on Japanese vector supercomputers would be a bad idea.

**April 2001:** Survey of DoD HPC requirements concludes that cryptanalysis computing requirements are not being met by commodity-based high-performance computers, although some DoD applications are being run reasonably well on commodity systems because of a significant investment by the DoD HPC Modernization Program to make their software compatible with the new breed of clusters. But the survey also reveals significant productivity issues with commodity clusters in almost all cases. The issues range from reduced scientific output due to complicated programming environments, to inordinately long run times for challenge applications.

**26 April 2001:** Results of the DoD HPC requirements survey are reviewed with Congressman Sabo. Dave Oliver, Delores Etter, John Landon, Charlie Holland, and George Cotter were the attendees from the DoD. The DoD commits to increasing its R&D funding to provide more diversity and increase the usefulness of high-performance computers for their applications.

**3 May 2001:** Commerce Department lifts tariffs on vector supercomputers from Japan.

***11 June 2001:*** *Release of the DoD Research and Development Agenda for High-Productivity Computing Systems White Paper, prepared for Dave Oliver and Charlie Holland. The white paper team was led by John Grosh (Office of the Deputy Under Secretary of Defense for Science and Technology) and included Robert Graybill (DARPA)), Dr. Bill Carlson (Institute for Defense Analysis Center for Computing Sciences) and Candace Culhane. The review team consisted of Dr. Frank Mello (DoD High-Performance Computing Modernization Office), Dr. Richard Games (The MITRE Corporation), Dr. Roman Kaluzniacki, Mr. Mark Norton (Office of the Assistant Secretary of Defense, Command, Control, Communications, and Intelligence), and Dr. Gary Hughes.*

***June 2001:*** *DARPA ITO sponsors an IDA Information Science and Technology (ISAT) summer study, 'The Last Classical Computer', chaired by Dr. William J. Dally from Stanford University.*

***July 2001:*** *DARPA approves High-Productivity Computing Systems Program based to a large extent on the HPCS white paper and ISAT studies. Robert Graybill is the DARPA program manger. The major goal is to provide economically viable high-productivity computing systems by the end of 2010. These innovative systems will address the inherent difficulties associated with the development and*

*use of current high-end systems and applications, especially programmability, performance, portability and robustness.*
*To achieve this aggressive goal, three program phases are envisioned: (1) concept study; (2) research and development and (3) design and development of a petascale prototype system. The program schedule is defined as follows:*

I. *June 2002–June 2003: Five vendors to develop concept studies for an HPC system to appear in 2010.*
II. *July 2003–June 2006: Expected down selection to 2–3 vendors (number depends on funding level) to develop detailed system designs for the 2010 system and to perform risk-reduction demonstrations.*
III. *July 2006–December 2010: Down selection to 1–2 vendors (number depends on funding level) to develop research prototypes and pilot systems.*

***January 2002:*** *DARPA's HPCS Phase I Broad Area Announcement (BAA) is released to industry.*

**February 2002:** Congress directs the DoD to conduct a study and deliver by 1 July 2002 a development and acquisition plan, including budgetary requirements for a comprehensive, long-range Integrated High-End Computing (IHEC) program. NSA is designated as the lead agency. DARPA, the DoD HPC Modernization Program, NIMA, NRO, DOE/NNSA and NASA are named as contributing organizations.

**8 March 2002:** NEC Corporation announces the delivery of its vector parallel computing system based on the NEC SX-6 architecture to the Japanese Earth Simulator Center. The system sustains 35.6 Tflop/s on the Linpack benchmark, making it the fastest computer in the world – approximately 5 times faster than the previous one, the DOE 'ASCI White' computer at the Lawrence Livermore National Laboratory. Jack Dongarra, who helps compile the Top500 computer list, compares the event's shock impact with the Sputnik launch, and dubs it 'Computenik'.

**May–June 2002:** The NSA-led Integrated High-End Computing (IHEC) study commences with a number of focused workshops.

***June 2002:*** *Phase I of the DARPA HPCS program begins with one-year study contracts awarded to Cray, HP, IBM, SGI and Sun. NSA provides additional funds for Phase I awards. The goal of the program is to develop a* ***new revolutionary generation*** *of* ***economically viable*** *high-productivity computing systems for national security and industrial user communities by 2010, in order to* ***ensure U.S. leadership, dominance and control*** *in this critical technology.*

*The vendors' conceptualizing efforts include a high degree of university participation (23), resulting in a wealth of novel concepts. In addition, a number of innovative technologies from DARPA's active embedded programs are considered by the vendors: Data Intensive Systems (DIS), Polymorphous Computing Architectures (PCA) and Power Aware Computing and Communications (PACC).*

**21 October 2002:** Sandia National Laboratories and Cray Inc. announce that they have finalized a multi-year contract, valued at approximately $90 million, under which Cray will collaborate with Sandia to develop and deliver a new supercomputer called Red Storm. The machine will use over 16 000 AMD Opteron microprocessors and have a peak processing rate of 100 trillion floating-point operations per second.

**21 November 2002:** Users of the Japanese Earth Simulator capture three out of five Gordon Bell prizes awarded at the Supercomputing 2002 conference. In one case, scientists run a 26.58 Tflop/s simulation of a complex climate system. This corresponds to 66% of the peak processing rate. Competing commodity systems in the U.S. deliver 10% or less of peak rates, illustrating one of the productivity issues that the DARPA HPCS program is proposing to address.

**December 2002:** The FY03 federal budget includes language proposing the development of an interagency R&D roadmap for high-end computing core technologies, along with a federal high-end computing capacity and accessibility improvement plan. In response to this guidance, the White House Office of Science and Technology Policy (OSTP), in coordination with the National Science and Technology Council, commissions the creation of the interagency High-End Computing Revitalization Task Force (HECRTF). The interagency HECRTF is charged with developing a five-year plan to guide future federal investments in high-end computing.

**June 2003:** Computing Research Association leads a workshop, chaired by Dr. Daniel A. Reed, on 'The Road for the Revitalization of High-End Computing', as part of the High-End Computing Revitalization Task Force's effort to solicit public comment on the planning process.

***July 2003:*** *DARPA HPCS Phase I down-select is completed and Phase II three-year research and development Other Transactions Authority (OTA) contracts are awarded to Cray, IBM and Sun.*

***July 2003:*** *A multi-agency initiative (DARPA, DOE Office of Science, NNSA, NSA, NSF, and NASA) funds a three-year HPCS productivity team effort led by Dr. Jeremy Kepner from MIT-Lincoln Laboratory. The productivity team comprised universities, laboratories, Federally Funded Research and Development Centers (FFRDCs) and HPCS Phase II vendors. Bi-annual public productivity conferences are held on a regular basis throughout the three-year Phase II program.*

**10 May 2004:** High-End Computing Revitalization Task Force (HPCRTF) Report is released by the Office of the Science and Technology policy (OSTP).

***May 2004:*** *DARPA sponsors the High Productivity Language System (HPLS) workshop, which is organized by Dr. Hans P. Zima from JPL to form the basis for the HPCS experimental language development activity. Experimental languages discussed include Chapel (Cray), X10 (IBM) and Fortress (Sun).*

***November 2004:*** *First formal public announcement is made at the Supercomputing Conference (SC2004) of the new HPC Challenge benchmarks, based on the work done under the HPCS Productivity Team efforts led by the University of Tennessee.*

**2004:** The National Research Council (NRC) releases a report, 'The Future of Supercomputing', sponsored by the DOE Office of Science.

**August 2005:** Completion of the report from the Joint UK Defense Scientific Advisory Council and U.S. Defense Science Board Study on Critical Technologies. High-Performance Computing is identified as a critical technology and the report makes key recommendations to maintain U.S./UK HPC superiority.

***September 2005:*** *The Army High Performance Computing Research Center (AHPCRC) and DARPA sponsor the first Parallel Global Address Space (PGAS) programming models conference in Minneapolis. Based on the interest level in the first conference, the plan is to turn this event into an annual conference.*

***November 2005:*** *First HPC Challenge performance and productivity awards are made at SC2005.*

***December 2005:*** *Dr. William Harrod becomes the HPCS program manager after Robert Graybill's six year DARPA term expires.*

***November 2006:*** *DARPA HPCS Phase II down-select is completed. Phase III multi-year prototype development Other Transaction Authority (OTA) cost-sharing contracts are awarded to Cray and IBM, with petascale prototype demonstrations planned for the end of 2010. This is a multi-agency effort involving DARPA (lead agency), NSA, DOE Office of Science, and NNSA (the HPCS mission partners), each contributing to Phase III funding.*

As this chronology suggests, this period represented a tumultuous transition period for supercomputing, resulting in no shortage of reports, recommendations and ideas on the roles of public and private sector in maintaining U.S. superiority from the national security and economic perspectives. There was also growing public awareness that theoretical ('peak') performance could no longer be a sufficient measure of computing leadership. During this period of public/private partnerships, the future of supercomputing has been altered by new wave of innovations and real sense that the real value of the computing is in achieving end-users' business objectives, agency mission and scientific discovery.

## 1.1 HPCS Motivation

As already noted, high-performance computing was at a critical juncture in the United States in the early 2000s, and the HPCS program was created by DARPA in partnership with other key government agencies to address HPC technology and application challenges for the next decade.

A number of DoD studies[1,2] stressed that there is a national security *requirement* for high-performance computing systems, and that, consistent with this requirement, DoD historically had provided partial funding support to assist companies with R&D for HPC systems. Without this government R&D participation, high-end computing might one day be available only through manufacturers of commodity clusters based on technologies developed primarily for mass-market consumer and business needs.

While driving U.S. superiority in high-end computing technology, the HPCS program will also contribute significantly to leadership in these and other critical DoD and industrial application areas: operational weather and ocean forecasting; planning for the potential dispersion of airborne contaminants; cryptanalysis; weapons (warheads and penetrators); survivability/stealth design; intelligence/surveillance/reconnaissance systems; virtual manufacturing/failure analysis of large aircraft, ships and structures; and emerging biotechnology applications. The HPCS program will create new systems and software tools that will lead to increased productivity of the applications used to solve these critical problems.

The critical mission areas are described below. Some descriptions were derived from a report submitted to Congress by the Office of the Secretary of Defense ('High Performance Computing for the National Security Community') Others came from a report created by MITRE[3]. The list is not exhaustive. HPCS systems are likely to be used for other missions – both military and commercial – if the systems provide a balanced architecture and are easy to use.

***Operational Weather and Ocean Forecasting.*** Provides worldwide 24-hour weather guidance to the military, CIA and Presidential Support Unit for current operations, weapons of mass destruction contingency planning, etc.

***Signals Intelligence.*** The transformation, cryptanalysis and intelligence analysis of foreign communications on the intentions and actions of foreign governments, militaries, espionage, sabotage, assassinations or international terrorism. There are both research and development and operational aspects of this activity.

[1] 'Task Force on DOD Supercomputing Needs', Defense Science Board Study, October 11, 2000.

[2] 'Survey and Analysis of the National Security High Performance Computing Architectural Requirements', Presentation by Dr. Richard Games, MITRE, April 26, 2001.

[3] 'DARPA HPCS Application Analysis and Productivity Assessment', MITRE, October 6, 2002.

***Intelligence, Surveillance and Reconnaissance.*** Processing the outputs of various types of sensors to produce battlespace situation awareness or other actionable intelligence. Includes target cueing, aided target recognition and other special exploitation products. These operational applications have to meet throughput and latency requirements as part of a larger system.

***Dispersion of Airborne Contaminants.*** Predicts the dispersion of hazardous aerosols and gasses in the atmosphere. Supports military operation planning and execution, intelligence gathering, counter terrorism and treaty monitoring.

***Weapons Design.*** Uses computer models to augment physical experimentation to reduce costs and explore new concepts that would be difficult to test. Computational mechanics are used to understand complex projectile – target interactions to develop advanced survivability and lethality technologies. Computational fluid dynamics is used for modeling flight dynamics of missiles and projectiles.

***Survivability and Stealth.*** Includes researches that are performed to reduce the radar signatures of airplanes such as the JSF and F22 and to provide technical support for acquisition activity. Uses computational electromagnetics for radar cross-section/signature prediction.

***Engineering Design of Large Aircraft, Ship and Structures.*** Applies computational structural mechanics used to do forensic analysis after terrorist bomb attacks and predictive analysis for the design of safer military and embassy structures. Augments aircraft wind tunnel experiments to reduce costs.

***Biotechnology.*** Uses information technology to create, organize, analyze, store, retrieve and share genomic, proteomic, chemical and clinical data in the life sciences. This area is not strictly considered a national security mission area, but it is of use to the military. More important, it is a growing field in private industry. If HPCS meets biotechnology users' needs, it may enhance the commercial viability of computer systems developed under the HPCS program.

## 1.2 HPCS Vision

The HPCS vision of developing economically viable high-productivity computing systems, as originally defined in the HPCS white paper, has been maintained throughout the life of the program. The vision of economically viable – yet revolutionary – petascale high-productivity computing systems led to significant industry and university partnerships early in the program and a heavy industry focus later in the program. To achieve the HPCS vision, DARPA created a three-phase program. A broad spectrum of innovative technologies and concepts were developed during Phase I. These were then evaluated and integrated with a balanced, innovative preliminary system design solution during Phase II. Now, in Phase III, the systems are under development, with prototype petascale demonstrations planned for late 2010.

The end product of the HPCS program will be systems with the ability to efficiently run a broad spectrum of applications and programming models in support of the national security and industrial user communities. HPCS is focusing on revolutionary, productivity-enhancing improvements in the following areas:

- **Performance:** Computational capability of critical national security applications improved by 10X to 40X over the 2002 capability.
- **Programmability:** Reduce time to develop, operate, and maintain HPCS application solutions to one-tenth of 2002's cost.
- **Portability:** Make available research and operational HPCS application software that is independent of specific hardware and software architectures.
- **Robustness (reliability):** Continue operating in the presence of localized hardware failure, contain the impact of software defects, and minimize the likelihood of operator error.

Achieving of the HPCS vision will require an optimum balance between revolutionary system requirements incorporating high-risk technology and features and functionality needed for a commercial viable computing system. The HPCS strategy has been to encourage the vendors not only to develop evolutionary systems, but also to make bold step *productivity* improvements, with the government helping to reduce the risks through R&D cost sharing. The assessment of productivity, by its very nature, is difficult because it depends upon the specifics of the end-user mission, applications, team composition and end use or workflow as shown in Fig. 1. A proper assessment requires a mixture of qualitative and quantitative (preferred) analysis to develop a coherent and convincing argument. The productivity goals of the HPCS Phase III system can be loosely grouped into **execution time and development time** goals. The goals of the program have been refined over the three phases as they have gone through this very challenging balancing process. The following refined goals have emerged from that process.

### *1.2.0.2 Productivity (Development Time) Goals.*

- Improve development productivity by 10X over 2002 development productivity for specified government workflows (workflows 1, 2, 4 and 5).
- Improve execution productivity to 2 petaflops sustained performance (scalable to greater than 4 petaflops) for workflow 3.

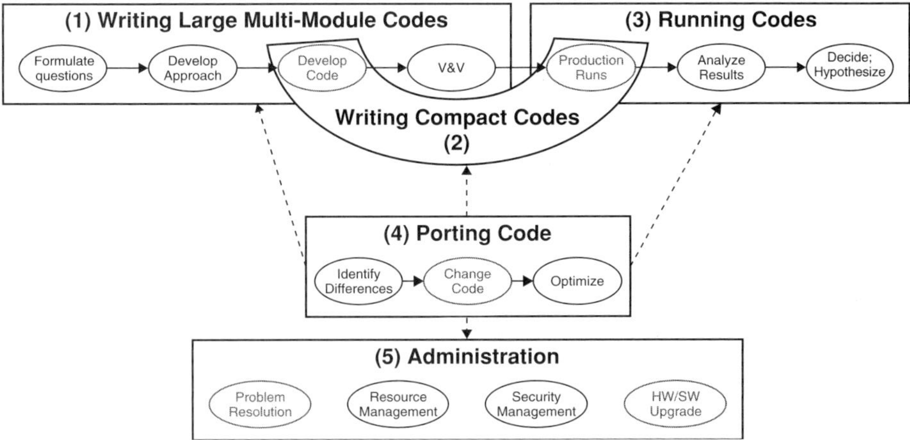


FIG. 1. Level 1 functional workflows. Workflows comprise several steps, with many steps overlapping. Items in red represent areas with highest HPC-specific interest.

No single productivity number applies to workflows for the 2002 starting point, or to 2010 workflows. Productivity will vary based on the specific machine, user and application. DoD and other government agencies will determine 2002 baseline productivity metrics for their government applications and mission requirements and will then evaluate the petascale prototype system to demonstrate the 10X improvement.

The HPCS program must address overarching issues impeding the development and utilization of high-end computational systems:

- Balanced system performance
- Improved software tools and methodologies
- Robustness strategy
- Performance measurement and prediction
- System tailorability (ability to scale up and out).

The following Table I lists the current and HPCS-targeted capabilities (execution time) for HPC systems. Note that 'current' is defined as 2007, rather than the program's 2002 starting point.

These future HPC systems will also have to operate as major subsystems of the HPCS mission partners' computing centers and meet their growing input/output and

TABLE I
PERFORMANCE (EXECUTION TIMES) DERIVED FROM HPC CHALLENGE BENCHMARKS

| Benchmark | Description | Current | HPCS |
|---|---|---|---|
| Global High-Performance LINPACK (G-HPL) (PF/s) | Sustained execution speed @ local nodes | $\sim 0.2$ | 2+ |
| STREAM (PB/s) | Data streaming mode – data processing rate | $\sim 0.1$ | 6.5 |
| Global Random Access (GUPS/s) | GUPS – random access across entire memory system | 35 | 64K |
| Bisection B/W (PB/s) | Min bandwidth connecting equal halves of the system | $\sim 0.001 - 0.01$ | 3.2 |

data storage requirements. The goals listed below represents the mission partners' requirements.

- 1 trillion files in a single file system
- 10 000 metadata operations per second
- Streaming I/O at 30 GB/sec full duplex
- Support for 30 000 nodes

These objectives cannot be met simply by tracking Moore's Law and leveraging evolutionary commercial developments, but will require revolutionary technologies and close partnerships between vendors and candidate procurement agencies. A fall back to evolutionary HPC systems with a focus on performance at the expense of productivity by vendor product organizations is not an acceptable alternative.

## 1.3 Program Overview

The HPCS acquisition strategy shown in Fig. 2 is designed to enable and encourage revolutionary innovation by the selected contractor(s) in close coordination with government HPC end users.

As Figure 2 illustrates, the DARPA-led HPCS program (denoted by the arrow labelled 'Vendor Milestones') is divided into three phases. Phase I, an industry concept study, was completed in 2003. DARPA awarded 12-month contracts to industry teams led by Cray, HP, IBM, SGI and Sun. The study provided critical technology assessments, revolutionary HPCS concept solutions, and new productivity metrics in order to develop a new class of high-end computers by the end of this decade. The outputs from Phase I convinced government decision-makers of the merits of continuing the program.

Phase II was a three-year effort that began with continuous awards to the Cray, IBM and Sun teams. These teams performed focused research, development and

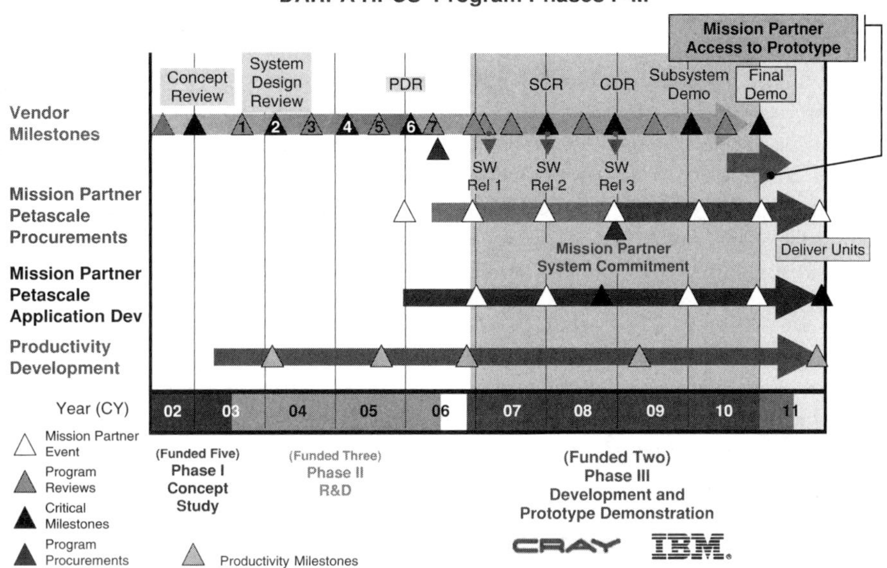


FIG. 2. HPCS program and acquisition strategy.

risk-reduction engineering activities. The technical challenges and promising solutions identified during the Phase I concept study were explored, developed, and simulated or prototyped. The work culminated in the contractors' preliminary HPCS designs. These designs, along with the vendors' risk-reduction demonstrations, analyses, lifecycle cost projections and their Phase III proposals were used by the decision-makers to determine whether it was technically feasible and fiscally prudent to continue to develop and procure HPCS systems.

Phase III, now under way, is a design, development and prototype demonstration effort that will last for four and a half years. The Phase III vendors, Cray and IBM, will complete the detailed design and development of a productive, petascale system and will provide a proof of out the system by demonstrating a petascale prototype. They will demonstrate the HPCS performance and productivity goals for an agreed-upon set of applications by the end of 2010. The Phase III mission partners will have access to these systems for the first six months in 2011. Fig. 2, in addition, outlines the relationship between the HPCS program and agency procurement programs aimed at addressing the petascale computing challenges of the DOE Office of Science, National Nuclear Security Agency, National Security Agency and the National Science Foundation.

## 1.4 Cray 'Cascade' and IBM 'PERCS' Overview

Cray and IBM have provided summaries of their proposed Phase III systems, with special emphasis on their revolutionary hardware and software architectures, resulting in significant improvement in overall user productivity. Detailed descriptions of the Phase III vendors' innovative architectures are not described here, due to the proprietary nature of the designs at this time. The authors encourage readers to inquire directly with Cray and IBM for fuller descriptions of their novel system architectures.

*1.4.0.3 The Cray Cascade System.* Cray's Cascade system is based on two observations regarding high-performance computing and productivity. The first is that no one processing technology is best for all applications. Application requirements and coding paradigms vary widely, and different forms of parallelism can be best exploited by different processor architectures. Effort spent trying to fit code onto a particular processing architecture is one of the largest drains on productivity. The second observation is that programming productivity starts with appropriate support at the architectural level. Machine characteristics such as the compute/bandwidth balance, overhead of synchronization and availability of threads and latency tolerance of processors have a significant impact on software's ability to efficiently exploit a variety of code constructs and allow programmers to express problems in the most natural way.

The cascade system is designed to be highly configurable and extensible. It provides a high-bandwidth, globally addressable memory and supports multiple types of compute blades that can be tailored for different application requirements. The interconnect can be dialed from low to very high local and global bandwidths and scales to well over 100 000 compute nodes with low network diameter. Compute blades in cascade use commodity microprocessors provided with both communication and computational accelerators. The communication accelerators extend the address space, address translation and communication concurrency of the commodity processors, and provide global synchronization and efficient message-passing support. The computational accelerators, based on massively multithreaded and vector technology, can adapt their mode of operation to the characteristics of the code, and provide significant speedup with little programmer intervention. Typical parallel architectures present numerous barriers to achieving high performance, largely related to memory access, and communication and synchronization between threads. The Cascade architecture removes many of these barriers, allowing programmers to write codes in a straightforward, intuitive manner and still achieve high performance. The key attributes of the architecture are motivated by a desire to both increased performance and improved programmability:

- Cascade provides a large, globally addressable memory and extremely high global bandwidth. This enables very low-overhead access to shared data, which allows programmers to express algorithms naturally, rather than labouring to reduce and lump together inter-processor communication.

To better serve a variety of application requirements and to support more natural parallel programming idioms, the system provides a set of heterogeneous processing capabilities, each optimized for executing a different style of computation. Serial and latency-sensitive computations are executed on commodity microprocessors, data-parallel computations with regular control flows are accelerated by vector processing and parallel computations with irregular control flows are accelerated via massive multi-threading.

The system supports low overhead, heavily pipelined communication and synchronization, allowing fine-grained parallelization and enhancing scalability.

The processor and system architecture support a programming environment that greatly simplifies the parallel programming task via higher productivity languages and programming models, and innovative tools that ease debugging and performance tuning at large scales. The Cascade programming environment supports MPI, OpenMP, pthreads, SHMEM and Global Arrays, as well as the global address space languages Unified Parallel C and Co-Array Fortran. For the most productive programming experience, Cascade supports global-view programming models, which provide a parallel programming experience more similar to uniprocessor programming. The new Chapel language provides data and controls abstractions that simplify parallel programming and create a clean separation between high-level algorithms and low-level details such as data decomposition and layout. This enables a programmer to first focus on expressing the parallelism inherent in the algorithm being implemented and to later redefine the critical data structures to exploit locality and processor affinity.

#### *1.4.0.4 The IBM PERC System.*

Figures 3 and 4 highlight the key features of IBM's PERC system that is under development through the HPCS program.

## 1.5 Productivity Initiatives

As stated earlier, productivity, by its very nature, is difficult to assess because it depends upon the specifics of the end-user mission, application, team composition and end use or workflow. The challenge is to develop a productivity assessment strategy based on a mixture of qualitative and quantitative (preferred) analysis-based metrics that will not only be used to evaluate the HPCS vendors but also adopted by the larger HPC community.

IBM HPCS

## IBM's Technical Approach for HPCS

- **Unprecedented focus on productivity**
  - Hardware/software co-design focused on improving system productivity by more than an order of magnitude and significantly expanding the number of productive users in a petascale environment
  - Application development: programming models, languages, tools
  - Administrative: automation, simplicity, ease of use
- **A holistic approach that encompasses all the critical elements of supercomputer system architecture and design (Hardware and Software)**
  - Processors, Caches, Memory subsystem, networking, storage, Operating systems, parallel/cluster file systems, programming models, application development environment, compilers, tools for debugging and performance tuning, libraries, schedulers, checkpoint-restart, high availability software, systems management
  - Balanced system architecture and design
- **Leverage IBM leadership in UNIX systems to provide petascale systems on commercially viable technology**
  - POWER, AIX/Linux, ISVs, ...
- **Focused effort on significantly enhancing the sustained performance experienced by applications at scale**
  - Maximize compute time spent on productive computation by minimization of overhead
  - Cluster network optimized for common communication patterns (collective, overlap of communication and computation...)
  - Tools to identify and correct load imbalance
- **General Purpose, flexible operating environment to address a large class of supercomputing applications**
- **Significant reductions in complexity and cost for large scale supercomputing infrastructure**

1

FIG. 3. IBM HPCS overview.

IBM HPCS

## IBM Hardware Innovations

- **Next generation POWER processor with significant HPCS enhancements**
  - Leveraged across IBM's server platforms
- **Enhanced POWER Instruction Set Architecture**
  - Significant extensions for HPCS
  - Leverage the existing POWER software eco-system
- **Integrated high speed network (very low latency, high bandwidth)**
- **Multiple hardware innovations to enhance programmer productivity**
- **Balanced system design to enable scalability**
- **Significant innovation in system packaging, footprint, power and cooling**

2

FIG. 4. IBM HPCS overview.

Figure 2 highlights a multi-year HPCS productivity initiative that was started in Phase II, funded by DARPA, DOE Office of Science, NNSA, NSA and NSF and led by Dr. Jeremy Kepner from MIT-Lincoln Laboratory. The Productivity Team was comprised of universities, laboratories, FFRDCs and HPCS Phase II vendors. Bi-annual public productivity conferences were held on a regular basis throughout the three-year Phase II program. The HPCS Phase II Productivity Team projects can be loosely grouped as execution-time and development-time research elements. **The next sections will delineate an expanded set of productive research elements and findings resulting from the HPCS Phase II Productivity Team projects.** The representative research elements presented are performance benchmarking, system architecture modelling, productivity workflows/metrics and new languages.

In summary, the HPCS program represents a very unique partnership between DARPA, industry and the government end users (mission partners). Since this partnership represents a very different model from the past, what 'it is not' is just as important as 'what it intends' to be. The items related to what the program is not are as follows:

- A One-off system. The HPCS system must be a viable commercial product.
- Meeting only one set of requirements. Aside from the varied requirements of the mission partners, the system must support a spectrum of a applications and configurations.
- Available only at petascale. The system must scale from a single cabinet to very large configurations.
- Using only new languages. The HPCS system must also support existing programming languages, including C, C++ and Fortran and MPI and existing PGAS languages.

## 2. Productivity Systems Modeling

The HPCS vision centers around the notion of computing systems with revolutionary hardware-software architectures that will enable substantially higher productivity than projected continuations of today's evolutionary system designs. Certainly, a crucial component of productivity is the actual ('sustained') performance the revolutionary computing systems will be able to achieve on applications and workloads. Because these architectures will incorporate novel technologies to an unusually large extent, prediction of application performance will be considerably more difficult than is the case for next-generation systems based on evolutionary architectures. Hence, the availability of sophisticated performance-modelling techniques will be critically important for designers of HPCS computing systems and for the success of the HPCS program as a whole.

Performance models allow users to predict the running time of an application based on the attributes of the application, its input and the target machine. Performance models can be used by system architects to help design supercomputers that will perform well on assorted applications. Performance models can also inform users which machines are likely to run their application fastest and alert programmers to performance bottlenecks which they can then attempt to remove.

The ***convolution problem*** in performance modelling addresses the prediction of the performance of an application on different machines, based on two things: (1) machine profiles consisting of rates at which a computer can perform various types of operations as measured by simple benchmarks and (2) an application signature consisting of counts of various types of operations performed by the application. The underlying notion is that the performance of an application can be represented by some combination of simple benchmarks that measure the ability of the target machine to perform different kinds of operations on the application's behalf.

There are three different methods for doing performance convolutions, each based on matrix operations, within the San Diego Supercomputing Center's Performance Modelling and Characterization (PmaC) framework for performance prediction. Each method is appropriate for answering a different set of questions related to correlation of application performance to simple benchmark results. Each requires a different level of human insight and intervention. And each, in its own way, can be used to predict the performance of applications on machines where the real runtime is unknown.

The first method uses Least Squares fitting to determine how good a statistical fit can be made between observed runtimes of applications on different machines, using a set of machine profiles (measured by using simple benchmarks); the resulting application signatures can then be used within the framework for performance prediction. This method has the virtue of being completely automated.

The second method uses Linear Programming to fit the same input data as those used by the first method (or similar input data). In addition, however, it can also mark input machine profiles and/or application runtimes as suspect. This corresponds to the real-world situation in which one wants to make sense out of benchmarking data from diverse sources, including some that may be flawed. While potentially generating more accurate application signatures that are better for performance prediction, this method requires some user interaction. When the solver flags data as suspect, the user must either discard the data, correct it, or insist that it is accurate.

Instead of inference from observed application runtimes, the third method relies on instrumented application tracing to gather application signatures directly. While arguably the most commonly used and the most accurate of the three methods, it is also the most labour intensive. The tracing step is expensive compared with the measurement of the un-instrumented application runtimes, as used by the Least Squares and Linear Programming methods to generate application signatures. Moreover, unlike the first two methods, formation of the performance model requires substantial expert interaction to 'train' the convolution framework, though subsequently performance predictions can be done automatically.

Finally, we demonstrate how a judicious mix of these methods may be appropriate for large performance-modelling efforts. The first two allow for broad workload and HPC asset characterizations, such as understanding what system attributes discriminate performance across a set of applications, while the last may be more appropriate for very accurate prediction and for guiding tuning efforts. To evaluate these methods, we tested them on a variety of HPC systems and on applications drawn from the Department of Defense's Technical Insertion 2006 (TI-06) application workload [5].

## 2.1 Problem Definition and Unified Framework

As an example of a simple pedagogical convolution, consider Equation 1. Equation 1 predicts the runtime of application $a$ on machine $m$ by combining three of application $a$'s operation counts (the number of floating-point, memory and communication operations) with the corresponding rates at which machine $m$ can perform those operations.

$$\text{Runtime}_{a,m} \approx \frac{\text{FloatOps}_a}{\text{FloatOpRate}_m} + \frac{\text{MemoryOps}_a}{\text{MemoryOpRate}_m} + \frac{\text{CommOps}_a}{\text{TransferRate}_m} \tag{1}$$

In practice, FloatOpRate, MemoryOpRate and TransferRate could be determined by running a set of simple synthetic benchmarks such as HPL, STREAM and EFF_BW, respectively, from the HPC Challenge benchmarks [10]. Likewise, FloatOps, MemoryOps and CommunicationOps could be measured for the application using hardware and software profiling tools such as the PMaC MetaSim Tracer [3] for floating and memory operations, and MPIDTrace[1] for communication events.

We could generalize Equation 1 by writing it as in Equation 2, where OpCount represents a vector containing the three operation counts for application $a$, Rate is a vector containing the corresponding three operation rates for machine $m$ and $\oplus$ represents a generic operator. This generic operator could, for example, take into account a machine's ability to overlap the execution of two different types of operations.

$$\text{Time}_{a,m} \approx P_{a,m} = \frac{\text{OpCount}(1)}{\text{Rate}(1)} \oplus \frac{\text{OpCount}(2)}{\text{Rate}(2)} \oplus \frac{\text{OpCount}(3)}{\text{Rate}(3)} \tag{2}$$

If the number of operation counts used in Equation 2 is expanded to include other performance factors, such as the bandwidth of strided accesses to L1 cache, the bandwidth of random-stride accesses to L1 cache, the bandwidth of strided accesses to main memory and network bandwidth, we could represent application $a$'s operation counts by making OpCount a vector of length $c$, where $c$ is the total number of different operation types represented for application $a$. We could further expand

OpCount to represent more than one application by making OpCount a matrix of dimension $c \times n$, where $n$ is the total number of applications that were characterized. Similar expansion could be done for Rate, making it a $k \times c$ matrix, where $k$ is the total number of machines, each of which is characterized by $c$ operation rates. This would make $P$ a $k \times n$ matrix in which $P_{ij}$ is the predicted runtime of application $i$ on machine $j$. That is, the generalized Equation 2 represents the calculation of predicted runtimes of $n$ different applications on $k$ different machines and can be expressed as $P = \text{Rate} \otimes \text{OpCount}$. Since each column in OpCount can also be viewed as the application signature of a specific application, we refer to OpCount as the application signature matrix, $A$. Similarly, each row of Rate is the machine profile for a specific machine, and so we refer to Rate as the machine profile matrix, $M$. Now the convolution problem can be written as $P = M \otimes A$. In expanded form, this looks like:

$$\begin{bmatrix} p_{1,1} & \cdots & p_{1,n} \\ p_{2,1} & \cdots & p_{2,n} \\ p_{3,1} & \cdots & p_{3,n} \\ \vdots & \ddots & \vdots \\ p_{k,1} & \cdots & p_{k,n} \end{bmatrix} = \begin{bmatrix} m_{1,1} & \cdots & m_{1,c} \\ m_{2,1} & \cdots & m_{2,c} \\ m_{3,1} & \cdots & m_{3,c} \\ \vdots & \ddots & \vdots \\ m_{k,1} & \cdots & m_{k,c} \end{bmatrix} \otimes \begin{bmatrix} a_{1,1} & \cdots & a_{1,n} \\ \vdots & \ddots & \vdots \\ a_{c,1} & \cdots & a_{c,n} \end{bmatrix} \tag{3}$$

Given Equation 3 as the general convolution problem, the relevant questions are how to determine the entries of $M$ and $A$, and what to use for the $\otimes$ operator to generate accurate performance predictions in $P$?

Populating $M$ is fairly straightforward, at least if the machine or a smaller prototype for the machine exists. Traditionally, this has been done by running simple benchmarks. It should be noted that determinination of $c$, the smallest number of benchmarks needed to accurately represent the capabilities of the machine, is generally considered an open research problem [3]. In this work, for populating $M$, we used the *netbench* and *membench* synthetic benchmarks from the TI-06 benchmark suite [22]. These benchmarks can be considered a superset of the HPC Challenge Benchmarks. For example, Figure 2 plots the results of running membench on an IBM system. We could then populate $M$ with several memory bandwidths corresponding to L1 cache bandwidth for strided loads, L1–L2 (an intermediate bandwidth), L2 bandwidth, etc., to represent the machine's capabilities to service strided load requests from memory; similarly, rates for random access loads, stores of different access patterns, floating-point and communication operations can be included in $M$. The results obtained when the STREAM benchmark is run from the HPC Challenge Benchmarks at different sizes ranging from small to large are shown by the upper curve in Fig. 2 and the lower curve gives the serial version of the RandomAccess benchmark run in the same way. (Some implementation details differ between the TI-06 synthetics and HPC Challenge, but the overall concepts and the rates they measure are the same.)

Populating of $A$ is less straightforward. While traditionally users have consulted performance counters to obtain operation counts, this may not reveal important operation subcategories such as the access pattern or locality of memory operations. For example, we can see from Fig. 2 that not all memory operations are equal; rates at which machines can complete memory operations may differ by orders of magnitude, depending on where in the memory hierarchy they fall. An alternative to performance counters is application tracing via code instrumentation. Tracing can, for example, discover memory addresses and locality, but is notoriously expensive [7]. The methods we propose in this section determine the entries of $A$ using three different methods, each with different trade-offs in accuracy versus effort.

## 2.2 Methods to Solve the Convolution Problem

In this work, we investigate three methods for calculating $A$ and determining the $\otimes$ operator. We classify the first two methods as *empirical* and the third one as *ab initio*. Empirical methods assume that $M$ and some values of $P$ are known, and then derive the matrix $A$. Matrix $A$ can then be used to generate more values of $P$. Ab initio methods, on the other hand, assume that both $M$ and $A$ are known and then calculate $P$ from first principles. In addition to this classification, the first two methods may be considered *top down* in that they attempt to resolve a large set of performance data for consistency, while the last may be considered *bottom up* as it attempts to determine general rules for performance modelling from a small set of thoroughly characterized loops and machine characteristics.

### *2.2.1 Empirical Method*

Although traditionally we assume that $P$ is unknown and its entries are to be predicted by the model, in practice some entries of $P$ are always measured directly by timing application runs on real machines. This may be done simply to validate a prediction, although the validation may be done some time in the future, as is the case when runtimes on proposed machines are predicted. A key observation is that running an application on an existing machine to find an entry of $P$ is generally significantly easier than tracing an application to calculate the $P$ entry through a model. This suggests that we treat some entries of $P$ as known for certain existing systems and $M$ as also known via ordinary benchmarking effort, rather than treating $P$ as an unknown and $A$ as a parameter that can be known only via extraordinary tracing effort. This, combined with assumptions about the structure of the convolution operator $\otimes$, allows us to provide a solution $A$. Once $A$ is known for the applications of interest, it can be convolved with a new $M'$ to predict performance on these other machines, where $M'$

is just $M$ with rows for the new machines, for which simple synthetic benchmarks may be known or estimated but for which full application running times are unknown.

We refer to the methods that treat $A$ as the unknown as *empirical* in the sense that one can deduce the entries of a column of $A$ by observing application runtimes on a series of machines that differ by known quantities in their ability to perform operations in each category. As an example, intuitively, if an application has very different runtimes on two systems that are identical except for their network latency, we may deduce that the application's sensitivity to network latency comes from the fact that it sends numerous small messages.

We formalize this intuition and demonstrate two different techniques for empirical convolution. In both methods, we assume that there is a set of machines on which we have gathered not only the synthetic benchmarks used to fill in the matrix $M$, but also actual runtimes for $n$ applications of interest in $P$. We further assume that the operator $\otimes$ is the matrix multiplication operator. We now describe two different approaches for using $P$ and $M$ to solve for entries of the application matrix, $A$, within a reasonable range of error.

The first empirical approach uses Least Squares to find the entries of $A$ and is particularly appropriate when the running times are known on more machines than those for which we have benchmark data. The second empirical approach uses Linear Programming to find the entries of $A$ and can be useful in the under-constrained case where we have real runtimes on fewer machines than those for which we have benchmark data. In addition to the determination of entries in the application matrix $A$, both methods can also be used to address questions such as:

- What is the best fit that can be achieved with a given assumption about the convolution? (For example, we may assume the convolution operator is a simple dot-product and operation counts are independent of machine for each application.)
- Can one automatically detect outliers, as a way to gain insight into the validity of benchmark and runtime data from various sources?
- Can one calculate application weights for a subset of the systems and use those weights to accurately predict runtimes on other systems?
- What properties of systems are most important for distinguishing their performance?

### 2.2.2 Solving for A Using Least Squares

Consider solving the matrix equality $P = MA$ for $A$. We can solve for each column of $A$ individually (i.e., $P_i = MA_i$), given the (plausible) assumption that the operation counts of one application do not depend on those of another application. If we further decide to compute application operation counts that minimize the 2-norm of the residual $P_i - MA_i$, then the problem becomes the much studied least squares problem. Furthermore, because only non-negative application operation counts have meaning, we can solve $P_i = MA_i$ as a non-negative least squares problem. These problems can be solved by a technique described in [9] and implemented as lsqnonneg in Matlab. In practice, before applying the non-negative least squares solver, we normalize both the rows and columns of the equation with respect to the largest entry in each column. Rescaling of the columns of $M$ so that the largest entry in each column is 1 allows us to weigh different operations similarly, despite the fact that the cost of different types of operations can vary by orders of magnitude (e.g., network latency versus time to access the L1 cache). Rescaling of the rows of $M$ and $P_i$ so that the entries of $P$ are all 1 allows us to normalize for different runtimes.

The least squares approach has the advantage of being completely automatic, as there are no parameters that need to be changed or no constraints that may need to be discarded. Thus, it also partially answers the question: if all the benchmark and runtime data are correct, how well can we explain the running times within the convolution framework? However, if some of the data are suspect, the least squares method will attempt to find a compensating fit rather than identifying the suspect data.

### *2.2.3 Solving for A Using Linear Programming*

Unlike the least squares method that seeks the minimum quadratic error directly, the linear programming method is more subtle – and it can also be more revealing. There are various ways to rephrase Equation 3 as a linear programming problem; in our implementation, for every $i$ and $j$ ($1 \leq i, j \leq n$), Equation 3 is relaxed to yield the following two inequalities:

$$p_{ij} \cdot (1 - \beta) \geq m_i \oplus a_j$$
$$p_{ij} \cdot (1 - \beta) \leq m_i \oplus a_j$$

where $0 < \beta < 1$ is an arbitrary constant and each element $a_j$ is a non-negative variable.

Therefore, each pair of inequalities defines a stripe within the solution space, and the actual solution must lie within the intersection of all $n$ stripes. Should any stripe fall completely outside the realm of the others, no solution that includes that machine–application pair exists. Given a simplifying assumption that similar architectures have similar frequencies of operations per type for a given application, it is expected that the intersection of the stripes will not be null, since the application execution time $p_{ij}$ will likely be a direct result of synthetic capability $m_i$ (when neglecting more complex, possibly non-deterministic execution properties such as overlapping operations, pre-fetching, and speculative execution). A null solution, therefore, suggests that an error may lie in one of the execution times or one of the synthetic capability measurements.

To determine the 'optimal' solution for $a_j$, the intersection of all stripes must result in a bounded space. In such a case, the intersection vertices are each tested via an objective function to determine the best solution. For this implementation, a minimum is sought for

$$f(a_j) = \sum_{i=1}^{k} (m_i \oplus a_j) \tag{4}$$

in order to force the estimate for the application times to be inherently faster than the actual application times. The error for each may then be associated with operation types such as I/O reads and writes that are not represented in the set of basic operations.

In applying the linear programming method, the value for $\beta$ was increased until all stripe widths were sufficiently large, in order to achieve convergence. Estimates for the application times were then calculated for each machine (1) to determine the overall extent of the estimation error and (2) to identify any systems with outlying error values when error percentages were clustered using a nearest-neighbor technique. Any system identified in (2) was removed from consideration, since an error in its application or synthetic benchmarks was suspected. This methodology was applied iteratively until the minimum value for $\beta$ that achieved convergence and the overall estimation error were both considered to be small.

### 2.2.4 Ab Initio Method

Methods that assume $P$ as unknown are referred to here as *ab initio,* in the sense that the performance of an application running on a system is to be determined from its first principles. The assumption, then, is that both $M$ and $A$ is known but the generic $\otimes$ operator and $P$ are not known.

To separate concerns we split the problem of calculating $P$ into two steps. The first step is to predict the execution time of the parallel processors between communication events. Following the format of Equation 3, memory and floating-point operations are gathered by tracing and are further fed through a simulator to propagate the corresponding entries of a matrix $A'$. Each column of $A'$ then holds floating-point operations and memory operations (but not communication operations), broken down into different types, access patterns, locality, etc., for a particular application. $P'$ is obtained by multiplying $A'$ with $M$, and thus a row of $P'$ represents the application's predicted time spent doing work on the processor during execution on the machines of $M$. In the second step, the Dimemas [6] simulator processes the

MPI trace data and $P'$ in order to model the full parallel execution time. The output from Dimemas is then the final calculated execution time for the application(s) on the target machine(s) $(P)$.

In the remainder of this section, we describe how the trace data is used to determine the entries of $A'$ and how $A'$ is used to calculate the entries of $P'$. Since the time spent doing floating-point operations tends to be small compared with the time spent doing memory operations in large-scale parallel applications, we focus on describing how we determine the entries of $A'$ related to memory performance.

Our approach is to instrument and trace the applications using the PMaC MetaSim Tracer and then to use the PMaC MetaSim Convolver to process the traces in order to find the entries in $A'$. Details of the PMaC MetaSim Tracer and the processing of the trace by the PMaC MetaSim Convolver can be found in [19].

Before proceeding, it is important to note that the ab initio methods relax two constraints of the least squares and linear programming methods. First, an application's trace, particularly its memory trace, is fed to a cache simulator for the machine(s) to be predicted. This means a column of $A'$ can be different on different machines. This represents a notable sophistication over the empirical methods: it is no longer assumed that operation category counts are the same on all machines (for example, machines with larger caches will get more operations that hit in cache). Second, rather than assuming a simple combining operator such as a dot product, the convolver can be trained to find a better operator that predicts performance with much smaller prediction errors. This operator may, for example, allow for overlapping of floating-point operations with memory operations – again a notable advancement in sophistication that is more realistic for modern machines.

Since tracing is notoriously expensive, we employ cross-platform tracing in which the tracing is done only once on a single system, but the cache structure of many systems is simulated during tracing. Figure 20 shows some of the information that MetaSim Tracer collects for every basic blocks (a basic block is a straight run of instructions between branches) of an application. Fields that are assumed under the cross-platform tracing assumption to be the same across all machines are collected or computed from direct observation; but fields in the second category are calculated by feeding the dynamic address stream on-the-fly to a set of cache simulators, unique to each machine.

The MetaSim Convolver predicts the memory performance of each basic block by mapping it to some linear combination of synthetic benchmark memory performance results (entries of $M$) using the basic block fields, such as simulated cache hit rates and stride access pattern, as shown in Fig. 5. This convolver mapping is implemented as a set of conditions to be applied to each basic block to determine the bandwidth region and curve of Figure 5 that need to be used for its estimated performance. A sample of one of these conditions for the L2 cache region on the ARL P690 system in

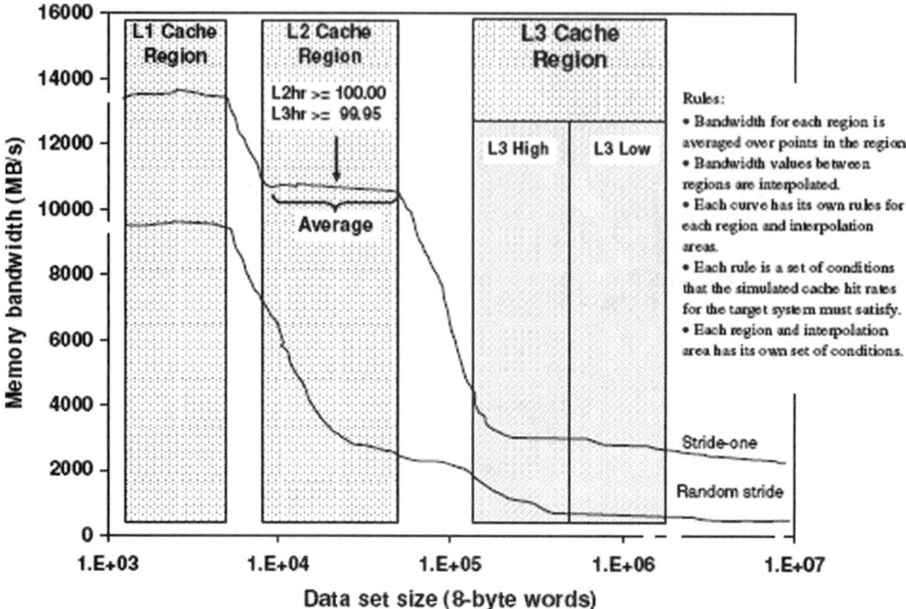


FIG. 5. The strided (upper) and random (lower) memory bandwidth test from membench taken from and IBM P690 system at Army research Laboratory (ARL), along with example rules for mapping a basic-block to its expected memory performance.

shown on Fig. 5. The main advancement of this method described in this work involve to refining of these conditions to improve prediction accuracy as described in the next section. The rules in Fig. 5 further exemplify the conditions that were developed for each region and interpolation area between regions of the membench curves.

In order to determine and validate the best set of conditions for minimizing prediction error, a small experimental $P^{measured} = MA'$ problem was defined. We chose several computational loops as a 'training set' to develop and validate the convolving conditions. We chose 40 computational loops from two parallel applications, HYCOM and AVUS, from the TI-06 application suite; then execution times for these loops on 5 systems were measured to propagate the entries of $P^{measured}$. The loops were chosen judiciously, based on their coverage of the trace data space: their constituent basic blocks contain a range of hit rates, different randomness, etc. We then performed a human-guided iteration, trying different sets of conditions the MetaSim Convolver could implement to determine each loop's $A'$ and thence entries in $P^{predicted}$. Thus, we were looking for rules to map basic blocks to expected performance; the rules were constrained to make sense in terms of first principles' properties of the target processors. For example, a loop's memory work cannot obtain a performance higher than the measured L1 memory performance or a performance lower than measured main memory performance. More subtly, the L1 hit rate value required to assign a basic block to get L1 cache performance could not be less than the hit rate value that would assign L3 cache performance.

We sought then to determine conditions in such a way that the generated elements of $A'$ would produce the most accurate calculated $P^{predicted}$. In other words, we looked for conditions to minimize:

$$\text{Total error} = \sum_{i,j}^{m,n} \left| \left( P_{i,j}^{measured} - P_{i,j}^{predicted} \right) / P_{i,j}^{measured} \right| \tag{5}$$

where $m$ is the number of machines (5) and $n$ is the number of loops (40).

Finally, having developed the conditions for the training set that minimized total error, we used the same conditions to convolve and to predict the full AVUS and HYCOM applications, as well as a larger set of applications on a larger set of machines.

## 2.2.5 Experimental Results

To evaluate the usefulness of the *empirical* and *ab initio* methods, we tested both on several strategic applications run at several processor counts and inputs on the systems listed in Table II. We chose several applications from the Technical Insertion 2006 (TI-06) application workload that covered an interesting space of computational properties, such as ratio of computation to communication time, ratio of floating-point operations to memory operations and memory footprint size. None of these codes on the inputs given are I/O intensive; thus we do not model I/O in the remainder.

The applications used are AVUS, a code used to determine the fluid flow and turbulence of projectiles and air vehicles; CTH, which models complex multi-dimensional, multiple-material scenarios involving large deformations or strong shock physics; HYCOM, which models all of the world's oceans as one global body of water; OVERFLOW, which is used for computation of both laminar and turbulent fluid flows over geometrically complex, non-stationary boundaries; and WRF, which is a next-generation mesoscale numerical weather prediction system designed to serve both operational forecasting and atmospheric research needs.

The applications were run on two different inputs each (DoD designations 'Standard' and 'Large') and on 3 different processor counts between 32 and 512 for each input on all 20 of the systems listed. More information on these applications can be found in [3] and [5]. It should be clear that populating the $P^{measured}$ matrix for the least squares and linear programming methods required the measurement of about 600 application runtimes in this case (20 systems, 5 applications, 2 inputs each,

3 cpu counts each). These are full applications that run, on average, about one or two hours each, depending on input and cpu count. The $P^{measured}$ values were therefore collected by a team of people from the Department of Defense High Performance Computing Modernization Program (HPCMP) centers. The authors populated the $M$ matrix by running the membench and netbench benchmarks on these same systems.

In testing the empirical methods, we tried several variants of the $M$ matrix, in part to explore the relationship between the number of columns in $M$ (and rows in $A$) and the resulting accuracy. This complements investigations in [3], where the authors studied the smallest number of benchmarks required to accurately represent the capabilities of machines. For example, we tried 10 and 18-column variants of the $M$ matrix, both based on the same machine benchmark data. The one with 10 columns had 8 measures pertaining to the memory subsystem from membench (i.e., drawn from plots similar to those in Fig. 5) and 2 being the off-node bandwidth and the latency of the interconnect from netbench, as described above. The set with 18 columns had 14 measures pertaining to the memory subsystem (i.e., taking more points from the membench curve in Fig. 5) 2 for off-node bandwidth and latency and 2 for on-node bandwidth and latency. From the synthetic measures pertaining to the memory subsystem, half were chosen from strided membench results and the other half were chosen from random access membench results.

We now discuss the data in Table II, which summarizes the results of using the empirical methods to understand our data set.

### 2.2.6 Fitting the Data Using Least Squares

Because the least squares method computes $A$ to minimize overall error, it can be used to answer the question of how well can we explain measured entries of $P$ as a function of measured entries of $M$, assuming a standard dot-product operator and machine-independent application signatures? The least squares column (denoted as *LS*) in Table II answers this question for our set of data. When averaged over all the applications and inputs and processor counts, we found that the performance and the performance differences of the applications on these machines could be represented within about 10% or 15%. As noted previously, we tested this method with both a 10- and an 18-column $M$ matrix. On looking at the errors averaged for each case separately, we found that the results were only slightly better than with the latter.

Overall, the LS results demonstrate that one can characterize the observed differences in performance of many applications on many different machines by using a small set of benchmark measurements (the $M$ matrix) whose entries pertain to each machine's memory and interconnect subsystems. The ERDC Cray X1 is the only machine where the least squares does not seem to fit well. This is discussed in the next section.

### 2.2.7 Detecting Outliers by Using Linear Programming

The linear programming method also tries to find the $A$ that best fits the entries in $M$ and $P$ under the same assumptions as those used in the least squares method, but linear programming has the advantage of being able to identify entries in $M$ and $P$ that seem as suspect.

When we first computed the errors given in Table II using the initial measured entries of $M$, large errors for the ASC SGI Altix and the ARL IBM Opteron led us to question the benchmark data on those machines. After rerunning the benchmarks on those machines and recalculating the errors using the least squares and linear programming methods, we ended up with the (much improved) results in Table II. The empirical methods were able to identify suspicious benchmark data. Upon further investigation, we found that the membench benchmark had originally been run on

TABLE II

AVERAGE ABSOLUTE ERROR FOR ALL APPLICATIONS TESTED ON 20 DOD SYSTEMS. FORMAT OF COLUMN 1 IS ACRONYM OF DEPARTMENT OF DEFENSE COMPUTER CENTER-COMPUTER MANUFACTURER-PROCESSOR TYPE

| Error Summary | Average Absolute Error | |
|---|---|---|
| Systems | LS | LP |
| ASC_SGI_Altix | 4% | 8% |
| SDSC_IBM_IA64 | 12% | — |
| ARL_IBM_Opteron | 12% | 8% |
| ARL_IBM_P3 | 4% | 4% |
| MHPCC_IBM_P3 | 6% | 6% |
| NAVO_IBM_P3 | 9% | 6% |
| NAVO_IBM_p655 (Big) | 5% | 6% |
| NAVO_IBM_p655 (Sml) | 5% | 5% |
| ARSC_IBM_p655 | 4% | 2% |
| MHPCC_IBM_p690 | 8% | 7% |
| NAVO_IBM_p690 | 7% | 9% |
| ARL_IBM_p690 | 10% | 6% |
| ERDC_HP_SC40 | 6% | 8% |
| ASC_HP_SC45 | 5% | 4% |
| ERDC_HP_SC45 | 5% | 6% |
| ARSC_Cray_X1 | 8% | 5% |
| ERDC_Cray_X1 | 51% | 3% |
| AHPCRC_Cray_X1E | 14% | — |
| ARL_LNX_Xeon (3.06) | 6% | 8% |
| ARL_LNX_Xeon (3.6) | 16% | 8% |
| **Overall Error** | % | % |

those two machines with a poor choice of compiler flags, resulting in unrealistically low bandwidths.

We note that in generating the results in Table II, the linear programming (denoted as *LS*) method still flagged the SDSC IBM IA64 and the AHPCRC Cray X1E was non-conforming (thus these machines are omitted from the LP column), suggesting that there are inconsistencies in either the benchmark data or the runtime data on those machines. Unfortunately, recollecting benchmark data on these machines did not improve the results, leading us to surmise that the problem lies in the application runtimes rather than in the benchmark. Looking specifically at the AHPCRC Cray X1, we observe that it was flagged when the ERDC Cray X1 was not. It is possible that the codes run on the AHPCRC Cray X1 were not properly vectorized. We have not tested our hypotheses yet, because rerunning the applications is a time-and resource-intensive process usually done by the teams at each center once in a year (unlike rerunning the benchmarks, which is much easier) and has not been completed at this time.

Both these sets of results could be further interpreted as saying that, if one is allowed to throw out results that may be due to errors in the input data (either benchmarks or application runtimes), one may attribute as much as 95% of the performance differences of these applications on these machines to their benchmarked capabilities on less than 20 simple tests. Results like these have implications on how much benchmarking effort is really required to distinguish the performance capabilities of machines.

Both these methods, taken together with the earlier results in [3], at least partially answer the question, 'what properties of systems are most important to distinguish performance'? In [3] it was shown that three properties (peak floating-point issue rate, bandwidth of strided main-memory accesses, and bandwidth of random main-memory accesses) can account for as much of 80% of observed performance on the TI-05 applications and machines (a set with substantial similarities to and overlap with TI-06). The results in this work can be seen as saying that another 10% (for 90% or more in total) is gained by adding more resolution to the memory hierarchy and by including communication.

## 2.3 Performance Prediction

We now describe how the empirical and ab initio convolution methods can be used to predict overall application performance. In what follows we refer to both a $P^{measured}$, which consists of measured runtimes that are used to generate either $A$ (for the empirical methods) or to improve the convolver conditions (for the ab initio method), and to a $P^{predicted}$, which consists of runtimes that are subsequently predicted.

### 2.3.1 Empirical Methods

To predict the performance of an application on a machine by using empirical convolution methods, we first determine the application signature by using runtimes in $P^{measured}$ that were collected on other machines. We then multiply the application signature with the characteristics of the new machine in order to arrive at a predicted runtime, $P^{predicted}$. If we have the actual measured runtime on the new machine, we can use it to evaluate the accuracy of the predicted time.

Generally, we found this method to be about 90% accurate if the machine being predicted was architecturally similar to machines in $P^{measured}$. For example, RISC-based architectures can be well predicted using an $A$ derived from runtimes and benchmark results of other RISC machines. As an example, Table III shows the error in $P^{predicted}$, using both the least squares and linear programming methods, with sets of 10 and 18 machine characteristics, to predict the performance of AVUS and HYCOM on the ERDC SC45. (In this case we report signed error, as we are not averaging, and so no cancellation in the error is possible.) The measured runtimes on the ERDC SC45 were not included in $P^{measured}$, but were used to calculate the error in $P^{predicted}$. We found the predictions using both methods to be generally within 10% of the actual runtimes.

In contrast, Table IV gives an example where $P^{measured}$ does not contain a machine that is architecturally similar to the machine being predicted. The results of using the least squares and linear programming methods to predict performance on the ASC SGI Altix are shown. Unlike almost all of the other machines in Table II, the Altix is neither a RISC-based machine nor a vector machine. Rather, it uses a VLIW and has other unique architectural features that are too extensive to be described here. So, once the ASC SGI Altix is removed from $P^{measured}$, there is no architecturally similar

TABLE III
SIGNED ERROR IN PREDICTING THE PERFORMANCE OF AVUS AND CTH ON DIFFERENT PROCESSOR COUNTS ON THE ERDC SC45, USING APPLICATION SIGNATURES GENERATED THROUGH EMPIRICAL METHODS

| | 10 Bin | | 18 Bin | |
|---|---|---|---|---|
| Error Application | LS | LP | LS | LP |
| avus 32 | 3% | 8% | −5% | 10% |
| avus 64 | 1% | 7% | −6% | 6% |
| avus 128 | 3% | 10% | −3% | 8% |
| cth 32 | −9% | −8% | 3% | −1% |
| cth 64 | −8% | −37% | 1% | 4% |
| cth 96 | −13% | −1% | −1% | 2% |

TABLE IV
SIGNED ERROR IN PREDICTING THE PERFORMANCE OF AVUS AND CTH ON DIFFERENT PROCESSOR COUNTS ON THE ASC ALTIX, USING APPLICATION SIGNATURES GENERATED THROUGH EMPIRICAL METHODS

| | 10 Bin | | 18 Bin | |
|---|---|---|---|---|
| Error Application | LS | LP | LS | LP |
| avus 32 | 27% | 42% | −117% | −117% |
| avus 64 | 18% | −27% | −135% | −100% |
| avus 128 | 16% | 32% | −129% | −80% |
| cth 32 | −108% | −64% | −56% | 8% |
| cth 64 | −98% | −30% | −35% | −35% |
| cth 96 | −171% | −170% | −47% | −44% |

machine other than the SDSC IA64 (already flagged as suspect). In this case, we see that the predicted runtime is only rarely within even 20% of the actual runtime. This seems to suggest that inclusion of an architecturally similar machine in $P^{measured}$ is crucial for determining a useful $A$ for subsequent prediction.

Tables III and IV demonstrate that empirical methods are particularly useful for prediction if the new machine has an architecture that is similar to those used in generating the application signature. However, if the new machine has a unique architecture, accurate prediction through these methods may be problematic.

### 2.3.2 Ab Initio Methods

Table V gives the results obtained by applying the convolver, trained against a 40-computational-loop training set, to predict the performance of all of the applications on all of the machines listed in Table V. So far, 9 RISC-based machines have been trained in the convolver, and work is ongoing to add additional systems and architecture classes. Once the convolver is trained for a system, any application trace can be convolved to produce a prediction. It should be clear from the table that this involved 270 predictions (5 applications, 2 inputs, 3 cpu counts, 9 machines) at an average of 92% accuracy. Since measured application runtimes can vary by about 5% or 10%, accuracy greater than that shown in Table V may not be possible unless performance models take into account contention on shared resources and other sources of variability.

Although the ab initio method 'knows' nothing about the performance of any application on any real machine, it is more accurate than the empirical methods. Thus, it seems the power and pure predictive nature of the ab initio approach may sometimes justify its added expense and complexity. Of further note is that the ab initio

TABLE V
ABSOLUTE ERROR AVERAGED OVER ALL APPLICATIONS FOR THE COMPUTATIONAL LOOP STUDY

| Systems | Average Error |
|---|---|
| ARL_IBM_Opteron | 11% |
| NAVO_IBM_P3 | 7% |
| NAVO_IBM_p655 (Big) | 6% |
| ARSC_IBM_p655 | 4% |
| MHPCC_IBM_p690 | 8% |
| NAVO_IBM_p690 | 18% |
| ASC_HP_SC45 | 7% |
| ERDC_HP_SC45 | 9% |
| ARL_LNX_Xeon (3.6) | 5% |
| **Overall Error** | % |

approach actually constructs an overall application performance model from many small models of each basic block and communications event. This means the models can be used to understand where most of the time is spent and where tuning efforts should be directed. The empirical methods do not provide such detailed guidance.

## 2.4 Related Work

Several benchmarking suites have been proposed to represent the general performance of HPC applications. Besides those mentioned previously, the best known are perhaps the NAS Parallel [2] and the SPEC [20] benchmarking suites, of which the latter is often used to evaluate micro-architecture features of HPC systems. A contribution of this work is to provide a framework for evaluating the quality of a spanning set for any benchmark suite (i.e., its ability to attribute application performance to some combination of its results).

Gustafson and Todi [8] performed seminal work relating 'mini-application' performance to that of full applications. They coined the term 'convolution' to describe this general approach, but they did not extend their ideas to large-scale systems and applications, as this work does. McCalpin [12] showed improved correlation between simple benchmarks and application performance, but did not extend the results to parallel applications as this work does.

Marin and Mellor-Crummey [11] show a clever scheme for combining and weighing the attributes of applications using the results of simple probes, similar to what is implemented here, but their application studies were focused primarily on 'mini application' benchmarks and were not extended to parallel applications and systems.

Methods for performance evaluations can be broken down into two areas [21]: structural models and functional/analytical models. A fairly comprehensive breakdown of the literature in these two areas is provided in the related work section of Carrington et al. [3], and we direct the reader's attention to that section for a more thorough treatment.

Saavedra [15–17] proposed application modelling as a collection of independent Abstract FORTRAN Machine tasks. Each abstract task was measured on the target machine and then a linear model was used to predict execution time. In order to include the effects of memory system, they measured miss penalties and miss rates for inclusion in the total overhead. These simple models worked well on the simpler processors and shallower memory hierarchies of the mid to late 1990s.

For parallel system predictions, Mendes [13, 14] proposed a cross-platform approach. Traces were used to record the explicit communications among nodes and to build a directed graph based on the trace. Sub-graph isomorphism was then used to study trace stability and to transform the trace for different machine specifications. This approach has merit and needs to be integrated with a full system for application tracing and modelling of deep memory hierarchies in order to be practically useful today.

## 2.5 Conclusions

We presented a general framework for the convolution problem in performance prediction and introduced three different methods that can be described in terms of this framework. Each method requires different amounts of initial data and user input, and each reveals different information.

We described two empirical methods which assume that some runtimes are known and used them to determine application characteristics in different ways. The least squares method determines how well the existing data can be explained, given that particular assumptions are made. The linear programming method can additionally correctly identify systems with erroneous benchmarking data (assuming that the architectures of the target systems are roughly similar). Both can generate plausible fits relating the differences in observed application performance to simple performance characteristics of a broad range of machines. Quantitatively, it appears they can attribute around 90% of performance differences to 10 or so simple machine metrics. Both empirical methods can also do fairly accurate performance prediction on machines whose architectures are similar to some of the machines used to determine application characteristics.

We then addressed the situation where real runtimes of the applications are not available, but where there is an expert who understands the target systems. We described how to use an ab initio approach in order to predict the performance of a range of applications on RISC machines with good accuracy, using just timings on a set of representative loops on representative applications (in addition to machine benchmarks) and a detailed report of the operations of the basic blocks that make up the loops used to train the convolver. This last method is capable of generating accurate predictions across a wide set of machines and applications.

It appears that empirical approaches are useful for determining how cohesive a large quantity of application and benchmarking performance data from various sources is, and that, further, reasonable effort may attribute 90% or so of observed performance differences on applications to a few simple machine metrics. The more fully predictive ab initio approach is more suitable for very accurate forecasting of application performance on machines for which little full application runtime data is available.

# 3. Productivity Evaluation on Emerging Architectures

The future systems from DARPA's High Productivity Computing Systems program will present a new level of architectural and programming diversity beyond existing multicore microprocessor designs. In order to prepare for the challenges of measuring productivity on these new devices, we created a project to study the performance and productivity of computing devices that will reflect this diversity: the STI Cell processor, Graphical Processing Units (GPU) and Cray's MTA multithreaded system.

We believe that these systems represent an architectural diversity more similar to the HPCS systems than do existing commodity platforms – which have generally been the focus of evaluations of productivity to date. Homogenous multi-core systems require coarse-grain, multi-threaded implementations, while GPUs and Cell systems require users to manage parallelism and orchestrate data movement explicitly. Taken together, these attributes form the greatest challenge for these architectures in terms of developer productivity, code portability and performance. In this project, we have characterized the relative performance improvements and required programming effort for two diverse workloads across these architectures: contemporary multi-core processors, Cell, GPU, and MTA-2. Our initial experiences on these alternative architectures lead us to believe that these evaluations may have to be very intricate and require a substantial investment of time to port and optimize benchmarks. These architectures will span the range of the parameters for development and execution time and will force us to understand the sensitivities of our current measurement methodologies. For example, consider the complexity of writing code for today's CELL system or graphics processors. Initial HPCS systems may be equally challenging.

Contemporary multi-paradigm, multi-threaded and multi-core computing devices can provide several orders-of-magnitude performance improvement over traditional single-core microprocessors. These devices include mainstream homogenous multi-core processors from Intel and AMD, the STI Cell Broadband Engine (BE) 44, Graphical Processing Units (GPUs) [30] and the Cray XMT [23] (Eldorado[39]) systems. These architectures have been developed for a variety of purposes, including gaming, multimedia and signal processing.

For productivity, our initial evaluations used source lines of code (SLOC) for the serial version against the target implementations using a tool called sloccount[4]; for performance, we measure algorithm time-to-solution. We were unable to use existing tools to measure many of the other metrics used in the HPCS productivity effort because they were incompatible with the programming environment or the architecture we were evaluating. We share the concerns of the entire HPCS community that the SLOC metric does not fully capture the level of effort involved in porting and optimizing an algorithm on a new system; however, it does provide a quantitative metric to compare and contrast different implementations in a high-level language – C – across the diverse platforms in our study.

## 3.1 Architecture Overviews

### *3.1.1 Homogeneous Multi-core Processors*

Our target commodity multi-core platforms are the dual-core and quad-core platforms from Intel. *Clovertown* is a quad-core Xeon 5300 series processor, which consists of two dual-core 64-bit Xeon processor dies, packaged together in a multi-chip module (MCM). Although a Level 2 cache is shared within each Xeon dual-core die, no cache is shared between both dies of an MCM. Like the Intel Xeon 5100 series dual-core processor known as *Woodcrest*, the Clovertown processor uses Intel's next-generation Core 2 microarchitecture [50]. The clock frequencies of our target platforms are 2.4 GHz for the Clovertown processor and 2.66 GHz for the Woodcrest processor.

Both Clovertown and Woodcrest systems are based on Intel's Bensley platform (shown in Fig. 6) for Xeon processors, which is expected to have sufficient capacity to handle the overheads of additional cores. The Blackford Memory Controller Hub (MCH) has dual, independent front-side busses, one for each CPU socket, and those FSBs run at 1333 MHz when coupled with the fastest Xeons, rated at approximately 10.5 GB/s per socket. Also, four memory channels of the Blackford MCH can host

[4] http://www.dwheeler.com/sloccount/.

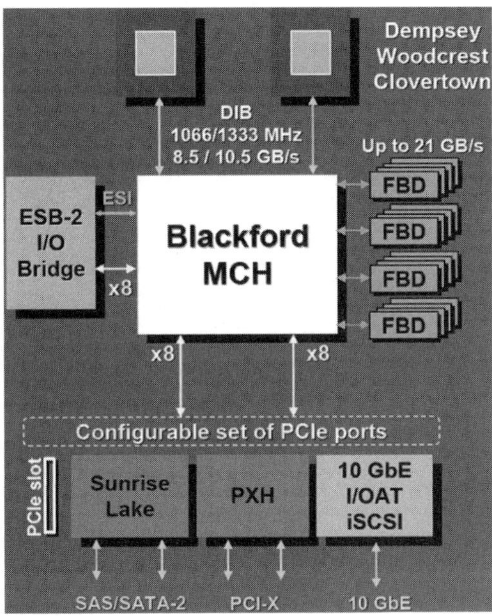


FIG. 6. The Bensley platform (Courtesy of Intel).

Fully Buffered DIMMs (FB-DIMMs) at clock speeds up to 667 MHz. The twin chips inside the Clovertown processor have no real provision for communicating directly with one another. Instead, the two chips share the front-side bus (FSB) with the Intel Blackford MCH, or north bridge.

The microarchitecture for both the Woodcrest and Clovertown processors supports Intel's Streaming SIMD Extension (SSE) instructions that operate on data values packed into 128-bit registers (e.g., four 32-bit values or two 64-bit values) in parallel. The microarchitecture used in the Clovertown processor can execute these SIMD instructions at a rate of one per cycle, whereas the previous-generation microarchitecture was limited to half that rate. The microarchitecture includes both a floating-point multiplication unit and a floating-point addition unit. Using SIMD instructions, each of these units can operate on two packed double-precision values in each cycle. Thus, each Clovertown core is capable of producing four double-precision floating-point results per clock cycle, for a theoretical maximum rate of sixteen double-precision floating-point results per clock cycle per socket in a Clovertown-based system.

### 3.1.2 Cell Broadband Engine

The Cell Broadband Engine processor is a heterogeneous multicore processor, with one 64-bit Power Processing Element (PPE) and eight Synergistic Processing Elements (SPEs), as shown in Fig. 7. The PPE is a dual-threaded Power Architecture core containing extensions for SIMD instructions (VMX) [41]. The SPEs are less traditional in that they are lightweight processors with a simple, heavily SIMD-focused instruction set, with a small (256 KB) fixed-latency local store (LS), a dual-issue pipeline, no branch prediction, and a uniform 128-bit, 128-entry register file [43]. The SPEs operate independently from the PPE and from each other, have an extremely high bandwidth DMA engine for transferring data between main memory and other SPE local stores and are heavily optimized for single-precision vector arithmetic. Regrettably, these SPEs are not optimized for double-precision floating-point

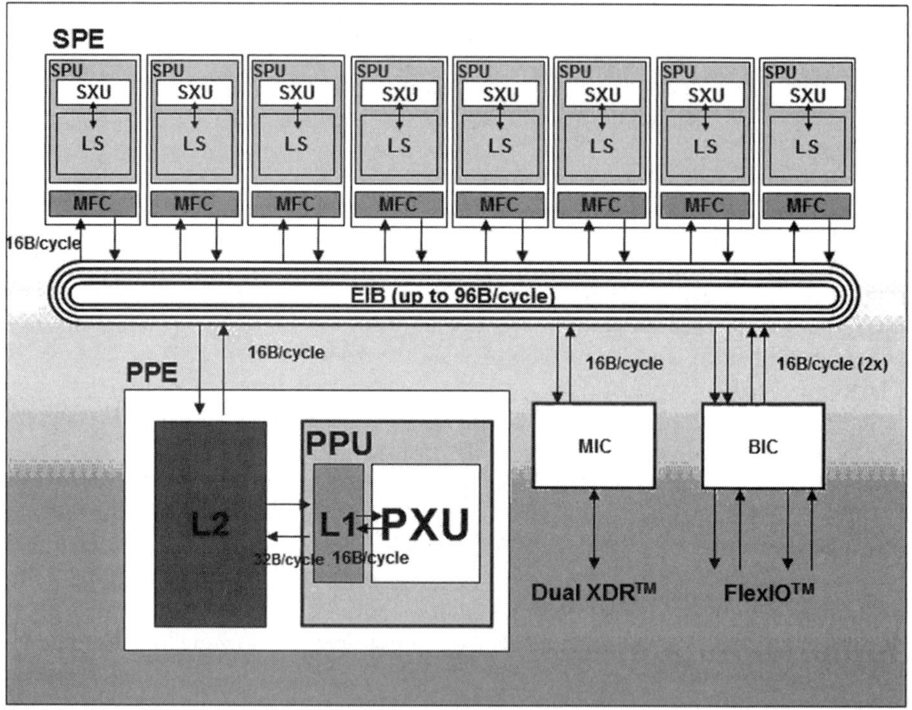


FIG. 7. Design components of the Cell BE [http://www.research.ibm.com/cell/heterogeneousCMO.html]. *Source:* M. Gschwind et al., Hot Chips-17, August 2005.

calculations, limiting Cell's applicability for a large number of scientific applications. The Cell processor architecture enables great flexibility with respect to programming models [27].

### 3.1.3 Graphics Processing Units

The origin of Graphics Processing Units, or GPUs, is attributed to the acceleration of the real-time graphics rendering pipeline. As developers demanded more power and programmability from graphics cards, these cards became appealing for general-purpose computation, especially as mass markets began to force even high-end GPUs into low price points [25]. The high number of FLOPS in GPUs comes from the parallelism in the architecture. Fig. 8 shows an earlier generation high-end part from NVIDIA, with 16 parallel pixel pipelines. It is these programmable pipelines that form the basis of general-purpose computation on GPUs. Moreover, in next-generation devices, the parallelism increased. The subsequent generation from NVIDIA contained up to 24 pipelines. Typical high-end cards today have 512 MB of local memory or more, and support from 8-bit integer to 32-bit floating-point data types, with 1-, 2- or 4-component SIMD operations.

There are several ways to program the parallel pipelines of a GPU. The most direct way is to use a GPU-oriented assembler or a compiled C-like language with graphics-related intrinsics, such as Cg from NVIDIA [30]. Accordingly, as GPUs are

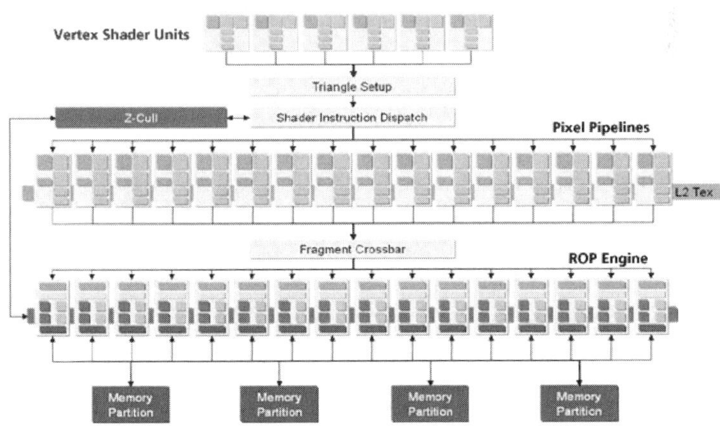


FIG. 8. The NVIDIA GeForce 6800 GPU.

coprocessors, they require interaction from the CPU to handle high-level tasks such as moving data to and from the card and setting up these 'shader programs' for execution on the pixel pipelines.

Inherently, GPUs are stream processors, as a shader program cannot read and write to the same memory location. Thus, arrays must be designated as either input or output, but not both. There are technical limitations on the number of input and output arrays addressable in any shader program. Together, these restrictions form a set of design challenges for accelerating a variety of algorithms using GPUs.

### *3.1.4 Cray MTA-2*

Cray's Multi-Threaded Architecture (MTA) uses a high degree of multi-threading instead of data caches to address the gap between the rate at which modern processors can execute instructions and the rate at which data can be transferred between the processor and main memory. An MTA-2 system consists of a collection of processor modules and a collection of memory modules, connected by an interconnection network. The MTA processors support a high degree of multi-threading when compared with current commercial off-the-shelf processors (as shown in Fig. 9). These processors tolerate memory access latency by supporting many concurrent streams of execution (128 in the MTA-2 system processors). A processor can switch between each of these streams on each clock cycle. To enable such rapid switching between streams, each processor maintains a complete thread execution context in hardware for each of its 128 streams. Unlike conventional designs, an MTA-2 processor module contains no local memory; it does include an instruction stream shared between all of its hardware streams.

The Cray MTA-2 platform is significantly different from contemporary, cache-based microprocessor architectures. Its differences are reflected in the MTA-2 programming model and, consequently, its software development environment [24]. The key to obtaining high performance on the MTA-2 is to keep its processors saturated, so that each processor always has a thread whose next instruction can be executed. If the collection of threads presented to a processor is not large enough to ensure this condition, then the processor will be under-utilized.

The MTA-2 is no longer an active product in the Cray product line. However, Cray has announced an extreme multi-threaded system – the Cray XMT system. Although the XMT system uses multithreaded processors similar to those of the MTA-2, there are several important differences in the memory and network architecture. The XMT will not have the MTA-2's nearly uniform memory access latency, so data placement and access locality will be important considerations when these systems are programmed.

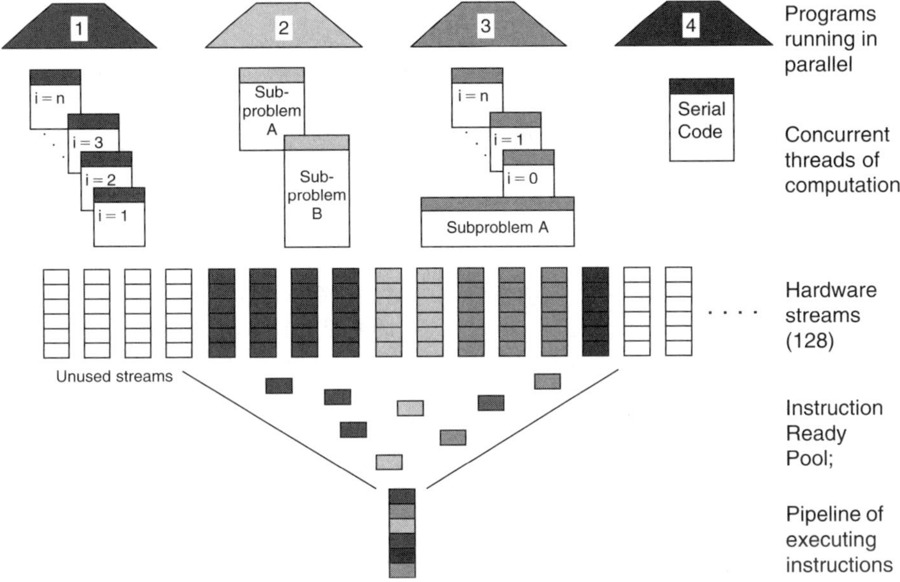


FIG. 9. Block diagram of the MTA-2 system.

## 3.2 Target Workloads

We target two algorithms for our initial evaluations: an imaging application and a floating-point-intensive scientific algorithm.

### 3.2.1 Hyperspectral Imaging (HSI)

*A covariance matrix* is created in a number of imaging applications, such as hyperspectral imaging (HSI). HSI, or image spectroscopy, can be described as the capture of imagery either with a large number of wavelengths or across a large number of pixels. Whereas black and white images are captured at one wavelength and color images at three (red, green and blue), hyperspectral images are captured in hundreds of wavelengths simultaneously. If a HSI data cube is $N$ by $M$ pixels, with L wavelengths, the covariance matrix is an L $\times$ L matrix, where the entry $\mathrm{Cov}_{a,b}$ at row $a$ and column $b$ in the covariance matrix can be represented as:

$$\mathrm{Cov}_{a,b} = \sum_{i=1}^{N} \sum_{j=1}^{M} \mathrm{input}_{i,j,a} \times \mathrm{input}_{i,j,b}.$$

### 3.2.2 Molecular Dynamics

The biological processes within a cell occur at multiple lengths and time scales. The processing requirements for bio-molecular simulations, particularly at large time scales, far exceed the available computing capabilities of the most powerful computing platforms today. Molecular dynamics (MD) is a computer-simulation technique where the time evolution of a set of interacting atoms is followed by integrating the equations of motion [45]. In the Newtonian interpretation of dynamics, the translational motion of a molecule is caused by force exerted by some external agent. The motion and the applied force are explicitly related through Newton's second law: $F_i = m_i a_i$. $m_i$ is the atom's mass, $a_i = \frac{d^2 r_i}{dt^2}$ is its acceleration, and $F_i$ is the force acting upon it due to the interactions with other atoms. MD techniques are extensively used in many areas of scientific simulations, including biology, chemistry and materials. MD simulations are computationally very expensive. Typically, the computational cost is proportional to $N^2$, where $N$ is the number of atoms in the system. In order to reduce the computational cost, a number of algorithm-oriented techniques such as a cutoff limit are used. It is assumed that atoms within a cutoff limit contribute to the force and energy calculations on an atom. As a result, the MD simulations do not exhibit a cache-friendly memory access pattern.

Our MD kernel contains two important parts of an MD calculation: force evaluation and integration. Calculation of forces between bonded atoms is straightforward and computationally less intensive, as there are only very small numbers of bonded interactions as compared with the non-bonded interactions. The effects of non-bonded interactions are modelled by a 6-12 Lennard-Jones (LJ) potential model: $V(r) = 4\varepsilon\left[\left(\frac{\sigma}{r}\right)^{12} - \left(\frac{\sigma}{r}\right)^{6}\right]$.

The Verlet algorithm uses positions and acceleration at time $t$ and positions from time $t + \delta t$ to calculate new positions at time $t + \delta t$. The pseudo code for our implementation is given in Fig. 10. Steps are repeated for $n$ simulation time steps.

```
1. advance velocities
2. calculate forces on each of the N atoms
   compute distance with all other N-1 atoms
   if(distance within cutoff limits)
   compute forces
3. move atoms based on their position,
   velocities & forces
4. update positions
5. calculate new kinetic and total energies
```

FIG. 10. MD kernel implemented on MTA-2.

The most time-consuming part of the calculation is step 2, in which an atom's neighbors are determined using the cutoff distance, and subsequently the calculations are performed ($N^2$ complexity). We attempt to optimize this calculation on the target platforms, and we compare the performance to the reference single-core system. We implement single-precision versions of the calculations on the Cell BE and the GPU accelerated system, while Intel OpenMP and MTA-2 implementation are in double-precision versions.

## 3.3 Evaluation

### 3.3.1 Homogeneous Multi-core Systems

#### 3.3.1.1 Optimization Strategies.

Since there are shared memory resources in Intel dual- and quad-core processors, we consider OpenMP parallelism in this study. Note that an additional level of parallelism is also available within individual Xeon cores in the form of SSE instructions. The Intel compilers are capable of identifying this parallelism with optimized flags, such as -fast -msse3 -parallel (-fast = -O3, -ipo, – static).

#### 3.3.1.2 Molecular Dynamics.

We inspected compiler reports and identified that a number of small loops in the initialization steps and subsequent calculations are automatically vectorized by the compiler. The complex data and control dependencies in the main phases of the calculation prevented the generation of optimized SSE instruction by the compiler. The next step was to introduce OpenMP parallelism in the main calculation phases. Figure 11 shows the results of an experiment with 8192 atoms. Overall, the performance of the Woodcrest system is higher than that of the Clovertown system, which could be attributed to the higher clock of the Woodcrest system, the shared L2 cache between the two cores and shared FSB between the two sockets in the Clovertown processor. We observe that the speedup increases with workload size (number of atoms). As a result, the runtime performance of 8 threads on Clovertown exceeds the performance of 4 threads on the Woodcrest system.

#### 3.3.1.3 HSI Covariance Matrix.

The OpenMP optimization applied for the covariance matrix calculations is similar to the MD optimization. The main loop is composed of largely data-independent calculations. We modified the innermost loop where a reduction operation is performed and then applied OpenMP parallel for construct. Figure 12 shows the results on a covariance matrix creation for a $256^3$ data cube. The results are qualitatively similar to those obtained from the molecular dynamics kernel: the Woodcrest system outperforms the Clovertown on the same number of threads, which is likely due to a higher clock speed and other architectural differences.

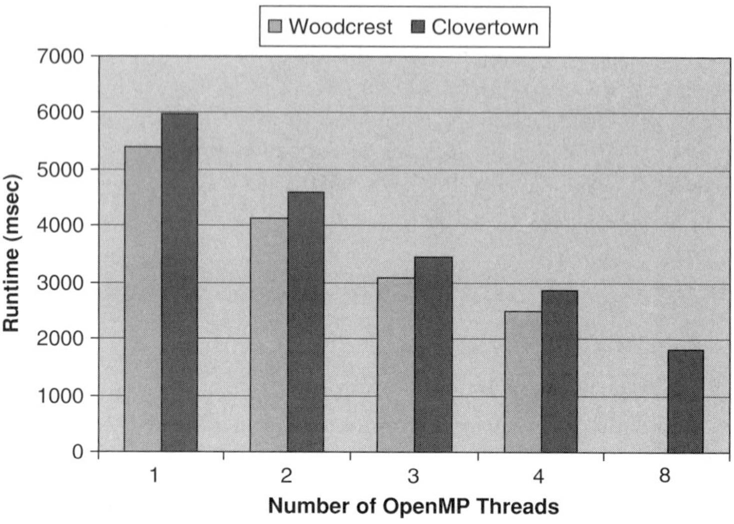


FIG. 11. MD experiments with 8192 atoms.

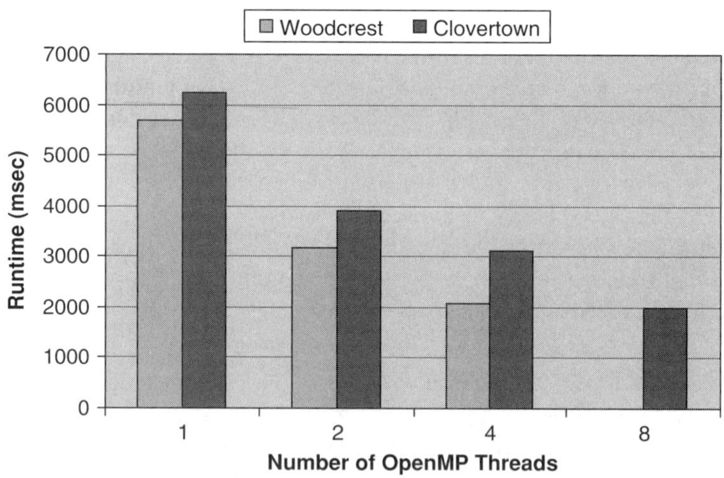


FIG. 12. Experiments with $256^3$ HSI covariance matrix.

In this case, the result of the 8-thread Clovertown shows a great improvement over the 4-thread Clovertown runtime, although it exceeds the performance of the 4-thread Woodcrest implementation by only a very small margin.

## 3.3.2 *Cell Broadband Engine*

### *3.3.2.1 Molecular Dynamics.*

Our programming model for the Cell processor involves the determination of time-consuming functions that map well to the SPE cores, and instead of calculating these functions on the PPE, we launch 'threads' on the SPEs to read the necessary information into their local stores, perform the calculations, and write the results back into main memory for the next calculation steps on the PPE. Because of its high percentage of the total runtime, the MD acceleration function alone was offloaded to SPEs.

The MD calculation deals with three-dimensional positions, velocities and forces, so the most natural way to make use of the 4-component SIMD operations on the SPE is to use the first three components of the inherent SIMD data types for the x, y and z components of each of these arrays. The communication between the PPE and SPEs is not limited to large asynchronous DMA transfers; there are other channels ('mailboxes') that can be used for blocking sends or receives of information of the order of bytes. As we are offloading only a single function, we can launch the SPE threads only on the first time step and signal them using mailboxes when there is more data to process. Hence, the thread launch overhead is amortized across all time steps.

Runtime results are listed in Table VI for a 4096-atom experiment that runs for 10 simulation time steps. Due the extensive use of SIMD intrinsics on the SPE, even a single SPE outperforms the PPE on the Cell processor by a significant margin. Further, with an efficient parallelization using all 8 SPEs, the total runtime is approximately 10 times faster than the PPE alone.

### *3.3.2.2 HSI Covariance Matrix.*

The covariance matrix creation routine transfers much more data through the SPEs for the amount of computation

TABLE VI
PERFORMANCE COMPARISON ON THE CELL PROCESSOR

| Number of Atoms | 4096 |
|---|---|
| Cell, PPE only | 4.664 sec |
| Cell, 1 SPE | 2.958 sec |
| Cell, 8 SPEs | 0.448 sec |

TABLE VII
PERFORMANCE COMPARISON ON THE CELL PROCESSOR

| Covariance Matrix | 256 × 256 × 256 |
|---|---|
| Cell, PPE only | 88.290 sec |
| Cell, 1 SPE | 5.002 sec |
| Cell, 8 SPEs | 0.662 sec |

performed than the MD application does. Specifically, the data set and tiling sizes used resulted in a total of 16 chunks that need to be processed, and this implementation must still stream the data set through each SPE to create each of the output chunks. Therefore, the time spent during data transfer has the potential for a noticeable impact on total performance. In this example, optimization of the thread launching, DMA overlapping and synchronization resulted in considerable improvement of the routine.

Table VII shows the performance improvement on the Cell processor. The disadvantage of the PPE as a computational processor is that it runs 18x slower than a single SPE. In addition, parallelization across SPEs was very effective, providing a 7.5x speedup on 8 SPEs.

### 3.3.3 GPU

#### 3.3.3.1 Molecular Dynamics.

As with the Cell, implementation for the GPU focused on the part of the algorithm that calculates new accelerations from only the locations of the atoms and several constants. For our streaming processor, then, the obvious choice is to have one input array comprising the positions and one output array comprising the new accelerations. The constants were compiled into the shader program source using the provided JIT compiler at program initialization.

We set up the GPU to execute our shader program exactly once for each location in the output array. That is, each shader program calculates the acceleration for one atom by checking for interaction with all other atoms and by accumulating forces into a single acceleration value for the target atom. Instruction length limits prevent us from searching more than a few thousand input atoms in a single pass, and so with 4096 atoms or more, the algorithm switches to use multiple passes through the input array. After the GPU is completeded, the resulting accelerations are read back into main memory, where the host CPU proceeds with the current time step. At the next time step, the updated positions are re-sent to the GPU and new accelerations computed again.

Figure 13 shows performance using an NVIDIA GeForce 7900GTX GPU. This figure includes results from the GPU's host CPU (a 2-GHz Opteron) as a reference for scaling comparisons. The readily apparent change in slope for the GPU below 1024 atoms shows the point at which the overheads associated with offloading this

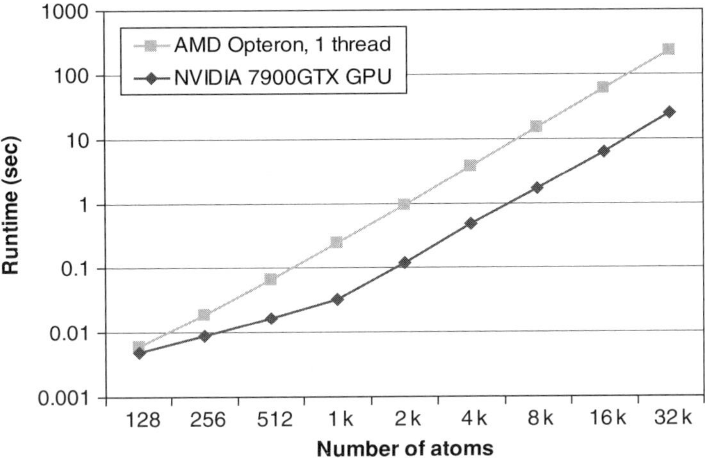


FIG. 13. Performance scaling results on GPU with CPU scaling for comparison.

acceleration computation to the GPU become a more significant fraction of the total runtime than the $O(N^2)$ calculation itself. These constant and $O(N)$ costs for each time step include sending the position array and reading the acceleration array across the PCIe bus at every time step, and these results show that there is a lower bound on problem size where a GPU will not be faster than a CPU. However, the massive parallelism of the GPU helps it maintain a consistent speedup above 1000 atoms.

*3.3.3.2 HSI Covariance Matrix.* The GPU architecture is generally well suited to image operations, and to some degree this extends to hyperspectral image data. However, as the SIMD nature of the pipelines in a GPU is well oriented toward 4-component images, this is not a direct match with an image with more than four components. However, the regular nature of the data does have an impact, and the SIMD nature of the GPU can be exploited to take advantage of the operations in the covariance matrix creation routine. Figure 14 shows the runtime of the GPU on the $256^3$ covariance matrix creation benchmark under several implementations. The implementation exploiting none of the SIMD instructions on the GPU naturally shows the worst performance. The fully SIMDized implementation is a drastic improvement, running several times faster than the unoptimized implementation.

Figure 14 also shows the effect of tile size on total runtime. With larger tile sizes, fewer passes need to be made over the same data. However, the larger the tile size, the longer is the stream program which needs to be run, and this can adversely impact memory access patterns. The competing effects lead to a moderate value for the ideal streaming tile size.

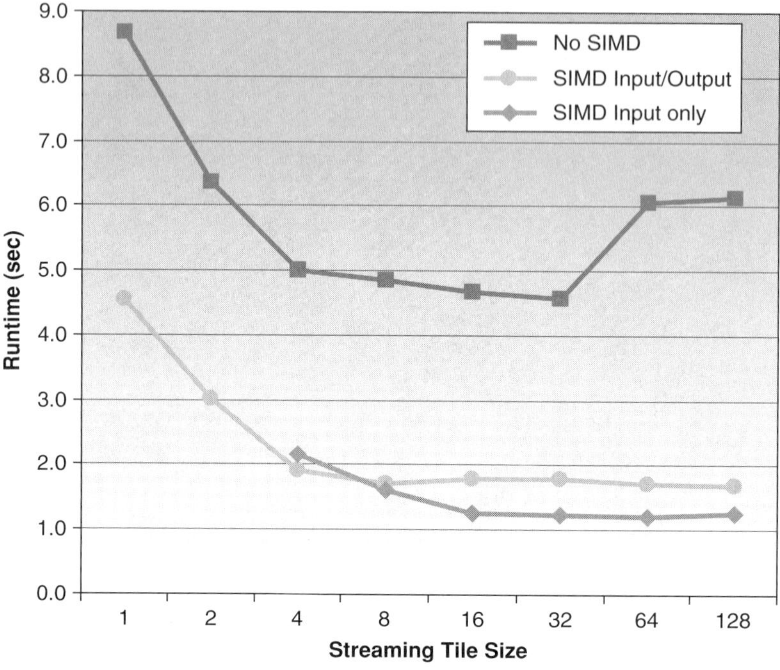


FIG. 14. Performance of the GPU on the $256^3$ covariance matrix creation under a variety of SIMDization optimizations and streaming tile sizes.

### *3.3.4 MTA-II*

***3.3.4.1 Molecular Dynamics.*** The MTA-2 architecture provides an optimal mapping to the MD algorithm because of its uniform memory latency architecture. In other words, there is no penalty for accessing atoms outside the cutoff limit or the cache boundaries, in an irregular fashion, as is the case in the microprocessor-based systems. In order to parallelize calculations in step 2, we moved the reduction operation inside the loop body. Figure 15 shows the performance difference before and after adding several pragmas to the code to remove phantom dependencies from this loop.

In order to explore the impact of the uniform memory hierarchy of the MTA-2 architecture, we compare its performance with the OpenMP multi-threaded implementation on the Intel quad-core Clovertown processor. Figure 16 shows runtime in milliseconds on the two systems when the number of OpenMP threads (number of Clovertown cores) and the number of MTA-2 processors for three workload sizes are increased. Although the performance of the Clovertown processor

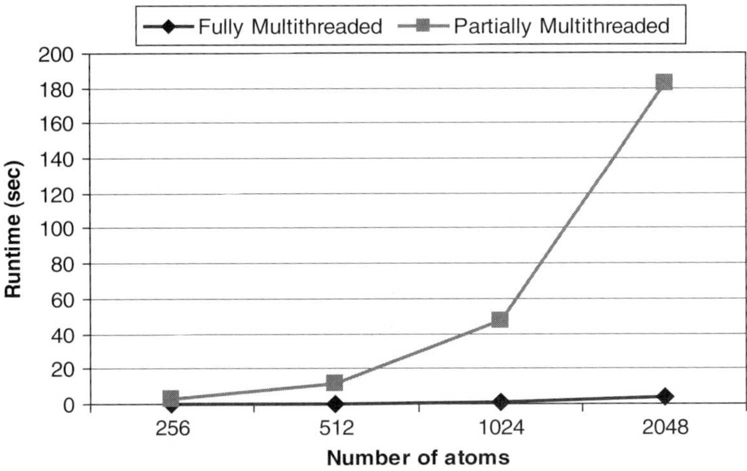


FIG. 15. Performance comparison of fully vs. partially multi-threaded versions of the MD kernel for the MTA-2.

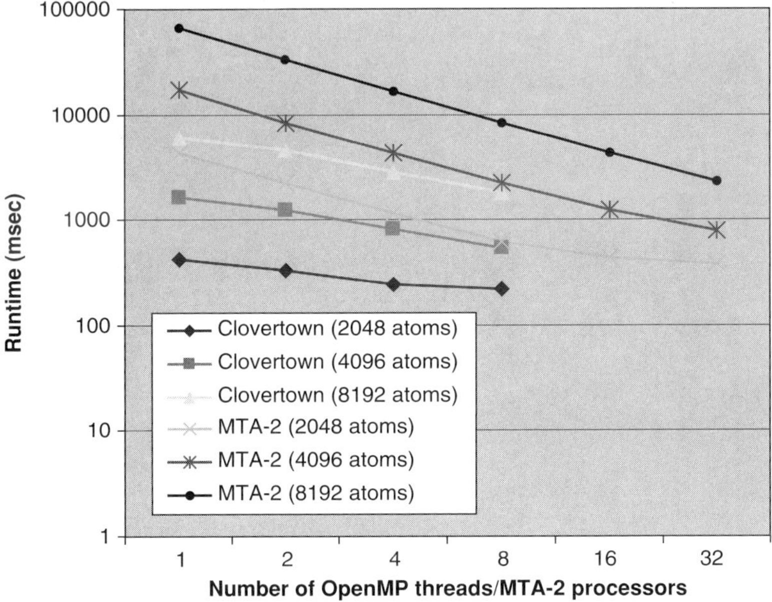


FIG. 16. Runtime in milli-seconds with multi-threaded implementation.

(released in November 2006) is significantly higher than that of the MTA-2 system (released in early 2002) for the same number of cores/MTA-2 processors, the MD workload scales almost linearly on the MTA-2 processor. Note that the clock frequency of MTA-2 is 200 MHz, while the Clovertown operates at 2.4 GHz clock frequency. Speedup (runtime on a single execution unit/runtime on $n$ execution units) shown in Fig. 17 confirms that the fine-grain multi-threading on the MTA-2 system provides relatively high scaling compared with the OpenMP implementation.

*3.3.4.2 HSI Covariance Matrix.* Similar to the MD application, the covariance matrix calculation was only partially optimized by the MTA-2 compiler. To enable full multi-threading, we moved the reduction operation outside the inner loop and introduced an array element. A full multi-threaded version of the application is then produced by the MTA-2 compiler. Figure 18 and 19 compare performance and relative speedup of the OpenMP multi-threaded implementation and MTA-2

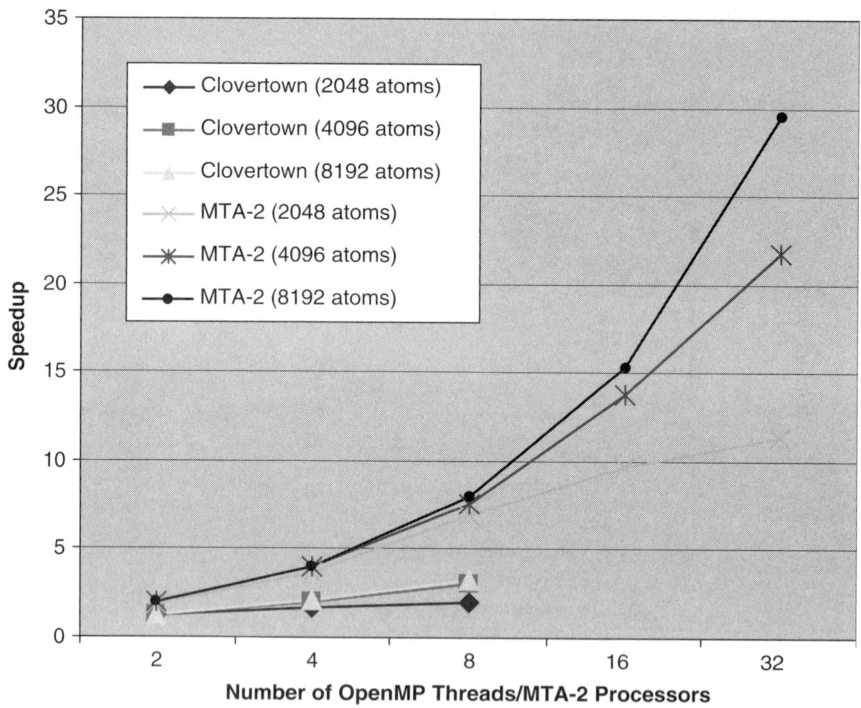


FIG. 17. Parallel efficiency on Clovertown cores (2 sockets) and MTA-2 processors.

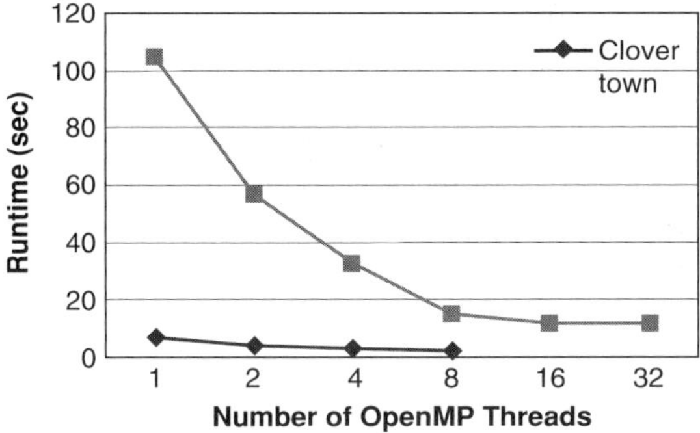


FIG. 18. Runtime in milli-seconds with multi-threaded implementation (HSI).

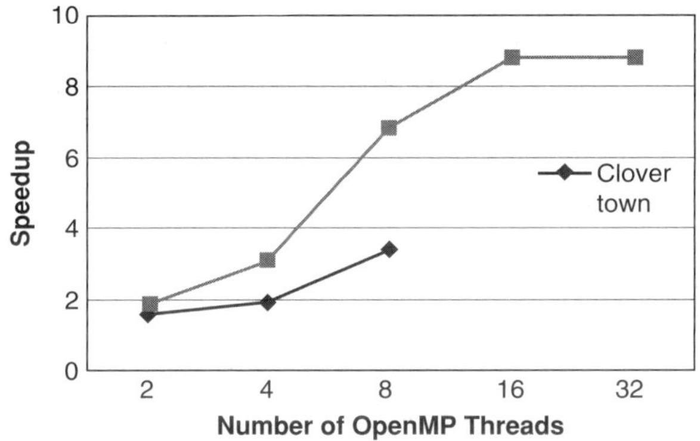


FIG. 19. Parallel efficiency on Clovertown cores and MTA-2 processors (HSI).

multi-threaded implementation, respectively. We observe that although the time-to-solution is much faster on the recent quad-core Clovertown system, the MTA-2 system provides high parallel efficiency on up to 16 threads.

## 3.4 Productivity

The preceding section reviewed a crucial aspect of the HPCS program's productivity goal – sustained performance on real-world codes – and presented performance and scaling results in terms of runtimes and parallel speedups. But another critical contributor to HPC productivity occurs before the codes are ever run. In this section, we discuss and compare relative performance improvement, and performance-to-productivity ratios, by taking into account the level of effort involved in optimizing the same molecular dynamics (MD) algorithm on the target architectures. Since it is not trivial to quantify the code development effort, which depends on a number of factors including the level of experience of the code developer, the degree of familiarity with the programming model and the attributes of the target system, we measure a quantifiable value called Source Lines of Code (SLOC). We recognize that SLOC does not encapsulate and fully represent the code optimization effort, but it has been extensively used and reported in a large number of productivity studies on parallel and high-performance computing systems. We further divide the SLOC into *effective* SLOC and *boilerplate* SLOC. The distinction is intended to quantify the learning curve associated with the unique architectures investigated here, as there is some amount of boilerplate code that one must write to get any application working and can typically be re-used on further applications. For example, code for SPE thread launches and DMA transfers on the Cell is highly reusable, and on the GPU this might include initialization of OpenGL and other graphics primitives. So the 'total' SLOC is close to what one might expect when presented with the architecture for the first time, and the 'effective' SLOC (with boilerplate code discounted) approximates to what one might expect with the platform.

We measure the relative performance of the optimized, SSE-enabled microprocessor (single-core Intel Woodcrest) version and the optimized implementation as $Performance_{ratio} = \frac{Runtime_{Woodcrest-core}}{Runtime_{emerging-architecure}}$, and we measure the productivity by comparing the SLOC ratio of the test suite as $SLOC_{ratio} = \frac{SLOC_{optimised-implementation}}{SLOC_{serial-implementation}}$. Although no code modification is performed in the serial version, we extensively studied the impact of various compile-time and runtime optimization flags offered by the Intel C compiler (version 9.1). These optimizations included operations such as Inter Procedural Optimization (IPO), auto-parallelization and SSE-enabled code generation/vectorization. Hence, our reference runtime results are optimal for the single-core Woodcrest platform. In order to quantify the trade-offs between time spent tuning a code versus the benefit seen via shorter runtimes, we introduce the concept of 'Relative Productivity', in the form of the relative development time productivity (RDTP) metric, defined as speedup divided by relative effort, i.e., the ratio of the first two metrics [42].

Some might observe that additional optimization can often result in fewer lines of code, and thus suggest that it is misleading to use SLOC as a productivity metric. While potentially true, that effect is greatly mitigated in this study. First, these devices ostensibly require adding code, not subtracting it, simply to get these devices to function as accelerators. Hence, an increase in the lines of code, when compared with the single-threaded CPU version, almost certainly requires an increase in the amount of effort. This is in dramatic contrast to other kinds of optimizations, such as within homogeneous CPU code and loop reordering, which can entail considerable effort with no increase in SLOC. Secondly, the fact that the added code was subject to these kinds of statement-level-optimizations, which have a non-linear impact on SLOC, does not invalidate the comparison, because the original single-threaded code was subject to these same transformations. In other words, because we are comparing optimized code with optimized code, SLOC remains a useful metric for the optimization effort.

In Table VIII, we list the ratio of source lines of code (SLOC), both in terms of effective SLOC and total SLOC, and the relative improvement in performance on our target platforms. The 'Performance Ratio' column in Table VIII is the speedup relative to the reference single-threaded implementation running on a 2.67-GHz Woodcrest Xeon compiled with the Intel 9.1 compiler, using the flags that achieved the best performance, including SSE3 instructions and inter-procedural optimization. The final column, 'Relative Productivity', is the relative development time productivity (RDTP) metric defined above, where a higher number indicates more benefit for less code development effort. The RDTP metric presented in Table VIII is calculated using effective SLOC, as the boilerplate code required no additional development effort.

First, we calculate RDTP for the OpenMP implementation on the Intel multi-core platforms. Since there is very little boilerplate code for the OpenMP implementation, the SLOC ratio compared with that of the serial implementation is not high. Performance is measured for 32K-atoms runs on the reference Woodcrest core against the 4 OpenMP thread and 8 OpenMP thread runs on Woodcrest and Clovertown, respectively. The RDTP for the Woodcrest is well over one and for the 8 cores, the ratio is greater than 2. We therefore conclude that the OpenMP implementation does not

TABLE VIII

PERFORMANCE AND PRODUCTIVITY OF AN MD CALCULATION ON THE EMERGING ARCHITECTURES RELATIVE TO THE SINGLE-CORE, SSE-ENABLED WOODCREST IMPLEMENTATION. NOTE THAT THE PERFORMANCES OF OPENMP AND MTA IMPLEMENTATIONS ARE GATHERED ON MULTIPLE CORES/PROCESSORS

| | SLOC Ratio (Total) | SLOC Ratio (Effective) | Performance Ratio | Relative Productivity |
|---|---|---|---|---|
| OpenMP (Woodcrest, 4 cores) | 1.07 | 1.059 | 1.713 | 1.618 |
| OpenMP (Clovertown, 8 cores) | 1.07 | 1.059 | 2.706 | 2.556 |
| Cell (8 SPEs) | 2.27 | 1.890 | 2.531 | 1.339 |
| GPU (NVIDIA 7900GTX) | 3.63 | 2.020 | 2.502 | 1.239 |
| MTA-2 (32 processors) | 1.054 | 1.054 | 1.852 | 1.757 |

TABLE IX

PERFORMANCE AND PRODUCTIVITY OF A COVARIANCE MATRIX CREATION ON THE EMERGING ARCHITECTURES RELATIVE TO THE SINGLE-CORE, SSE-ENABLED WOODCREST IMPLEMENTATION. NOTE THAT THE PERFORMANCES OF OPENMP AND MTA IMPLEMENTATIONS ARE GATHERED ON MULTIPLE CORES/PROCESSORS

| | SLOC Ratio (Total) | SLOC Ratio (Effective) | Performance Ratio | Relative Productivity |
|---|---|---|---|---|
| OpenMP (Woodcrest, 4 cores) | 1.070 | 1.047 | 2.746 | 2.624 |
| OpenMP (Clovertown, 8 cores) | 1.070 | 1.047 | 2.859 | 2.732 |
| Cell (8 SPEs) | 5.605 | 3.442 | 8.586 | 2.495 |
| GPU (NVIDIA 7900GTX) | 11.302 | 1.977 | 4.705 | 2.380 |
| MTA-2 (32 processors) | 1.093 | 1.093 | 0.481 | 0.440 |

have a negative performance-to-productivity ratio, as this implementation can utilize the target system resources effectively.

For the Cell processor, our final performance numbers were obtained using the latest XLC compiler. Our implementation limited us to a comparison at 4 K atoms, but effective parallelization and use of SIMD instructions nevertheless resulted in good performance, even when the problem was smaller. However, manual handling of the decomposition and the various aspects of SPE coding did result in a noticeable increase in SLOC, and as such the RDTP for the Cell processor was approximately 1.3.

The GPU had comparable performance to the Cell – though the parallelization is handled at a finer granularity, the SIMD instructions were utilized in a similar fashion. Though we rely on the GPU to handle the distribution of the parallel work among the shader units, collection of the results and setting up of the graphics primitives in a way the GPU can process still takes some coding effort, even after most boilerplate routines are discounted. As such, the effective SLOC ratio is the highest of all platforms, and the RDTP, though still greater than one, is the lowest among the platforms.

Finally, we compare the fine-grain multi-threaded implementation on the MTA-2 system. Due to a highly optimizing compiler, very few code modifications are required to optimize the time-critical loop explicitly; the remaining loops were automatically optimized by the compiler, resulting in very low code development overheads. We compare performance of a 32 K-atoms run on 32 MTA-2 processors. Note that the uniform memory hierarchy for 32 processors provides for good scaling and somewhat compensates for the difference in the clock rates of the two systems. Like the OpenMP implementation, the RDTP for the fine-grain multi-threading on MTA-2 is greater than 1; in fact, it is close to the dual-core (4 cores in total) Woodcrest system's RDTP.

Note that we have not utilized multiple sockets and processors for all our target devices. However, it is possible to utilize more than one Cell processor in parallel, as blade systems have two sockets on the board, and similarly one can place two GPUs in a node with more than one PCI-Express slot. So, with additional effort one could include an additional level of parallelism for these platforms. As such, we introduce Table X to show the comparison of performance and productivity when limited to a single 'socket' or 'processor', with as much inherent parallelism (cores, shaders, SPEs) as this implies. For Woodcrest, this means we are limited to one socket and thus two cores; for Clovertown, four cores; and for MTA-2, 128 streams. In these comparisons, only the Clovertown, Cell and GPU sustained RDTP metrics greater than one. The Cell and the GPU implementation, on the other hand, provide over 2x speedup over the reference optimized serial implementation.

We would like to emphasize that the results presented in Tables VIII, IX, X, and XI should not be considered the absolute performance measures of the targeted devices. First, the level of maturity in the software stack for scientific code development is not consistent across all platforms. Second, some target devices presented in the paper do not represent the state-of-the-art devices in the field, while others were released very recently. For instance, the Clovertown and Woodcrest systems are the most recent releases among all the platforms. In contrast, the 2.4-GHz Cell processor used here is over one year old, the 7900GTX has already been supplanted by its successor GPU

TABLE X
PERFORMANCE AND PRODUCTIVITY OF A 4K-ATOM MD CALCULATION (SINGLE SOCKET/PROCESSOR COMPARISONS)

| | Performance Ratio | Relative Productivity |
|---|---|---|
| OpenMP (Woodcrest, 2 cores) | 1.031 | 0.973 |
| OpenMP (Clovertown, 4 cores) | 1.407 | 1.329 |
| Cell (8 SPEs) | 2.531 | 1.339 |
| GPU (NVIDIA 7900GTX) | 2.367 | 1.172 |
| MTA-2 (1 processor, 128 streams) | 0.0669 | 0.063 |

TABLE XI
PERFORMANCE AND PRODUCTIVITY FOR A $256^3$ HSI DATA CUBE (SINGLE SOCKET/PROCESSOR COMPARISONS)

| | Performance Ratio | Relative Productivity |
|---|---|---|
| OpenMP (Woodcrest, 2 cores) | 1.794 | 1.714 |
| OpenMP (Clovertown, 4 cores) | 1.823 | 1.742 |
| Cell (8 SPEs) | 8.586 | 2.495 |
| GPU (NVIDIA 7900GTX) | 4.705 | 2.380 |
| MTA-2 (1 processor, 128 streams) | 0.054 | 0.050 |

from NVIDIA and the MTA-2 system was released in early 2002 and is not an active product from Cray.

# 4. The DARPA HPCS Language Project

Another important goal of the HPCS project has been to improve the productivity of software designers and implementers by inventing new languages that facilitate the creation of parallel, scalable software. Each of the three Phase II vendors proposed a language – Chapel from Cray, X10 from IBM, Fortress from Sun – for this purpose. (Sun was not funded in Phase III, so Fortress is no longer being supported by DARPA. Nonetheless, it remains a significant contribution to the HPCS goals, and we include it here.) Before we consider these 'HPCS languages' themselves, we provide the context in which this development has taken place. Specifically, we discuss current practice, compare some early production languages with the HPCS languages, and comment on previous efforts to introduce new programming languages for improved productivity and parallelism.

## 4.1 Architectural Developments

Language development for productivity is taking place at a time when the architecture of large-scale machines is still an area of active change. Innovative network interfaces and multi-processor nodes are challenging the ability of current programming model implementations to exploit the best performance the hardware can provide, and multicore chips are adding another level to the processing hierarchy. The HPCS hardware efforts are at the leading edge of these innovations. By combining hardware and languages in one program, DARPA is allowing language designs that may take advantage of unique features of one system, although this design freedom is tempered by the desire for language ubiquity. It is expected that the new HPCS programming models and languages will exploit the full power of the new architectures, while still providing reasonable performance on more conventional systems.

*4.1.0.3 Current Practice.* Most parallel programs for large-scale parallel machines are currently written in a conventional sequential language (Fortran-77, Fortran-90, C or C++) with calls to the MPI message-passing library. The MPI standard [63, 64] defines bindings for these languages. Bindings for other languages (particularly Java) have been developed and are in occasional use but are not part of the MPI standard. MPI is a realization of the message-passing model, in which processes with completely separate address spaces communicate with explicit calls to send and receive functions. MPI-2 extended this model in several ways (parallel I/O, remote memory access and dynamic process management), but the bulk of MPI programming utilizes only the MPI-1 functions. The use of the MPI-2 extensions is more limited, but usage is increasing, especially for parallel I/O.

#### *4.1.0.4 The PGAS Languages.*

In contrast to the message-passing model, the Partitioned Global Address Space (PGAS) languages provide each process direct access to a single globally addressable space. Each process has local memory and access to the shared memory.[5] This model is distinguishable from a symmetric shared-memory model in that shared memory is logically partitioned, so there is a notion of near and far memory explicit in each of the languages. This allows programmers to control the layout of shared arrays and of more complex pointer-based structures.

The PGAS model is realized in three existing languages, each presented as an extension to a familiar base language: UPC (Unified Parallel C) [58] for C; Co-Array Fortran (CAF) [65] for Fortran, and Titanium [68] for Java. The three PGAS languages make references to shared memory explicit in the type system, which means that a pointer or reference to shared memory has a type that is distinct from references to local memory. These mechanisms differ across the languages in subtle ways, but in all three cases the ability to statically separate local and global references has proven important in performance tuning. On machines lacking hardware support for global memory, a global pointer encodes a node identifier along with a memory address, and when the pointer is dereferenced, the runtime must deconstruct this pointer representation and test whether the node is the local one. This overhead is significant for local references and is avoided in all three languages due to expressions that are statically known to be local. This allows the compiler to generate code that uses a simpler (address-only) representation and avoids the test on dereference.

These three PGAS languages share with the strict message-passing model a number of processes fixed at job start time, with identifiers for each process. This results in a one-to-one mapping between processes and memory partitions and allows for very simple runtime support, since the runtime has only a fixed number of processes to manage and these typically correspond to the underlying hardware processors. The languages run on shared memory hardware, distributed memory clusters and hybrid architectures. Each of these languages is the focus of current compiler research and implementation activities, and a number of applications rely on them. All three languages continue to evolve based on application demand and implementation experience, a history that is useful in understanding requirements for the HPCS

[5] Because they access shared memory, some languages use the term 'thread' rather than 'process'.

languages. UPC and Titanium have a set of collective communication operations that gang the processes together to perform reductions, broadcasts and other global operations, and there is a proposal to add such support to CAF. UPC and Titanium do not allow collectives or barrier synchronization to be done on subsets of processes, but this feature is often requested by users. UPC has parallel I/O support modelled after MPIs, and Titanium has bulk I/O facilities as well as support to checkpoint data structures, based on Java's serialization interface. All three languages also have support for critical regions and there are experimental efforts to provide atomic operations.

The distributed array support in all three languages is fairly rigid, a reaction to the implementation challenges that plagued the High Performance Fortran (HPF) effort. In UPC, distributed arrays may be blocked, but there is only a single blocking factor that must be a compile-time constant; in CAF, the blocking factors appear in separate 'co-dimensions'; and Titanium does not have built-in support for distributed arrays, but they are programmed in libraries and applications using global pointers and a built-in all-to-all operation for exchanging pointers. There is an ongoing tension in this area of language design, most visible in the active UPC community, between the generality of distributed array support and the desire to avoid significant runtime overhead.

*4.1.0.5 The HPCS Languages.* As part of Phase II of the DARPA HPCS Project, three vendors – Cray, IBM, and Sun – were commissioned to develop new languages that would optimize software development time as well as performance on each vendor's HPCS hardware, which was being developed at the same time. Each of the languages – Cray's Chapel [57], IBM's X10 [66] and Sun's Fortress [53] – provides a global view of data (similar to the PGAS languages), together with a more dynamic model of processes and sophisticated synchronization mechanisms.

The original intent of these languages was to exploit the advanced hardware architectures being developed by the three vendors and in turn to be particularly well supported by these architectures. However, in order for these languages to be adopted by a broad sector of the community, they will also have to perform reasonably well on other parallel architectures, including the commodity clusters on which much parallel software development takes place. (The advanced architectures will also have to run 'legacy' MPI programs well in order to facilitate the migration of existing applications.)

Until recently, the HPCS languages were being developed quite independently by the vendors; however, DARPA also funded a small, academically based effort to consider the languages together, in order to foster vendor cooperation and perhaps eventually to develop a framework for convergence to a single high-productivity language [61]. (Recent activities on this front are described below.)

*4.1.0.6 Cautionary Experiences.* The introduction of a new programming language for more than research purposes is a speculative activity. Much effort can be expended without creating a permanent impact. We mention two well-known cases.

In the late 1970s and early 1980s, an extensive community effort was mounted to produce a complete, general-purpose language expected to replace both Fortran and COBOL, the two languages in most widespread use at the time. The result, called Ada, was a large, full-featured language and even had constructs to support parallelism. It was required for many U.S. Department of Defense software contracts, and a large community of programmers eventually developed it. Today, Ada is used within the defense and embedded systems community, but it did not supplant the established languages. A project with several similarities to the DARPA HPCS program was the Japanese '5th Generation' project of the 1980s. Like the DARPA program, it was a ten-year project involving both a new programming model, presented as a more productive approach to software development and new hardware architectures designed by multiple vendors to execute the programming model efficiently and in parallel. The language realizing the model, called CLP (Concurrent Logic Programming), was a dialect of Prolog and was specifically engineered for parallelism and high performance. The project was a success in training a generation of young Japanese computer scientists, but it has had no lasting influence on the parallel computing landscape.

*4.1.0.7 Lessons.* Programmers *do* value productivity, but reserve the right to define it. Portability, performance and incrementality seem to have mattered more in the recent past than did elegance of language design, power of expression or even ease of use, at least when it came to programming large scientific applications. Successful new sequential languages have been adopted in the past twenty-five years, but each has been a modest step beyond an already established language (from C to C++, from C++ to Java). While the differences between each successful language have been significant, both timing of the language introduction and judicious use of familiar syntax and semantics were important. New 'productivity' languages have also emerged (Perl, Python, and Ruby); but some of their productivity comes from the interpreted nature, and they neither show high performance nor show specific suitability to parallelism.

The PGAS languages, being smaller steps beyond established languages, thus present serious competition for the HPCS languages, despite the advanced, and even elegant, features exhibited by Chapel, Fortress and X10. The most serious competition, however, comes from the more established message-passing interface, MPI, which has been widely adopted and provides a base against which any new language must compete. In the next section, we describe some of the 'productive' features of MPI, as a way of setting the bar for the HPCS languages and providing some opportunities for improvement over MPI as we progress. New approaches to scalable parallel programming must offer a significant advantage over MPI and must not omit critical features that have proven useful in the MPI experience.

## 4.2 The HPCS Languages as a Group

The detailed, separate specifications for the HPCS languages can be found in [60]. In this section, we consider the languages together and compare them along several axes in order to present a coherent view of them as a group.

***Base Language.*** The HPCS languages use different sequential bases. X10 uses an existing object-oriented language, Java, inheriting both good and bad features. It gains Java support for multi-dimensional arrays, value types and parallelism and gains tool support from IBM's extensive Java environment. Chapel and Fortress use their own, new object-oriented languages. An advantage of this approach is that the language can be tailored to science (Fortress even explores new, mathematical character sets), but the fact that a great intellectual effort is required in order to get the base language right has slowed development and may deter users.

***Creating Parallelism.*** Any parallel programming model must specify how the parallelism is initiated. All three HPCS languages have parallel semantics; that is, there is no reliance on automatic parallelism, nor are the languages purely data parallel with serial semantics, like the core of HPF. All of them have dynamic parallelism for loops as well as tasks and encourage the programmer to express as much parallelism as possible, with the idea that the compiler and runtime system will control how much is actually executed in parallel. There are various mechanisms for expressing different forms of task parallelism, including explicit spawn, asynchronous method invocation and futures. Fortress is unusual in that it makes parallelism the default semantics for both loops and for argument evaluation; this encourages programmers to 'think in parallel', which may result in very highly parallel code, but it could also prove surprising to programmers. The dynamic parallelism exhibits the most significant semantic difference between the HPCS language and the existing PGAS languages with their static parallelism model. It presents the greatest opportunity to improve performance and ease of use relative to these PGAS languages and MPI. Having dynamic thread support along with data, parallel operators may encourage a higher degree of parallelism in the applications and may allow for simply expressing this parallelism directly rather than mapping it to a fixed process model in the application. The fine-grained parallelism can be used to mask communication latency, reduce stalls at synchronization points and take advantage of hardware extensions such as SIMD units and hyperthreading within a processor.

The dynamic parallelism is also the largest implementation challenge for the HPCS languages, since it requires significant runtime support to manage. The experience with Charm++ shows the feasibility of such runtime support for a class of very dynamic applications with limited dependencies [62]. A recent UPC project that involved the application of multi-threading to a matrix factorization problem reveals some of the challenges that arise from more complex dependencies between tasks. In that UPC code, the application-level scheduler manages user-level threads on top of UPC's static process model: it must select tasks on the critical path to avoid idle time, delay allocating memory for non-critical tasks to avoid running out of memory and ensure that tasks run long enough to gain locality benefits in the memory hierarchy. The scheduler uses application-level knowledge to meet all of these constraints, and performance depends critically on the quality of that information; it is not clear as to how such information would be communicated to one of the HPCS language runtimes.

***Communication and Data Sharing.*** All three of the HPCS languages use a global address space for sharing state, rather than an explicit message-passing model. They all support shared multi-dimensional arrays as well as pointer-based data structures. X10 originally allowed only remote method invocations rather than direct reads and writes to remote values, but this restriction has been relaxed with the introduction of 'implicit syntax', which is syntactic sugar for a remote read or write method invocation.

Global operations such as reductions and broadcasts are common in scientific codes, and while their functionality can be expressed easily in shared memory using a loop, they are often provided as libraries or intrinsics in parallel programming models. This allows for tree-based implementations and the use of specialized hardware that exists on some machines. In MPI and some of the existing PGAS languages, these operations are performed as 'collectives': all processes invoke the global operation together so that each process can perform the local work associated with the operation. In data parallel languages, global operations may be converted to collective operations by the compiler. The HPCS languages provide global reductions without explicitly involving any of the other threads as a collective: a single thread can execute a reduction on a shared array. This type of one-sided global operation fits nicely in the PGAS semantics, as it avoids some of the issues related to processes modifying the data involved in a collective while others are performing the collective [58]. However, the performance implications are not clear. To provide tree-based implementation and to allow work to be performed locally, a likely implementation will be to spawn a remote thread to reduce the values associated with each process. Since that thread may not run immediately, there could be a substantial delay in waiting for the completion of such global operations.

***Locality.*** The HPCS languages use a variation of the PGAS model to support locality optimizations in shared data structures. X10's 'places' and Chapel's 'locales' provide a logical notion of memory partitions. A typical scenario maps each memory partition at program startup to a given physical compute node with one or more processors and its own shared memory. Other mappings are possible, such as one partition per processor or per core. Extensions to allow for dynamic creation of logical memory partitions have been discussed, although the idea is not fully developed. Fortress has a similar notion of a 'region', but regions are explicitly tied to the machine structure rather than being virtualized, and regions are hierarchical to reflect the design of many current machines.

All three languages support distributed data structures, in particular distributed arrays that include user-defined distributions. These are much more general than those in the existing PGAS languages. In Fortress, the distribution support is based on the machine-dependent region hierarchy and is delegated to libraries rather than being in the language itself.

***Synchronization Among Threads and Processes.*** The most common synchronization primitives used in parallel applications today are locks and barriers. Barriers are incompatible with the dynamic parallelism model in the HPCS languages, although their effect can be obtained by waiting for the completion of a set of threads. X10 has a sophisticated synchronization mechanism called 'clocks', which can be thought of as barriers with attached tasks. Clocks provide a very general form of global synchronization that can be applied to subsets of threads.

In place of locks, which are viewed by many as cumbersome and error prone, all three languages support atomic blocks. Atomic blocks are semantically more elegant than locks, because the syntactic structure forces a matching 'begin' and 'end' to each critical region, and the block of code is guaranteed to be atomic with respect to all other operations in the program (avoiding the problems of acquiring the wrong lock or deadlock). Atomic blocks place a larger burden on runtime support: one simple legal implementation involves a single lock to protect all atomic blocks[6], but the performance resulting from such an implementation is probably unacceptable. More aggressive implementations will use speculative execution and rollback, possibly relying on hardware support within shared memory systems. The challenge comes from the use of a single global notion of atomicity, whereas locks may provide

[6] This assumes atomic blocks are atomic only with respect to each other, not with respect to individual reads and writes performed outside an atomic block.

atomicity on two separate data structures using two separate locks. The information that the two data structures are unaliased must be discovered dynamically in a setting that relies on atomics. The support for atomics is not the same across the three HPCS languages. Fortress has abortable atomic sections, and X10 limits atomic blocks to a single place, which allows for a lock-per-place implementation.

The languages also have some form of a 'future' construct that can be used for producer–consumer parallelism. In Fortress, if one thread tries to access the result of another spawned thread, it will automatically stall until the value is available. In X10, there is a distinct type for the variable on which one waits and its contents, so the point of potential stalls is more explicit. Chapel has the capability to declare variables as 'single' (single writer) or 'sync' (multiple readers and writers).

*4.2.0.8 Moving Forward.* Recently, a workshop was held at Oak Ridge National Laboratory, bringing together the three HPCS language vendors, computer science researchers representing the PGAS languages and MPI, potential users from the application community and program managers from DARPA and the Department of Energy's Office of Advanced Scientific Computing. In this section, we describe some of the findings of the workshop at a high level and present the tentative plan for further progress that evolved there.

The workshop was organized in order to explore the possibility of converging the HPCS languages to a single language. Briefings were presented on the status of each of the three languages and an effort was made to identify the common issues involved in completing the specifications and initiating the implementations. Potential users offered requirements for adoption, and computer science researchers described recent work in compilation and runtime issues for PGAS languages. One high-level finding of the workshop was the considerable diversity in the overall approaches being taken by the vendors, the computer science research relevant to the HPCS language development and the application requirements.

***Diversity in Vendor Approaches.*** Although the three vendors are all well along the path towards the completion of designs and prototype implementations of these languages that are intended to increase the productivity of software developers, they are not designing three versions of the same type of object. X10, for example, is clearly intended to fit into IBM's extensive Java programming environment. As described earlier, it uses Java as a base language, allowing multiple existing tools for parsing, compiling and debugging to be extended to the new parallel language. Cray's approach is more revolutionary, with the attendant risks and potential benefits; Chapel is an attempt to design a parallel programming language from the basic language. Sun is taking a third approach, providing a framework for experimentation with parallel language design, in which many aspects of the language are to be defined by the user and many of the features are expected to be provided by libraries instead of by the language itself. One novel feature is the option of writing code with symbols that, when displayed, can be typeset as classical mathematical symbols, improving the readability of the 'code'.

***Diversity in Application Requirements.*** Different application communities have different expectations and requirements for a new language. Although only a small fraction of potential HPC applications were represented at the workshop, there was sufficient diversity to represent a wide range of positions with respect to the new languages.

One extreme is represented by those applications for which the current programming model – MPI together with a conventional sequential language – is working well. In many cases, MPI is being used as the MPI Forum intended: the MPI calls are in libraries written by specialists, and the application programmer sees these library interfaces rather than MPI itself, thus bypassing MPI's ease-of-use issues. In many of the applications content with the status quo, the fact that the application may have a long life (measured in decades) amortizes the code development effort and makes development convenience less of an issue.

The opposite extreme is represented by those for whom rapidity of application development is *the* critical issue. Some of these codes are written in a day or two for a special purpose and then discarded. For such applications, the MPI model is too cumbersome and error prone, and the lack of a better model is a genuine barrier to development. Such applications cannot be deployed at all without a significant advancement in the productivity of programmers.

Between these extremes is, of course, a continuously variable range of applications. Such applications would welcome progress in the ease of application development and would adopt a new language in order to obtain it, but any new approach must not come at the expense of qualities that are essential in the status quo: portability, completeness, support for modularity and at least some degree of performance transparency.

***Diversity in Relevant Computer Science Research.*** The computer science research most relevant to the HPCS language development is the one that is being carried out related to the various PGAS language. Similar to the HPCS languages, PGAS languages offer a global view of data, with explicit control of locality in order to provide performance. Their successful implementation has involved research on compilation techniques that are likely to be useful as the language design is finalized for the HPCS languages and as production compilers, or at least serious prototypes, are beginning to be developed. The PGAS languages, and associated research, also share with the HPCS languages the need for runtime systems that support lightweight communication of small amounts of data. Such portable runtime libraries are being developed in both the PGAS and MPI implementation research projects [55, 56].

The PGAS languages are being used in applications to a limited extent, while the HPCS languages are still being tested for expressiveness on a number of example kernels and benchmarks.

The issue of the runtime system is of particular interest, because its standardization would bring multiple benefits. A standard syntax and semantics for a low-level communication library that could be efficiently implemented on a variety of current communication hardware and firmware would benefit the entire programming model implementation community: HPCS languages, PGAS languages, MPI implementations and others. A number of such portable communications exist now (GASNet [54], ADI-3, ARMCI), although most have been developed with a particular language or library implementation in mind.

***Immediate Needs.*** Despite the diverse approaches to the languages being taken by the vendors, some common deficiencies were identified in the workshop. These are areas were not focused up on while the initial language designs were being formulated, but at present there is really a need to address these areas if the HPCS languages need to attract the attention of the application community.

*4.2.0.9 Performance.* The Fortress [59] and X10 [67] implementations are publicly available and an implementation of Chapel exists, but is not yet released. So far these prototype implementations have focused on expressivity rather than performance. This direction has been appropriate up to this point, but now that one can see how various benchmarks and kernels can be expressed in these languages, one wants to see how they can be compiled for performance competitive with the performance of existing approaches, especially for scalable machines. While the languages may not reach their full potential without the HPCS hardware being developed by the same vendors, the community needs some assurance that the elegant language constructs, such as those used to express data distributions, can indeed be compiled into efficient programs for current scalable architectures.

*4.2.0.10 Completeness.* The second deficiency involves completeness of the models being presented. At this point, none of the three languages has an embedded parallel I/O model. At the very least, the languages should define how to read and write distributed data structures from and into single files, and the syntax for doing so should enable an efficient implementation that can take advantage of parallel file systems.

Another feature that is important in multi-physics applications is modularity in the parallelism model, which allows subsets of processors to act independently. MPI has 'communicators' to provide isolation among separate libraries or separate physics models. The PGAS languages are in the process of introducing 'teams' of processes to accomplish the same goals. Because the HPCS languages have a dynamic parallel operator combined with data parallel operators, this form of parallelism should be expressible, but more work is needed to understand the interactions between the abstraction mechanisms used to create library interfaces and the parallelism features.

***A Plan for Convergence.*** On the last day of the workshop, a plan for the near future emerged. It was considered too early to force a convergence on one language in the near term, given that the current level of diversity seemed to be beneficial to the long-term goals of the HPCS project, rather than harmful. The level of community and research involvement could be increased by holding a number of workshops over the next few years in specific areas, such as memory models, data distributions, task parallelism, parallel I/O, types, tools and interactions with other libraries. Preliminary plans were made to initiate a series of meetings, loosely modelled on the MPI process, to explore the creation of a common runtime library specification.

An approximate schedule was proposed at the workshop. In the next eighteen months (i.e., by the end of the calendar year 2007), the vendors should be able to freeze the syntax of their respective languages. In the same time frame, workshops should be held to address the research issues described above. Vendors should be encouraged to establish 'performance credibility' by demonstrating the competitive performance of some benchmark on some high-performance architecture. This would not necessarily involve the entire language, nor would it necessarily demand better performance of current versions of the benchmark. The intent would be to put to rest the notion that a high-productivity language precludes high performance. Also during this time, a series of meetings should be held to determine whether a common communication subsystem specification can be agreed upon.

The following three years should see the vendors improve performance of all parts of their languages. Inevitably, during this period the languages will continue to evolve independently with experience. At the same time, aggressive applications should get some experience with the languages. After this period, when the languages have had an opportunity to evolve in both design and implementations while applications have had the chance to identify strengths and weaknesses of each, the consolidation period would begin. At this point (2010–2011), an MPI forum-like activity could be organized to take advantage of the experience now gained, in order to cooperatively design a single HPCS language with the DARPA HPCS languages as input (much as the MPI Forum built on, but did not adopt any of, the message-passing library interfaces of its time).

By 2013, then, we could have a new language, well vetted by the application community, well implemented by HPCS vendors and even open-source developers, which could truly accelerate productivity in the development of scientific applications.

*4.2.0.11 Conclusion.* The DARPA HPCS language project has resulted in exciting experimental language research. Excellent work is being carried out by each of the vendor language teams, and it is to be hoped that Sun's language effort will not suffer from the end of Sun's hardware development contract with DARPA. Now is the time to get the larger community involved in the high-productivity programming model and language development effort, through workshops targeted at outstanding relevant research issues and through experimentation with early implementations of all the 'productivity' languages. In the long run, acceptance of any new language for HPC is a speculative proposition, but there is much energy and enthusiasm for the project, and a reasonable plan is in place by which progress can be made. The challenge involves a transition of the HPCS language progress made to-date into the future community efforts.

# 5. Research on Defining and Measuring Productivity

Productivity research under the HPCS program has explored better ways to define and measure productivity. The work that was performed under Phase 1 and Phase 2 of the HPCS program had two major thrusts. The first thrust was in the study and analysis of software development time. Tools for accomplishing this thrust included surveys, case studies and software evaluation tools. The second thrust was the development of a productivity figure of merit, or metric. In this section, we will present the research that occurred in Phase 1 and Phase 2 of the HPCS program in these areas. This research has been described in depth in [69] and [70]. This section will provide an overview of the research documented in those publications and will provide pointers to specific articles for each topic.

## 5.1 Software Development Time

Much of the architectural development in the past decades has focused on raw hardware performance and the technologies responsible for it, including faster clock speeds, higher transistor densities, and advanced architectural structures for exploiting instruction-level parallelism. Performance metrics, such as GFLOPS/second and

MOPS/watt, were exclusively employed to evaluate new architectures, and to reflect this focus on hardware performance.

A key, revolutionary aspect of the HPCS program is its insistence that software be included in any performance metric used to evaluate systems. The program participants realized early that true time for achieving a solution on any HPC system is not just the execution time, but is in fact the sum of development time and execution time. Not only are both important, but the piece of the puzzle that has always been ignored, development time, has always dominated time-to-solution – usually by orders of magnitude. This section describes the ground-breaking research done in understanding and quantifying development time and its contribution to the productivity puzzle.

## *5.1.1 Understanding the Users*[7]

Attempts to evaluate the productivity of an HPC system require an understanding of what productivity means to all its users. For example, researchers in computer science work to push the boundaries of computational power, while computational scientists use those advances to achieve increasingly detailed and accurate simulations and analysis. Staffs at shared resource centers enable broad access to cutting-edge systems while maintaining high system utilization. While each of these groups use HPC resources, their differing needs and experiences affect their definitions of productivity.

Computational scientists and engineers face many challenges when writing codes for high-end computing systems. The HPCS program is developing new machine architectures, programming languages and software tools to improve the productivity of scientists and engineers. Although the existence of these new technologies is important for improving productivity, they will not achieve their stated goals if individual scientists and engineers are not able to effectively use them to solve their problems. A necessary first step in determining the usefulness of new architectures, languages and tools is to gain a better understanding of what the scientists and engineers do, how they do it and what problems they face in the current high-end computing development environment. Because the community is very diverse, it is necessary to sample different application domains to be able to draw any meaningful conclusions about the commonalities and trends in software development in this community.

Two important studies were carried out during Phases 1 and 2 of the HPCS program to better identify the needs and characteristics of the user and application spaces that are the targets for these new architectures. The first team worked with the San Diego Supercomputer Center (SDSC) and its user community [73]. This team analyzed

[7] Material taken from [73] and [76].

data from a variety of sources, including SDSC support tickets, system logs, HPC developer interviews and productivity surveys distributed to HPC users, to better understand how HPC systems are being used, and where the best opportunities for productivity improvements are. The second team analyzed 10 large software projects from different application domains to gain deeper insight into the nature of software development for scientific and engineering software [76]. This team worked with ASC-Alliance projects, which are DOE-sponsored computational science centers based at five universities across the country, as well as codes from the HPCS mission partners.

Although the perspectives and details of the two studies were quite different, a number of common conclusions emerged with major relevance for the community of HPCS tool developers. Table XII and Table XIII summarize the conclusions of the two studies.

Common themes from these two studies are that end results are more important than machine performance (we're interested in the engine, but we drive the car!); visualization and easy-to-use tools are key; and HPC programmers are primarily domain experts driven by application needs, not computer scientists interested in fast computers. The implications for HPCS affect both the types of tools that should be developed and how productivity should ultimately be measured on HPCS systems from the user's perspective.

### 5.1.2 Focusing the Inquiry[8]

Given the difficulty in deriving an accurate general characterization of HPC programmers and their productivity characteristics, developing a scientific process for

TABLE XII
SDSC STUDY CONCLUSIONS

| SDSC Study Conclusions |
| --- |
| HPC users have diverse concerns and difficulties with productivity. |
| Users with the largest allocations and most expertise are not necessarily the most productive. |
| Time to solution is the limiting factor for productivity on HPC systems, not computational performance. |
| Lack of publicity and education are not the main roadblocks to adoption of performance and parallel debugging tools–ease of use is more significant. |
| HPC programmers do not require dramatic performance improvements to consider making structural changes to their codes. |
| A computer science background is not crucial to success in performance optimization. |
| Visualization is the key to achieving high productivity in HPC in most cases. |

[8] Material taken from [79] and [88].

TABLE XIII
ASC/HPCS PROJECT SURVEY

| Goals and drivers of code development |
|---|
| • Code performance is not the driving force for developers or users; the science and portability are of primary concern.<br>• Code success depends on customer satisfaction. |
| **Actions and characteristics of code developers** |
| • Most developers are domain scientists or engineers, not computer scientists.<br>• The distinction between developer and user is blurry.<br>• There is high turnover in the development team. |
| **Software engineering process and development workflow** |
| • There is minimal but consistent use of software engineering practices.<br>• Development is evolutionary at multiple levels.<br>• Tuning for a specific system architecture is rarely done, if ever.<br>• There is little reuse of MPI frameworks.<br>• Most development effort is focused on implementation rather than maintenance. |
| **Programming languages** |
| • Once selected, the primary languages does not change.<br>• Higher level languages (e.g., Matlab) are not widely adopted for the core of applications. |
| **Verification and validation** |
| • Verification and validation are very difficult in this domain.<br>• Visualization is the most common tool for validation. |
| **Use of support tools during code development** |
| • Overall, tool use in lower than in other software development domains.<br>• Third party (externally developed) software and tools are viewed as a major risk factor. |

evaluating productivity is even more difficult. One team of researchers responded with two broad commitments that could serve more generally to represent the aims of the productivity research team as a whole: [79]

1. Embrace the broadest possible view of productivity, including not only machine characteristics but also human tasks, skills, motivations, organizations and culture, to name just a few; and
2. Put the investigation of these phenomena on the soundest scientific basis possible, drawing on well-established research methodologies from relevant fields, many of which are unfamiliar within the HPC community.

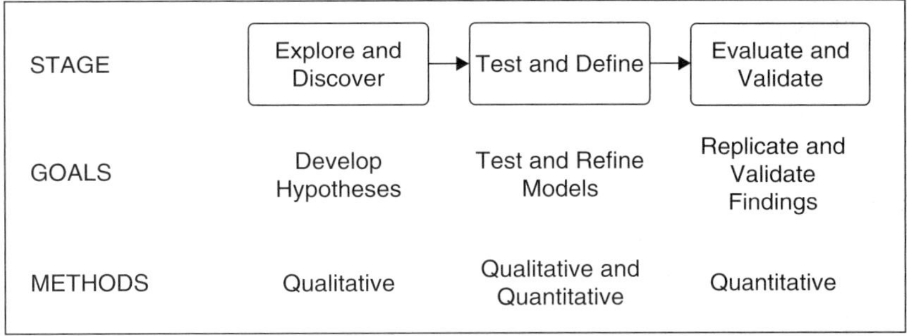


FIG. 20. Research framework.

This team of researchers outlined a three-stage research design shown in Fig. 20. For the first stage, exploration and discovery, case studies and other qualitative methods are used to produce the insights necessary for hypothesis generation. For the second stage, qualitative and quantitative methods are combined to test and refine models. The quantitative tool used by this team in the second stage was HackyStat, an in-process software engineering measurement and analysis tool. Patterns of activity were used to generate a representative workflow for HPC code development. In the third stage, the workflows were validated via quantitative models that were then used to draw conclusions about the process of software development for HPC systems.

A number of case studies were produced in the spirit of the same framework, with the goal of defining a workflow that is specific to large-scale computational scientific and engineering projects in the HPC community [88]. These case studies identified seven development stages for a computational science project:

1. Formulate questions and issues
2. Develop computational and project approach
3. Develop the program
4. Perform verification and validation
5. Make production runs
6. Analyze computational results
7. Make decisions.

These tasks strongly overlap with each other, with a lot of iteration among the steps and within each step. Life cycles for these projects are very long, in some cases 30–40 years or more, far longer than typical IT projects. Development teams are large and diverse, and individual team members often do not have working experience with the modules and codes being developed by other module sub-teams, making software engineering challenges much greater than those of typical IT projects. A typical project workflow is shown in Fig. 21.

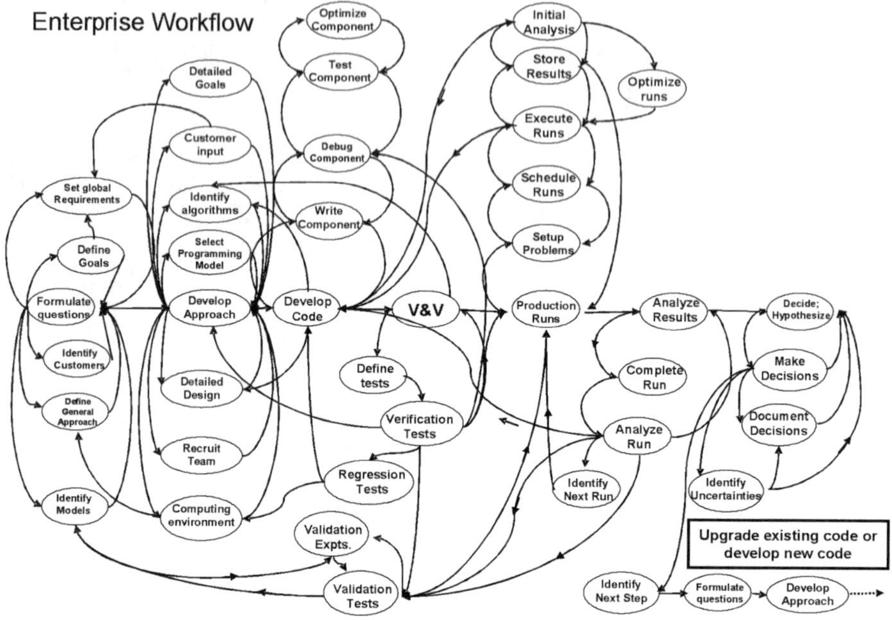


FIG. 21. Comprehensive workflow for large-scale CSE project.

With these projects, we begin to see the development of frameworks and representations to guide the productivity evaluation process. The derivation of workflows is the key to understanding any process, and a disciplined understanding is necessary before any improvements can be made or assessed. The workflows for software development could be as complex as the projects they reflect and as diverse as the programmers who implement them. In the next section, we will see some examples of the types of tools that can be used once formal representations, specific measurements, and quantifiable metrics have been defined.

## 5.1.3 Developing the Evaluation Tools[9]

A pre-requisite for the scientific and quantified study of productivity in HPC systems is the development of tools and protocols to study productivity. As a way to understand the particular needs of HPC programmers, prototype tools were developed in Phases 1 and 2 of the HPCS program to study productivity in the HPC community. The initial focus has been on understanding the effort involved in coding for HPC systems and

[9] Material taken from [75], [78], and [82].

the defects that occur in developing programs. Models of workflows that accurately explain the process that HPC programmers use to build their codes were developed. Issues such as time involved in developing serial and parallel versions of a program, testing and debugging of the code, optimizing the code for a specific parallelization model (e.g., MPI, OpenMP) and tuning for specific machine architectures were all topics of the study. Once those models are developed, the HPCS system developers can then work on the more crucial problems of what tools and techniques will better optimize a programmer's ability to produce quality code more efficiently.

Since 2004, studies of programmer productivity have been conducted, in the form of human-subject experiments, at various universities across the U.S. in graduate-level HPC courses. [75] Graduate students in HPC classes are fairly typical of novice HPC programmers who may have years of experience in their application domain but very little experience in HPC-style programming. In the university studies, multiple students were routinely given the same assignment to perform, and experiments were conducted to control for the skills of specific programmers (e.g., experimental meta-analysis) in different environments. Due to their relatively low cost, student studies are an excellent environment for debugging protocols that might be later used on practising HPC programmers. Limitations of student studies include the relatively short programming assignments, due to the limited time in a semester, and the fact that these assignments must be picked for their educational value to the students as well as their investigative value to the research team.

Using the experimental environment developed under this research, various hypotheses about HPC code development can be tested and validated (or disproven!). Table XIV shows some sample hypotheses and how they would be tested using the

TABLE XIV
HPC CODE DEVELOPMENT HYPOTHESES

| Hypothesis | Test Measurement |
|---|---|
| The average time to fix a defect due to race conditions will be longer in a shared memory program compared with a message-passing program. | Time to fix defects due to race conditions |
| On average, shared memory programs will require less effort than message-passing models, but the shared memory outliers will be greater than the message-passing outliers. | Total development time |
| There will be more students who submit incorrect shared memory programs compared with message-passing programs. | Number of students who submit incorrect solutions |
| An MPI implementation will require more code than an OpenMP implementation. | Size of code for each implementation |

various tools that have been developed. In addition to the verification of hypotheses about code development, the classroom experiments have moved beyond effort analysis and started to look at the impact of defects (e.g., incorrect or excessive synchronization, incorrect data decomposition) on the development process. By understanding how, when, and what kinds of defects appear in HPC codes, tools and techniques can be developed to mitigate these risks and to improve the overall workflow. Automatic determination of workflow is not precise, so these studies involved a mixture of process activity (e.g., coding, compiling, executing) and source code analysis techniques.

Some of the key results of this effort include:

- Productivity measurements of various workflows, where productivity is defined as relative speedup divided by relative effort. Relative speedup is reference (sequential) execution time divided by parallel execution time, and relative effort is parallel effort divided by reference (sequential effort). The results of student measurements for various codes show that this metric behaves as expected, i.e., good productivity means lower total effort, lower execution time and higher speedup.
- Comparison of XMT-C (a PRAM-like execution model) with MPI-based codes in which, on average, students required less effort to solve the problem using XMT-C compared with MPI. The reduction in mean effort was approximately 50%, which was statistically significant according to the parameters of the study.
- Comparison of OpenMP and MPI defects did not yield statistically significant results, which contradicts a common belief that shared memory programs are harder to debug. Since defect data collection was based on programmer-supplied effort forms, which are not accurate, more extensive defect analysis is required.
- Collection of low-level behavioral data from developers in order to understand the workflows that exist during HPC software development. A useful representation of HPC workflow could help both characterize the bottlenecks that occur during development and support a comparative analysis of the impact of different tools and technologies upon workflow. A sample workflow would consist of five states: serial coding, parallel coding, testing, debugging and optimization.

Figure 22 presents results of the relative development-time productivity metric, using the HPCChallenge benchmark described in the next section in this chapter. With the exception of Random Access (the implementation of which does not scale well on distributed memory computing clusters), the MPI implementations all fall into the upper-right quadrant of the graph, indicating that they deliver some level of

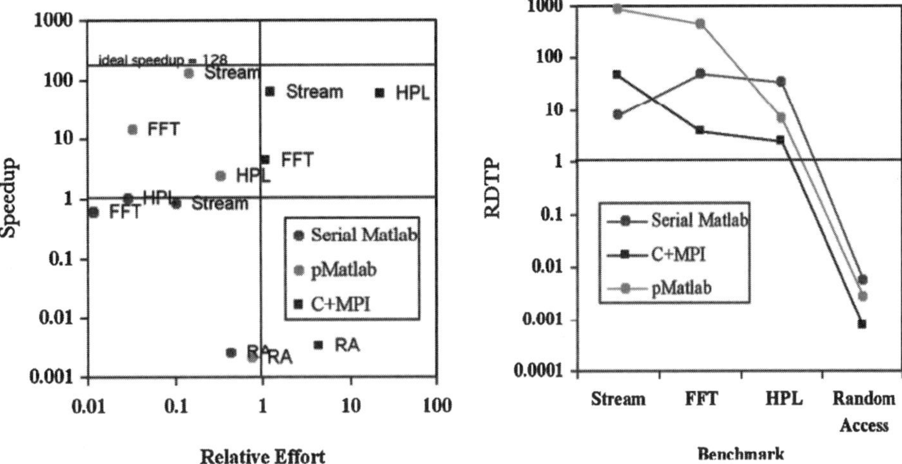


FIG. 22. Speedup vs. relative effort and RDTP for the HPC challenge.

parallel speedup, while requiring greater effort than the serial code. As expected, the serial Matlab implementations do not deliver any speedup, but all require less effort than the serial code. The pMatlab implementations (except Random Access) fall into the upper-left quadrant of the graph, delivering parallel speedup while at the same time requiring less effort.

In another pilot study [78], students worked on a key HPC code using C and PThreads in a development environment that included automated collection of editing, testing and commanding line data using Hackystat. The 'serial coding' workflow state was automatically inferred as the editing of a file not containing any parallel constructs (such as MPI, OpenMP or PThread calls) and the 'parallel coding' workflow state as the editing of a file containing these constructs. The 'testing' state was inferred as the occurrence of unit test invocation using the CUTest tool. In the pilot study, the debugging or optimization workflow states could not be inferred, as students were not provided with tools to support either of these activities that we could instrument. On the basis of these results, researchers concluded that inference of workflow may be possible in an HPC context and hypothesize that it may actually be easier to infer these kinds of workflow states in a professional setting, since more sophisticated tool support that can help support conclusions regarding the intent of a development activity is often available. It is also possible that a professional setting may reveal that the five states initially selected are appropriate for all HPC development contexts. There may be no 'one size fits all' set of workflow states and that custom sets of states for different HPC organizations will be required in order to achieve the goal of accurately modelling the HPC software development process.

To support the tools and conclusions described in this section, an Experiment Manager was developed to more easily collect and analyze data during the development process. It includes effort, defect and workflow data, as well as copies of every source program used during development. Tracking effort and defects should provide a good data set for building models of productivity and reliability of high-end computing (HEC) codes. Fig. 23 shows the components of the Experiment Manager and how they interact.

Another key modelling tool developed in Phases 1 and 2 of the HPCS program involves the analysis of an HPC development workflow using sophisticated mathematical models. [82] This work is based on the observation that programmers go through an identifiable, repeated process when developing programs, which can be characterized by a directed graph workflow. Timed Markov Models (TMMs) are one way to quantify such directed graphs . A simple TMM that captures the workflows of programmers working alone on a specific problem was developed. An experimental setup was constructed in which the student's homework in a parallel computing class was instrumented. Tools were developed for instrumentation, modelling, and simulating different what-if scenarios in the modelled data. Using our model and tools, the workflows of graduate students programming the same assignment in C/MPI4 and

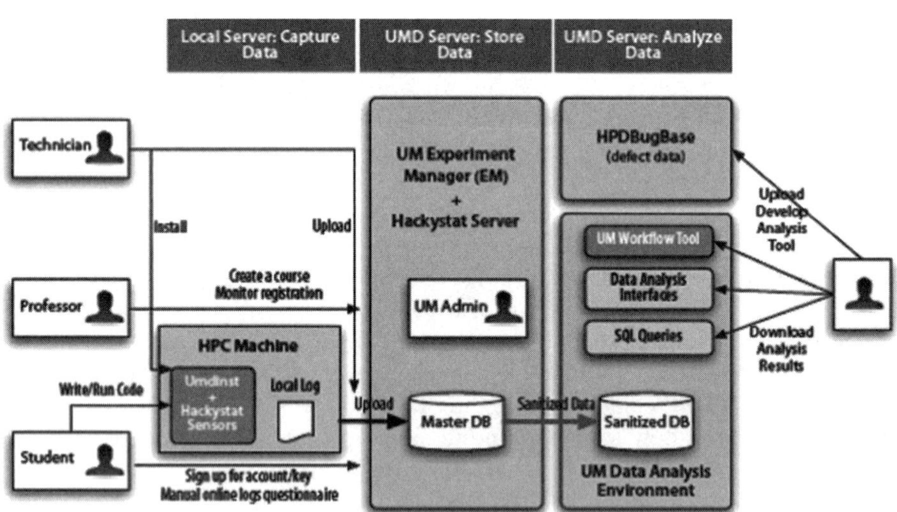


FIG. 23. Experiment manager structure.

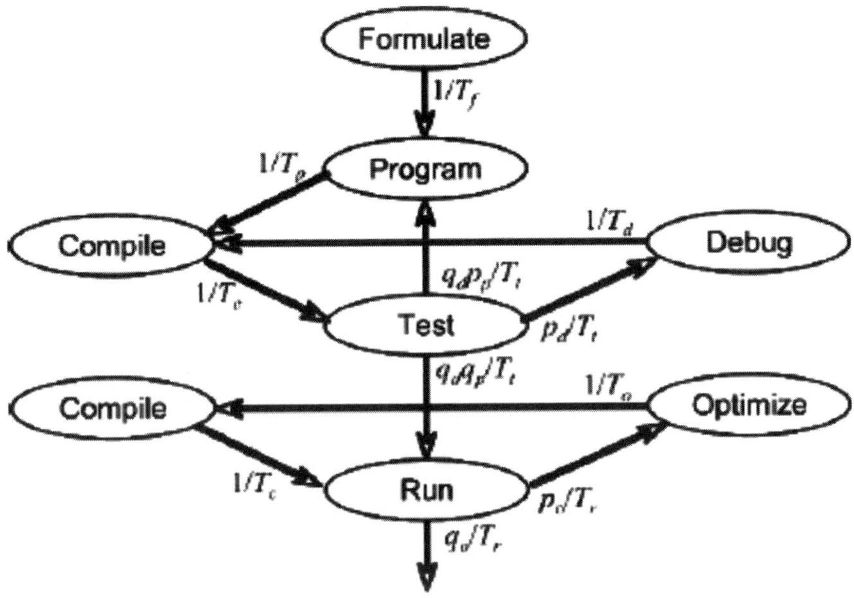


FIG. 24. Lone programmer workflow.

UPC5 were compared – something that is not possible without a quantitative model and measurement tools. Figure 24 shows the workflow used, where:

- $T_f$ represents the time taken to formulate the new algorithmic approach.
- $T_p$ is the time necessary to implement the new algorithm in a program.
- $T_c$ is the compile time.
- $T_t$ is the time necessary to run a test case during the debugging phase.
- $T_d$ is the time the programmer takes to diagnose and correct the bug.
- $T_r$ is the execution time for the performance-tuning runs. This is the most obvious candidate for a constant that should be replaced by a random variable.
- $T_o$ is the time the programmer takes to identify the performance bottleneck and to program an intended improvement.
- $P_p$ is the probability that debugging will reveal a necessity to redesign the program.
- $P_d$ is the probability that more debugging will be necessary.
- $P_o$ is the probability that more performance optimization will be necessary.
- $q_p$, $q_d$ and $q_o$ are $1 - P_p$, $1 - P_d$ and $1 - P_o$, respectively.

Using the TMM, the workflow of UPC programs was compared to that of C/MPI programs on the same problem. The data collection process gathers enough data at compile time and run time so that programmer experience can be accurately recreated offline. A tool for automatic TMM generation from collected data, as well as a tool for representing and simulating TMMs was built. This allowed replay of the sequence of events (every compile and run) and collection-specific data that may be required by the modelling process but was not captured while the experiment was in progress. The resulting data showed that a 'test' run is successful 8% of the time for C/MPI and 5% of the time for UPC; however, in the optimization cycle, 28% of C/MPI runs introduced new bugs compared to only 24% in case of UPC runs. It is not clear whether these differences are significant, given this small sample size. A programmer spends much longer to attempt an optimization (763 seconds for UPC and 883 seconds for C/MPI) than to attempt to remove a bug (270–271 seconds). The time to optimize UPC (763 seconds) is smaller that for MPI (883 seconds), suggesting perhaps that UPC optimization is carried out in a more small-granularity, rapid-feedback way.

The research presented in this section takes the formalisms and representations developed under productivity research and begins the scientific process of gathering measurements, building and verifying models, and then using those models to gain insight into a process, either via human analysis or via formal, mathematical methods. This is where the leap from conjecture to scientific assertion begins, and the measurements and insights presented here represent a breakthrough in software engineering research. The immediate goal for the HPCS program is to use these analytical tools to compare current HPC systems with those that are being developed for HPCS. However, we see a broader applicability for these types of methods in the computing industry. Future work in this area has the potential to take these models and use them not only to gain insight, but also to predict the performance of a given process. If we can build predictive models and tailor those models to a particular user base or application class, the gains in productivity could eventually outstrip the capability to build faster machines and may have a more lasting impact on software engineering for HPC as a whole.

### *5.1.4 Advanced Tools for Engineers*

Several advanced tools were developed under HPCS productivity research that should be mentioned here but cannot be described in detail because of space constraints. These are briefly described in the following paragraphs; more detailed information can be found in [70].

**Performance complexity (PC) metric:** [81] an execution-time metric that captures how complex it is to achieve performance and how transparent are the performance results. PC is based on performance results from a set of benchmark experiments and related performance models that reflect the behavior of a program. Residual modelling errors are used to derive PC as a measure for how transparent program performance is and how complex the performance appears to the programmer. A detailed description for calculating compatible P and PC values is presented and uses results from a parametric benchmark to illustrate the utility of PC for analyzing systems and programming paradigms.

**Compiler-guided instrumentation for application behavior understanding:** [83] an integrated compiler and runtime approach that allows the extraction of relevant program behavior information by judiciously instrumenting the source code and deriving performance metrics such as range of array reference addresses, array access stride information or data reuse characteristics. This information ultimately allows programmers to understand the performance of a given machine in relation to rational program constructs. The overall organization of the compiler and run-time instrumentation system is described and preliminary results for a selected set of kernel codes are presented. This approach allows programmers to derive a wealth of information about the program behavior with a run-time overhead of less than 15% of the original code's execution time, making this approach attractive for instrumenting and analyzing codes with extremely long running times where binary-level approaches are simply impractical.

**Symbolic performance modelling of HPCS:** [84] a new approach to performance model construction, called modelling assertions (MA), which borrows advantages from both the empirical and analytical modelling techniques. This strategy has many advantages over traditional methods: isomorphism with the application structure; easy incremental validation of the model with empirical data; uncomplicated sensitivity analysis; and straightforward error bounding on individual model terms. The use of MA is demonstrated by designing a prototype framework, which allows construction, validation and analysis of models of parallel applications written in FORTRAN or C with the MPI communication library. The prototype is used to construct models of NAS CG, SP benchmarks and a production-level scientific application called Parallel Ocean Program (POP).

**Compiler approaches to performance prediction and sensitivity analysis:** [86] the Source Level Open64 Performance Evaluator (SLOPE) approaches performance prediction and architecture sensitivity analysis by using source-level program analysis and scheduling techniques. In this approach, the compiler extracts the computation's high-level data-flow-graph information by inspection of the source code. Taking into account the data access patterns of the various references in the code, the tool uses a list-scheduling algorithm to derive performance bounds for the program under various architectural scenarios. The end result is a very fast prediction of what the performance could be and, more importantly, why the predicted performance is what it is. This research experimented with a real code that engineers and scientists use. The results yield important qualitative performance sensitivity information. This can be used to allocate computing resources to the computation in a judicious fashion, for maximum resource efficiency and to help guide the application of compiler transformations such as loop unrolling.

## 5.2 Productivity Metric[10]

Another key activity in the HPCS productivity research was the development of productivity metrics that can be used to evaluate both current and future HPCS systems. The former is necessary to establish a productivity baseline against which to compare the projected improvements of the latter. In either case, the metric must be quantifiable, measurable and demonstrable over the range of machines competing in the program.

Establishing a single, reasonably objective quantitative framework to compare competing high-productivity computing systems has been difficult to accomplish. There are many reasons for this, not the least of which is the inevitable subjective component of the concept of productivity. Compounding the difficulty, there are many elements that make up productivity and these are weighted and interrelated differently in the wide range of contexts into which a computer may be placed. But because significantly improved productivity for high-performance government and scientific computing is the key goal of the HPCS program, evaluation of this critical characteristic across these contexts is clearly essential.

This is not entirely a new phenomenon. Anyone who has driven a large-scale computing budget request and procurement has had to address the problem of turning a set of preferences and criteria, newly defined by management, into a budget justification and a procurement figure of merit that will pass muster with agency (and OMB) auditors. The process of creating such a procurement figure of merit helps to focus the mind and cut through the complexity of competing user demands and computing options. The development of productivity metrics was addressed from both a business and a system-level perspective in Phase 1 and Phase 2 research. The results of both phases are summarized in the following sections.

### *5.2.1 Business Perspective*[11]

High performance computing (HPC), also known as supercomputing, makes enormous contributions not only to science and national security, but also to business

[10] Material drawn from [72], [77] and [80].

[11] Material drawn from [72] and [77].

innovation and competitiveness – yet senior executives often view HPC as a cost, rather than as a value investment. This is largely due to the difficulty businesses and other organizations have had in determining the return on investment (ROI) of HPC systems.

Traditionally, HPC systems have been valued according to how fully they are utilized (i.e., the aggregate percentage of time that each of the processors of the HPC system is busy); but this valuation method treats all problems equally and does not give adequate weight to the problems that are most important to the organization. Due to inability to properly assess problems having the greatest potential for driving innovation and competitive advantage, organizations risk purchasing inadequate HPC systems or, in some cases, forego purchases altogether because they cannot be satisfactorily justified.

This stifles innovation within individual organizations and, in the aggregate, prevents the U.S. business sector from being as globally competitive as it could and should be. The groundbreaking July 2004 'Council on Competitiveness Study of U.S. Industrial HPC Users', sponsored by the Defense Advanced Research Projects Agency (DARPA) and conducted by market research firm IDC, found that 97% of the U.S. businesses surveyed could not exist, or could not compete effectively, without the use of HPC. Recent Council on Competitiveness studies reaffirmed that HPC typically is indispensable for companies that exploit it.

It is increasingly true that to out-compete, companies need to out-compute. Without a more pragmatic method for determining the ROI of HPC hardware systems, however, U.S. companies already using HPC may lose ground in the global competitiveness pack. Equally important, companies that have never used HPC may continue to miss out on its benefits for driving innovation and competitiveness.

To help address this issue, we present an alternative to relying on system utilization as a measure of system valuation, namely, capturing the ROI by starting with a benefit – cost ratio (BCR) calculation. This calculation is already in use at the Massachusetts Institute of Technology, where it has been proven to be effective in other contexts.

As part of the HPCS productivity research, two versions of the productivity metric were developed based on benefit-to-cost ratios. Numerical examples were provided to illustrate their use. The goal is to use these examples to show that HPC assets are not just cost items, but that they can contribute to healthy earnings reports as well as more productive and efficient staff. Detailed results are described in [72].

Another important barrier preventing greater HPC use is the scarcity of application software capable of fully exploiting current and planned HPC hardware systems. U.S. businesses rely on a diverse range of commercially available software from independent software vendors (ISVs). At the same time, experienced HPC business users want to exploit the problem-solving power of contemporary HPC hardware systems with hundreds, thousands or (soon) tens of thousands of processors to boost innovation and competitive advantage. Yet few ISV applications today can exploit ('scale to') even 100 processors, and many of the most popular applications scale to only a few processors in practice.

Market forces and technical challenges in recent years have caused the ISVs to pull away from creating new and innovative HPC applications, and no other source has arisen to satisfy this market need. For business reasons, ISVs focus primarily on the desktop computing markets, which are much larger and therefore promise a better return on R&D investments. ISVs can sometimes afford to make modest enhancements to their application software so that it can run faster on HPC systems, but substantially revising existing applications or creating new ones typically does not pay off. As a result, the software that is available for HPC systems is often outdated and incapable of scaling to the level needed to meet industry's needs for boosting problem-solving performance. In some cases, the applications that companies want simply do not exist.

This need for production-quality application software and middleware has become a soft spot in the U.S. competitiveness armor; a pacing item in the private sector's ability to harness the full potential of HPC. Without the necessary application software, American companies are losing their ability to aggressively use HPC to solve their most challenging problems and risk ceding leadership in the global marketplace. Market and resource barriers are described in detail in [77].

### 5.2.2 System Perspective[12]

Imagining that we were initiating a procurement in which the primary criterion would be productivity, defined as utility/cost, we developed figure of merit for total productivity. This framework includes such system measurables as machine performance and reliability, developer productivity and administration overhead and effectiveness of resource allocation. These are all applied using information from the particular computing site that is proposing and procuring the HPCS computer. This framework is applicable across the broad range of environments represented by HPCS mission partners and others with science and enterprise missions that are candidates for such systems. The productivity figure of merit derived under this research is shown in Fig. 25. As a convention, the letters $U$, $E$, $A$, $R$, $C$ are used to denote the variables of utility, efficiency, availability, resources and cost, respectively. The subscripts indicate the variables that address system-level (including administrative and utility) and job-level factors.

As is evident from this formulation, some aspects of the system-level efficiency will never be amenable to measurement and will always require subjective evaluation.

[12] Material drawn from [80].

$$P = \frac{U_{sys} E_{proj} E_{adm} E_{job} A_{sys} R}{C}$$

FIG. 25. System-wide productivity figure of merit.

Only subjective evaluation processes can address the first two variables in the utility numerator, for example. In principle, one can measure the last four variables, and the HPCS research program is addressing such measurements. A description of the steps required for using the overall system-level productivity figure of merit can be found in [80].

## 5.3 Conclusions

In this section, we have given a broad overview of the activities performed under Phase 1 and Phase 2 HPCS Productivity Research, in enough detail to communicate substantial results without misrepresenting the inherent complexity of the subject matter. In reality, the productivity of HPC users intrinsically deals with some of the brightest people on the planet, solving very complex problems, using the most complex computers in the world. The HPCS program has performed ground-breaking research into understanding, modelling, quantifying, representing and analyzing this complex and difficult arena; and although much has been accomplished, the surface of productivity research has barely been scratched. The tools and methodologies developed under the HPCS program are an excellent base on which a full understanding of HPC productivity can be built; but in the final analysis, those tools and methodologies must be applied to an area of human endeavour that is as diverse, specialized, individualistic, inconsistent, and even eccentric as the people who are its authors and creators. If HPCS productivity research is to have a hand in transforming the world of high-performance computing, it must evolve from a set of tools, equations and experiments into a comprehensive understanding of HPC software development in general. Such understanding will require enlarging its experimental space, both for statistical reasons and also for the purpose of refining, deepening and making mature the models and assumptions inherent in the experimental methodologies. It will require clever engineering of test conditions to isolate factors of interest and demonstrate true cause and effect relationships. It will require long-term investment in research, since experiments are difficult to 'set up' and take a long time to produce results. Finally, it will require a new generation of researchers who grasp the vital importance of understanding and improving HPC software productivity and are committed to creating a legacy for future generations of HPC systems and their users. It is the hope of the authors and all who participate in HPCS productivity research that such a vision will come into being.

## 6. The HPC Challenge Benchmark Suite

As noted earlier, productivity – the main concern of the DARPA HPCS program – depends both on the programming effort and other 'set up' activities that precede the running of application codes, and on the sustained, runtime performance of the codes. Approaches to measuring programming effort were reviewed in a prior section of this work. This section discusses the HPC Challenge (HPCC) benchmark suite, a relatively new and still-evolving tool for evaluating the performance of HPC systems on various types of tasks that form the underpinnings for most HPC applications.

The HPC Challenge[13] benchmark suite was initially developed for the DARPA HPCS program, [89] to provide a set of standardized hardware probes based on commonly occurring computational software kernels. The HPCS program involves a fundamental reassessment of how we define and measure performance, programmability, portability, robustness and, ultimately, productivity across the entire high-end domain. Consequently, the HPCC suite aimed both to give conceptual expression to the underlying computations used in this domain and to be applicable to a broad spectrum of computational science fields. Clearly, a number of compromises needed to be embodied in the current form of the suite, given such a broad scope of design requirements. HPCC was designed to approximately bound computations of high and low spatial and temporal locality (see Fig. 26, which

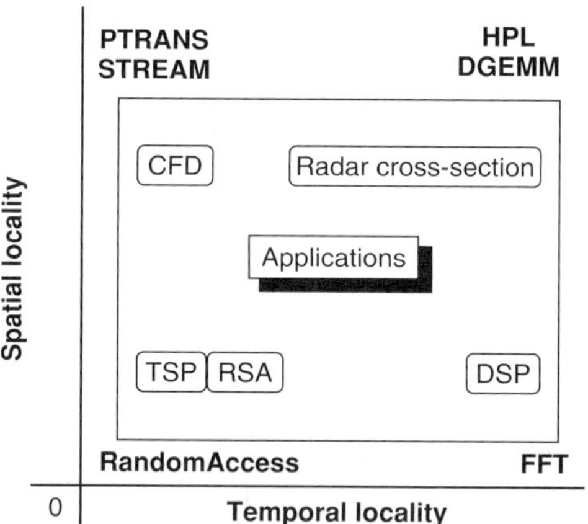


FIG. 26. The application areas targeted by the HPCS program are bound by the HPCC tests in the memory access locality space.

[13] This work was supported in part by the DARPA, NSF and DOE through the DARPA HPCS program under grant FA8750-04-1-0219 and SCI-0527260.

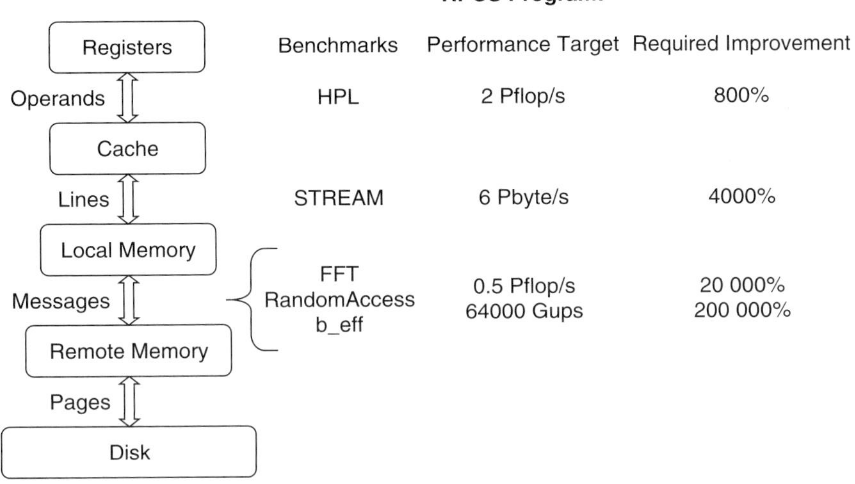


FIG. 27. HPCS program benchmarks and performance targets.

gives the conceptual design space for the HPCC component tests). In addition, because the HPCC tests consist of simple mathematical operations, HPCC provides a unique opportunity to look at language and parallel programming model issues. As such, the benchmark is designed to serve both the system user and designer communities [90].

Figure 27 shows a generic memory subsystem and how each level of the hierarchy is tested by the HPCC software, along with the design goals for the future HPCS system (i.e., the projected target performance numbers that are to come out of the wining HPCS vendor designs).

## 6.1 The TOP500 Influence

The most commonly known ranking of supercomputer installations around the world is the TOP500 list [91]. It uses the equally well-known LINPACK benchmark [92] as a single figure of merit to rank 500 of the world's most powerful supercomputers. The often-raised question about the relation between the TOP500 list and HPCC can be addressed by recognizing the positive aspects of the former. In particular, the longevity of the TOP500 list gives an unprecedented view of the high-end arena across the turbulent era of Moore's law [93] rule and the emergence of today's prevalent computing paradigms. The predictive power of the TOP500 list is likely to have a lasting influence in the future, as it has had in the past. HPCC extends the

TABLE XV
ALL OF THE TOP-10 ENTRIES OF THE 27TH TOP500 LIST THAT HAVE RESULTS IN THE HPCC DATABASE

| Rank | Name | Rmax | HPL | PTRANS | STREAM | FFT | Random Access | Lat. | B/w |
|---|---|---|---|---|---|---|---|---|---|
| 1 | BG/L | 280.6 | 259.2 | 4665.9 | 160 | 2311 | 35.47 | 5.92 | 0.16 |
| 2 | BG W | 91.3 | 83.9 | 171.5 | 50 | 1235 | 21.61 | 4.70 | 0.16 |
| 3 | ASC Purple | 75.8 | 57.9 | 553.0 | 44 | 842 | 1.03 | 5.11 | 3.22 |
| 4 | Columbia | 51.9 | 46.8 | 91.3 | 21 | 230 | 0.25 | 4.23 | 1.39 |
| 9 | Red Storm | 36.2 | 33.0 | 1813.1 | 44 | 1118 | 1.02 | 7.97 | 1.15 |

TOP500 list's concept of exploiting a commonly used kernel and, in the context of the HPCS goals, incorporates a larger, growing suite of computational kernels. HPCC has already begun to serve as a valuable tool for performance analysis. Table XV shows an example of how the data from the HPCC database can augment the TOP500 results.

## 6.2 Short History of the Benchmark

The first reference implementation of the HPCC suite of codes was released to the public in 2003. The first optimized submission came in April 2004 from Cray, using the then-recent X1 installation at Oak Ridge National Lab. Since then, Cray has championed the list of optimized HPCC submissions. By the time of the first HPCC birds-of-a-feather session at the Supercomputing conference in 2004 in Pittsburgh, the public database of results already featured major supercomputer makers – a sign that vendors were participating in the new benchmark initiative. At the same time, behind the scenes, the code was also being tried out by government and private institutions for procurement and marketing purposes. A 2005 milestone was the announcement of the HPCC Awards contest. The two complementary categories of the competition emphasized performance and productivity – the same goals as those of the sponsoring HPCS program. The performance-emphasizing Class 1 award drew the attention of many of the biggest players in the supercomputing industry, which resulted in populating the HPCC database with most of the top10 entries of the TOP500 list (some exceeding their performances reported on the TOP500 – a tribute to HPCC's continuous results update policy). The contestants competed to achieve the highest raw performance in one of the four tests: HPL, STREAM, RANDA and FFT. The Class 2 award, by solely focusing on productivity, introduced a subjectivity factor into the judging and also into the submission criteria, regarding what was appropriate for the contest. As a result, a wide range of solutions were submitted, spanning various programming languages (interpreted and compiled) and paradigms (with explicit and implicit parallelism). The Class 2 contest featured openly available as well as proprietary technologies, some of which were arguably confined to niche markets and some of which were widely used. The financial incentives for entry turned out to be all but needless, as the HPCC seemed to have gained enough recognition within the high-end community to elicit entries even without the monetary assistance. (HPCwire provided both press coverage and cash rewards for the four winning contestants in Class 1 and the single winner in Class 2.) At the HPCCs, second birds-of-a-feather session during the SC07 conference in Seattle, the former class was dominated by IBM's BlueGene/L at Lawrence Livermore National Lab, while the latter class was split among MTA pragma-decorated C and UPC codes from Cray and IBM, respectively.

### 6.2.1 The Benchmark Tests' Details

Extensive discussion and various implementations of the HPCC tests are available elsewhere [94, 95, 96]. However, for the sake of completeness, this section provides the most important facts pertaining to the HPCC tests' definitions.

All calculations use *double precision* floating-point numbers as described by the IEEE 754 standard [97], and no mixed precision calculations [98] are allowed. All the tests are designed so that they will run on an arbitrary number of processors (usually denoted as $p$). Figure 28 shows a more detailed definition of each of the seven tests included in HPCC. In addition, it is possible to run the tests in one of three testing scenarios to stress various hardware components of the system. The scenarios are shown in Fig. 29.

### 6.2.2 Benchmark Submission Procedures and Results

The reference implementation of the benchmark may be obtained free of charge at the benchmark's web site[14]. The reference implementation should be used for the base run: it is written in a portable subset of ANSI C [99] using a hybrid programming model that mixes OpenMP [100, 101] threading with MPI [102, 103, 104] messaging. The installation of the software requires creating a script file for Unix's make(1) utility. The distribution archive comes with script files for many common computer architectures. Usually, a few changes to any of these files will produce the script file for a given platform. The HPCC rules allow only standard system compilers and libraries to be used through their supported and documented interface, and the build procedure should be described at submission time. This ensures repeatability of the results and serves as an educational tool for end users who wish to use a similar build process for their applications.

[14] http://icl.cs.utk.edu/hpcc/

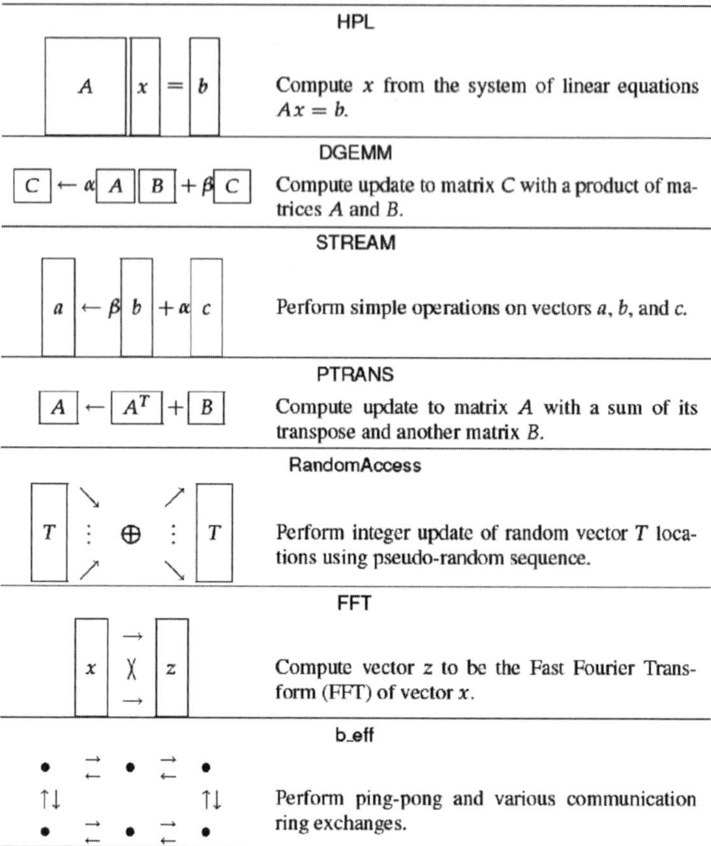


FIG. 28. Detailed description of the HPCC component tests ($A$, $B$, $C$ – matrices, $a$, $b$, $c$, $x$, $z$ – vectors, $\alpha$, $\beta$- scalars, $T$-array of 64-bit integers).

After a successful compilation, the benchmark is ready to run. However, it is recommended that changes be made to the benchmark's input file that describes the sizes of data to be used during the run. The sizes should reflect the available memory on the system and the number of processors available for computations.

There must be one baseline run submitted for each computer system entered in the archive. An optimized run for each computer system may also be submitted. The baseline run should use the reference implementation of HPCC, and in a sense it represents the scenario when an application requires use of legacy code – a code that cannot be

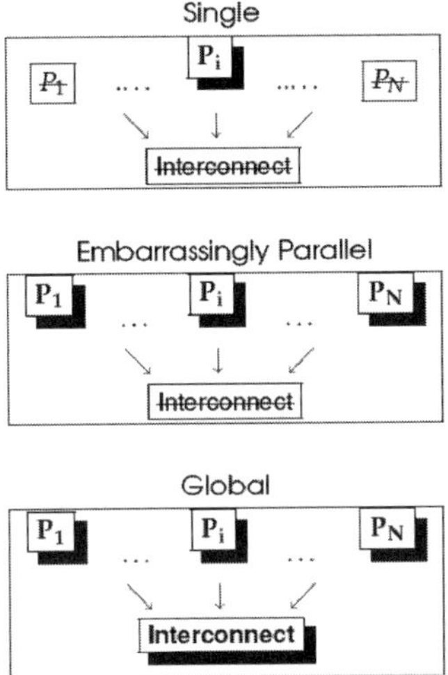


FIG. 29. Testing scenarios of the HPCC components.

changed. The optimized run allows the submitter to perform more aggressive optimizations and use system-specific programming techniques (languages, messaging libraries, etc.), but at the same time still includes the verification process enjoyed by the base run.

All of the submitted results are publicly available after they have been confirmed by email. In addition to the various displays of results and exportable raw data, the HPCC web site also offers a kiviat chart display for visual comparison systems using multiple performance numbers at once. A sample chart that uses actual HPCC results data is shown in Fig. 30.

Figure 31 show performance results of some currently operating clusters and supercomputer installations. Most of the results come from the HPCC public database.

### *6.2.3 Scalability Considerations*

There are a number of issues to be considered for benchmarks such as HPCC that have scalable input data. These benchmarks need to allow for proper stressing of arbitrary sized systems in the benchmark run. The time to run the entire suite is a major concern for institutions with limited resource allocation budgets. With these considerations in mind, each component of HPCC has been analyzed from the

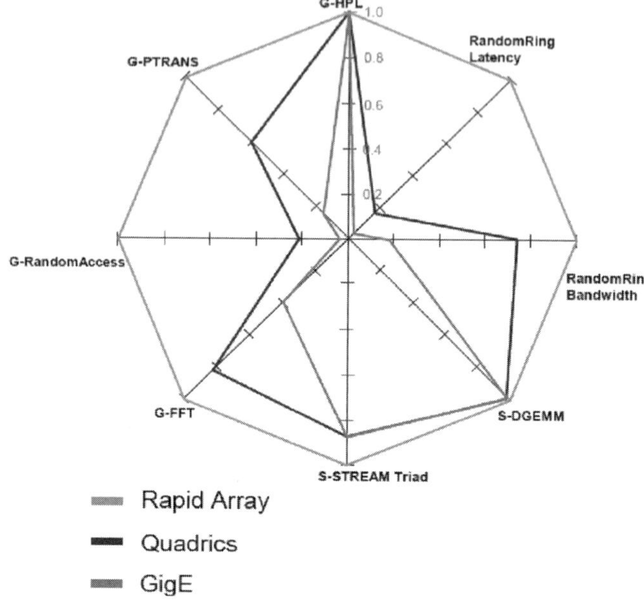


FIG. 30. Sample Kiviat diagram of results for three different interconnects that connect the same processors.

scalability standpoint, and Table XVI shows the major time complexity results. In the following tables, it is assumed that:

- $M$ is the total size of memory,
- $m$ is the size of the test vector,
- $n$ is the size of the test matrix,
- $p$ is the number of processors,
- $t$ is the time to run the test.

Clearly, any complexity formula that shows a growth faster than linear growth for any system size raises concerns about the time-scalability issue. The following HPCC tests have had to be looked at with this concern in mind:

- HPL, because it has computational complexity $O(n^3)$.
- DGEMM, because it has computational complexity $O(n^3)$.
- b_eff, because it has communication complexity $O(p^2)$.

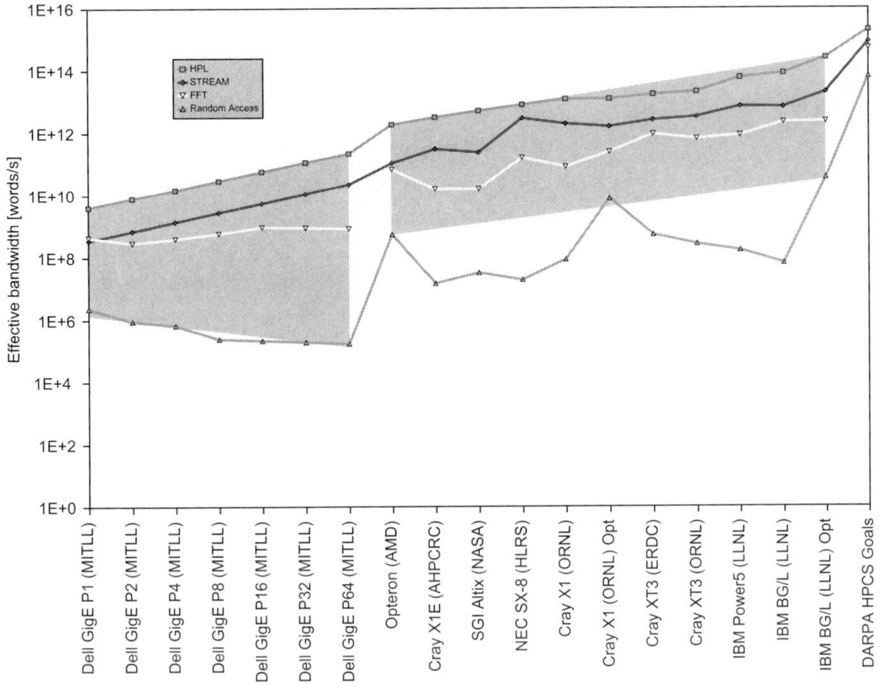


FIG. 31. Sample interpretation of the HPCC results.

TABLE XVI
TIME COMPLEXITY FORMULAS FOR VARIOUS PHASES OF THE HPCC TESTS ($m$ AND $n$ CORRESPOND TO THE APPROPRIATE VECTOR AND MATRIX SIZES, RESPECTIVELY; $p$ IS THE NUMBER OF PROCESSORS.)

| Name | Generation | Computation | Communication | Verification | Per-processor data |
|---|---|---|---|---|---|
| HPL | $n^2$ | $n^3$ | $n^2$ | $n^2$ | $p^{-1}$ |
| DGEMM | $n^2$ | $n^3$ | $n^2$ | 1 | $p^{-1}$ |
| STREAM | m | m | 1 | m | $p^{-1}$ |
| PTRANS | $n^2$ | $n^2$ | $n^2$ | $n^2$ | $p^{-1}$ |
| RandomAccess | m | m | m | m | $p^{-1}$ |
| FFT m | m | $\log_2$m | m | m $\log_2 m$ | $p^{-1}$ |
| *b_eff* | 1 | 1 | $p^2$ | 1 | 1 |

The computational complexity of HPL of order $O(n^3)$ may cause excessive running time because the time will grow proportionately to a high power of total memory size:

$$\textbf{Equation 1}\ t_{HPL} \sim n^3 = (n^2)^{3/2} \sim M^{3/2} = \sqrt{M^3}$$

To resolve this problem, we have turned to the past TOP500 data and analyzed the ratio of Rpeak to the number of bytes for the factorized matrix for the first entry on all the lists. It turns out that there are on average 6±3 Gflop/s for each matrix byte. We can thus conclude that the performance rate of HPL remains constant over time ($r_{HPL} \sim M$), which leads to a formula that is much better than Equation 1:

$$\textbf{Equation 2}\ t_{HPL} \sim n^3/r_{HPL} \sim \sqrt{M^3}/M = \sqrt{M}$$

There seems to be a similar problem with the DGEMM, as it has the same computational complexity as HPL; but fortunately, the $n$ in the formula is related to a single process memory size rather than the global one, and thus there is no scaling problem.

The b_eff test has a different type of problem: its communication complexity is $O(p^2)$, which is already prohibitive today as the number of processes of the largest system in the HPCC database is 131072. This complexity comes from the ping-pong component of b_eff that attempts to find the weakest link among all nodes and thus, theoretically, needs to look at all possible process pairs. The solution to the problem was made in the reference implementation by adapting the runtime of the test to the size of the system tested.

## 6.3 Conclusions

No single test can accurately compare the performance of any of today's high-end systems, let alone those envisioned by the HPCS program in the future. Thus, the HPCC suite stresses not only the processors, but the memory system and the interconnect. It is a better indicator of how a supercomputing system will perform across a spectrum of real-world applications. Now that the more comprehensive HPCC suite is available, it can be used in preference to comparisons and rankings based on single tests. The real utility of the HPCC benchmarks is that it can describe architectures with a wider range of metrics than just flop/s from HPL. When only HPL performance and the TOP500 list are considered, inexpensive build-your-own clusters appear to be much more cost-effective than more sophisticated parallel architectures. But the tests indicate that even a small percentage of random memory accesses in real applications can significantly affect the overall performance of that application on architectures not designed to minimize or hide memory latency. The HPCC tests provide users with additional information to justify policy and purchasing decisions. We expect to expand the HPCC suite (and perhaps remove some existing components) as we learn more about the collection and its fit with evolving architectural trends.

## 7. Summary: The DARPA HPCS Program

This document reviews the historical context surrounding the birth of the High Productivity Computing Systems (HPCS) program, including DARPA's motivation for launching this long-term high-performance computing initiative. It discusses HPCS-related technical innovations, productivity research and the renewed commitment by key government agencies to advancing leadership computing in support of national security and large science and space requirements at the start of the $21^{st}$ century.

To date, the HPCS vision of developing economically viable high-productivity computing systems, as originally defined in the HPCS white paper, has been carefully maintained. The vision of economically viable – yet revolutionary – petascale high-productivity computing systems led to significant industry and university partnerships early in the program and to a heavier industry focus later in the program. The HPCS strategy has been to encourage the vendors to not simply develop evolutionary systems, but to attempt bold *productivity* improvements, with the government helping to reduce the risks through R&D cost sharing. Productivity, by its very nature, is difficult to assess because its definition depends upon the specifics of the end-user mission, applications, team composition and end use. On the basis of the productivity definition outlined in this work, specific research results, performed by multi-agency/university HPCS productivity team, that address the challenge of providing some means of predicting, modeling and quantifying the end value 'productivity' of complex computing systems to end users were presented. The productivity research to date represents the beginning and not the end of this challenging research activity.

History will ultimately judge the progress made under HPCS during this period, but will no doubt concede that these years produced renewed public/private support and recognition for the importance of supercomputing and the need for a better path forward. It has become abundantly clear that theoretical ('peak') performance can no longer suffice for measuring computing leadership. The ability to use supercomputing to improve a company's bottom line, enhance national security, or accelerate scientific discovery has emerged as the true standard for technical leadership and national competitiveness. However, the battle for leadership is far from over. Programming large-scale supercomputers has never been easy, and the near-term prospect of systems routinely having 100 000 or more processors has made the programming challenge even more daunting.

A number of agencies, including the DOE Office of Science, National Nuclear Security Agency (NNSA), National Security Agency (NSA) and National Science Foundation (NSF) now have active programs in place to establish and maintain leadership-class computing facilities. These facilities are preparing to meet the challenges of running applications at sustained petaflop speeds (one quadrillion calculations per second) in areas ranging from national security to data analysis and scientific discovery.

The challenge through this decade and beyond is to continue the renewed momentum in high-end computing and to develop new strategies to extend the benefits of this technology to many new users, including the tens of thousands of companies and other organizations that have not moved beyond desktop computers to embrace HPC. Meeting this challenge would not only boost the innovation and competitiveness of these companies and organizations, but in the aggregate would lead to the advancement of the economic standing of the nation.

## References


[1] Badia R., Rodriguez G., and Labarta J. 2003. Deriving analytical models from a limited number of runs. In *Parallel Computing: Software Technology, Algorithms, Architectures, and Applications (PARCO 2003)*, pp. 769–776, Dresden, Germany.

[2] Bailey D. H., Barszcz E., Barton J. T., Browning D. S., Carter R. L., Dagum D., Fatoohi R. A., Frederickson P. O., Lasinski T. A., Schreiber R. S., Simon H. D., Venkatakrishnan V., and Weeratunga S. K., Fall 1991. The NAS parallel benchmarks. *The International Journal of Supercomputer Applications*, **5**(3):63–73.

[3] Carrington L., Laurenzano M., Snavely A., Campbell R., and Davis L., November 2005. How well can simple metrics predict the performance of real applications? In *Proceedings of Supercomputing (SCé05)*.

[4] Carrington L., Snavely A., Wolter N., and Gao X., June 2003. A performance prediction framework for scientific applications. In *Proceedings of the International Conference on Computational Science (ICCS 2003)*, Melbourne, Australia.

[5] Department of Defense High Performance Computing Modernization Program. Technology Insertion-06 (TI-06). http://www.hpcmo.hpc.mil/Htdocs/TI/TI06, May 2005.

[6] European Center for Parallelism of Barcelona. Dimemas. http://www.cepba.upc.es/dimemas.

[7] Gao X., Laurenzano M., Simon B., and Snavely A., September 2005. Reducing overheads for acquiring dynamic traces. In *International Symposium on Workload Characterization* (ISWC05).

[8] Gustafson J. L., and Todi R., 1999. Conventional benchmarks as a sample of the performance spectrum. *The Journal of Supercomputing*, **13**(3):321–342.

[9] Lawson C. L., and Hanson R. J., 1974. Solving least squares problems, volume 15 of Classics in Applied Mathematics. SIAM, Philadelphia, PA, 1995. An unabridged, revised republication of the original work published by Prentice-Hall, Englewood Cliffs, NJ.

[10] Luszczek P., Dongarra J., Koester D., Rabenseifner R., Lucas B., Kepner J., McCalpin J., Bailey D., and Takahashi D., March 2005. Introduction to the HPC challenge benchmark suite. Available at http://www.hpccchallenge.org/pubs/.

[11] Marin G., and Mellor-Crummey J., June 2004. Crossarchitecture performance predictions for scientific applications using parameterized models. In *Proceedings of SIGMETRICS/Performance'04*, New York, NY.
[12] McCalpin J. D., December 1995. Memory bandwidth and machine balance in current high performance computers. *IEEE Technical Committee on Computer Architecture Newsletter.*
[13] Mendes C. L., and Reed D. A., 1994. Performance stability and prediction. In *IEEE/USP International Workshop on High Performance Computing.*
[14] Mendes C. L., and Reed D. A., 1998. Integrated compilation and scalability analysis for parallel systems. In *IEEE PACT.*
[15] Saavedra R. H., and Smith A. J., 1995. Measuring cache and tlb performance and their effect on benchmark run times. In *IEEE Transactions on Computers*, **44**(10):1223–1235.
[16] Saavedra R. H., and Smith A. J., 1995. Performance characterization of optimizing compilers. In TSE21, vol. **7**, pp. 615–628.
[17] Saavedra R. H., and Smith A. J., 1996. Analysis of benchmark characteristics and benchmark performance prediction. In TOCS14, vol. **4**, pp. 344–384.
[18] Simon J., and Wierum J., August 1996. Accurate performance prediction for massively parallel systems and its applications. In *Proceedings of 2nd International Euro-Par Conference*, Lyon, France.
[19] Snavely A., Carrington L., Wolter N., Labarta J., Badia R., and Purkayastha A., November 2002. A framework for application performance modeling and prediction. In *Proceedings of Supercomputing (SC2002)*, Baltimore, MD.
[20] SPEC: Standard Performance Evaluation Corporation. http://www.spec.org, 2005.
[21] Svobodova L., 1976. Computer system performance measurement and evaluation methods: analysis and applications. In Elsevier N.Y.
[22] TI-06 benchmarking: rules & operational instructions. Department of defense high performance computing modernization program. http://www.hpcmo.hpc.mil/Htdocs/TI/TI06/ti06 benchmark inst. May 2005.
[23] Cray Inc., Cray XMT Platform, available at http://www.cray.com/products/xmt/index.html.
[24] Cray Inc., Cray MTA-2 Programmer's Guide, Cray Inc. S-2320-10, 2005.
[25] GPGPU, General Purpose computation using GPU hardware, http://www.gpgpu.org/.
[26] GROMACS, http://www.gromacs.org/.
[27] International Business Machines Corporation, Cell Broadband Engine Programming Tutorial Version 1.0, 2005.
[28] LAMMPS, http://lammps.sandia.gov/.
[29] NAMD, http://www.ks.uiuc.edu/Research/namd/.
[30] NIVDIA, http://www.nvidia.com.
[31] OpenMP specifications, version 2.5, http://www.openmp.org/drupal/mp-documents/spec25.pdf.
[32] Alam S. R., et al., 2006. Performance characterization of bio-molecular simulations using molecular dynamics, ACM Symposium of Principle and Practices of Parallel Programming.
[33] Bader D. A., et al., 2007. On the design and analysis of irregular algorithms on the cell processor: a case study of list ranking, IEEE Int. Parallel and Distributed Processing Symp. (IPDPS).
[34] Bokhari S., and Sauer J., 2004. Sequence alignment on the Cray MTA-2, Concurrency and Computation: Practice and Experience (Special issue on High Performance Computational Biology), **16**(9):823–39.
[35] Bower J., et al., 2006. Scalable algorithms for molecular dynamics: simulations on commodity clusters, *ACM/IEEE Supercomputing Conference.*
[36] Blagojevic F., et al., 2007. RAxML-cell: parallel phylogenetic tree inference on the cell broadband engine, IPDPS.

[37] Buck I., 2003. Brook-data parallel computation on graphics hardware, Workshop on Parallel Visualization and Graphics.

[38] Faulk S., et al., 2004. Measuring HPC productivity, *International Journal of High Performance Computing Applications*, **18**(4):459–473.

[39] Feo J., et al., 2005. ELDORADO, Conference on Computing Frontiers. ACM Press, Italy.

[40] Fitch B. J., et al., 2006. Blue Matter: Approaching the limits of concurrency for classical molecular dynamics, *ACM/IEEE Supercomputing Conference*.

[41] Flachs B., et al., 2006. The microarchitecture of the synergistic processor for a cell processor. *Italy:IEEE Journal of Solid-State Circuits*, **41**(1):63–70.

[42] Funk A., et al., 2006. Analysis of parallel software development using the relative development time productivity metric, CTWatch Quarterly, **2**(4A).

[43] Hwa-Joon, Mueller S. M., et al., 2006. A fully pipelined single-precision floating-point unit in the synergistic processor element of a CELL processor. *IEEE Journal of Solid-State Circuits*, **41**(4): 759–771.

[44] Kahle J. A., et al., 2005. Introduction to the Cell Microprocessor, IBM J. of Research and Development, **49**(4/5):589–604.

[45] Leach A. R., 2001. Molecular modeling: Principles and Applications, 2nd edn, Prentice Hall.

[46] Liu W., et al., 2006. Bio-sequence database scanning on a GPU, IEEE Int. Workshop on High Performance Computational Biology.

[47] Liu Y., et al., 2006. GPU accelerated Smith-Waterman. *International Conference on Computational Science*.

[48] Oliver S., et al., 2007. Porting the GROMACS molecular dynamics code to the cell processor, Proc. of 8th IEEE Intl. Workshop on Parallel and Distributed Scientific and Engineering Computing (PDSEC-07).

[49] Petrini F., et al., 2007. Multicore surprises: lessons learned from optimizing Sweep3D on the cell broadband engine, IPDPS.

[50] Ramanthan R. M., Intel Multi-core processors: Making the move to quad-core and beyond, white paper available at http://www.intel.com/technology/architecture/downloads/quad-core-06.pdf

[51] Villa et al., 2007. Challenges in mapping graph exploration algorithms on advanced multi-core processors, IPDPS.

[52] Zelkowitz M., et al., 2005. Measuring productivity on high performance computers, *11th IEEE International Symposium on Software Metric*.

[53] Allen E., Chase D., Hallett J., Luchangco V., Maessen J.-W., Ryu S., Steele G., and Tobin- Hochstadt S., The Fortress Language Specification. Available at http://research.sun.com/projects/plrg/.

[54] Bonachea D., GASNet specification. Technical Report CSD-02-1207, University of California, Berkeley, October 2002. Instructions for Typesetting Camera-Ready Manuscripts.

[55] Buntinas D., and Gropp W., Designing a common communication subsystem. In Beniamino Di Martino, Dieter Kranzlu¨uller, and Jack Dongarra, editors, Recent Advances in Parallel Virtual Machine and Message Passing Interface, volume LNCS 3666 of Lecture Notes in Computer Science, pp. 156–166. Springer, September 2005. 12th European PVM/MPI User's Group Meeting, Sorrento, Italy.

[56] Buntinas D., and Gropp W., 2005. Understanding the requirements imposed by programming model middleware on a common communication subsystem. Technical Report ANL/MCS-TM-284, Argonne National Laboratory.

[57] Chapel: The Cascade High Productivity Language. http://chapel.cs.washington.edu/.

[58] UPC Consortium. UPC language specifications v1.2. Technical Report, Lawrence Berkeley National Lab, 2005.

[59] Project Fortress code.

[60] HPCS Language Project Web Site. http://hpls.lbl.gov/.
[61] HPLS. http://hpls.lbl.gov.
[62] Kale L. V., and Krishnan S., CHARM++: a portable concurrent object oriented system based on C++. In *Proceedings of the Conference on Object Oriented Programming Systems, Languages and Applications*, September–October 1993. ACM Sigplan Notes, **28**(10):91–108.
[63] Message passing interface forum. MPI: A message-passing interface standard. *International Journal of Supercomputer Applications*, **8**(3/4):165–414, 1994.
[64] Message passing interface forum. MPI2: a message passing interface standard. *International Journal of High Performance Computing Applications*, **12**(1–2):1–299, 1998.
[65] Numrich R., and Reid J., 1998. Co-Array Fortran for parallel programming. In *ACM Fortran Forum* **17**(2):1–31.
[66] The X10 programming language. http://www.research.ibm.com/x10.
[67] The X10 compiler. http://x10.sf.net.
[68] Yelick K., Semenzato L., Pike G., Miyamoto C., Liblit B., Krishnamurthy A., Hilfinger P., Graham S., Gay D., Colella P., and Aiken A., 1998. Titanium: a high-performance Java dialect. Concurrency: Practice and Experience, **10**:825–836.
[69] Cyberinfrastructure Technology Watch (CTWatch) Quarterly, http://www.ctwatch.org, Volume 2, Number 4A, November 2006: High Productivity Computing Systems and the Path Towards Usable Petascale Computing, Part A: User Productivity Challenges, Jeremy Kepner, guest editor.
[70] Cyberinfrastructure Technology Watch (CTWatch) Quarterly, http://www.ctwatch.org, Volume 2, Number 4B, November 2006: High Productivity Computing Systems and the Path Towards Usable Petascale Computing, Part B: System Productivity Technologies, Jeremy Kepner, guest editor.
[71] Kepner J., Introduction: High Productivity Computing Systems and the Path Towards Usable Petascale Computing, MIT Lincoln Laboratory, in [69] p. 1.
[72] Making the Business Case for High Performance Computing: A Benefit-Cost Analysis Methodology Suzy Tichenor (Council on Competitiveness) and Albert Reuther (MIT Lincoln Laboratory), in [69], pp. 2–8.
[73] Wolter N., McCraacken M. O., Snavely A., Hochstein L., Nakamura T., and Basili V., What's Working in HPC: Investigating HPC User Behavior and Productivity, in [69] pp. 9–17
[74] Luszczek P., Dongarra J., and Kepner J., Design and Implementation of the HPC Challenge Benchmark Suite, in [69] pp. 18–23.
[75] Hochstein L., Nakamura T., Basili V. R., Asgari S., Zelkowitz M. V., Hollingsworth J. K., Shull F., Carver J., Voelp M., Zazworka N., and Johnson P., Experiments to Understand HPC Time to Development, in [69] pp. 24–32.
[76] Carver J., Hochstein L. M., Kendall R. P., Nakamura T., Zelkowitz M. V., Basili V. R., and Post D. E., Observations about Software Development for High End Computing, in [69] pp. 33–38.
[77] Tichenor S., Application Software for High Performance Computers: A Soft Spot for U.S. Business Competitiveness, in [69] pp. 39–45.
[78] Funk A., Basili V., Hochstein L., and Kepner J., Analysis of Parallel Software Development using the Relative Development Time Productivity Metric, in [69] pp. 46–51.
[79] Squires S., Van de Vanter M. L., and Votta L. G., Software Productivity Research in High Performance Computing, in [69] pp. 52–61.
[80] Murphy D., Nash T., Votta L., and Kepner J., A System-wide Productivity Figure of Merit, in [70] pp. 1–9.
[81] Stromaier E., Performance Complexity: An Execution Time Metric to Characterize the Transparency and Complexity of Performance, in [70] pp. 10–18.
[82] Funk A., Gilbert J. R., Mizell D., and Shah V., Modelling Programmer Workflows with Timed Markov Models, in [70] pp. 19–26.

[83] Diniz P. C., and Krishna T., A Compiler-guided Instrumentation for Application Behavior Understanding, in [70] pp. 27–34.
[84] Alam S. R., Bhatia N., and Vetter J. S., Symbolic Performance Modeling of HPCS Applications, in [70] pp. 35–40.
[85] Bader D. A., Madduri K., Gilbert J. R., Shah V., Kepner J., Meuse T., and Krishnamurthy A., Designing Scalable Synthetic Compact Applications for Benchmarking High Productivity Computing Systems, in [70] pp. 41–51.
[86] Diniz P. C., and Abramson J., SLOPE – A Compiler Approach to Performance Prediction and Performance Sensitivity Analysis for Scientific Codes, in [70] pp. 52–48.
[87] Chen T.-Y., Gunn M., Simon B., Carrington L., and Snavely A., Metrics for Ranking the Performance of Supercomputers, in [70] pp. 46–67.
[88] Post D. E., and Kendell R. P., Large-Scale Computational Scientific and Engineering Project Development and Production Workflows, in [70] pp. 68–76.
[89] Kepner J., HPC productivity: an overarching view. *International Journal of High Performance Computing Applications*, **18**(4), November 2004.
[90] Kahan W., 1997. The baleful effect of computer benchmarks upon applied mathematics, physics and chemistry. The John von Neumann Lecture at the 45th Annual Meeting of SIAM, Stanford University.
[91] Meuer H. W., Strohmaier E., Dongarra J. J., and Simon H. D., TOP500 Supercomputer Sites, 28th edition, November 2006. (The report can be downloaded from http://www.netlib.org/benchmark/top500.html).
[92] Dongarra J. J., Luszczek P., and Petitet A., 2003. The LINPACK benchmark: past, present, and future. Concurrency and Computation: Practice and Experience, 15:1–18.
[93] Moore G. E., April 19, 1965. Cramming more components onto integrated circuits. Electronics, **38**(8).
[94] Dongarra J., and Luszczek P., 2005. Introduction to the HPC challenge benchmark suite. Technical Report UT-CS-05-544, University of Tennessee.
[95] Luszczek P., and Dongarra J., 2006. High performance development for high end computing with Python Language Wrapper (PLW). *International Journal of High Perfomance Computing Applications*, Accepted to Special Issue on High Productivity Languages and Models.
[96] Travinin N., and Kepner J., 2006. pMatlab parallel Matlab library. *International Journal of High Perfomance Computing Applications*, Submitted to Special Issue on High Productivity Languages and Models.
[97] ANSI/IEEE Standard 754–1985. Standard for binary floating point arithmetic. Technical report, Institute of Electrical and Electronics Engineers, 1985.
[98] Langou J., Langou J., Luszczek P., Kurzak J., Buttari A., and Dongarra J., Exploiting the performance of 32 bit floating point arithmetic in obtaining 64 bit accuracy. In Proceedings of SC06, Tampa, Florida, November 11–17 2006. See http://icl.cs.utk.edu/iter-ref.
[99] Kernighan B. W., and Ritchie D. M., The C Programming Language. Prentice-Hall, Upper Saddle River, New Jersey, 1978.
[100] OpenMP: Simple, portable, scalable SMP programming. http://www.openmp.org/.
[101] Chandra R., Dagum L., Kohr D., Maydan D., McDonald J., and Menon R., 2001. Parallel Programming in OpenMP. Morgan Kaufmann Publishers.
[102] Message Passing Interface Forum. MPI: a message-passing interface standard. *The International Journal of Supercomputer Applications and High Performance Computing*, **8**, 1994.
[103] Message Passing Interface Forum. MPI: A Message-Passing Interface Standard (version 1.1), 1995. Available at: http://www.mpi-forum.org/.
[104] Message Passing Interface Forum. MPI-2: Extensions to the Message-Passing Interface, 18 July 1997. Available at http://www.mpi-forum.org/docs/mpi-20.ps.

# Productivity in High-Performance Computing

THOMAS STERLING

CHIRAG DEKATE

*Department of Computer Science*
*Louisiana State University, Baton Rouge, LA 70803, USA*

**Abstract**

Productivity is an emerging measure of merit for high-performance computing. While pervasive in application, conventional metrics such as flops fail to reflect the complex interrelationships of diverse factors that determine the overall effectiveness of the use of a computing system. As a consequence, comparative analysis of design and procurement decisions based on such parameters is insufficient to deliver highly reliable conclusions and often demands detailed benchmarking to augment the more broad system specifications. Even these assessment methodologies tend to exclude important usage factors such as programmability, software portability and cost. In recent years, the HPC community has been seeking more advanced means of assessing the overall value of high-end computing systems. One approach has been to extend the suite of benchmarks typically employed for comparative examination to exercise more aspects of system operational behavior. Another strategy is to devise a richer metric for evaluation that more accurately reflects the relationship of a system class to the demands of the real-world user workflow. One such measure of quality of computing is 'productivity', a parameter that is sensitive to a wide range of factors that describe the usage experience and effectiveness of a computational workflow. Beyond flops count or equivalent metrics, productivity reflects elements of programmability, availability, system and usage cost and the utility of the results achieved, which may be time critical. In contrast to a single measure, productivity is a class of quantifiable predictors that may be adjusted to reveal best understanding of system merit and sensitivity to configuration choices. This chapter will discuss the set of issues leading to one or more formulations of the productivity, describe such basic formulations and their specific application and consider the wealth of system and usage parameters that may contribute to

ADVANCES IN COMPUTERS, VOL. 72
ISSN: 0065-2458/DOI: 10.1016/S0065-2458(08)00002-8



Copyright © 2008 Elsevier Inc.
All rights reserved.

ultimate evaluation. The paper will conclude with a discussion of open issues that still need to be resolved in order to enable productivity to serve as a final arbiter in comparative analysis of design choices for system hardware and software.



# 1. Introduction

Productivity is emerging as a new metric which can be used to evaluate the effectiveness of high-performance computing systems. Conventionally, the measure of quality for such systems is given in terms of some metric of performance such as peak floating-point operations per second (flops) or the sustained performance for a given benchmark program (e.g., Linpack) also quantified as flops. But such simplistic parameters fail to provide useful tools for assessing the real value of a system for the end purpose of its application to an individual or institution and do not provide the basis for devising a method of comparing and contrasting alternative systems for possible application or procurement. In the most extreme case, these traditional metrics are insufficient to determine realisability of some critical strategic goal within finite time and cost. Other challenges to conventional methods also dictate a need for transition to a more meaningful criterion of comparative evaluation. One among these challenges is that increased measured flops rates may not actually correlate with improved operation. There are a number of means (tricks when done by intent) by which the flops rate is increased, whereas the actual rate at which a given application or workload is accomplished decreases. Hence, performance as typically determined fails to reveal real worth in terms of getting the computing work done. Productivity is being considered as a valid replacement for previous flawed performance metrics to provide a means of deriving higher confidence in decision-making related to choices in high-performance computing.

Perhaps more importantly than its inconsistency as a measure of quality, performance does not reflect all of the key factors that must influence difficult choices in procurement and application. Among these are total cost and total time to deliver a solution to a given problem. In particular, time and costs required for developing software are not considered, while experience shows that software can contribute the greatest component of getting a final answer. The ease of programming can vary dramatically among system classes such that the fastest machine may not be the best machine for a given purpose or place. In the real sense, this is made more challenging by the wide variance of the skills of different programmers and the inadequate means by which the rate of program development is measured. Measurement of costs, too, is non-trivial although this is better understood by the related professions of accounting and economics.

The final challenge to establishing a useful measure of productivity is the strong degree of subjectivity applied to the assessment of the value of the outcome (i.e., getting a particular result) and how quickly such a result is obtained through computational means. Such worth can be as insignificant as one of convenience, to the other extreme of blocking an entire domain of science without it. In some cases in the financial market or interactive services (e.g., web servers), competitive production of answers may result in major financial gain or loss. In other cases such as those found in the military context or those of emergency services, it may mean something even worse: literally life or death. Thus in the broadest sense, there can be no absolute measures but rather only qualitative measures sensitive to subjective relative importance.

This complicated interplay of uncertain factors and formulation is the subject of current exploration by a community of researchers motivated, in part, by the basic needs for an improved means of assessing value to high-performance computing systems and also through the DARPA HPCS (High-Productivity Computing Systems) program [9]. This ambitious program was established more than five years ago to sponsor the development of a class of innovative Petascale system architectures by the end of this decade. As a consequence of this program and complimenting programs by other Federal agencies, most notably the Department of Energy, a series of studies in benchmarking, software development and productivity modeling has been undertaken to achieve a fundamental understanding of the nature of productivity, its determination and its application for the purposes of measurement, comparative evaluation and trade-off decisions. At this time, there is no single codification of productivity as a formal method but rather a collection of partial models that provide insight but no single complete representation definition. In fact, not even the units of measure for productivity as a metric are defined. Nonetheless, productivity provides a rich trade-off space to consider procurement, allocation, and application decisions and in so doing justifies its study in spite of its current limitations.

This treatise will examine the issues defining productivity and will provide some practical guidance with respect to its determination and use. In so doing, while acknowledging the broadest scope of interpretation of the term and citing the worthy work of other contributors in this new field, this discussion will focus on a more narrow specification that may be more readily applied to high-performance computing. Where possible, specific observable metrics will be employed in all aspects of the discussion, and where not, quantifiable parameters will be considered. In certain cases, not even this relaxed degree of explicit quantification will be readily apparent, in which cases the basic contributing factors will be described, recognizing their qualitative nature.

The goal of an effective model of productivity is to provide a useful framework for performing comparative quantitative analysis between alternative systems, the combination of hardware and software, in a repeatable manner that relates all key elements of the workflow, yielding a final solution to an initial question. Such a productivity model can be used to perform trade-off studies among alternative choices of such systems to produce an ordered set of preferences among available alternatives. It is recognized that software development is an important part of such a workflow and therefore must be represented in a productivity model.

This paper will discuss the principal factors that contribute to productivity in high-performance computing including key quantifiable parameters, some of which are observable metrics. A distinction will be made between the perspective of the productivity of a system and the perspective of the user's productivity in the derivation of an answer via computation. Relationships for both will be derived within the context of assumed measure of value in achieving the results. This will constitute a Special Theory of Productivity that eliminates many of the uncertainties of a broader interpretation at the cost of generality.

## 2. A General Formulation

Performance is the rate at which computational work is performed with such metrics as Giga instructions per second (Gips), Tera floating point operations per second (Tflops) and Million instructions per second (Mips) as representative units. But two systems with the same performance for a given application with significant differences in cost cannot be distinguished by these measures alone. And how would one compare one system that is 20% slower but 50% lower in cost to a second system? If one extends the comparison between two systems, one system having a running time that is one-tenth of the other but taking ten times as long to program, how would these two systems be compared as well? Productivity is intended to provide at least a framework to consider these issues and in restricted favourable cases to give a direct quantitative comparison.

With the assumption that a positive shift in productivity is a reflection of an improvement in the state of the total system, several qualitative observations can be made concerning the formulation of productivity as a formal predictor of system value:

1. Productivity is a positive function of the value (to the user) of the results produced. The value may vary depending on the time required to produce the results.
2. It is a function of the effective rate of producing such results; that is, it is inversely proportional to the time required to produce the results.
3. It is a function of the cost-effectiveness of producing such results; that is, it is inversely proportional to the cost required to produce the results.

A relationship that satisfies these conditions is:

$$\Psi = \frac{U(T)}{C \times T}$$

where:

$$\begin{aligned} \Psi &\equiv \text{productivity} \\ C &\equiv \text{cost} \\ T &\equiv \text{time} \\ U(T) &\equiv \text{utility} \end{aligned}$$

The value of $U$ is the utility function which is subjective and therefore its quantification is the most difficult aspect of this relation. Often, it is a function of time, either having some positive value for a bounded time and no value at a later stage or having some more complicated function with respect to time, which may not even be monotonically decreasing in certain cases. It should be noted that this relation for productivity is a more restricted case of the more general definition derived from the field of economics which is generally given as:

$$\Psi = U(T)/C,$$

where the selected equation previously given is derived through a redefinition of the utility function to incorporate the inverse time factor. This is made explicit in this more applied formulation to emphasize the role of performance, the rate at achieving an end goal, in the definition of productivity for high-performance computing.

There are two perspectives with which productivity may be considered for high-performance computing. The first is with regards to the system. This examines how useful a given system is in performing the total workload, likely to comprise many different user applications over the lifetime of the machine. Here cost includes that of the machine, its programming and its operation, whereas time relates to the lifetime of the machine. Time may also play a role in establishing the utility function for each of the application programs supported by the machine.

The second perspective is with regards to a specific application or user program that is created, run, and analyzed by a group of users working together. In this case, there is a single utility function related to the specific application. Time relates to the total workflow for the user group from problem definition, through program creation and testing, to one or more execution runs, to produce the desired computed results, culminating in a final stage of data analysis to derive the final answers to the original question posed. Cost in this scenario relates to some amortized fraction of the total machine cost and its operation for the period of usage, as well as the cost of the code development. There is a subtlety in that the cost and time of software development are interrelated. But this is important. Imagine two programmers that work at exactly the same rate on a code that is conveniently partitioned into two separate and clearly delineated pieces of equal size. One of the programmers can write the entire code or both programmers can work on it together. For both cases, the cost of code development is the same (assuming one programmer takes twice as long to write the program as the two programmers together) while the time differs by a factor of two. This would not affect the evaluation of productivity for the system perspective but will have a potentially profound effect on the evaluation of productivity for the user program perspective.

It is interesting to consider the actual units of measure for productivity. The challenge is (as suggested earlier) that the utility function is highly subjective and its units can vary dramatically among different cases. Therefore, there can be no single metric for productivity. On the other hand, if we abstract the utility value function, we could define an artificial unit: UDDS (utility divided by dollar seconds). The issue of units of measure will be considered in greater and more accurate detail when a special model of productivity is considered for high-performance computing.

# 3. Factors Determining HPC Productivity

Many aspects of the workflow leading to a final outcome of a computation determine the overall productivity experienced. In this section, the dominant factors that influence the observed productivity are considered. As previously stated, practical considerations and limitations on our understanding require that we distinguish among three levels of such factors: 1) metrics – which are factors that are both quantifiable and can be directly measured, 2) parameters – which are quantifiable, but may not be observable, and 3) factors – which influence productivity but may be limited to qualitative description being neither measurable or quantifiable. For convenience, it is assumed that metrics are a special case of parameters and likewise that parameters are a special case of factors.

## 3.1 Dominant Factors

Here four principal factors that dominate the determination of productivity are introduced. Each contributes to the time to solution, the cost of solution, or both. They can be represented as an expanding tree with Productivity the root node at the far left and the dominant factors at the next level of the tree as shown in Fig. 1. But each of these in turn can be further subdivided into contributing factors and minor factors, yet another level (to the right). Nor is this characterization of productivity a true tree because some factors influence multiple superior factors forming a directed graph. However, we will examine only the primary relationships.

*Performance* of a system represents the peak capability of a machine in a number of respects. It specifies the peak number of operations that it can perform at any one time and reflects the best (not to be exceeded) ability that is available to a user program. Inversely, it determines the minimum time that a user program requires, given the

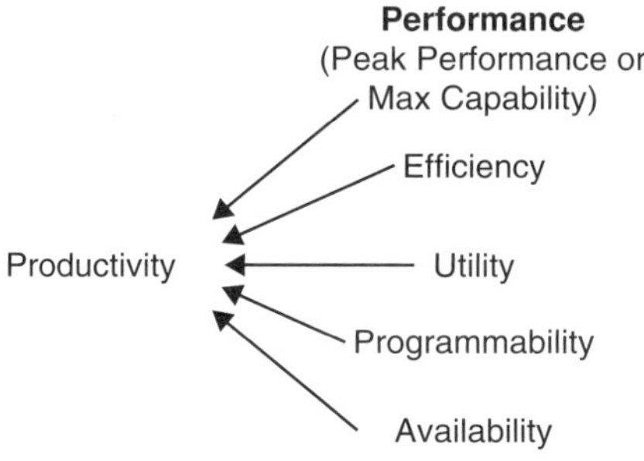


FIG. 1. Dominant factors of productivity.

total workload requirement and intrinsic parallelism of the applications. Performance is a metric. An array of factors contributing to performance will be discussed in the next section.

*Efficiency* is that portion (between 0.0 and 1.0) of the peak performance that is actually achieved as the sustained performance for a given system for a given user application program. Efficiency is measured with respect to assumed peak performance parameters which itself may vary in terms of the kind of operations of interest. For example, the efficiency of a floating-point-intensive application may be determined with respect to peak flops rate, whereas a problem with little or no floating-point operations would be measured against its peak integer operation rate (ips), or in the case of a data-intensive application its updates per second (ups). Efficiency is a metric. Factors influencing a system's efficiency will be discussed in Section 3.3.

*Availability* is that portion of time or duty cycle (between 0.0 and 1.0) of the full life of a machine or bounded epoch during which a system can be applied to a given user problem. While some representations of productivity would highlight robustness or reliability as dominant factors, in this study, these and other important issues are integrated within this one measurable quality. Availability is insensitive to the details of the application program as it would be to efficiency except where problem resource requirements influence resource-allocation policy decisions concerning scheduling. Availability is a measurable metric although all the factors influencing it are not measurable. Availability will be considered in greater detail in Section 3.5.

*Programmability* is the fourth dominant factor determining overall productivity of a system and application workflow. Programmability is neither a metric nor a parameter. But it is a critical factor; some would say that it is the critical factor in determining the overall productivity of system performance applications.

Finally, *Utility* is the subjective factor that establishes the relative value to a customer of the outcome of a computational process. Utility addresses the question of how significant the successful result is and its sensitivity to the amount of time it takes to get that result or sequence of results. Real-time control systems and theater-of-war contexts have highly time-sensitive utility functions, while there is broad latitude when a cosmology application such as the simulation of two spiral galaxies (e.g., the Milky Way with Andromeda in approximately 5 billion years) is considered. Utility will be discussed in more detail in Section 3.6.

## 3.2 Performance

The specification and quantification of peak performance of a system is among the easiest because it is a function of the physical elements and their attributes that comprise the system. However, peak performance may be established with respect to one or more parameters including floating-point performance, integer performance, memory-access performance, global-data-movement performance such as a global matrix transpose, and other more obscure measures (e.g., peak logical inferences per second). Conventionally, the high-performance-computing community uses peak floating-point operations per second or flops as the measure of choice. However, other attributes of system organization also falls into the broadest definition such as memory capacity which defines the size of problem that may be performed by a given system. The factors that have the highest influence on the determination of the peak capability of a system are illustrated in Fig. 2.

It is noted that the vast majority of HPC systems are organized in a hierarchy with an intermediate building block, the node, being integrated by one or more System-wide Area Network (SAN) and each containing the combination of processing and memory resources that in the aggregate determine the total system capability and capacity. Therefore, a metric contributing to the peak performance of the system is the 'number of nodes'. The primary computing resource of the system is provided by the multiplicity of processors in the system. With the advent of multicore systems, this will be referred to as the 'processor cores' or simply 'core'. Another emerging term is the 'socket'. Together, the following metrics determine the number of computing elements in a system: 1) 'number of cores per socket', 2) 'number of sockets per node', and 3) 'number of nodes' (as before). To determine the peak performance, the product of these is combined with the 'peak performance per core', which may be a short vector based on operation type (e.g., a two-tuple of floating point and integer operation types). With the gaining popularity of heterogeneous system structures into which accelerators such as graphical processing units (GPU) have been incorporated, the 'number of cores' metric may be a vector based on types of cores so that a node may have one or more of each of one or more type.

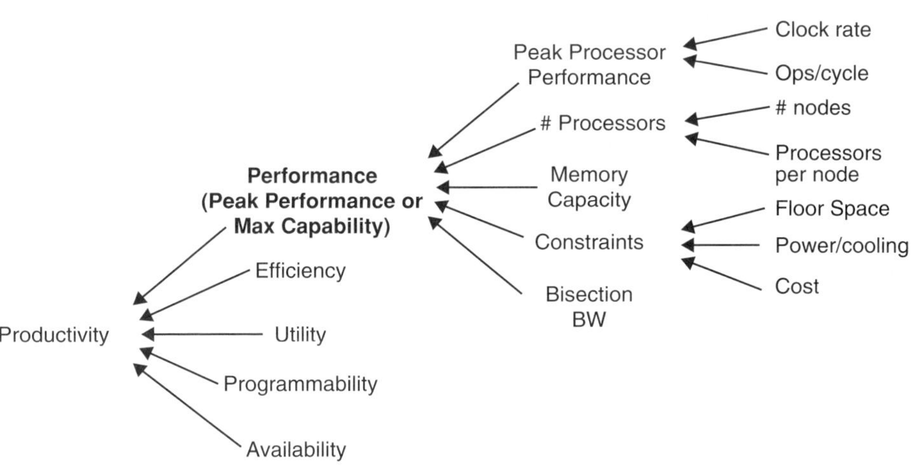


FIG. 2. Performance factors of productivity.

Other critical factors that influence both the value of a system and indirectly its performance are memory capacity and bandwidth as well as system bi-section network bandwidth. These are peak capabilities in their own right and suggest that performance is also a short n-tuple vector. Peak memory capacity is determined by the product of 'number of nodes per system' and the 'memory capacity per node'. Similarly, a measure of peak bandwidth is derived from the product of the factors 'number of nodes per system', 'number of network ports per node' and the 'peak bandwidth per network port'. It should be noted that there can be more than one type of network and multiple ports of each per node.

Practical constraints are factors that contribute to the determination of peak performance of a system. These include size, power and cost. System size is literally limited by the available floor space area in an organization's machine room. Machines may require thousands of square feet, with the largest machine rooms exceeding 20,000 square feet and some facilities having more than one such machine room. National laboratories have been known to build entirely new buildings for the express purpose of housing new machines. Equally constraining is power consumption. Some user agencies consider power consumption and the need to remove the waste heat, demanding even more power for cooling to be their number one constraint in fixing the scale of their future systems. Finally, cost is a determining factor. Government funding is usually based on bounded cost for specific procurements. Thus, all these practical constraints limit the peak performance and capacity of a new system. An interesting trade-off involves balancing of the number of processors with the amount of memory: less memory means that more processors can be afforded, but this has an effect on the ultimate user utility. No effective formulation of these subtle interrelationships is available. But the exchange of funding for different resources is a real part of the equation.

## 3.3 Efficiency

### *3.3.1 Efficiency Factors*

Efficiency can be deceptively simply defined, can be relatively directly measured, but its diagnosis id difficult. This section offers one possible model of efficiency through a delineation of factors that contribute to efficiency as shown in Fig. 3. Other models are also possible. In its most simple form, 'efficiency' is defined as the ratio of observed sustained performance to specified peak performance for some metric of performance such as, but not limited to, flops. Efficiency can be measured by determining the number of operations performed by the application of the type considered and by averaging these across the measured execution time of the application. The ratio of this to the peak performance of the system is a measure of the efficiency.

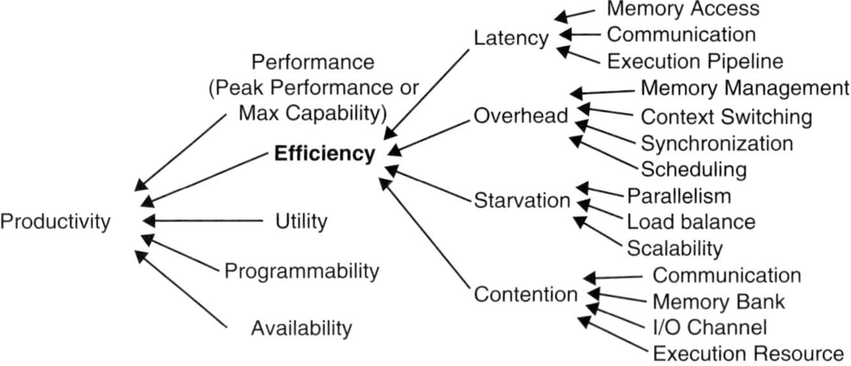


FIG. 3. Efficiency factors of productivity.

A set of four factors that determine (or at least appreciatively contribute to) the observed system efficiency is identified: latency, overhead, starvation and contention.

### 3.3.2 Latency

Latency is the distance measured in processor cycles that is required for relatively remote services such as remote (other node) memory accesses and remote procedure calls. Remote is relative to the synchronous register and registers execution times that are ordinarily pipelined and therefore ideally provides that level of latency hiding. Latency can be experienced even within a single node. Accessing main memory in a node may require hundreds of cycles. Efficiency in the presence of latency can be achieved through a number of strategies for locality management and latency hiding. System latency is typically addressed by ensuring that most of the computation is performed in coarse grained blocks, each almost entirely performed on its respective resident node. Memory latency on most processors is countered through the use of cache hierarchies which exploit temporal locality to manage automatically useful copies of data close to the processor, thus significantly reducing the average observed latency. When temporal locality is poor and cache miss rate is high, alternative methods come to play. Prefetching, both hardware and software driven, can result in the overlapping of memory accesses with computation when the right accesses can be guessed ahead of time. More arcane techniques include vector processing and multi-threading, among others. To some degree, latency to remote nodes can be addressed by the aforementioned methods. However, beyond a certain size, these methods may prove inadequate and the user once again may be required to resort to explicit locality management from the application code. Advanced concepts in message-driven computation are being pursued to hide the effects of system-wide latency but these are of an experimental nature and not embodied in programming tools and environments readily available to the programmer. Latency-hiding techniques exploit parallelism, which is therefore not available to additional hardware resources to further reduce time to execution. Ultimately, latency limits scalability.

### 3.3.3 Overhead

Overhead is the critical time required to manage the parallel resources and the concurrent tasks of a parallel computing system. This is the work that would not be required in a sequential execution of the same problem, so it is referred to as wasted work. Examples include such functions as memory management, context switching, synchronization and scheduling; the last three being interrelated. Memory management controls the virtualization of the user namespace and its mapping to the physical namespace. On a single processor, this is done with a translation lookaside buffer (TLB) when there is good access behavior. Otherwise, it is performed by the operating system. For large parallel computing systems, there should be a combination of middleware with user-explicit intervention to decide the allocation, mapping and load balancing of objects in physical memory. This work is a form of overhead. Context switching changes the attention of a processor from one task to another. The work required to do this is overhead. In many systems, a single process or thread is assigned to each processor (or hardware thread) so that no context switching is required, thus avoiding the overhead cost, at least for this cause. Specialty multithreaded hardware architectures such as the Cray XT3 and the Sun Niagara have hardware support for single-cycle context switching that minimized the overhead. Processes and Pthreads in Unix-like operating systems leave the context switching to the operating system. This is relatively costly with regards to the number of cycles, but it is not conducted frequently, so the overall overhead experienced is low on an average. Synchronization when performed by a global barrier can be costly, essentially stopping the entire machine (or assigned subsection) based on the slowest sub-process. This can be a costly overhead and limits the granularity of parallelism that can be effectively exploited. Even finer grained synchronization methods, if they block other actions, can have a serious impact on efficiency. Scheduling, if done by software and if done dynamically, say for load-balancing purposes, can be an expensive overhead function offsetting the advantage of the scheduling policy. Many other forms of overhead can be encountered in parallel processing. But the effect is not simply that of wasted work. Because it can be in the critical path of the useful work, overhead actually imposes an upper bound on scalability of fixed-sized problems (strict scaling), which is independent of the amount of hardware one throws at the problem. Thus, overhead is a fundamental limitation on efficiency and ultimately on productivity.

### 3.3.4 Starvation

Starvation is the phenomenon of an execution unit experiencing idle cycles, cycles in which it performs no useful action and hence is wasted, because there is no pending work to be performed. This is distinct from idle cycles caused by latency or overhead. Starvation occurs because of an inadequacy of the amount of useful work at an execution site. This is generally caused by an overall insufficiency of parallel work, an issue of scalability or an insufficiency of work local to the execution site while there is an abundance of pending work elsewhere in the system. This latter form of starvation is a product of inadequate load balancing. Starvation is addressed within a core by hardware support for out-of-order execution using reservation stations and the Tomasulo algorithm. Like overhead, starvation imposes an upper bound on scalability of a fixed-sized problem (strict scaling, again). Vector architectures employ dense-matrix operations to expose fine grain parallelism. Multithreaded architectures support an additional level of parallelism to maintain multiple threads per core. But often the issue of sufficient parallelism is as much a software issue. Either the programmer has the means to expose algorithm parallelism through the programming language being used. Or the compiler is able to analyze an apparently sequential code and extracts parallelism from it. In extreme cases, the application algorithm is intrinsically and fundamentally sequential, permitting no exploitation of parallelism. Here, Amdahl's Law [11] takes hold and efficiency drops precipitately. The most general method of reducing starvation by increasing parallelism is to increase the problem size, availability of memory-capacity permitting. This is a form of weak scaling. Resources are more efficiently used and the measured performance increases, but the response time of the original problem (fixed size) is not reduced. Much of the successful usage of ensemble systems comprising large collections of microprocessors in MPP or commodity cluster (e.g., Beowulf [8, 10]) structures are achieved through weak scaling and the avoidance of starvation (or at least reduction) through increased problem size.

### 3.3.5 Contention

Contention is the idle time, measured in processor cycles, incurred due to waiting for shared resources. The two classical examples of contention are bank conflicts of two requesting agents for the same memory bank, and network contention. In the latter case, the network bandwidth is insufficient to handle all of the demand for remote access to other nodes. Contention is often handled by increasing a particular resource when possible. However, contention is usually a 'bunching' phenomenon rather than an average continuous behavior. Increase of a resource may result in a substantial increase in cost and leads to considerably little improvement in the overall performance. This is attributed to the fact that such rare peaks in demand for a resource often greatly exceeds the average usage.

## 3.4 Availability

### 3.4.1 Availability Factors

A number of factors restrict the usage of a system 100% of the time. These are due to mundane operational functions such as planned maintenance and upgrades or crisis events such as a major hardware failure or power outage. Some such possible factors are depicted in Fig. 4 and are given in three broad categories: Reliability, Maintainability and Accessibility.

### 3.4.2 Reliability

Reliability deals with issues related to failures in hardware and software. MTBF or mean time between failure is a metric that gives the average time between successive faults that halts productive use of the system. MTBF is generally proportional to increase in the number of system components including chips and cables, but is

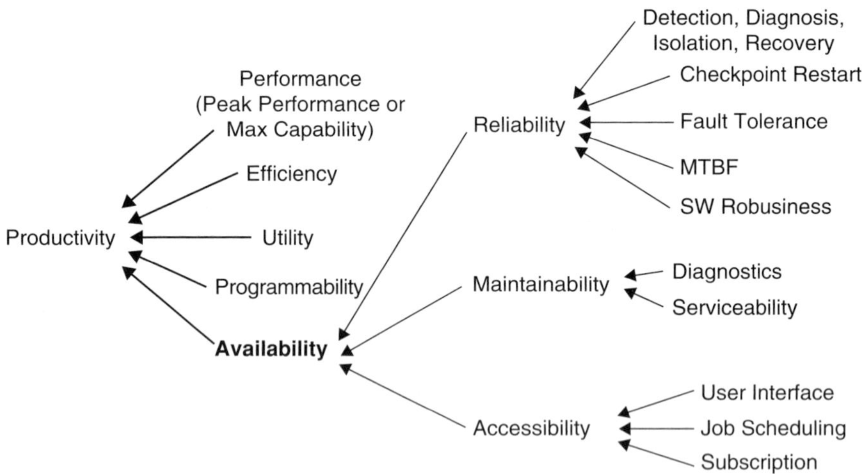


FIG. 4. Availability factors of productivity.

often very sensitive as well to mechanical elements such as fans and disk drives. Even in the case of a fault, the system need not terminate its operation if it incorporates mechanisms of immediate self-repair. This is achieved through redundancy of resources and information. Memories have extra hardware to recover from a cell or string of cells being damaged, for example, from cosmic rays. Communication channels employ bit codes that can detect and correct or detect and resend a message between nodes. There are many other such examples. In the presence of a transient fault, the system need not terminate operation but the application may have suffered fatal error as a result and therefore must be restarted. If checkpointing is employed where intermediate application state is stored usually on secondary storage, then the application need not be started from the beginning but rather from the last known good state. How frequently checkpointing is performed will determine how much computation is lost. But checkpointing itself is a form of overhead and in the extreme can consume a significant amount of the execution time. Impact of reliability on availability is a product of both the MTBF not covered by fault tolerance and the time required to restart the system. This latter is a function of a number of interrelated mechanisms that must operate together quickly and effectively. These include detection of the fault, determination (diagnosis) of its cause, isolating the consequences of the fault to minimize corruption of program (and machine system) state and recovery from the fault.

### 3.4.3 Maintainability

System maintenance whether scheduled or in response to a failure leads to the detraction of the availability of the system to perform useful work. Maintainability breaks down to two basic functions: diagnostics and serviceability. Diagnosis can be very time-consuming, especially for transient errors where the symptoms of the failure are not always repeatable. Also, errors may not be a result of a simple single broken piece of hardware or software but rather may be due to the subtle interplay of multiple functions coinciding with improper behavior at the same time. Slight variations in clock or transmission rates may have no serious consequences, except on occasion when some other aspect is slightly outside margins. Test vectors and other forms of regression testing are particularly important when changes to a system such as updates in hardware or software, seemingly benign, elicit these unanticipated effects. Once a needed system modification is identified, the ease with which the system can be modified, its serviceability, impacts the overall effect of its maintainability on productivity. Serviceability can be as mundane as how quickly one can gracefully power down a system, how easy is it (how much time does it take) to extract a system module such as a blade, replace it, and power the system back up. With the reinsertion of water-cooled elements back into high-end systems, plumbing is again proving to be a challenge both to the design and the serviceability of such systems.

### 3.4.4 Accessibility

If an application programmer or team owned their own system, and small clusters have made this a reality for many groups, then their accessibility to that system would be essentially 100%, baring internal usage conflicts. But in the real world of very large-scale systems, availability to a given user is as much a function of user demand and scheduling priority policies as it is a consequence of failure rates and repair times. Accessibility is the third factor that contributes to availability. It is a function of the degree of subscription or user demand, the job-scheduling policies of resources in time and space (what partition of the entire machine can one get) and the ease of getting on the machine itself. The last factor may be trivial or it may involve travelling to a selected site, entering a special facility or room or waiting in a queue of other programmers submitting decks of cards (ok, so this has not happened in thirty years or more, but some of us remember doing so). Together, these contribute to appreciable delay in getting a job run once it is ready. For real environments, delays of many days can occur for jobs that might otherwise only take hours to execute.

## 3.5 Programmability

### 3.5.1 Programmability Factors

While the previous dominant factors discussed have all been demonstrated to meet the criteria of metrics with quantifiable and measurable units, the next and potentially most important factor, 'programmability', does not. The ultimate arbiters of programmability are clear: time and cost as a function of level of effort. Furthermore, the key factors governing programmability are also well understood as shown in Fig. 5:

1. Parallelism representation,
2. Resource management,
3. Portability and reuse,
4. Debugging, and testing.

However, there is no consistent and comprehensive model of programmability and no parameter or units to quantify it. This is not due to the fact that there was lack of any attempt from researchers. Being able to estimate the cost and time do deliver a major piece of software is an important ability in commerce and government. In a later section, some of these tentative and empirical results, such as the Constructive Cost

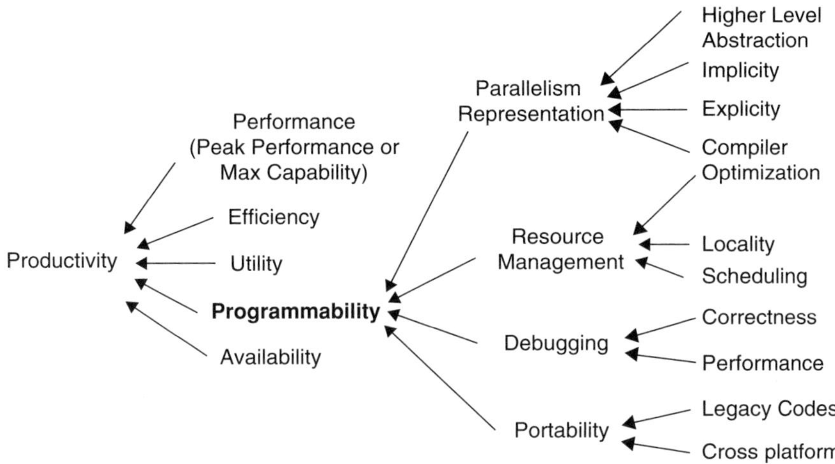


FIG. 5. Programmability factors of productivity.

model (COCOMO) [7], will be discussed. But while such methods have had some practical application in the field, they are not robust in building a cohesive productivity model. Here, these contributing factors are discussed to expose and clarify the issues related to programmability even if they are not formally defined.

It may appear surprising that a number of issues such as programming languages and problem formulation are not directly identified. Language is a formalistic way of controlling essentially all aspects of the above while representing an underlying programming strategy and model. Thus, how the language does these is an important methodology. But it is these foundation factors that are the ultimate determinant of programmability and its contribution to productivity. Problem formulation can be a significant part of the level of effort in the critical path of achieving the results. However, the workflow model that is used to investigate the derivation of productivity presumes this to have been accomplished prior to initiating the procedures of developing the end programs and performing the necessary computations.

### *3.5.2 Parallelism Representation*

Parallelism representation is critical to the success of high-performance computing. Historically, machine types could be defined in terms of the primary form of parallelism that was used to achieve performance gain with respect to sequential execution. Most recently, process parallelism under user control and instruction-level parallelism under compiler control has proven the dominant paradigm with some special-purpose processors using SIMD and systolic structures for higher ALU density. Currently, rapid migration to multicore and heterogeneous (e.g., general-purpose computing on graphic processing units (GPGPU) [6]) system structures may lead to the exploitation of multi-threading and dataflow-like parallelism in future massively parallel machines. The ease with which such parallelism is expressed or discovered through automatic means is a critical aspect of programmability and ultimately impacts efficiency as it addresses starvation as well. The breakthrough accomplishment of a community-wide standard, MPI, more than ten years ago provided an accepted semantics and syntax based on the message-passing model for representing process-oriented parallelism in distributed memory machines. A second standard, OpenMP, although somewhat less widely, had a similar effect for the multiple thread parallelism in shared-memory multiprocessing (SMP) systems of bounded scalability. Experimental languages for other forms of parallelism such as Sisal and Haskel for the dataflow model have also been devised although they have experienced little usage in standard practice. Exposure of parallelism is made much more difficult in shared memory contexts where anti-dependencies through aliased variable names may dictate worst-case scenarios that restrict parallelism. In other cases as discussed before, even when parallelism can be made explicit, if the overhead to manage it is too large for the granularity of the concurrent action, then it cannot be effectively exploited.

### *3.5.3 Resource Management*

Resource management probably should not be part of the responsibility of the programmer or programming. But during the last two decades, in most practical cases it has been. This is because the class of machines that have been the mainstream supercomputer have been ensembles of sequential microprocessors integrated with COTS (commodity clusters) or custom (MPPs) networks. These system architectures have had essentially no support for runtime resource management and have had to rely on the programmer to explicitly manage the allocation of resources to the user program's data and computing requirements. This has been a major burden on the programmer and is a critical factor to programmability. It has also been aggravated by the need for cross-system platform portability (discussed below), either of different architectures or of the same architecture but of different scales. The two driving issues are 1) locality management to minimize impact on communication latency and on synchronization overheads and 2) scheduling to determine what phases of the total workload get priority access to the system resources to ensure best overall throughput and response time.

### 3.5.4 Debugging and Testing

In many studies, the single most expensive part of the development of new codes and to a greater extent the modification of old codes has been proven to be testing and the consequent debugging when testing fails. Even a small change to a code block may require a complete retesting of the entire program against test vectors and regression testing sequences. This can be very time-consuming and is proportional to the size of the entire code, not to the degree of the change made. Debugging of parallel programs has never been satisfactorily achieved although tools to facilitate this have been developed. Debugging of parallel programs has been extended beyond correctness debugging to relate to performance debugging as well. Again, visualization tools have been developed and disseminated to let the programmer see what is happening in time. But it is still a challenge to determine the root causes, sometimes very subtle, and to figure out how to restructure the code to achieve significant performance improvements.

### 3.5.5 Portability and Reuse

Mitigation of the cost and time of code development is related to the portability of programs or code blocks across platforms and between different applications. Libraries, templates and frameworks provide varying degrees of portability and flexibility. Ideally, a piece of code may be directly applied to the needs of a new program-creation project, eliminating the need to implement at least that piece of the total code base. But even when this is possible, testing is still required to verify the results and the correct integration of the old reused code with the new. The two major constituents to portability are 1) the availability and applicability of existing legacy codes and 2) the generality of such codes to show correct and effective performance across disparate computing platform types. Libraries make up a large body of legacy codes defined for ease of use in other programs and optimized for different computer-system architecture types and scale. Templates allow codes to be built up by exploiting known patterns and idioms of program structure to reduce the burden of writing a program entirely from scratch. Cross-platform portability can be readily achieved between target micro-architecture instruction sets but is much harder to achieve between system classes. Conversion of a code between two clusters, one using an Intel Xeon and the other using an IBM Power-5 architecture, along with some refinement and optimization for adjusting certain key parameters such as cache block size can be achieved with good compiler technology and some judicious recoding at critical points. But to port a code written for a cluster in MPI to a vector system such as the NEC SX-8 is a far more challenging task if optimal performance on the latter target platform is to be achieved and requires a complete rewrite of key code blocks or the restructuring of the entire program. Therefore, portability is an important factor in principle, but potentially very difficult to achieve broadly in practice at least without a substantial level of effort. This is one of the reasons that libraries such as LAPACK and *P* are of such importance as their developers over many years have invested the necessary effort to achieve this goal.

## 3.6 Utility

The ultimate value of productivity of a workflow must be proportional to the worth of the computational product derived. In the broadest sense, this is subjective, that is it is purely determined by the needs of the entity to carrying out the computation series. The entity can be a person, group of collaborators, an institution, a national agency, a nation, or all of humanity. In the first case, it could be a spin of a CAD program seeking a local optima of some engineering design. In the last case, it could be the need to predict accurately the course of a medium-sized asteroid that is in jeopardy of impacting the Earth. A Hollywood company may need thousands of hours to do the special effects for a hundred-million dollar blockbuster movie. In the US typically, agencies such as DOE or NSA have applications which are critical to their mission, which is in turn essential for the national security. Clearly, by some undefined metric, some applications have a net worth far greater than others. But all can be important in some context.

How utility is measured is the big challenge to any meaningful, quantifiable and usable model of productivity. Yet in the most general sense, it is beyond current understanding, although such fields as economics suggest frameworks and methods for addressing it. One approach is to form a single ordered list of all of the applications to be run and then order them in terms of the highest value. This can be surprisingly effective. Pair-wise orders for most elements can be readily achieved through subjective appraisal. Most people would rate saving the planet as more important than making a movie. But the economic benefit in commerce of such a movie would likely outweigh that of a particular design point in an optimization trade-off space. Yet such an advance does not yield even the units of productivity let alone their quantitative evaluation. In the field of economics, an attempt to put dollar values on the outcome does provide one possible path for establishing units and in some special cases actual values. While the value of a Harry Potter movie can be quantified, the measurement of the dollar value of a mega-death event is more problematic. How much was the extinction of the dinosaurs worth 65 million years ago, or the loss of the trilobites 250 million years ago?

In a later section, we will take an alternative strategy to quantifying utility based on the computational work being performed. This does not satisfy the big problem. But it does provide a rational and justifiable basis for establishing quantifiable units and for assessing worth; one which could even be translated to economic value. This method fails to capture the subtleties of the time domain for degree of urgency other than to note that there is a timeout associated with each problem; beyond a certain point, the solution has no value, for example, predicting the weather for the next day (a result that takes two days to compute is of little but academic interest in this case) or performing a cosmological simulation (the scientist needs the result at least before the end of his/her life to be useful). Many actual utility functions can have far richer value relationships with respect to time other than this simplistic band-bang formulation. But there is one other aspect to the methodology already imposed (section 2) compared with the more general case (Snir et al.). Faster is better as implied by the explicit use of time as part of the denominator; less time means more productivity, all other things being equal. While this may not be true in the most general case, it is implicit in the domain of high-performance computing.

In conclusion, at this time the community does not have a single consensus model of utility as it relates to productivity in high-performance computing. But some progress has been made in domain-specific cases including the work-based model presented later in this chapter as a 'special theory'. Further work is required urgently in this area before a robust and rigorous conceptual framework can be employed with confidence by the community. Given its potential importance in decision-making processes that govern commerce and national defense, it is unfortunate that at the time of this writing, those US agencies that had been sponsoring research towards this end have now terminated such support.

## 4. A Special Theory of Productivity

While in the most general case, utility [12, 13] is ill defined other than as a qualitative factor reflecting subjective worth or value of a delivered result; more narrow definitions may be applied that not only clarify the meaning of utility at least for the domain of high-performance computing, but also permit both quantifiable units to be applied and its value to be measured. One such example is referred to here as the 'special theory of HPC productivity'. In this section, one particular instance of the special theory is presented that reflects the system-based model. This is distinguished from the user-based model which is presented in the following section.

### 4.1 A Work-based Model of Utility

It can be argued that, at least in the field of high-performance technical computing, the value of an outcome of a computation is a function of the amount of resources dedicated to its production. To a first measure, resources include the scale of the system in memory and processors integrated over the period of execution. In today's systems as previously mentioned, the structure of multiple nodes comprising a given system and the likely allocation of resources through space partitioning along the dimension of number of nodes and the ratio of memory to peak processor performance is highly proportional for different scales of the same machine class. Admittedly, across systems the ratio may vary by some unit (usually a power of two) but this can be adjusted through a constant of proportionality. Therefore, through this fundamental assumption, a measure of utility based on resource utilization can be devised.

An application execution can be represented as a trace (a set of multiple connected sequences) of primitive operations. These operations may be allocated to the basic work required by any implementation of the algorithm and the additional overhead work required to perform the application on a specific parallel system. Work will be defined as the basic algorithm operations that are system independent and excludes the overhead work including replicated operations that are a consequence of the use of a specific parallel computer. This work can be defined by post-mortem analysis of an application run or measured directly through on-chip counters supported by infrastructure software. There is an expectation that beyond a user specified period of time, the result is no longer of value. This is a very simple way of incorporating some time dependence of the worth of the application result into the utility function. But other than checking for this criterion being satisfied, the special theory of productivity employs a flat value for the utility of a specific application.

There is a subtle implication of this model which comes from the specific definition of productivity as previously described. Because time is in the denominator, this version of the productivity model assumes that faster is better or that the worth of a result is inversely proportional to the amount of time taken for computation. While this version is a somewhat more narrow definition of the most general form of productivity, this model is consistent with the foundations of high-performance computing and therefore is noted as the HPC productivity model. Utility measured as the total amount of useful work, then is the special model of HPC productivity.

Let $w_i$ represent the basic work of a particular job $i$, such that the worth of the result of job $I$, $u_i$, is equal to $w_i$. Then, $U$ is the sum of $u$ over $i$ and is equal to the sum of all $w$.

$$U = \sum_i u_i$$

$$W = \sum_i w_i$$

$$U = W$$

The implications of this definition of utility for HPC productivity will be explored in the next subsection.

## 4.2 Machine Throughput Utility

A simple example of productivity can be formulated in relation to the overall throughput of the machines during its lifetime. This trivializes certain aspects of the overall workload, but is valid and in the process gives a rigourous, albeit narrow, formulation of productivity based on the value of the utility function presented above. $i$ indicates the set of all jobs performed on a machine in its lifetime, $T_{\mathrm{L}}$, and the total utility function for this duration is $W$ according to definitions from the previous subsection. The third fundamental factor in conjunction with utility and time reflects the cost of both the program development and the machine that performs the computation. However, this is the only factor that represents the impact of programming; there is no time aspect in the machine throughput model.

For each program run, $i$, the work $w_i$ performed in time $t_i$ is a fraction of the maximum work that could have been accomplished, given the system's peak performance, $S$. This fraction is assessed as the efficiency of system operation for the program, $e_i$.

$$w_i = S \times e_i \times t_i$$
$$W = \sum_i w_i = \sum_i (S \times e_i \times t_i) = S \times \sum (e_i \times t_i)$$

The time that is available to execution of the user program is less than the lifetime of the machine. Scheduled maintenance, servicing of failures, upgrades and reserved systems usage all contribute to lower than 100% system availability. This total available time then is given as:

$$T_{\mathrm{A}} = A \times T_{\mathrm{L}} = \sum_i t_i$$

Average system efficiency, $E$, is defined as the ratio of the useful work or the utility, $W$, previously specified to be the peak work for the available time:

$$W = S \times E \times T_{\mathrm{A}} = S \times E \times A \times T_{\mathrm{L}}$$
$$E = \sum_i \left(e_i \times \frac{t_i}{T_{\mathrm{A}}}\right) = \left(\frac{1}{T_{\mathrm{A}}}\right) \times \sum_i e_i \times t_i$$
$$E \times A \times T_{\mathrm{L}} = \sum_i e_i \times t_i$$

This confirms that the average efficiency over the lifetime of the system is equivalent to the sum of the individual job efficiencies weighted by the ratio of their respective execution times and available time for user programs.

### 4.3 Cost

The cost, $C$, of achieving the computational results is the sum of the costs of developing the programs, $C_P$, and performing the computations on the system, $C_S$. Without proof, it will be asserted that the costs of the individual programs, amortized over the cost of the partition in space and time per program of the machine does sum to the cost of machine deployment, $C_M$, and operation, $C_O$, over its lifetime. Thus:

$$C = C_P + C_S$$
$$C_S = C_M + C_O$$

Later, one possible breakdown of cost of programming will be considered. But for the system model of productivity, it is sufficient to note that all software-development costs in the denominator are additive.

### 4.4 Productivity for the Machine Model

Here the elements of the formulation for the machine-based special theory of HPC productivity are brought together in a single relationship, starting with the original definition of productivity.

$$\Psi = \frac{U}{C \times T}$$

Substituting for each of these over the lifetime of the machine:

$$\Psi = \frac{U}{C \times T} = \frac{W}{C \times T_L} = \frac{S \times E \times A \times T_L}{(C_P + C_S) \times T_L} = \frac{S \times E \times A}{C_P + C_M + C_O}$$

This model is a function of a set of quantifiable parameters. If, as is typically done, peak performance for HPC systems is specified in flops, then the units for productivity are flops/$ for the special theory of productivity for the case of the machine model.

## 5. A User-based Model of Productivity

The system-based model described in the previous section provided a precise representation of productivity as viewed from the perspective of the machine and within the narrow measure of utility based on work. It is encouraging that a model of productivity, albeit so constrained, can be formulated rigorously to yield quantifiable measures. However, productivity beyond performance is motivated by the need to reflect the programmer and system workflow factors into a single viable representation from the user perspective as well. In particular, the time to obtain the solution of a posed question must incur the effects related to program development time, not just its cost as was the case in the machine-based model. Under specific conditions, the time to implement a new program can take years while the execution time may take hours, days or weeks, with some runs lasting for several months. But even in these extreme execution times, the program development time may dominate. Programming is also much harder to measure than are machine operational properties. As will be further discussed in a later section, just quantifying the size of a program is challenging due to non-robust measures such as the popular SLOC or source lines of code. For a given execution program, its source code may vary substantially in terms of the SLOC measure depending on the programmers involved, the language being used, the degree of resource management optimization incorporated explicitly in the code and simple style issues. Yet, the result values may be equivalent. Finally, the length of time to derive a code for execution can vary dramatically independent of length by the original source material chosen as a starting point. Most programs are not written from scratch, at least not entirely, but rather are based on other related codes, libraries and system services. Construction of a final program usually involves a mix of methods and sources and the means to integrate them. Ironically, the hardest part about creating a complete, robust, performance-tuned code is not its writing but its testing. Even the smallest change to a user program may require extensive testing to verify that the program will run without faults and validate the correctness of the results delivered. For codes incorporating highly non-linear relationships, this is actually impossible with the degree of confidence in a code, a function of the degree of testing applied. In this section, another simple model is devised founded on many of the previous assumptions but reflects the user perspective. While correct within the narrow scope of its formulation, many subtleties at the detailed level are abstracted away. These are areas of active research within the community.

## 5.1 A Workflow for a User-based Productivity Model

The machine-based model assumed a 'throughput' workflow where the resource being utilized was driven by a non-empty queue of pending tasks. This is a multi-task workflow. The time was infinite, or more precisely, the lifetime of the system and only the costs of program development was considered, not their time. A user-based model of productivity reflects a single-task workflow, although the task may comprise many iterations or runs of the same program to deliver a sequence of results rather than a single result. The principal distinction between the two models is that the machine-based model does not reflect program development time, except implicitly as a factor in determining cost, whereas the user-based model makes program development time explicit. A second distinction between the two models is that the user-based model is a 'response time' oriented model rather than a throughput model. The time domain is finite over the duration of a single task rather than quasi infinite normalized over the lifetime of the machine. Time starts with the specification of the problem to be resolved or the question to be answered through computational means and ends when the results contributing to the answer is delivered by the computation. This workflow is illustrated in Fig. 6.

While somewhat simplified from real-world experience, this workflow captures the major constituent factors contributing to the time domain of the model. $T_D$ is the time taken to develop the program code. The sub-factors contributing to the program development time will be discussed in greater detail in the following section. $T_{Qi}$ is the initialization or setup time required for a particular run $i$ of the application code. For some applications requiring complex input data sets, such as a 3-D data grid for a variable geometry airframe of a fighter aircraft, this can be a very time-consuming (and computation-consuming) aspect of the total workflow. For other problems, it may

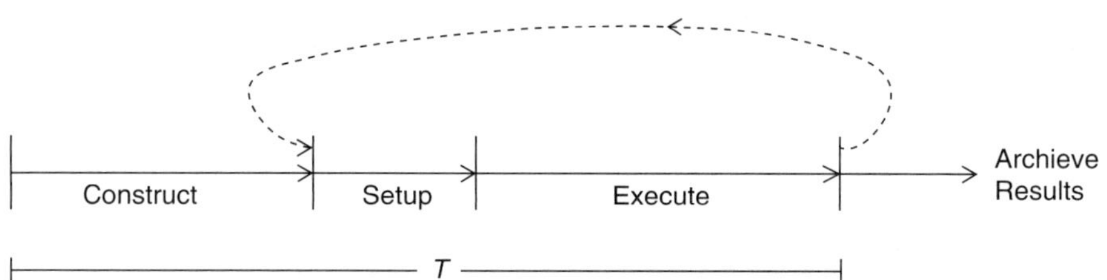


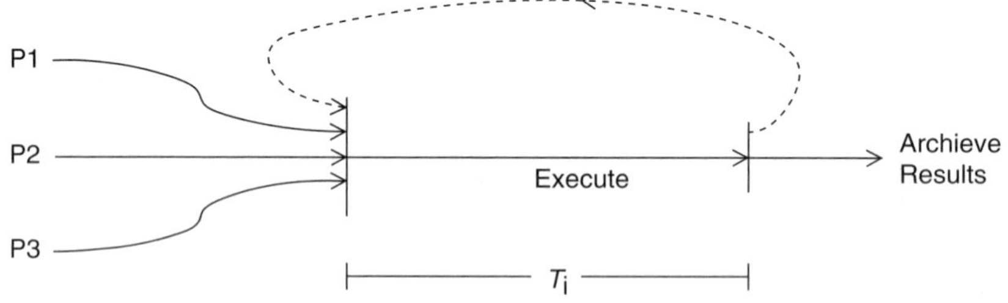


FIG. 6. User-based productivity model & cost.

amount to little more than a handful of initialization parameters and take essentially no time at all. $T_{\text{Ri}}$ is the execution time for a given run $i$ of the application code. If there are a total of $K$ runs of the application code for the user task, then the total time for the task is given as:

$$T = T_{\text{D}} + \sum_{i}^{K} (T_{\text{Qi}} + T_{\text{Ri}})$$

Note that in the workflow described, the setup time is put in the critical timeline of the workflow. This is valid when the setup of one run is dependent on the results of the previous run. However, there are valid situations when the setup times can be overlapped with the execution times, minimizing their impact on the critical workflow time, although still contributing to the cost (see below).

## 5.2 Cost for User-based Model

The cost factor for the user-based model is similar to that of each task in the machine-based model. It combines the cost of program development, $C_{\text{D}}$, with the cost of the execution of the task, $C_{\text{Ri}}$, over the number of $K$ runs. In addition, the cost must also reflect the level of effort applied to the input data initialization, i.e., the setup cost, $C_{\text{Qi}}$. Similar to the total time, $T$, the total cost $C$ can be derived from the workflow.

$$C = C_{\text{D}} + \sum_{i}^{K} (C_{\text{Qi}} + C_{\text{Ri}})$$

It is clear that cost is not an independent factor but is strongly related to time. For example, the cost of the task execution is proportional to the length of time that the machine platform is employed by the application. For the labour-intensive aspects of the program development (there are also ancillary costs related to machine usage for debugging and testing), the cost of program development is a direct function of the average number of programmers and the time for completion of the application. Similarly, setup cost is related to the number of computational scientists involved (these may be different from the code developers) and the time required for assembling the input data set.

$$C_{\text{D}} = c_{\text{d}} \times n_{\text{d}} \times T_{\text{D}}$$
$$C_{\text{Qi}} = c_{\text{q}} \times n_{\text{q}} \times T_{\text{Qi}}$$
$$C_{\text{Ri}} = c_{\text{r}} \times T_{\text{Ri}}$$

Here $c_{\mathrm{d}}$ and $c_{\mathrm{q}}$ are coefficients in units of dollars per person-time (e.g., manhour) for code development and input setup time, respectively. Also, $n_{\mathrm{d}}$ and $n_{\mathrm{q}}$ are the average number of persons for code development and input setup, respectively. The coefficient $c$ is that parameter that specifies cost per unit time of system usage which combines the amortized cost of the machine deployment combined with the per-unit-time cost of operation. A simplification that has been assumed in this discussion is that the entire machine is used for each program. Typically, the largest machines are space partitioned so that more than one program is run at one time with different subsets of system nodes employed for each concurrent application.

## 5.3 User-based Productivity

Combination of these results provides an initial formulation of a relation for user-based productivity. As mentioned before, the utility function is equated to useful work performed over the $K$ runs of the single application.

$$\Psi = \frac{U}{C \times T}$$

$$\Psi = \frac{\sum_i^K w_i}{\left[C_{\mathrm{D}} + \sum_i^K (C_{\mathrm{Qi}} + C_{\mathrm{Ri}})\right] \times \left[T_{\mathrm{D}} + \sum_i^K (T_{\mathrm{Qi}} + T_{\mathrm{Ri}})\right]}$$

$$\Psi = \frac{\sum_i^K w_i}{\left[c_{\mathrm{d}} \times n_{\mathrm{d}} \times T_{\mathrm{D}} + \sum_i^K (c_{\mathrm{q}} \times n_{\mathrm{q}} \times T_{\mathrm{Qi}} + c_{\mathrm{r}} \times T_{\mathrm{Ri}})\right] \times \left[T_{\mathrm{D}} + \sum_i^K (T_{\mathrm{Qi}} + T_{\mathrm{Ri}})\right]}$$

Using similar conversions as was done with the earlier machine model, the useful work can be translated to efficiency measures.

$$\sum_i^K w = \sum_i^K (S \times e_i \times T_{\mathrm{Ri}}) = S \times e_{\mathrm{A}} \times K \times T_{\mathrm{RA}}$$

$$\Psi = \frac{S \times e_{\mathrm{A}} \times K \times T_{\mathrm{RA}}}{\left[c_{\mathrm{d}} \times n_{\mathrm{d}} \times T_{\mathrm{D}} + \sum_i^K (c_{\mathrm{q}} \times n_{\mathrm{q}} \times T_{\mathrm{Qi}} + c_{\mathrm{r}} \times T_{\mathrm{Ri}})\right] \times \left[T_{\mathrm{D}} + \sum_i^K (T_{\mathrm{Qi}} + T_{\mathrm{Ri}})\right]}$$

In this formulation, the subscript ‘A’ indicates the average values of the efficiencies per run and the execution times per run.

### 5.4 Limiting Properties

The formulation of the user-based model while reflecting the dominant factors at least within the HPC utility function adopted does not lend itself to easy analysis or interpretation in closed form. If we were to carry out the product in the denominator, there would be nine separate product elements. This does not lend itself to intuitive understanding. To better understand the user-based model, we will examine the limits of the formulation with respect to the two most critical time parameters: $T_D$ and $T_R$.

For many tasks, existing codes are used whenever possible. For this class of workflow, it is assumed that $T_R$ is much greater than $T_D$ and $T_Q$. In this case, the machine execution time dominates the workflow and an approximate measure of productivity is given by:

$$\Psi_{TR} = \frac{S \times e \times K \times T_{RA}}{\left(c_r \times \sum_i^K T_{Ri}\right) \times \sum_i^K T_{Ri}} = \frac{S \times e \times K \times T_{RA}}{(c_r \times K \times T_{RA}) \times (K \times T_{RA})}$$

$$= \frac{S \times e}{(c_r \times K \times T_{RA})}$$

This simple relation shows that in the limit for execution-dominated workflows, productivity is inversely proportional to the runtime. A somewhat more complicated expression captures the productivity for those workflows that are dominated by program development time. In this case, $T_D$ is much greater than $T_R$.

$$\Psi_{TD} = \frac{S \times e \times K \times T_{RA}}{(c_d \times n_d \times T_D) \times T_D} = \left[\frac{S \times e}{c_d \times n_d}\right] \times \left[\frac{K \times T_{RA}}{T_D^2}\right]$$

This shows the importance of program development time to productivity. When code development dominates, productivity is inversely proportional to the square of the development time.

## 6. Software Development & Productivity

Application development for HPC systems affects productivity at several levels including time and overall cost of the application. Traditionally, significant lines of code (SLOC) has been used as a metric for measuring software development productivity. An SLOC-based approach fails to take into account the software development process (reuse/write from scratch etc.), complexities associated with various parallel programming and computational models, cost and time associated with debugging and testing etc. In summary, there are no widely accepted metrics that comprehensively capture the complexities of software development processes. Earlier section (3.5) detailed the programmability factors affecting productivity. In this section, we discuss the process of code development, issues related to programming languages and tools used to develop complex codes and finally the nature of machines and associated programming model decisions.

***Degree of Reuse.*** Development of source code for any program usually involves varying degreeS of reuse of existing codes. A programmer developing source code to solve a problem could: 1) write the entire application from scratch, 2) reuse parts of existing codes and write the glue code, and in the scenario of maximum reuse and 3) use existing codes without modification to the source code but with new/varying parameters during runtime. In practice, programmers use a combination of the above three methods depending on the case of specific software development use. Each of these techniques has temporal features associated with it; writing complex HPC programs from scratch would lead to customized solutions for the problem at hand; however, such an approach might increase the time to production code and associated cost. Reuse of existing codes (such as libraries or frameworks) to provide parts of the desired functionality could potentially reduce the time to development; however, the involved developers would require wide range of expertise and hence increased associated cost. Reuse of existing codes without modification except for their input parameters requires little or no time for development; however, it requires expert users who are aware of the intricacies of the code and hence could affect the overall cost.

***Programming Language.*** Selection of programming language impacts every aspect of complex program development. Some programming languages, particularly object-oriented languages, lend themselves naturally to extremely complex problems involving large teams. Legacy languages that still pervade most of HPC codes require additional effort to enable code sharing across large teams. Programming language also affect the degree of reuse of existing codes. High-level languages are extremely easy to learn and provide fast turn-around of production level code at the expense of performance. Related research (Ken Kennedy's research) elucidates the trade-off between programming language abstraction and performance.

***Development and Debugging Tools.*** Majority of the costs in software engineering have been known to come from testing and maintenance of software. HPC codes are particularly large and involve complex interactions between communicating processes. In addition, many of these codes run on distributed homogenous systems that provide unpredictable execution environments. Debugging such complex codes is an extremely challenging endeavour, hence availability of debugging codes influences, to a large extent, the choice of programming language and parallelization techniques. In addition to debugging tools, compilation tools also have a large role to play in selection of the right technologies for the problem to be solved. Compilers for languages such as C and FORTRAN are available by default on most production-scale supercomputers. In addition, many of these compilers are optimized for the particular system architecture of the supercomputer, for instance, availability of xlc and xlf on IBM supercomputers, PGI or Intel compilers on production supercomputers etc. Wider selection of compilers allows developers to utilize the supercomputing system efficiently while ensuring faster time to provide solution for their applications.

## 7. Related Works

Emerging discipline of productivity is being studied across by large number of research groups. In this section, we briefly highlight the works that provide other approaches to productivity and have helped us better understand the problem space

***Snir Model.*** Snir's [2] model defines supercomputing productivity as the ratio between the utility of the output computed by the system to the overall cost of the system. This productivity model is represented using:

$$\Psi(P, S, T, U) = \frac{U(P, T)}{C(P, S, T)}$$

where $\Psi(P, S, T, U)$ represents the productivity of the supercomputing system $S$ used; $P$ the problem solved in time $T$ and the corresponding utility function $U$ representing the preferences controlling the outcomes. Each time to solution $T$ is associated with a utility function $U(P, T)$. Overall cost of computing the solution on a system $S$ for a problem $P$ in time $T$ is captured using the cost function $C(P, S, T)$. The utility function $U(P, T)$ is characterized as a decreasing function of $T$. The overall cost function $C(P, S, T)$ is characterized as a combination of development cost $C_D(P, S, T_D)$ and execution cost $C_E(P, S, T_E)$ where the overall time to solution is $T = T_D + T_E$.

***Ken Kennedy Model.*** Kennedy's [1] attempts to define the productivity of programming interfaces using two dimensionless ratios: relative power and relative efficiency. In doing so, the model exposes the trade-offs between abstraction and performance in programming interfaces. This model defines productivity as the problem of minimizing time to solution $T(P)$, where $P$ is the problem. The time to solution is defined as $T(P) = I(P) + r_1C(P) + r_2E(P)$, where $I(P)$ is the implementation time for the program $P$, $C(P)$ is the compilation time, $r_1$ is the number of compilations, $E(P)$ is the execution time per run of the program $P$ and $r_2$ is the number of runs.

The cost to solution for a problem is denoted using $c(P)$ and is defined as the sum of cost of developing the application code $\mathrm{D}(P)$ and average cost of machine time for one run of the application. Relative power ($\rho_\mathrm{L}$) of a programming language is defined as the ratio of implementation time of a given program written ($P_0$) in a standard programming language, to the implementation time of the same program written ($P_\mathrm{L}$) using the new programming language. The relative efficiency ($\varepsilon_\mathrm{L}$) of a programming language is defined as the ratio between the execution times of the programs (standard vs. new)

$$\rho_\mathrm{L} = \frac{I(P_0)}{I(P_\mathrm{L})}$$

$$\varepsilon_\mathrm{L} = \frac{\mathrm{E}(P_0)}{\mathrm{E}(P_\mathrm{L})}$$

Relative power is inversely proportional to efficiency, highlighting the trade-off between abstraction and performance for programming languages (for high-level languages, $\rho_\mathrm{L} > 1$ and $\varepsilon_\mathrm{L} < 1$). On the basis of these concepts, productivity of a programming interface is defined as:

$$productivity = \frac{\rho - \varepsilon X}{1 - X}$$

Where $X$ is defined as a problem-dependent parameter that helps combine relative power and efficiency of a programming language and is defined as $X = r\mathrm{E}(P_\mathrm{L})/I(P_\mathrm{L})$.

***Kepner's (SK)$^3$ Synthesis Model.*** Kepner's [5] model combines prior works (Snir, Sterling, Ken Kennedy, Charles Koelbel, Rob Schriber) to provide a unified look at productivity using (SK)$^3$ model. Productivity is expressed as:

$$\Psi = \frac{S_\mathrm{P} \varepsilon_\mathrm{L} \mathrm{EA}}{C_\mathrm{S}/\rho_\mathrm{L} + C_\mathrm{O} + C_\mathrm{M}}$$

where $\rho_\mathrm{L}$ and $\varepsilon_\mathrm{L}$ are described in Kennedy's model. $C_\mathrm{S}$, $C_\mathrm{O}$ and $C_\mathrm{M}$ are costs associated with software on a system, ownership and machine, respectively. $S_\mathrm{P}$ is the peak processing speed (operations per unit time), $E$ is efficiency and $A$ is availability of the system.

***Other Works.*** Post and Kendell [4] present the comprehensive experience of developing production-level complex high-performance computing programs at National Labs. Their work also highlights lateral issues such as code development team composition and software engineering issues. Bob Numrich's [3] model defines productivity as an evolution of work as a function of time. In order to do so, the model uses the concept of computational action.

# 8. Conclusions

Productivity is a far richer measure of value of a computing methodology than are conventional flops or benchmark-based metrics. It reflects the entire workflow involved in the derivation of computationally derived answers to posed questions. It captures the utility or worth of the result for the user institution, the time to derive the answer, and the cost in doing so. With a valid formulation of productivity for a given context, sensitivity studies may be performed and choices made among alternative approaches for reaching the end goal. For example, when does it make sense to invest more time in refining an already working code for performance tuning? Should a larger system be employed to solve a computational problem? Should more people be put on a software development project? These and other questions may be considered within the analytical framework provided by productivity. This chapter, while introducing the most general definition of productivity, has focused on a narrower representation targeted to the realm of high-performance computing and its response time and throughput-oriented bias. The model was further constrained through the adoption of a specific work-based utility function, asserting that the worth of a result is proportional to the amount of basic computational work required to derive that answer independent of the ancillary work performed as a result of the system characteristics employed. This is not to assume this is by any means to only class of utility function to apply nor necessarily the best for comparative evaluation of alternative strategies. However, it is relevant to high-performance computing, typical of the major determining factor in scheduling policies and in enabling a quantifiable productivity metric. This strategy was applied to two related but distinct perspectives on system usage and its productivity: the machine-based and user-based models. The machine-based model allowed us to consider the productivity of a given high-performance computing platform or system. This is important because institutions make major commitments in the procurement of such systems and their productivity determines the ultimate value of such systems to the mission of the deploying organization and its sponsoring agency (government or corporate). The user-based model allowed us to consider the productivity of a specific user or team working on a single application. This is the more common viewpoint in which productivity is considered and looks at the end-to-end workflow from the point of posing the question to the time that all of the results required to address it are determined through computational means. Again, this model of productivity yielded quantitative metrics of productivity and also exposed distinct modes of operation depending on the dominance of either code development or execution. This distinction was made with respect to time. A different limits formulation would have been possible in terms of cost, suggesting somewhat different trade-offs.

However, as the early discussion on factors demonstrated, there is significant uncertainty on how to characterize the time and cost of software development a priori. How hard is it to write a program? The use of lines of code is hardly an adequate representation of a program in terms of its difficulty of development. Yet, it is the most widely used metric and there is no good alternative. This is just one of many aspects of productivity that demand further substantial research. Adoption of productivity as a valid measure of quality still requires future research. It will be some time when computational scientists will be willing to accept poorer performance in place of reduced code development time, especially when many such codes achieve less than 10% efficiency measured as floating-point utilization against peak performance as used here. The issues of scalability and the difference between weak scaling and strict scaling make the existing issues more complex. When the availability of a larger system immediately results in the execution of larger programs rather than current programs with shorter response time, it is hard to compare the productivity of two system of different sizes. The understanding of productivity and its effective use in the field of high-performance computing will rely on resolution of these difficult albeit practical issues.

## References

[1] Kennedy K., Koelbel C., and Schreiber R., 2004. *International Journal of High Performance Computing*, **18**:441.

[2] Snir M., and Bader D. A., 2004. *International Journal of High Performance Computing*, **18**:417.

[3] Numrich R. W., 2004. *International Journal of High Performance Computing*, **18**:449.

[4] Post D. E., and Kendall R. P., 2004. *International Journal of High Performance Computing*, **18**:399.

[5] Kepner J., 2004. *International Journal of High Performance Computing*, **18**:505.

[6] Owens J. D., Luebke D., Govindaraju N., Harris M., Krüger J., Lefohn A. E., and Purcell T., 2007. *Computer Graphics Forum*, **26(1)**:80–113.

[7] Boehm B., Abts, Brown A. W., Chulani C., Clark B. K., Horowitz E., Madachy R., Reifer D., and Steece B., 2000. Software Cost Estimation with COCOMO II. Englewood Cliffs, Prentice-Hall, NJ, ISBN 0-13-026692-2.

[8] Sterling T., 2001. *Beowulf Cluster Computing with Linux*. MIT Press, Cambridge, MA.

[9] Kepner J., November 2006. *High Productivity Computing Systems and the Path towards Usable Petascale Computing*, CTWatch **2(4A)**.

[10] Sterling T., Becker D., Savarese D., Dorband J. E., Ranawake U. A., and Packer C. V., August 1995. BEOWULF: a parallel workstation for scientific computation. *Proceedings of the International Conference on Parallel Processing (ICPP)*.

[11] Amdahl G., 1967. Validity of the single processor approach to achieving large-scale computing capabilities, *AFIPS Conference Proceedings*, **30**, pp. 483–485.

[12] Peter C. F., 1970. *Utility Theory for Decision Making*, in Robert E (ed.), Huntington, NY, Krieger Publishing Co.

[13] von Neumann J., and Morgenstern O., 1944. *Theory of Games and Economic Behavior*, Princeton University Press, Princeton, NJ, 2nd edition, 1947.

# Performance Prediction and Ranking of Supercomputers

TZU-YI CHEN

*Department of Computer Science*
*Pomona College*
*Claremont, CA 91711*
*tzuyi@cs.pomona.edu*

OMID KHALILI

*Department of Computer Science and Engineering*
*University of California, San Diego*
*9500 Gilman Drive, Mail Code 0404*
*La Jolla, CA 92093-0404*
*okhalili@cs.ucsd.edu*

ROY L. CAMPBELL, JR.

*Army Research Laboratory*
*Major Shared Resource Center*
*Aberdeen Proving Ground, MD 21005*
*rcampbell@arl.army.mil*

LAURA CARRINGTON, MUSTAFA M. TIKIR, AND ALLAN SNAVELY

*Performance Modeling and Characterization (PMaC) Lab, UCSD*
*9500 Gilman Dr*
*La Jolla, CA 92093-0505*
*{lcarring,mtikir,allans}@sdsc.edu*

ADVANCES IN COMPUTERS, VOL. 72
ISSN: 0065-2458/DOI: 10.1016/S0065-2458(08)00003-X



Copyright © 2008 Elsevier Inc.
All rights reserved.

**Abstract**

Performance prediction indicates the time required for execution of an application on a particular machine. Machine ranking indicates the set of machines that is likely to execute an application most quickly. These two questions are discussed within the context of large parallel applications run on on supercomputers. Different techniques are surveyed, including a framework for a general approach that weighs the results of machine benchmarks run on all systems of interest. Variations within the framework are described and tested on data from large-scale applications run on modern supercomputers, helping to illustrate the trade-offs in accuracy and effort that are inherent in any method for answering these two questions.

# 1. Introduction

Given a parallel application, consider answering the following two questions: how much time is needed for the execution of application on a particular machine, and which of a set of machines is likely to execute the application most quickly? Answers to these questions could enable users to tune their applications for specific machines, or to choose a machine on which to run their applications. Answers could help a supercomputing center schedule applications across resources more effectively, or provide them data for decisions regarding machine acquisitions. More subtly, answers might enable computer architects to design machines on which particular applications are likely to run quickly.

But it is not easy to get an answer to these questions. Since the performance of a parallel application is a function of both the application and the machine it runs on, accurate performance prediction has become increasingly difficult as both applications and computer architectures have become more complex. Consider Fig. 1, which plots the normalized relative runtimes of 8 large-scale applications on 6 supercomputers, both described in Section 4.[1] The plot shows that across these applications, no single machine is always the fastest, suggesting that there is no trivial way to predict even relative performance across a set of machines.

Since different machines can be best for different applications, this chapter discusses techniques for answering the original two questions:

- How can one accurately predict the running time of a specific application, on a given input, on a particular number of processors, on a given machine? (performance prediction)
- How can one accurately predict which of a set of machines is likely to execute an application fastest? (machine ranking)

[1] Since the machines shown are only a subset of those on which each application was run, the highest bar is not at 1 for every application. In addition, not all applications were run on all machines with the chosen number of processors.

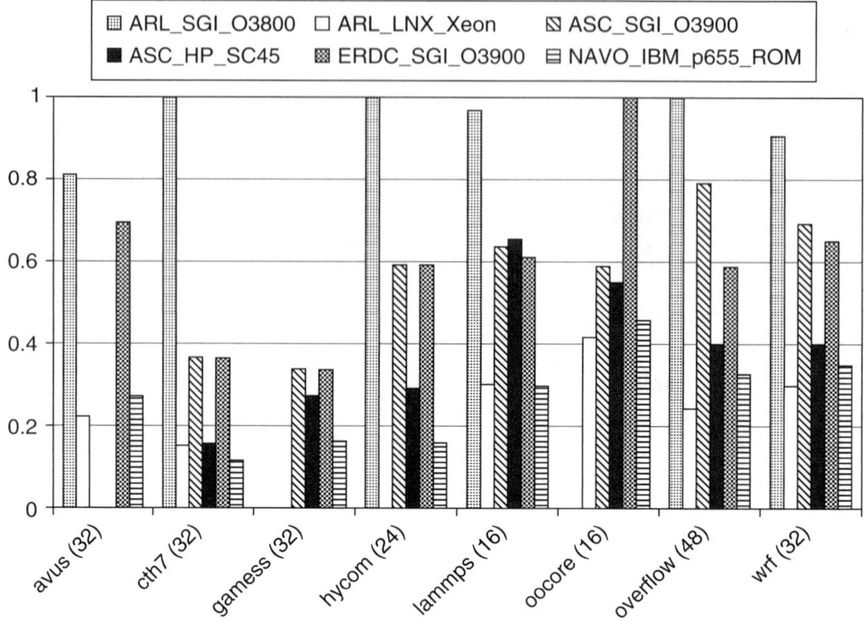


FIG. 1. This graph shows the relative runtimes of 8 applications on 6 supercomputers. The x-axis gives the name of the application, with the number of processors on which it was run in parentheses. The y-axis gives the runtime divided by the maximum time taken by any of a larger set of 14 machines to run the particular application.

Note that while the ability to do the former gives us a way to do the latter, the reverse is not true. In practice, however, while any method for predicting performance (including the many that are described in Section 2) could also be used to rank machines, users may consider the work required for the initial prediction to be excessive. Since sometimes the only information desired is that of expected relative performance across a set of machines, this scenario is also addressed. In addition, Section 7 considers an even further generalization where the goal is to find an application-*independent* machine ranking that is sufficiently accurate for providing useful information.

The rest of this chapter is laid out as follows. Section 2 surveys some general approaches for both performance prediction and machine ranking, organized by the type of information and level of expertise required for each. The trade-offs inherent in choosing a particular performance prediction technique or a particular ranking technique are studied in the context of a methodology that attempts to achieve a balance between accuracy and effort in Sections 3 through 6. The basic framework for the methodology is covered in Section 3, details are addressed in Section 4, and examples of how different techniques fit into this framework are discussed in Sections 5 and 6. An exploration of how to apply the techniques to generate application-independent machine rankings is presented in Section 7. The results are given and analyzed in each section.

## 2. Methods for Predicting Performance

Methods for predicting the performance of an application on a parallel machine begin with the assumption that the running time is a function of application and system characteristics. Currently, the most accurate predictions are made by creating detailed models of individual applications which describe the running time as a function of system characteristics. These characteristics can then be carefully measured on all systems of interest. However, in many situations the time and/or expertise required to build a detailed model of an individual application are not available, and sometimes even the system characteristics cannot be measured (for example, when performance predictions are used to help decide which of a number of proposed supercomputers to build). And even when data are available, there are situations in which precise performance prediction is unnecessary: for example, when the question is which of a set of machines is expected to run a particular application most quickly.

In this section, we give an overview of some of the approaches to performance prediction, noting connections to ranking as appropriate. The techniques are distinguished by the amount of information they use about a system and an application, as well as by the sophistication of the ways in which they use that information to predict the performance of an application.

While the focus here is on predicting the performance of large-scale applications on parallel machines, there has also been considerable work on predicting the performance of single processor applications (see, for example, [30]).

### 2.1 Benchmarks

At one extreme are benchmarks, which can be used to predict performance using only information about the machine. Consider that low-level performance metrics such as processor speed and peak floating-point issue rate are commonly reported, even in mass-market computer advertisements. The implication is that these numbers can be used to predict how fast applications will run on different machines, hence faster is better. Of course, manufacturer specifications such as theoretical peak floating-point issue rates are rarely achieved in practice, so simple benchmarks may more accurately predict relative application performance on different machines.

A particularly well-known parallel benchmark is described by Linpack [14] and has been used since 1993 to rank supercomputers for inclusion on the Top 500 list [45]. The Top 500 list is popular partly because it is easy to read, is based on a simple metric that is easy to measure (essentially peak FLOPS), and is easy to update. Unfortunately, simple benchmarks such as Linpack may not be sufficient for accurately predicting runtimes of real applications [7]. This is not surprising, since Linpack gives a single number for a machine which, at best, allows the execution time to be modelled as some application-specific number divided by that particular system's performance on Linpack.

To better predict the performance of individual applications, two approaches have been taken. One is to provide benchmarks which more closely mimic actual applications. The best known of these is perhaps the NAS Parallel Benchmark suite [3], which consists of scaled-down versions of real applications. The other is to provide benchmarks which take into consideration the performance of multiple system components. An early example of the latter considered the ratio of FLOPS to memory bandwidth [31], which has the advantage of allowing simple comparisons between machines since it also gives a single number for each machine.

More recently, benchmark suites that give multiple performance numbers measuring assorted system characteristics have been proposed. These include the IDC Balanced Rating [20], which has been used to rank machines based on measurements in the broad areas of processor performance, memory system capability, and scaling capabilities; and the HPC Challenge (HPCC) benchmark [29], which consists of 7 tests measuring performance on tasks such as dense matrix multiplication and the Fast Fourier Transform. Of course, with such benchmark suites it becomes incumbent on the user to decide which measurements are most relevant for predicting the performance of a particular application.

Note that a benchmark such as Linpack, which generates a single number for each machine, produces an application-independent ranking of machines. While their usefulness is limited, such rankings are still of significant interest, as the use of Linpack in generating the popular Top 500 list [45] demonstrates. Alternative methods for generating application-independent rankings are explored in Section 7. In contrast, a benchmark suite that generates multiple numbers for each machine has the potential to produce more useful application-specific rankings, but requires a user to interpret the benchmark numbers meaningfully.

## 2.2 Weighted Benchmarks

If several benchmarks are run on a machine, a user must determine how to interpret the collection of results in light of an individual application. With a benchmark such as the NAS Parallel Benchmarks [3], a user can choose the benchmark that most closely resembles their particular application. For lower level benchmark suites such as HPCC [19], users can turn to research on performance prediction techniques that consist of weighting the results of simple benchmarks. The amount of information assumed to be available about the application in generating the weights can range from end-to-end runtimes on a set of machines to more detailed information.

For example, Gustafson and Todi [16] used the term *convolution* to describe work relating "mini-application" performance to that of full applications. McCalpin [31] showed improved correlation between simple benchmarks and application performance, though the focus was on sequential applications rather than the parallel applications of interest here. Other work focussing on sequential applications includes that of Marin and Mellor-Crummey [30], who described a clever scheme for combining and weighting the attributes of applications by the results of simple probes. Using a full run of an application on a reference system, along with partial application runtimes on the reference and a target system, Yang et al. [48] describe a technique for predicting the full application performance using the relative performance of the short runs. While the reported accuracy is quite good, this type of approach could miss computational behavior that changes over the runtime of the application; in addition, the accuracy was reduced when the partial runtime was used to predict the application's performance on a different problem size or number of processors.

Section 3 in this chapter discusses another general method for weighting benchmark measurements. Sections 4 and 5 discuss the use of a least squares regression to calculate weights for any set of machine benchmarks and demonstrate their use for both performance prediction and machine ranking.

## 2.3 Building Detailed Performance Models

For the most accurate performance predictions, users must employ time and expertise to build detailed models of individual applications of interest.

With this approach, the user begins with an in-depth understanding of how the application works, including details about the computational requirements, the communication patterns, and so on. This understanding is then used to build a performance model consisting of a potentially complex equation that describes the running time in terms of variables that specify, for example, the size of the input, processor characteristics and network characteristics. While this approach can generate highly accurate predictions, building the model is generally acknowledged to be a time-consuming and complex task [43]. Nevertheless, if there is significant interest in a critical application, the investment may be deemed worthwhile.

Other research focusses on highly accurate modelling of specific applications [17, 18, 23, 28]. The very detailed performance models built as a result have been used both to compare advanced architectures [22, 24] and to guide the performance optimizations of applications on specific machines [35].

Due to the difficulty of constructing detailed models, an assortment of general techniques for helping users build useful performance models has also been proposed.

Many of these methods are based on a hierarchical framework that is described in [1]. First, the application is described at a high level as a set of tasks that communicate with one another in some order determined by the program. The dependencies are represented as a graph, which is assumed to expose all the parallelism in the application. This task graph is then used to predict the overall performance of the application, using low-level information about how efficiently each task can be executed.

Examples that can be fit into this framework include work on modelling applications as collections of independent abstract Fortran tasks [36–38], as well as using graphs that represent the dependencies between processes to create accurate models [32, 33, 39]. Other work describes tools for classifying overhead costs and methods for building performance models based on an analysis of those overheads [11]. Another technique that also begins by building graphs that reveal all possible communication continues by measuring the potential costs on the target machine and uses those partial measurements for predicting the performance of the overall application [47].

## 2.4 Simulation

One way to try and approach the accuracy of detailed performance models, but without the need for human expertise, is through simulation.

For example, one could use cycle accurate simulations of an application [4–6, 27, 34, 44]. Of course, the main drawback of this approach is the time required. Due to the level of detail in the simulations, it could take several orders of magnitude more time to simulate an application than to run it. Again, if there is significant interest in a single application, this expense may be considered acceptable.

A related technique described in detail in [42] and briefly referred to in Section 6 starts by profiling the application to get memory operation counts and information on network messages. This model is coarser than the detailed models described previously in that there is no attempt to capture the structure of the application; rather, the data collected provides a higher level model of what the application does. This information can later be convolved with the rates of memory operations — possibly by modelling the cache hierarchy of the target architecture on the application trace — and combined with a simulation of the network messages in order to predict the performance of the given application on the specified machine.

Other methods that attempt to avoid the overhead of cycle accurate simulations include those that instrument the application at a higher level [12, 15] in order to predict performance.

### 2.5 Other Approaches

It is also worth noting other approaches that have been proposed for predicting the performance of large-scale applications.

For example, attempts have been made to employ machine-learning techniques. In [10], the authors examine statistical methods for estimating machine parameters and then describe how to use these random variables in a performance model. Neural networks are used in [21, 40] to make performance predictions for an application as a function of its input parameter space, without building performance models. This methodology can find nonlinear patterns in the training input in order to make accurate performance predictions; however, first it requires that the target application is run numerous times (over 10,000 in the example in [21]) with a range of input parameters, which may not always be practical.

## 3. A Method for Weighting Benchmarks

The rest of this chapter explores a few methods for predicting performance and for ranking machines. These methods are unified by their assumption that all knowledge regarding machine characteristics are obtained from results of simple benchmark probes. That this is enough to distinguish the machines is demonstrated in Fig. 2, which shows that different machines are best at different types of operations. For example, when compared to the other machines, the machine labelled ARL_Xeon_36 has a very high FLOPS rate (as one would expect from its clock speed, shown in Table I in Section 4.1), but poor network bandwidth.

Almost all of the methods discussed also assume that information about the application is limited to end-to-end runtimes (although Sections 6 and 7 consider what can be done through incorporating the results of lightweight traces). Just as Fig. 2 shows that different machines are best at different operations, Fig. 3 demonstrates that different applications stress different types of machine operations. As a result, changing the behavior of a single system component can affect the overall performance of two applications in very different ways.

### 3.1 Machine and Application Characteristics

As noted previously, methods for predicting performance and generating machine rankings typically assume that performance is a function of machine and application characteristics. The question is then how to get the most accurate predictions and rankings using data about the machines and applications that is as cheap as possible to gather.

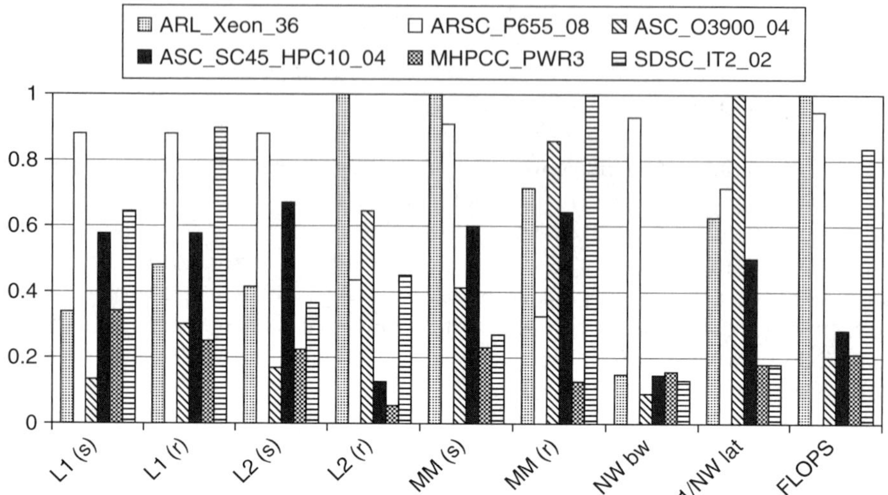


FIG. 2. A plot of machine characteristics for a set of supercomputers. The characteristics along the x-axis are described in Table II in Section 4.1. The highest count for each characteristic is normalized to 1.

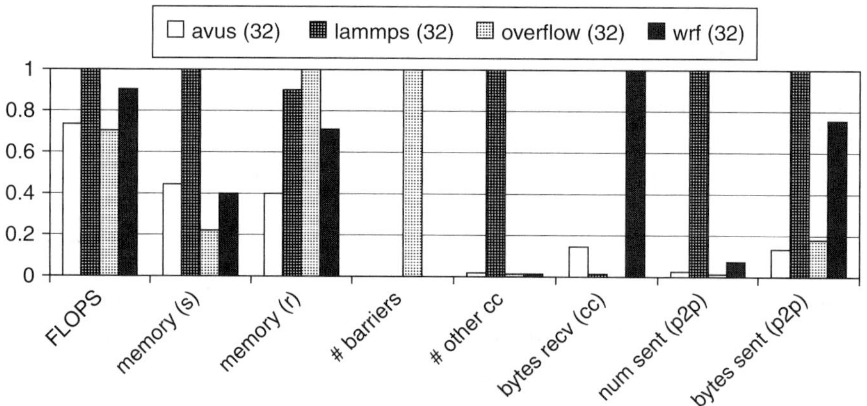


FIG. 3. A plot of application characteristics for a set of parallel applications. From left to right, the x-axis refers to the average count over all processors of floating-point operations, strided memory accesses, random memory accesses, barriers, other collective communications, the total number of bytes received as a result of those collective communications, the number of point to point messages sent, and the number of bytes sent as a result of those point-to-point communications. The highest count for each application characteristic is normalized to 1.

The examples explored in the rest of this chapter assume that basic benchmark measurements can be taken on all machines of interest (or, at a minimum, accurately estimated, as in the case where the system of interest has yet to be built). The same benchmarks must be run across all the machines, although no further assumptions are made. In particular, these benchmarks could consist of microbenchmarks (e.g., a benchmark measuring the network latency between two nodes), or computational kernels (e.g., the FFT component of the HPC Challenge suite [19]), or something even closer to full-scale applications (e.g., the NAS Parallel Benchmarks [3]). This assumption is reasonable since, by their nature, these benchmarks tend to be easy to acquire and to run.

The examples in this chapter are of two types when it comes to the data needed regarding the applications. Those discussed in Section 5 require only end-to-end runtimes on some small number of machines; those discussed in Sections 6 and 7 use simple trace information about the application, including the number of floating-point operations and/or the number of memory references. Memory and network trace information can be collected using tools such as the PMaC MetaSim Tracer [8] and MPIDTrace [2] tools, respectively. All the techniques also assume that the input parameters to the application during tracing and measurement of runtimes are the same across all machines. Note that while these techniques could be used even if the above assumption was not true, the resulting accuracy of the predictions could be arbitrarily poor.

## 3.2 General Performance Model

The other, more fundamental, assumption made by the techniques described in this chapter is that the performance of an application can be modelled to an acceptable accuracy as a linear combination of the benchmark measurements. As a small example, say three benchmarks are run on some machine and that the benchmarks take $m_1$, $m_2$ and $m_3$ seconds, respectively. Then the assumption is that the running time $P$ of any application (with some specified input data and run on some specific number of processors) on that machine can be approximated by the following equation:

$$P \approx m_1 w_1 + m_2 w_2 + m_3 w_3 = \mathbf{m} \cdot \mathbf{w} \tag{1}$$

Here $w_1$, $w_2$ and $w_3$ are constants that may depend on the application, the machine, the input and the number of processors with which the application was run.

This model helps illustrate the trade-off between expertise/time and accuracy. While the linear model is appealingly simple, it could have difficulty capturing, say, the benefits of overlapping communication and computation in an application.

Given application runtimes on a set of machines and benchmark measurements on those machines, Section 5 describes how to use a least squares regression to obtain weights $w$ that are optimal in the sense that they minimize the sum of the squares of the errors in the predicted times over a set of machines.

A less restrictive approach to the performance model can also be taken; an example is the method briefly summarized in Section 6. Instead of the dot product in Equation 1, this method combines machine and application characteristics using a more complex convolution function.

## 3.3 Evaluating Performance Predictions

To test the methods that are based on linear regression, cross-validation is used. In other words, each machine in the data set is considered individually as the target machine for performance prediction. That machine is not included when the weights $w$ in Equation 1 are calculated. Then, after the weights are calculated using only the other machines, those weights are used to predict the performance on the target machine. The absolute value of the relative error in the predicted time (given by Equation 2) is then calculated.

$$\left| \frac{predictedRT - actualRT}{actualRT} \right| \tag{2}$$

After repeating this process for each machine in the data set, the average of all the relative errors is reported. This process becomes clearer when examples in Section 5 is considered.

Note that cross-validation simulates the following real-world usage of the method: a researcher has run his/her application on different systems, has access to the benchmark measurements on both those systems and a target system, and would like to predict the running time of the application on the target system without having to actually run the application on that machine.

Sections 5.3 and 6 briefly describe two other methods for performance prediction. There, again, the absolute value of the relative error is calculated, and the average over all the machines is reported.

## 3.4 Evaluating Rankings

The performance prediction models can also be used to rank a set of machines in order of the predicted runtimes of an application on those systems. Those rankings, or rankings generated in any other way, can be evaluated using the metric of *threshold inversions*, proposed in [9] and summarized here.

### 3.4.1 Predicting Runtimes for Ranking

Testing a predicted ranking requires predicting the performance on more than one machine at a time. So, instead of removing a single target machine as is done with the cross-validation procedure described previously, now a set of machines is randomly selected and the performance on all of those machines is predicted using some performance prediction methodology. Once the predicted runtimes are calculated, the number of threshold inversions between the predictions and the true runtimes can be determined. This is repeated 5000 times, each time choosing a random set of machines to rank and to count thresholded inversions, to get a strong mix of randomly selected validation machines. While some sets may be repeated in the 5000 trials, because they are chosen at random, this should not greatly affect the average accuracies reported.

### 3.4.2 Thresholded Inversions

A simple inversion occurs when a machine ranking predicts that machine A will be faster than machine B on some application, but actual runtimes on the two machines show that the opposite is true. For example, if machine A has larger network bandwidth than machine B, then the ranking based on network bandwidth would contain an inversion if, in practice, some application runs faster on machine B. The number of inversions in a ranking, then, is the number of pairs of machines that are inverted. In the above example, this is the number of pairs of machines for which the interprocessor network bandwidth incorrectly predicts which machine should execute a given application faster. Note that if there are $n$ machines, the number of inversions is at least 0 and is no larger than $n(n-1)/2$.

A threshold is added to the concept of an inversion in order to account for variations in collected application runtimes and/or benchmark measurements. These variations can be due to several reasons including, for example, system architectural and design decisions [26].

For evaluating the ranking methods presented here, two thresholds are used. One ($\alpha$) accounts for variance in the measured runtimes, while the other ($\beta$) accounts for variance in the benchmark measurements. Both $\alpha$ and $\beta$ are required to have values between 0 and 1, inclusive. For example, let the predicted runtimes of $A$ and $B$ be $\hat{RT}_{\mathrm{A}}$ and $\hat{RT}_{\mathrm{B}}$ and the measured runtimes be $RT_{\mathrm{A}}$ and $RT_{\mathrm{B}}$. If the predicted runtimes $\hat{RT}_{\mathrm{A}} < \hat{RT}_{\mathrm{B}}$, then $A$ would be ranked better than $B$, and, if the measured runtimes $RT_{\mathrm{A}} > RT_{\mathrm{B}}$, then there is an inversion. Yet, when using threshold inversions with $\alpha$, that would only count as an inversion if $RT_{\mathrm{A}} > (1+\alpha) \times RT_{\mathrm{B}}$. $\beta$ is used in a similar fashion to allow for variance in benchmark measurements and is usually set to be less than $\alpha$. The different values for $\alpha$ and $\beta$ are attributed to the fact that one generally expects less variance in benchmark times than in full application runtimes because benchmarks are typically simpler than large-scale real applications and so their execution times are more consistent.

The examples in this chapter use values of $\alpha = .01$ (which means that a difference of up to 1% in the application runtimes is considered insignificant) and $\beta = .001$ (which means a difference of up to .1% in the benchmark times is considered insignificant). In addition, Table VII in Section 5 demonstrates the effect of changing the threshold values on the number of inversions for a particular scenario.

This metric based on thresholded inversions is particularly appealing because it is monotonic in the sense that adding another machine and its associated runtime cannot decrease the number of inversions in a ranking. Within our context of large parallel applications, this feature is highly desirable because often only partial runtime data is available: in other words, rarely have all applications of interest been run with the same inputs and on the same number of processors on all machines of interest.

# 4. Examples

While the techniques described in the following sections could be used for any set of benchmarks in order to study any parallel application, the examples in this chapter use the following machines, benchmarks and applications. To see the application of these techniques to other combinations of benchmarks and applications, see [25].

## 4.1 Machines

Table I summarizes the set of machines on which benchmark timings were collected and applications were run; the locations are abbreviations for the sites noted in the Acknowledgements at the end of the chapter. Regarding the benchmarks, information was collected about the FLOPS, the bandwidth to different levels of the memory hierarchy, and network bandwidth and latency.

To determine the FLOPS, results from the HPC Challenge benchmarks [19] were used. Although the HPC Challenge benchmarks were not run directly on the machines in Table I, results on similar machines (determined based on their processor type, the processor frequency, and the number of processors) were always available and so were used instead. In practice, memory accesses always take significantly longer than floating-point operations and so getting the exact FLOPS measurement on each machine would unlikely make a significant difference in the results presented in this chapter.

Because increases in clock speed have far outpaced increases in the bandwidth between processors and memory, the bottleneck for today's applications is as, if not more, likely to be memory bandwidth than FLOPS [46]. As a result, the

TABLE I
SYSTEMS USED FOR THE EXAMPLES IN THIS CHAPTER

| Location | Vendor | Processor | Frequency | # Processors |
|---|---|---|---|---|
| ASC | SGI | Altix | 1.600 GHz | 2000 |
| SDSC | IBM | IA64 | 1.500 GHz | 512 |
| ARL | IBM | Opteron | 2.200 GHz | 2304 |
| ARL | IBM | P3 | 0.375 GHz | 1024 |
| MHPCC | IBM | P3 | 0.375 GHz | 736 |
| NAVO | IBM | P3 | 0.375 GHz | 928 |
| NAVO | IBM | p655 | 1.700 GHz | 2832 |
| NAVO | IBM | p655 | 1.700 GHz | 464 |
| ARSC | IBM | p655 | 1.500 GHz | 784 |
| MHPCC | IBM | p690 | 1.300 GHz | 320 |
| NAVO | IBM | p690 | 1.300 GHz | 1328 |
| ARL | IBM | p690 | 1.700 GHz | 128 |
| ERDC | HP | SC40 | 0.833 GHz | 488 |
| ASC | HP | SC45 | 1.000 GHz | 768 |
| ERDC | HP | SC45 | 1.000 GHz | 488 |
| ARSC | Cray | X1 | 0.800 GHz | 504 |
| ERDC | Cray | X1 | 0.800 GHz | 240 |
| AHPCRC | Cray | X1E | 1.130 GHz | 960 |
| ARL | LNX | Xeon | 3.060 GHz | 256 |
| ARL | LNX | Xeon | 3.600 GHz | 2048 |

FLOPS measurement was augmented by the results of the MAPS benchmark in Membench [7], which measures the bandwidth to different levels of the memory hierarchy for both strided and random accesses. Note that the fundamental difference between strided and random memory references is that the former are predictable and thus prefetchable. Because random memory references are not predictable, the bandwidth of random accesses actually reflects the latency of an access to some particular level of the memory hierarchy. As an example, Fig. 4 demonstrates the result of running MAPS on an IBM p690 node to measure the bandwidth of strided accesses. As the size of the array increases, eventually it will no longer fit into smaller, faster caches — as a result, the effective bandwidth drops. A region for a memory level is defined as a range of data array sizes where the array fits into the level and achievable bandwidth from the level that is fairly stable (each plateau in the MAPS curve). Once the regions for L1, L2, L3 caches and those for main memory have been identified by a human expert, a single point in each region is used as the bandwidth metric for that level of the memory hierarchy.

Finally, Netbench [7] was used to measure network bandwidth and latency.

The benchmark metrics used for the examples in this chapter are summarized in Table II.

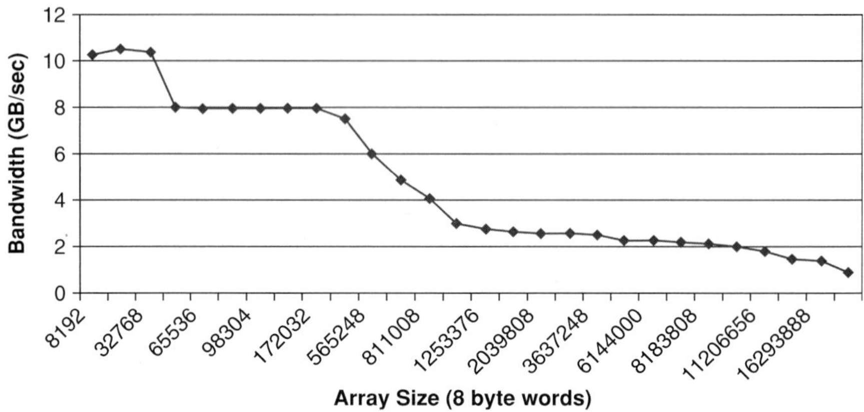


FIG. 4. MAPS bandwidth measurements (in Gigabytes/second) for an IBM p690 node as a function of array size.

TABLE II
BENCHMARK METRICS USED FOR THE EXAMPLES IN THIS CHAPTER

| Abbreviation | Description | Benchmark Suite |
|---|---|---|
| L1 (s) | Bandwidth of strided accesses to L1 cache | MAPS |
| L1 (r) | Bandwidth of random accesses to L1 cache | MAPS |
| L2 (s) | Bandwidth of strided accesses to L2 cache | MAPS |
| L2 (r) | Bandwidth of random accesses to L2 cache | MAPS |
| L3 (s) | Bandwidth of strided accesses to L3 cache | MAPS |
| L3 (r) | Bandwidth of random accesses to L3 cache | MAPS |
| MM (s) | Bandwidth of strided accesses to main memory | MAPS |
| MM (r) | Bandwidth of random accesses to main memory | MAPS |
| NW bw | Bandwidth across interprocessor network | Netbench |
| NW lat | Latency for interprocessor network | Netbench |
| FLOPS | Floating point operations per second | HPCC |

## 4.2 Applications

The applications used in this chapter are from the Department of Defense's Technical Insertion 2006 (TI-06) program [13]. The following are short descriptions of the eight applications:

**AVUS:** Developed by the Air Force Research Laboratory, AVUS is used to determine the fluid flow and turbulence of projectiles and air vehicles. The parameters used calculate 100 time-steps of fluid flow and turbulence for wing, flap and end plates using 7 million cells.

**CTH:** The CTH application measures the effects of multiple materials, large deformation, strong shock wake, solid mechanics and was developed by the Sandia National Laboratories. CTH models multi-phase, elastic viscoplastic, porous and explosive materials on 3-D and 2-D rectangular grids, as well as 1-D rectilinear, cylindrical and spherical meshes.

**GAMESS:** Developed by the Gordon research group at Iowa State University, GAMESS computes *ab initio* molecular quantum chemistry.

**HYCOM:** HYCOM models all of the world's oceans as one global body of water at a resolution of one-fourth of a degree measured at the Equator. It was developed by the Naval Research Laboratory, Los Alamos National Laboratory and the University of Miami.

**LAMMPS:** Developed by the Sandia National Laboratories, LAMMPS is generally used as a parallel particle simulator for particles at the mesoscale or continuum levels.

**OOCORE:** An out-of-core matrix solver, OOCORE was developed by the SCALAPACK group at the University of Tennessee at Knoxville. OOCORE has been included in past benchmark suites and is typically I/O bound.

**OVERFLOW:** NASA Langley and NASA Ames developed OVERFLOW to solve CFD equations on a set of overlapped, adaptive grids, so that the resolution near an obstacle is higher than that near other portions of the scene. With this approach, computations of both laminar and turbulent fluid flows over geometrically complex non-stationary boundaries can be solved.

**WRF:** A weather forecasting model that uses multiple dynamical cores and a 3-D variational data assimilation system with the ability to scale to many processors. WRF was developed by a partnership between the National Center for Atmospheric Research, the National Oceanic and Atmospheric Administration, the Air Force Weather Agency, the Naval Research Laboratory, Oklahoma University and the Federal Aviation Administration.

These eight applications were each run multiple times with a variety of processor counts ranging from 16 to 384 on the HPC systems summarized in Table I. Each application was run using the DoD 'standard' input set. Each application was run on no fewer than 10, and no more than 19, of the machines. Sometimes applications were not run on particular machines with particular processor counts either because those systems lacked the required number of processors or because the amount of main memory was insufficient. But, more generally, the examples in this chapter were meant to reflect real-world conditions and, in the real-world, it is not unusual for timings that have been collected at different times on different machines by different people to be incomplete in this way.

At a minimum, for each run, the end-to-end runtime was collected. This is the cheapest data to collect and is the only information used by the methods discussed in

Section 5. However, in some cases trace information was also collected and used, in varying levels of detail, for the methods described in Sections 6 and 7.

In addition to counting the number of FLOPS and memory accesses, some of the methods required partitioning the memory accesses between strided and random accesses. Since there is a standard understanding of what it means to count the total number of memory accesses in an application, but not of what it means to partition memory accesses into strided and random accesses, a little more detail is presented on how this was done.

These examples categorize memory accesses by using the Metasim tracer [8], which partitions the code for an application into non-overlapping basic blocks. Each block is then categorized as exhibiting either primarily strided or primarily random behavior using both dynamic and static analysis techniques. For the examples in this chapter, if either method classifies the block as containing at least 10% random accesses, all memory accesses in that block are counted as random. While the number 10% is somewhat arbitrary, it is based on the observation that on many machines the sustainable bandwidth of random accesses is less than the sustainable bandwidth of strided accesses by an order of magnitude.

The dynamic method for determining if a block exhibits primarily random or strided behavior uses a trace of the memory accesses in each basic block and considers each access to be strided if there has been an access to a sufficiently nearby memory location within some small number of immediately preceding memory accesses. The advantage of a dynamic approach is that every memory access is evaluated, so nothing is overlooked. The disadvantage is that the number of preceding accesses considered must be chosen carefully. If the size is too small, some strided accesses may be misclassified as random. If the size is too large, the process becomes too expensive computationally. In contrast, the static analysis method searches for strided references based on an analysis of dependencies in the assembly code. Static analysis is less expensive than dynamic analysis and also avoids the potential for misclassifying accesses due to a window size that is too small. On the other hand, static analysis may miss some strided accesses because of the difficulty of analysing some types of indirect accesses. Since the two types of analysis are predisposed to misclassify different types of strided accesses as random, both methods are applied and an access is considered to be strided if either method classifies it as such.

## 5. Using End-to-End Runtimes

If the only information available for the applications are end-to-end runtimes on some set of machines, then the weights in Equation 1 can be estimated by finding $w$ in the equation $M \times w = \boldsymbol{P}$, where $M$ is a matrix containing the benchmark measurements for a set of machines. Written out in matrix form, the equation looks as follows:

$$\begin{pmatrix} m_{1,1} & \dots & m_{1,b} \\ m_{2,1} & \dots & m_{2,b} \\ m_{3,1} & \dots & m_{3,b} \\ . & & . \\ . & \dots & . \\ . & & . \\ m_{n,1} & \dots & m_{n,b} \end{pmatrix} \times \begin{pmatrix} w_1 \\ w_2 \\ w_3 \\ \dots \\ w_b \end{pmatrix} = \begin{pmatrix} p_1 \\ p_2 \\ p_3 \\ . \\ . \\ . \\ p_n \end{pmatrix} \tag{3}$$

Again, the matrix $M$ contains all the benchmark measurements on all the machines. Each row represents a single machine and each column a particular benchmark. Hence, for the $M$ in Equation 3, there are benchmark measurements for $b$ resources on $n$ machines. The vector $\boldsymbol{P}$ contains the end-to-end, measured runtimes for the target application on the $n$ machines in $M$. (Note the assumption that each of these times was gathered running on the same number of processors, on the same input.) Furthermore, in addition to assuming that the linear model described in Section 3.2 holds, the assumption is also made that the weight vector $\boldsymbol{w}$ varies relatively little across machines. Obviously, this is a simplifying assumption which affects the accuracy of the predictions; the techniques in Section 6 relax this assumption.

Some basic preprocessing is done before proceeding with any of the techniques described here. First, since all measurements must be in the same units, the inverse of all non-latency measurements (e.g., FLOPS, memory and network bandwidths) must be used. Next, the measurements in $M$ are normalized by scaling the columns of $M$ so that the largest entry in each column is 1. This allows us to weigh different operations similarly, despite the fact that the cost of different types of operations can vary by orders of magnitude (e.g., network latency versus time to access the L1 cache).

After the preprocessing step, the weights for the benchmark measurements can be estimated by finding the 'best' $\boldsymbol{w}$ in $M \times \boldsymbol{w} = \boldsymbol{P}$ (Equation 3). If $n < b$, then the system is underdetermined and there is not enough data to choose a single 'best' value for $\boldsymbol{w}$. As a result, this technique assumes that $n \geq b$. Since this means that equality in Equation 3 may not be achievable, the metric for evaluating the quality of any given value of $\boldsymbol{w}$ must be specified.

Finally, having obtained $\boldsymbol{w}$, it can be used to make predictions for a new set of machines which have benchmark measurements captured in a matrix $M_{new}$. The runtime prediction for the application on the new set of machines is then $\boldsymbol{P_{new}} = M_{new} \times \boldsymbol{w}$. Machine ranking can be done on the new machines by sorting their respective application runtimes in $\boldsymbol{P_{new}}$.

## 5.1 Basic Least Squares

Perhaps the most natural way to find $\boldsymbol{w}$ is by using a least squares regression, also known as solving the least squares problem, which computes the $\boldsymbol{w}$ that minimizes the 2-norm of the residual $r = \boldsymbol{P} - M \times \boldsymbol{w}$.

With this technique, the entire set of machine benchmarks given in Table II, also referred to here in this chapter as 'the full basis set', is used. This set consists of:

$$< [FLOPS], L1(s), L2(s), L3(s), MM(s), L1(r), L2(r), L3(r), MM(r), NWbw, NWlat >$$

FLOPS is given in brackets because sometimes it is included in the full basis set and sometimes not. The distinction should always be clear from the context.

### 5.1.1 Results for Performance Prediction

The results shown in Table III were computed using a tool that reads the benchmark data and application runtimes for a set of machines and performs the above analysis [25]. Because of the requirement that the number of machines be no less than the number of machine benchmarks, some entries in the table could not be computed.

Using just the MAPS and Netbench measurements, the performance predictions are worse than those obtained using FLOPS alone. However, using a combination of the FLOPS, MAPS and Netbench measurements provides generally better performance

TABLE III
AVERAGE ABSOLUTE RELATIVE ERROR FOR TI-06 APPLICATIONS USING FLOPS, THE FULL MAPS + NETBENCH SET AND THE FULL FLOP + MAPS + NETBENCH SET

| | FLOPS | MAPS + Netbench | FLOPS + MAPS + Netbench |
|---|---|---|---|
| avus | 73.9 | 213.4 | – |
| cth | 61.2 | 64.8 | 59.2 |
| gamess | 72.6 | – | – |
| hycomm | 67.6 | 70.8 | – |
| lammps | 58.4 | 54.3 | 84.8 |
| oocore | 62.9 | 33.3 | 40.2 |
| overflow | 74.8 | 23.2 | 28.6 |
| wrf | 58.2 | 69.6 | 45.2 |
| Average | 66.2 | 72.4 | 51.6 |

TABLE IV
AVERAGE NUMBER OF THRESHOLDED INVERSIONS FOR TI-06 APPLICATIONS USING FLOPS, THE FULL MAPS + NETBENCH SET AND THE REDUCED MAPS + NETBENCH SET. ($\alpha = .01$ AND $\beta = .001$)

| | FLOPS | MAPS + Netbench | FLOPS + MAPS + Netbench |
|---|---|---|---|
| cth | 2.9 | – | – |
| lammps | 2.9 | 3.6 | – |
| oocore | 3.1 | 3.1 | 2.9 |
| overflow | 3.3 | 2.2 | 2.2 |
| wrf | 3 | 3.6 | – |
| Average | 3.0 | 3.2 | 2.6 |

predictions than using FLOPS alone. But regardless of the set of benchmarks used, the performance predictions are poor, with average errors ranging from 51.6% to 72.4%.

### 5.1.2 Results for Ranking

The least-squares performance prediction method can be extended to make predictions for several machines at a time and then to rank the machines based on the predicted performance using the methodology described in Section 3.4.

In Table IV, the average number of thresholded inversions is reported. For each entry, 5 machines are chosen at random for ranking; hence the maximum number of inversions is 10.

Use of the MAPS and Netbench measurements provides more thresholded inversions in these tests than the use of the FLOPS alone, similar to the results for performance prediction, which were worse. However, when FLOPS was included with the MAPS and Netbench measurements, not only did the accuracy of the performance predictions generally improve, but the rankings also became more accurate. Taken together, this suggests that FLOPS cannot be completely ignored for accurate performance predictions.

## 5.2 Least Squares with Basis Reduction

One drawback of applying least squares in such a straightforward way to solve Equation 3 is that the benchmark measurements may not be orthogonal. In other words, if $M$ contains several benchmarks whose measurements are highly correlated, the redundant information may have an unexpected effect on the accuracy of predicted runtimes on new systems.

This redundant information can be removed using the method of *basis reduction* [25]. After computing the correlations of all pairs of benchmark measurements across all the machines in $M$, highly correlated pairs are identified and one of each pair is dropped. For the purposes of this chapter, pairs are considered to be highly correlated if the correlation coefficient between them is greater than 0.8 or less than $-0.8$.

In the cross-validation tests, basis reduction is run on $M$ after the inverse of non-latency measurements is taken, but before the columns are normalized. $M$ is reduced to $M_r$, where $M_r$ has equal or fewer columns than $M$, depending on the correlation coefficients of the columns in $M$. From here, $M_r$ is normalized and the cross-validation tests are conducted in the same way as before, using $M_r$ instead of $M$.

### 5.2.1 Results for Prediction

Since the applications were run on subsets of the single set of 20 machines, basis reduction was run on all machines, instead of for each application's set of machines. Recall that the full basis set consisted of the following:

$$<[\text{FLOPS}], \text{L1}(s), \text{L2}(s), \text{L3}(s), \text{MM}(s), \text{L1}(r), \text{L2}(r), \text{L3}(r), MM(r), NWbw, NWlat>$$

On the machines in Table I, measurements for strided access to L1 and L2 caches were highly correlated, and only L1-strided bandwidths were kept. In addition, both strided access to L3 cache and main memory along with random access to L3 cache and main memory were highly correlated, and only main memory measurements were kept. The correlation between L3 cache and main memory is not surprising since not all of the systems have L3 caches. As a result, when the human expert looked at the MAPS plot (as described in Section 4.1) and had to identify a particular region as representing the L3 cache, the region chosen tended to have very similar behavior to that of the region identified for the main memory.

While different combinations of eliminated measurements were tested, in practice different combinations led to only minor differences in the results. As a result, the first predictor in each highly correlated pair was always dropped. This led to a reduced basis set consisting of:

$$<[\text{FLOPS}], \text{L1}(s), \text{MM}(s), \text{L1}(r), \text{L2}(r), \text{MM}(r), NWbw, NWlat>$$

Note that, in addition to using just the MAPS and Netbench measurements, the FLOPS measurement was also included in the full basis set. FLOPS was not correlated

TABLE V

AVERAGE ABSOLUTE RELATIVE PREDICTION ERROR FOR TI-06 APPLICATIONS USING FLOPS, THE FULL MAPS + NETBENCH SET WITH AND WITHOUT FLOPS AND THE REDUCED MAPS + NETBENCH SET WITH AND WITHOUT FLOPS

| | FLOPS | MAPS + Netbench | | FLOPS + MAPS + Netbench | |
|---|---|---|---|---|---|
| | | Full | Reduced | Full | Reduced |
| avus | 73.9 | 213.4 | **43.5** | – | 60.4 |
| cth | 61.2 | 64.8 | 36.0 | 59.2 | **33.4** |
| gamess | 72.6 | – | 55.0 | – | **35.2** |
| hycomm | 67.6 | 70.8 | 60.4 | – | **58.4** |
| lammps | 58.4 | 54.3 | **32.4** | 84.8 | 34.6 |
| oocore | 62.9 | 33.3 | **24.0** | 40.2 | 27.4 |
| overflow | 74.8 | **23.2** | 27.9 | 28.6 | 31.9 |
| wrf | 58.2 | 69.6 | 17.4 | 45.2 | **16.6** |
| Average | 66.2 | 72.4 | **37.1** | 51.6 | 42.4 |

with any of the other measurements, and so its inclusion had no effect on whether other metrics were included in the reduced basis set.

Table V presents the prediction results using the least squares solver (results in bold are the most accurate predictions in their row). Reducing the full set of measurements helps provide more accurate performance predictions for all applications with and without including FLOPS in the basis set.

### 5.2.2 Results for Ranking

The average number of inversions for each application is presented in Table VI. The table shows that use of FLOPS alone provides the best ranking only for CTH. Although the use of the reduced FLOPS, MAPS and Netbench basis set did not provide better performance predictions, it provides the best rankings, on average, for the systems. Moreover, whether or not FLOPS is included in the full basis set, after basis reduction the reduced basis set always provides more accurate rankings than the full one.

Table VII shows the effects on the number of inversions as $\alpha$ and $\beta$ are varied. This is only shown for the case where the MAPS and Netbench measurements, not including FLOPS, are used. As $\alpha$ and $\beta$ increases, larger variances in the collected runtimes and benchmark measurements are considered insignificant. As a result, the number of thresholded inversions declines. Nonetheless, when averaged over all the applications, the reduced basis set always provides more accurate rankings compared with FLOPS alone or the full basis set.

TABLE VI
AVERAGE NUMBER OF THRESHOLDED INVERSIONS FOR TI-06 APPLICATIONS USING FLOPS, THE FULL MAPS + NETBENCH SET AND THE REDUCED MAPS + NETBENCH SET. ($\alpha = .01$ AND $\beta = .001$)

| | FLOPS | MAPS + Netbench | | FLOPS + MAPS + Netbench | |
|---|---|---|---|---|---|
| | | Full | Reduced | Full | Reduced |
| cth | **2.9** | – | 3.2 | – | 3.4 |
| lammps | 2.9 | 3.6 | 3.1 | – | **2.8** |
| oocore | 3.1 | 3.1 | 2.4 | 2.9 | **2.4** |
| overflow | 3.3 | 2.2 | 2.1 | 2.2 | **2.0** |
| wrf | 3.0 | 3.6 | 1.9 | – | **1.8** |
| Average | 3.0 | 3.2 | 2.6 | 2.6 | **2.5** |

TABLE VII
THE NUMBER OF THRESHOLDED INVERSIONS, AVERAGED OVER ALL APPLICATIONS, WITH DIFFERENT VALUES OF $\alpha$ AND $\beta$ FOR THE TI-06 APPLICATIONS USING THE MAPS AND NETBENCH BENCHMARKS

| ($\alpha$, $\beta$) | (.01, .001) | (.1, .01) | (.2, .02) | (.5, .05) |
|---|---|---|---|---|
| FLOPS | 3.0 | 2.5 | 2.2 | 1.7 |
| Full basis set | 3.2 | 2.9 | 2.8 | 2.3 |
| Reduced basis set | 2.6 | 2.3 | 2.1 | 1.6 |

## 5.3 Linear Programming

In [41] a method that uses linear programming to solve Equation 1 is described. This method uses no more benchmark or application information than the least squares methods described previously, but it adds the ability to incorporate human judgement and so demonstrates the impact that expert input can have.

The basic idea is to add a parameter $\gamma$ to Equation 1 so that it is changed from:

$$P \approx m_1 w_1 + m_2 w_2 + m_3 w_3, \tag{4}$$

to:

$$P(1 - \gamma) \geq m_1 w_1 + m_2 w_2 + m_3 w_3 \tag{5}$$

$$P(1 + \gamma) \leq m_1 w_1 + m_2 w_2 + m_3 w_3. \tag{6}$$

The goal is to find non-negative weights $w$ that satisfy the above constraints, while keeping $\gamma$ small. When some constraints are determined to be difficult to satisfy, a human expert can decide that either the end-to-end application runtime measurement, or the benchmark measurements, are suspect and can simply eliminate that machine and the corresponding two constraints. Alternatively, the decision could be made to rerun the application and/or benchmarks in the hopes of getting more accurate measurements.

### 5.3.1 Results

The linear programming method tries to find the weights that best fit the entries in $M$ and $P$ under the same assumptions as with the least squares methods. However, with human intervention, it can also identify entries in $M$ and $P$ that seem to be suspect and either ignore or correct them.

On the set of test data used here, a few runtimes and benchmark measurements were found to be suspect. After correcting those errors, the linear programming method was run again, giving the overall results presented in Table VIII. The fact that these predictions are so much more accurate than those in Table V using the least squares

TABLE VIII
AVERAGE ABSOLUTE ERROR OVER ALL APPLICATIONS USING LINEAR PROGRAMMING FOR PERFORMANCE PREDICTION. THE SYSTEMS ARE IDENTIFIED BY A COMBINATION OF THE DEPARTMENT OF DEFENSE COMPUTER CENTER, THE COMPUTER MANUFACTURER, AND THE PROCESSOR TYPE

| Systems | Average Error |
|---|---|
| ASC_SGI_Altix | 8% |
| SDSC_IBM_IA64 | – |
| ARL_IBM_Opteron | 8% |
| ARL_IBM_P3 | 4% |
| MHPCC_IBM_P3 | 6% |
| NAVO_IBM_P3 | 6% |
| NAVO_IBM_p655(Big) | 6% |
| NAVO_IBM_p655 (Sml) | 5% |
| ARSC_IBM_p655 | 2% |
| MHPCC_IBM_p690 | 7% |
| NAVO_IBM_p690 | 9% |
| ARL_IBM_p690 | 6% |
| ERDC_HP_SC40 | 8% |
| ASC_HP_SC45 | 4% |
| ERDC_HP_SC45 | 6% |
| ARSC_Cray_X1 | 5% |
| ERDC_Cray_X1 | 3% |
| AHPCRC_Cray_X1E | – |
| ARL_LNX_Xeon (3.06) | 8% |
| ARL_LNX_Xeon (3.6) | 8% |
| **Overall Average Error** | **6%** |

method reflects the power of allowing a human expert to examine the results and to eliminate (or to rerun and recollect) suspicious benchmark measurements and application runtimes. Significantly more detail and analysis can be found in [41].

### 5.4 Discussion

A simple approach for obtaining benchmark weights is to use least squares. Using this method is quick and simple, assuming that end-to-end runtimes of the application on different machines, along with the results of simple machine benchmarks, are available. Although the accuracy of the performance prediction (at best a relative error of 37% averaged over all TI-06 applications) may be insufficient for scenarios such as a queue scheduler, they are accurate relative to each other and so can be useful for ranking a set of machines.

Simply using the full set of benchmark measurements is not the best approach for the least squares method. For example, when using the full set of MAPS and Netbench measurements, the average relative error for predictions was as high as 72.4%, and there were an average of 3.2 thresholded inversions when a set of 5 systems was ranked. But, once the full set of measurements were reduced using basis reduction to an orthogonal set, the performance predictions improved to an average relative error of 37% and the thresholded inversions reduced to an average of 2.6. In all cases but one, use of the reduced set of benchmark measurements for making performance predictions and ranking systems is better than the use of FLOPS alone. The only exception to this is ranking systems for CTH.

The combination of MAPS and Netbench measurements with and without FLOPS show similar performance: the performance predictions are better by 5% when FLOPS are not included in the set. Although the average number of thresholded inversions are lower when FLOPS is included in the set, the difference between the two is quite small.

The linear programming method used exactly the same information about the machines and the applications as the least squares methods, but added the ability to factor in human expertise. This improved the results significantly, indicating the power of having access to human expertise (in this case, the ability to throw out results judged to be due to errors in either the benchmark measurements or the measured application runtimes).

## 6. Using Basic Trace Data

As noted previously, different applications with the same execution time on a given machine may stress different system components. As a result, applications may derive varying levels of benefit from improvements to any single system component. The techniques described in Section 5 do not take this into consideration.

In contrast, this section discusses some techniques that incorporate more application-specific information, in particular the lightweight trace data described in Section 4.2. Note that the types of traces used are considerably cheaper than those used for the cycle-accurate simulations described in Section 2.4.

## 6.1 Predicting Performance

In [41] the authors describe methods for performance prediction that assume that both $M$ and $w$ in Equation 3 are known, but the operation for combining them is significantly more complex than matrix multiplication. In addition, whereas $M$ is determined as before, $w$ is determined by tracing the application. Most notably, $w$ is allowed to vary depending on the system. To keep costs down, the application is only traced on a single system, but the data collected (summarized in Fig. 5)

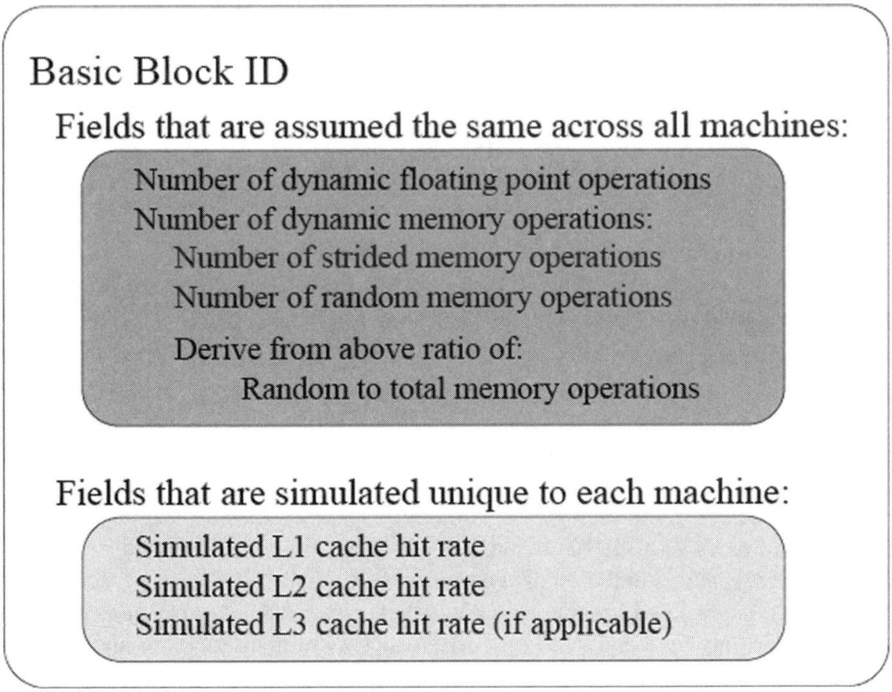

FIG. 5. Data collected on each basic block using the MetaSim Tracer.

TABLE IX
ABSOLUTE ERROR AVERAGED OVER ALL APPLICATIONS

| Systems | Average Error |
|---|---|
| ARL_IBM_Opteron | 11% |
| NAVO_IBM_P3 | 7% |
| NAVO_IBM_p655 (Big) | 6% |
| ARSC_IBM_p655 | 4% |
| MHPCC_IBM_p690 | 8% |
| NAVO_IBM_p690 | 18% |
| ASC_HP_SC45 | 7% |
| ERDC_HP_SC45 | 9% |
| ARL_LNX_Xeon (3.6) | 5% |
| **Overall Average Error** | **8%** |

TABLE X
SUM OF THE NUMBER OF THRESHOLDED INVERSIONS FOR ALL APPLICATIONS AND NUMBERS OF PROCESSORS, FOR EACH OF THE NINE PERFORMANCE-PREDICTION STRATEGIES DESCRIBED IN [7]

| Methodology (case #) | 1 | 2 | 3 | 4 | 5 | 6 | 7 | 8 | 9 |
|---|---|---|---|---|---|---|---|---|---|
| # Thresh. inversions | 165 | 86 | 115 | 165 | 76 | 53 | 55 | 44 | 44 |

is then simulated on other systems of interest in order to generate $w$ for those other machines.

A detailed description of the technique can be found in [41]; here it suffices to note simply that the results they attained (presented in Table IX) are quite accurate, with an average absolute error of below 10%.

## 6.2 Ranking

As in Section 5, once performance predictions have been made for each system, the times can be used to generate a machine ranking. In [7] the quality of performance predictions using 9 methodologies of different sophistications are evaluated. Using the methodologies and the data from [7], Table X gives the summed number of thresholded inversions in the predicted runtimes.

The first 3 cases should produce rankings that are equivalent to rankings based on only FLOPS, only the bandwidth of strided accesses to main memory and only the bandwidth of random accesses to main memory, respectively. The ranking based on the bandwidth of strided access to main memory is the best of these three. As expected from the description in [7], the first and fourth cases produce equivalent rankings.

Case 5 is similar to a ranking based on a combination of FLOPS and the bandwidth of strided and random accesses to memory. Case 6 is similar to Case 5, but with a different method for partitioning between strided and random accesses. Table X shows that both of these rankings are significantly better than those produced by the first four cases. As the rankings in these cases are application dependent, it is not surprising that they outperform the application-independent rankings discussed in Section 7.

Cases 7 through 9 use more sophisticated performance-prediction techniques. These calculations consider combinations of FLOPS, MAPS memory bandwidths (case 7), Netbench network measurements (case 8) and loop and control flow dependencies for memory operations (case 9). As expected, they result in more accurate rankings.

### 6.3 Discussion

Although the methods in this section do not use any information about the actual end-to-end runtimes of an application across a set of machines, the trace information that these methods employ instead allows them to achieve high accuracy. This represents another point on the trade-off line between accuracy and expense/complexity. As with the other, more detailed, model-based methods summarized in Section 2, this approach constructs an overall application performance model from many small models of each basic block and communications event. This model can then be used to understand where most of the time is spent and where tuning efforts should be directed. The methods described in Section 5 do not provide such detailed guidance.

Furthermore, generating more accurate predictions using these methods also gives improved (application dependent) machine rankings.

## 7. Application-Independent Rankings

Thus far, the techniques discussed have focussed on application-specific performance prediction and rankings. When it comes to ranking machines, this means one is given a set of machines and a specific application, and the goal is to predict which of those machines will execute the application fastest. However, there is also interest in application-independent rankings (e.g., the Top 500 list [45]), in which a set of machines is ranked and the general expectation is that the machine ranked, say, third, will execute most applications faster than the machine ranked, say, tenth.

The Top 500 list ranks supercomputers based solely on their performance on the Linpack benchmark, which essentially measures FLOPS. This section studies whether it is possible to improve on that ranking and what is the cost of doing so.

## 7.1 Rankings Using Only Machine Metrics

With the metric described in Section 3.4 for evaluating the quality of a ranking, it is possible to evaluate objectively how FLOPS is compared with other machine benchmarks as a way for generating machine rankings. All rankings in this section are tested on the set of applications described in Section 4.2, run on subsets of the machines described in Section 4.1.

The first experiment considers the quality of rankings generated by the machine benchmarks summarized in Table II: bandwidth of strided and random accesses to L1 cache, bandwidth of strided and random accesses to L2 cache, bandwidth of strided and random accesses to main memory, interprocessor network bandwidth, interprocessor network latency and peak FLOPS.

Table XI sums the number of thresholded inversions over all the applications and all the processor counts on which each was run. Because each application is run on a different set of processor counts and not every application has been run on every machine, the numbers in Table XI should not be compared across applications, but only on an application-by-application basis, across the rankings by different machine characteristics.

The last row of Table XI shows that the bandwidth of strided accesses to main memory provides the single best overall ranking, with 309 total thresholded inversions (in contrast, there is also a machine ranking that generates over 2000 thresholded inversions on this data). The ranking generated by the bandwidth of random accesses to L1 cache is a close second; however, it is also evident that there is no single ranking that is optimal for all applications. Although the bandwidth of strided accesses to

TABLE XI

SUM OF THE NUMBER OF THRESHOLDED INVERSIONS ($\alpha = .01$ AND $\beta = .001$) FOR ALL PROCESSOR COUNTS FOR EACH APPLICATION. THE SMALLEST NUMBER (REPRESENTING THE BEST METRIC) FOR EACH APPLICATION IS GIVEN IN BOLD. THE LAST ROW IS A SUM OF EACH COLUMN AND GIVES A SINGLE NUMBER REPRESENTING THE OVERALL QUALITY OF THE RANKING PRODUCED USING THAT MACHINE CHARACTERISTIC

| Metric | L1(s) | L1(r) | L2(s) | L2(r) | MM(s) | MM(r) | 1/NW lat | NW bw | FLOPS |
|---|---|---|---|---|---|---|---|---|---|
| avus | 51 | 26 | 44 | 42 | **1** | 61 | 19 | 30 | 22 |
| cth | 32 | **18** | 30 | 82 | 21 | 117 | 63 | 37 | 35 |
| gamess | 25 | **16** | 40 | 55 | 48 | 76 | 65 | 35 | 25 |
| hycom | 26 | **10** | 26 | 83 | 17 | 126 | 65 | 28 | 35 |
| lammps | 136 | 107 | 133 | 93 | 80 | 157 | 95 | 116 | **68** |
| oocore | 44 | **31** | 56 | 71 | 61 | 91 | 75 | 50 | 52 |
| overflow | 71 | **39** | 79 | 91 | 47 | 104 | 108 | 81 | 44 |
| wrf | 99 | 63 | 92 | 134 | **34** | 203 | 103 | 83 | 60 |
| overall sum | 484 | 310 | 500 | 651 | **309** | 935 | 593 | 460 | 341 |

main memory is nearly perfect for avus and does very well on hycom, wrf and cth, it is outperformed by the bandwidth of both strided and random accesses to L1 cache for ranking performance on gamess. One interpretation of the data is that these applications fall into three categories:

- codes dominated by time to perform floating-point operations,
- codes dominated by time to access main memory,
- and codes dominated by time to access L1 cache.

With 20 machines, there are 20! possible distinct rankings. Searching through the subspace of 'feasible' rankings reveals one that gives only 195 inversions (although this number cannot be directly compared with those in Table XI since the parameter values used were $\alpha = .01$ and $\beta = 0$). In this optimal ranking the SDSC Itanium cluster TeraGrid was predicted to be the fastest machine. However, across all of the benchmarks, the Itanium is only the fastest for the metric of bandwidth of random access to main memory – and Table XI shows using random access to main memory alone to be the poorest of the single-characteristic ranking metrics examined. This conundrum suggests trying more sophisticated ranking heuristics.

Testing various simple combinations of machine metrics — for example, the ratio of flops to the bandwidth of both strided and random accesses to different levels of the memory hierarchy — gave rankings that were generally significantly worse than the ranking based solely on the bandwidth of strided accesses to main memory. This suggests a need to incorporate more information.

## 7.2 Rankings Incorporating Application Characteristics

As in Section 6, one might try improving the rankings by incorporating application characteristics and using those characteristics to weight the measured machine characteristics. However, in order to generate a single application-independent ranking, this requires either choosing a single representative application, or using values that represent an 'average' application. This section considers the former approach.

Since the goal is to use as little information as possible, the first example presented uses only the number of memory accesses $m$ and the number of floating-point operations $f$. Recall that the goal is an application-independent ranking, so while we evaluate the rankings generated by each of the applications, only the best result over all the applications is reported. In other words, this is the result of taking the characteristics of a single application and using it to generate a ranking of the machines that is evaluated for all the applications in the test suite.

If a memory reference consists of 8 bytes, $m$ and $f$ can be used in a natural way by computing the following number for each machine $m_i$:

$$r_i = \frac{8m}{\text{bw\_mem}(i)} + \frac{f}{\text{flops}(i)}. \tag{7}$$

Within Equation 7, $m$ (and $f$) could be either the average number of memory accesses over all the processors, or the maximum number of memory accesses over all the processors. In addition, bw_mem can be the strided or random bandwidth of accesses to any level of the memory hierarchy.

Using the bandwidth of strided accesses to main memory for bw_mem, regardless of whether the average or the maximum counts for $m$ and $f$ are used, leads to a ranking that is identical to a ranking based only on the bandwidth of strided accesses to main memory. Since the increase in memory bandwidth has not kept pace with the increase in processor speed, it is not surprising that the memory term in Equation 7 overwhelms the processor term. The effect would be even greater if the bandwidth of random accesses to main memory for bw_mem$(i)$ was used, since the disparity between the magnitude of the two terms would be even greater. Moreover, using the measurement that has the fastest access time of all levels of the memory hierarchy, bandwidth of strided accesses to L1, for bw_mem in Equation 7 results in a ranking that is independent of $f$.

This suggests a model that accommodates more detail about the application, perhaps by partitioning the memory accesses. One possibility would be to partition $m$ into $m = m_{l1} + m_{l2} + m_{l3} + m_{mm}$, where $m_{l1}$ is the number of accesses that hit in the L1 cache, and so on. Another is to partition $m$ into $m = m_1 + m_r$, where $m_1$ is the number of strided accesses and $m_r$ is the number of random accesses to memory. Partitioning into levels of the hierarchy is dependent on the architecture chosen, which suggests trying the latter strategy (using the technique described in Section 4 to partition the memory accesses).

Once the $m$ memory accesses are partitioned into random ($m_r$) and strided ($m_1$), Equation 8 can be used to compute the numbers $r_1, r_2, \ldots, r_n$ from which the ranking is generated:

$$r_i = \frac{8m_1}{\text{bw\_mem}_1(i)} + \frac{8m_r}{\text{bw\_mem}_r(i)} + \frac{f}{\text{flops}(i)}. \tag{8}$$

Note that there is again a choice to be made regarding what to use for $\text{bw\_mem}_1$ and $\text{bw\_mem}_r$. There are several options including: using the bandwidths of strided and random accesses to main memory; the bandwidths of strided and random accesses to L1 cache; or considering the data in Table XI, the bandwidth of strided access to main memory and of random access to L1 cache. Furthermore, since the goal is a single, fixed ranking that can be applied to all applications, a choice also has to made

TABLE XII
SUM OF THE NUMBER OF THRESHOLDED INVERSIONS FOR ALL NUMBERS OF PROCESSORS FOR EACH APPLICATION, WITH $\alpha = .01$ AND $\beta = .001$. THE SMALLEST NUMBER (REPRESENTING THE BEST METRIC) FOR EACH APPLICATION IS GIVEN IN BOLD

| Metric | l1(1,r) | mm(1,r) | mm(1), l1(r) |
|---|---|---|---|
| avus | 12 | 21 | **9** |
| cth | 14 | 80 | **9** |
| gamess | **16** | 77 | 26 |
| hycom | **2** | 44 | **2** |
| lamps | 107 | 148 | **81** |
| oocore | **31** | 100 | 44 |
| overflow2 | **34** | 78 | **34** |
| wrf | 63 | 158 | **44** |
| overall sum | 279 | 706 | **249** |

about which application's $m_1$, $m_r$, and $f$ are to be used for generating the ranking. In theory, one could also ask what processor count of which application to use for the ranking; in practice, performance of these tasks take time, and so $m_1$ and $m_r$ counts were only gathered for one processor count per application.

Table XII shows the results of these experiments. Each column shows the number of thresholded inversions for each of the 8 applications using the specified choice of strided and random access bandwidths. In each column, the results use the application whose $m_1$, $m_r$, and $f$ led to the smallest number of inversions for all other applications. When using the random and strided bandwidths to L1 cache, the most accurate ranking was generated using overflow2; when using the bandwidths to main memory, the best application was oocore; and when using a combination of L1 and main memory bandwidths, avus and hycom generated equally good rankings.

Comparison of the results in Table XII with those in Table XI reveals that partitioning of the memory accesses is useful as long as the random accesses are considered to hit in L1 cache. Using the bandwidth of random access to L1 cache alone did fairly well, but the ranking is improved by incorporating the bandwidth of strided accesses to L1 cache and is improved even more by incorporating the bandwidth of strided accesses to main memory. When we use the bandwidth of accesses to main memory only, the quality of the resulting order is between those of rankings based on the bandwidth of random accesses and those based on the bandwidth of strided accesses to main memory.

In [9] the authors discuss possible reasons why the combined metric based on mm(1) and l1(r) works so well. One observation is that this may be representative of a more general fact: applications with a large memory footprint that have many strided accesses benefit from high bandwidth to main memory because the whole cache line is used and prefetching further utilizes the full main memory bandwidth. For many of these codes, main memory bandwidth is thus the limiting performance factor. On the other hand, applications with many random accesses waste most of the cache line and these accesses do not benefit from prefetching. The performance of these codes is limited by the latency-hiding capabilities of the machine's cache, which is captured by measuring the bandwidth of random accesses to L1 cache.

### 7.3 Discussion

Two things that might further improve on the ranking would be partitioning memory accesses between the different levels of the memory hierarchy and allowing different rankings based on the processor count. The two possibilities are not entirely independent since running the same size problem on a larger number of processors means a smaller working set on each processor and therefore different cache behaviors. However, allowing different rankings for different processor counts takes us away from the original goal of finding a single fixed ranking that can be used as a general guideline.

This leaves partitioning memory accesses between the different levels of the memory hierarchy. As noted previously, this requires either choosing a representative system or moving towards a more complex model that allows for predictions that are specific to individual machines, as is done in [7, 30]. Therefore, given the level of complexity needed for a ranking method that incorporates so much detail, we simply observe that we achieved a ranking with about 28% more thresholded inversions than the brute-force obtainable optimal ranking on our data set, without resorting to anything more complex than partitioning each application's memory accesses into strided and random accesses. This represents a significant improvement over the ranking based on FLOPS, which was about 75% worse than the optimal ranking.

## 8. Conclusion

This chapter addressed two related issues of interest to various parties in the world of supercomputing: performance prediction and machine ranking. The first is a long-standing problem that has been studied extensively, reflected in part by the survey of work in Section 2. The second, while not as well studied, is still of interest both when the goal is a machine ranking for a particular application, and when the goal is a more general application-independent ranking.

To illustrate the trade-offs between accuracy and effort that are inherent in any approach, one framework for both prediction and ranking is presented. The main assumption in this framework is that simple benchmarks can be run (or accurately estimated) on all systems of interest. Then, several variations within the framework are examined: ones that use only end-to-end runtimes for an application on any set of machines (Section 5), and those that also employ basic trace data about an application (Section 6). Using trace data is more expensive and, not surprisingly, gives significantly more accurate predictions than a completely automatic method that is based on least squares and uses only end-to-end runtimes. However, a linear programming method that also only uses end-to-end runtimes can partially compensate by allowing human expert intervention. Finally, in Section 7 the question of application-independent machine rankings is addressed, again within the same framework. Once again, reasonable results can be obtained using only the results of simple benchmark measurements, but the results can be improved by incorporating limited application trace information.

## Acknowledgments

We would like to thank Michael Laurenzano and Raffy Kaloustian for helping to collect trace data and Xiaofeng Gao for writing the dynamic analysis tool used in Section 4.2. The applications benchmarking data used in this study was obtained by the following members of the Engineering Research and Development Center (ERDC), Computational Science and Engineering Group: Mr. Robert W. Alter, Dr. Paul M. Bennett, Dr. Sam B. Cable, Dr. Alvaro A. Fernandez, Ms. Carrie L. Leach, Dr. Mahin Mahmoodi, Dr. Thomas C. Oppe and Dr. William A. Ward, Jr. This work was supported in part by a grant from the DoD High-Performance Computing Modernization Program (HPCMP) along with HPCMP-sponsored computer time at the Army Research Laboratory (ARL), the Aeronautical Systems Center (ASC), the Engineering Research and Development Center (ERDC), and the Naval Oceanographic Office (NAVO), Major Shared Resource Centers (MSRCs) and the Army High Performance Computing Research Center (AHPCRC), the Artic Region Supercomputing Center (ARSC), and the Maui High Performance Computing Center (MHPCC). Computer time was also provided by SDSC. Additional computer time was graciously provided by the Pittsburgh Supercomputer Center via an NRAC award. This work was supported in part by a grant from the National Science Foundation entitled 'The Cyberinfrastructure Evaluation Center' and by NSF grant #CCF-0446604. This work was sponsored in part by the Department of Energy Office of Science through SciDAC award 'High-End Computer System Performance: Science and Engineering' and through the award entitled 'HPCS Execution Time Evaluation.'

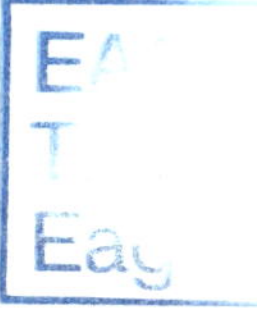

## References


[1] Adve V., 1993. *Analyzing the Behavior and Performance of Parallel Programs*. PhD thesis, University of Wisconsin, Madison.

[2] Badia R., Rodriguez G., and Labarta J., 2003. Deriving analytical models from a limited number of runs. In *Parallel Computing: Software Technology, Algorithms, Architectures, and Applications (PARCO 2003)*, pp. 769–776, Dresden, Germany.

[3] Bailey D. H., Barszcz E., Barton J. T., Browning D. S., Carter R. L., Dagum D., Fatoohi R. A., Frederickson P. O., Lasinski T. A., Schreiber R. S., Simon H. D., Venkatakrishnan V., and Weeratunga S. K., Fall 1991. The NAS parallel benchmarks. *Intl. J. Supercomp. Appl.*, **5**(3):63–73.

[4] Ballansc R. S., Cocke J. A., and Kolsky H. G., 1962. *The Lookahead Unit, Planning a Computer System*. McGraw-Hill, New York, NY.

[5] Boland L. T., Granito G. D., Marcotte A. V., Messina B. V., and Smith J. W., 1967. The IBM system 360/model9: storage system. *IBM J. Res. and Dev.*, **11**:54–79.

[6] Burger D., Austin T. M., and Bennett S., 1996. Evaluating future microprocessors: the simplescalar tool set. Technical Report CS-TR-1996-1308, University of Wisconsin-Madison.

[7] Carrington L., Laurenzano M., Snavely A., Campbell R. L. Jr., and Davis L., November 2005. How well can simple metrics predict the performance of real applications? In *Proceedings of Supercomputing (SC|05)*.

[8] Carrington L., Snavely A., Wolter N., and Gao X., June 2003. A performance prediction framework for scientific applications. In *Proceedings of the International Conference on Computational Science (ICCS 2003)*, Melbourne, Australia.

[9] Chen T. -Y., Gunn M., Simon B., Carrington L., and Snavely A., November 2006. Metrics for ranking the performance of supercomputers. *CTWatch Quarterly*, **2**(4B).

[10] Clement M. J., and Quinn M. J., 1995. Multivariate statistical techniques for parallel performance prediction. In *HICSS'95: Proceedings of the 28th Hawaii International Conference on System Sciences*, pp. 446–455.

[11] Crovella M. E., and LeBlanc T. J., 1994. Parallel performance prediction using lost cycles analysis. In *Supercomputing'94: Proceedings of the 1994 ACM/IEEE Conference on Supercomputing*, pp. 600–609, Washington, D.C.

[12] Culler D., Karp R., Patterson D., Sahay A., Schauser K. E., Santos E., Subramonian R., and von Eicken T., May 1993. LogP: Towards a realistic model of parallel computation. In *Proceedings of the Fourth ACM SIGPLAN Symposium on Principles and Practice of Parallel Programming*, pp. 1–12, San Diego, CA.

[13] Department of Defense High Performance Computing Modernization Program. May 2005. Technology Insertion-06 (TI-06). http://www.hpcmo.hpc.mil/Htdocs/TI/TI06.

[14] Dongarra J., Luszczek P., and Petitet A., 2003. The LINPACK benchmark: past, present and future. *Concurr. Comput.: Pract. Exper.*, **15**:1–18.

[15] Faerman M., Su A., Wolski R., and Berman F., 1999. Adaptive performance prediction for distributed data-intensive applications. In *Supercomputing'99: Proceedings of the 1999 ACM/IEEE Conference on Supercomputing (CDROM)*, p. 36, Portland, OR.

[16] Gustafson J. L., and Todi R., 1999. Conventional benchmarks as a sample of the performance spectrum. *J. Supercomp.*, **13**(3):321–342.

[17] Hoisie A., Lubeck O. M., and Wasserman H. J., 1999. Performance analysis of wavefront algorithms on very-large scale distributed systems. In *Workshop on Wide Area Networks and High Performance Computing*, pp. 171–187, London, UK, Springer-Verlag. Also Lecture Notes in Control and Information Sciences, Vol. **249**.

[18] Hoisie A., Lubeck O. M., and Wasserman H. J., February 1999. Scalability analysis of multidimensional wavefront algorithms on large-scale SMP clusters. In *FRONTIERS'99: Proceedings of the The 7th Symposium on the Frontiers of Massively Parallel Computation*, pp. 4–15, Annapolis, MD.

[19] HPC Challenge Benchmarks. http://icl.cs.utk.edu/hpcc/.

[20] IDC reports latest supercomputer rankings based on the IDC Balanced Rating test., December 2002. In EDP Weekly's IT Monitor.

[21] Ipek E., de Supinski B. R., Schulz M., and McKee S. A., 2005. *Euro-Par 2005 Parallel Processing*, volume 3648, chapter An approach to performance prediction for parallel applications, pp. 196–205. Springer Berlin/Heidelberg.

[22] Kerbyson D. J., Hoisie A., and Wasserman H. J., 2005. A performance comparison between the Earth Simulator and other terascale systems on a characteristic ASCI workload. *Concurr. Comput.: Pract. Exper.*, **17**(10):1219–1238.

[23] Kerbyson D. J., and Jones P. W., Summer 2005. A performance model of the parallel ocean program. *Intl. J. High Perf. Comput. Appl.*, **19**(3):261–276.

[24] Kerbyson D. J., Wasserman H. J., and Hoisie A., 2002. Exploring advanced architectures using performance prediction. In *IWIA'02: Proceedings of the International Workshop on Innovative Architecture for Future Generation High-Performance Processors and Systems*, pp. 27–40.

[25] Khalili O., June 2007. Performance prediction and ordering of supercomputers using a linear combination of benchmark measurements. Master's thesis, University of California at San Diego, La Jolla, CA.

[26] Kramer W. T. C., and Ryan C., June 2003. Performance variability of highly parallel architectures. In *Proceedings of the International Conference on Computational Science (ICCS 2003)*, Melbourne, Australia.

[27] Lo J., Egger S., Emer J., Levy H., Stamm R., and Tullsen D., August 1997. Converting thread-level parallelism to instruction-level parallelism via simultaneous multithreading. *ACM Trans. Comput. Sys.*

[28] Luo Y., Lubeck O. M., Wasserman H., Bassetti F., and Cameron K. W., 1998. Development and validation of a hierarchical memory model incorporating CPU- and memory-operation overlap model. In *WOSP'98: Proceedings of the 1st International Workshop on Software and Performance*, pp. 152–163, Santa Fe, NM, ACM Press.

[29] Luszczek P., Dongarra J., Koester D., Rabenseifner R., Lucas B., Kepner J., McCalpin J., Bailey D., and Takahashi D., March 2005. Introduction to the HPC challenge benchmark suite. Available at http://www.hpccchallenge.org/pubs/.

[30] Marin G., and Mellor-Crummey J., June 2004. Cross-architecture performance predictions for scientific applications using parameterized models. In *Proceedings of SIGMETRICS/Performance'04*, New York, NY.

[31] McCalpin J. D., December 1995. Memory bandwidth and machine balance in current high performance computers. IEEE Technical Committee on Computer Architecture Newsletter.

[32] Mendes C. L., and Reed D. A., 1994. Performance stability and prediction. In *Proceedings of the IEEE/USP International Workshop on High Performance Computing.*

[33] Mendes C. L., and Reed D. A., 1998. Integrated compilation and scalability analysis for parallel systems. In *PACT'98: Proceedings of the 1998 International Conference on Parallel Architectures and Compilation Techniques*, pp. 385–392.

[34] Murphey J. O., and Wade R. M., 1970. The IBM 360/195. *Datamation*, **16**(4):72–79.

[35] Petrini F., Kerbyson D. J., and Pakin S., November 2003. The case of the missing supercomputer performance: achieving optimal performance on the 8,192 processors of ASCIQ. In *Proceedings of Supercomputing (SC'03)*, Phoeniz, AZ.

[36] Saavedra R. H., and Smith A. J., 1995. Measuring cache and TLB performance and their effect on benchmark runtimes. *IEEE Trans. Comput.*, **44**(10):1223–1235.

[37] Saavedra R. H., and Smith A. J., 1995. Performance characterization of optimizing compilers. *IEEE Trans. Softw. Eng.*, **21**(7):615–628.

[38] Saavedra R. H., and Smith A. J., 1996. Analysis of benchmark characteristics and benchmark performance prediction. *ACM Trans. Comput. Sys.*, **14**(4):344–384.

[39] Simon J., and Wierun J., August 1996. Accurate performance prediction for massively parallel systems and its applications. In *Proceedings of the 2nd International Euro-Par Conference*, Lyon, France.

[40] Singh K., Ipek E., McKee S. A., de Supinski B. R., Schulz M., and Caruana R., 2007. Predicting parallel application performance via machine learning approaches. To appear in Concurrency and Computation: Practice and Experience.

[41] Snavely A., Carrington L., Tikir M. M., Campbell R. L. Jr., and Chen T. -Y., 2006. Solving the convolution problem in performance modeling. Unpublished manuscript.

[42] Snavely A., Carrington L., Wolter N., Labarta J., Badia R., and Purkayastha A., November 2002. A framework for application performance modeling and prediction. In *Proceedings of Supercomputing (SC 2002)*, Baltimore, MD.

[43] Spooner D., and Kerbyson D., June 2003. Identification of performance characteristics from multi-view trace analysis. In *Proceedings of the International Conference on Computational Science (ICCS 2003)*, Melbourne, Australia.

[44] Tjaden G. S., and Flynn M. J., 1970. Detection and parallel execution of independent instruction. *IEEE Trans. Comput.*, C-19:889–895.

[45] Top500 supercomputer sites. http://www.top500.org.

[46] Wulf W. A., and McKee S. A., 1995. Hitting the memory wall: implications of the obvious. *SIGARCH Comput. Arch. News*, **23**(1):20–24.

[47] Xu Z., Zhang X., and Sun L., 1996. Semi-empirical multiprocessor performance predictions. *J. Parallel Distrib. Comput.*, **39**(1):14–28.

[48] Yang L. T., Ma X., and Mueller F., 2005. Cross-platform performance prediction of parallel applications using partial execution. In *SC'05: Proceedings of the 2005 ACM/IEEE Conference on Supercomputing*, p. 40, Seattle, WA.

# Sampled Processor Simulation: A Survey

LIEVEN EECKHOUT*

*Department of Electronics and Information Systems (ELIS), Ghent University, Sint-Pietersnieuwstraat 41, B-9000 Gent, Belgium*

**Abstract**

Simulation of industry-standard benchmarks is extremely time-consuming. Sampled processor simulation speeds up the simulation by several orders of magnitude by simulating a limited number of sampling units rather than the execution of the entire program.

This work presents a survey on sampled processor simulation and discusses solutions to the three major challenges to sampled processor simulation: how to choose representative sampling units; how to establish efficiently a sampling unit's architecture starting image; and how to efficiently establish an accurate sampling unit's microarchitecture starting image.



* Corresponding author. *Email address:* leeckhou@elis.ugent.be (Lieven Eeckhout).

ADVANCES IN COMPUTERS, VOL. 72
ISSN: 0065-2458/DOI: 10.1016/S0065-2458(08)00004-1



Copyright © 2008 Elsevier Inc.
All rights reserved.

# 1. Introduction

Designing of a microprocessor is extremely time-consuming and takes several years to complete (up to seven years, [72]). This is partly attributed to the fact that computer designers and architects heavily rely on simulation tools for exploring the huge microprocessor design space. These simulation tools are at least three or four orders of magnitude slower than real hardware. In addition, architects and designers use long-running benchmarks that are built after real-life applications; today's industry-standard benchmarks such as SPEC CPU have several hundreds of billions of dynamically executed instructions. The end result is that the simulation of a single benchmark can take days to weeks, which in this case involves the simulation of only a single microarchitecture configuration. As a result, the exploration of a huge design space in order to find an optimal trade-off between design metrics of interest—such as performance, cost, power consumption, temperature, and reliability—is impossible through detailed simulation.

This is a well-recognized problem and several researchers have proposed solutions for it. The *reduced input sets* as proposed by KleinOsowski and Lilja [53] and Eeckhout et al. [33] strive at reducing simulation time by reducing the dynamic instruction count of benchmarks by providing reduced inputs. The challenge in building these reduced inputs is to reduce the dynamic instruction count without affecting the overall performance characteristics compared to the reference inputs. *Analytical models* as proposed by Sorin et al. [99], Karkhanis and Smith [50,51], Lee and Brooks [65] and Ipek et al. [45] present themselves as a number of simple equations, typically in an algebraic form. The inputs to these models are program characteristics and a microarchitecture configuration description; the output is a performance prediction. The main benefit of these analytical models is that they are intuitive, insightful and extremely fast to use. These models enable chief architects to make high-level design decisions in a limited amount of time early in the design cycle. *Statistical simulation* as described by Eeckhout et al. [27, 31], Nussbaum and Smith [81, 82], Oskin et al. [83], Genbrugge and Eeckhout [37], and Bell, Jr. and John [8] is a recently proposed approach to make quick performance estimates. Statistical simulation characterizes a benchmark execution in terms of a number of key performance metrics, and these performance metrics are subsequently used to generate a synthetic trace or benchmark; the synthetic trace or benchmark then serves as a proxy for the original program. Another approach is to parallelize the simulator engine and take advantage by running the *parallelized simulator* on existing multithreaded and multiprocessor hardware, as proposed by Reinhardt et al. [91]. Recent work in this area focuses on speeding up of the simulation through hardware acceleration as proposed by Penry et al. [85], Chiou et al. [16, 17] and the Research Acceleration for Multiple Processor (RAMP) project by Arvind et al. [2].

Yet another approach, namely, *sampled simulation*, which is the topic of this survey, only simulates a limited number of well-chosen sampling units, i.e., instead of simulating the entire instruction stream as executed by the program, only a small number of sampling units are simulated in full detail. This leads to dramatic simulation speedups compared to the detailed simulation of entire benchmarks, reducing weeks of simulation to just a few minutes, with performance prediction errors on the order of only a few percentages compared to entire benchmark simulation.

To achieve these spectacular improvements in simulation speed with high accuracy, there are three major challenges to be addressed. The sampling units should provide an accurate and representative picture of the entire program execution. Second, the architecture state (registers and memory) needs to be established as fast as possible so that the sampled simulation can quickly jump from one sampling unit to the next. Third, the microarchitecture state (caches, branch predictor, processor core structures, etc.) at the beginning of a sampling unit should be as accurate as possible and should be very close to the microarchitecture state should the whole dynamic instruction stream prior to the sampling unit be simulated in detail. Addressing all of these challenges in an accurate and efficient manner is far from trivial. In fact, researchers have been studying this area for over 15 years, and it is only until recently that researchers have been capable of achieving dramatic simulation time savings with high accuracy.

The objective of this work is to provide a survey on sampled processor simulation. Such a survey is feasible given that it is a well-studied research topic, and in addition, is a very popular simulation speedup approach; in fact, it probably is the most widely used simulation acceleration approach to date. This survey paper describes solutions to the sampled processor simulation challenges as outlined above and could serve as a work of reference for researchers working in this area, or for practitioners looking for implementing state-of-the-art sampled simulation techniques.

## 2. Trace-Driven versus Execution-Driven Simulation

Before detailing on sampled processor simulation, we first revisit five commonly used architectural simulation methodologies: functional simulation, specialized trace-driven simulation, trace-driven simulation, execution-driven simulation and full-system simulation.

*Functional simulation* is the simplest form of simulation and models the functional behavior of an instruction set architecture (ISA). This means that instructions are simulated one at a time by taking input operands and by computing output values. In other words, a functional simulator basically is an ISA emulator. Functional simulation is extremely useful for determining whether a software program or operating system is implemented correctly. Functional simulators are also extremely useful for architectural simulation since these tools can generate instruction and address *traces* which can be used by other tools in the design flow. A trace is a linear sequence of instructions that a computer program produces when it gets executed. The length of such a trace is called the *dynamic instruction count* of the application. Examples of functional simulators and tracing tools are SimpleScalar's sim-safe and sim-fast as described by Burger and Austin [13] and Austin et al. [3], SHADE by Cmelik and Keppel [18], and QPT by Larus [59].

*Specialized cache and branch predictor simulators* take instruction and address traces as input and simulate cache behavior and branch prediction behavior in isolation. The performance metric that these tools typically produce is *a miss rate*, or the number of cache misses of branch mispredictions per access to the cache and to the branch predictor. These tools are widely available, see for example cheetah by Sugumar and Abraham [100], DineroIV by Edler and Hill [26], and cachesim5 by Cmelik and Keppel [18].

*Trace-driven simulation* also takes as input instruction and address traces but simulates a complete microarchitecture in detail instead of isolated units. Since the microarchitecture is modeled in a more or less cycle-accurate way, this kind of simulation is also referred to as *timing simulation*. A trace-driven simulation methodology thus separates functional simulation from timing simulation. This approach has the important benefit that functional simulation needs to be done only once, whereas timing simulation has to be done multiple times to evaluate various processor configurations. This can reduce the total simulation time. An important disadvantage of trace-driven simulation is that the traces need to be stored on disk. These traces can be very long since the number of instructions that need to be stored in a trace file equals the dynamic instruction count. For current applications, the dynamic instruction count can be several hundreds of billions of instructions. For example, the dynamic instruction count for the industry-strength SPEC CPU2000 benchmark suite is in the range of several hundreds of billions of instructions per benchmark; for SPEC CPU2006, the dynamic instruction count is in the range of several trillions of instructions per benchmark. Storing these huge trace files might be impractical in some situations. However, trace compression can reduce the required disk space, see for example Johnson et al. [49] and Burtscher et al. [15]. Another disadvantage of trace-driven simulation is of particular interest when contemporary superscalar microprocessors are modelled. Superscalar microarchitectures predict the outcome of branches and speculatively execute instructions along the predicted path. In case of a branch misprediction, the speculatively executed instructions need to be nullified. These speculatively executed instructions do not show up in a trace file and as such, do not get simulated in a trace-driven simulator. These instructions, however, can have an impact on overall performance because they require resources that need to be shared with instructions along the correct path. Also, these speculatively executed instructions can result in prefetching effects or cache contention; see Bechem et al. [6] and Mutlu et al. [77].

*Execution-driven simulation* is similar to trace-driven simulation but combines functional simulation with timing simulation. As a consequence, trace files do not need to be stored and speculatively executed instructions get simulated accurately. In recent years, execution-driven simulation has become the method of choice. A well-known and widely used execution-driven simulator is SimpleScalar's out-of-order simulator sim-outorder described by Burger and Austin [13] and Austin et al. [3]. This simulator is widely used in computer architecture research in academia. Other execution-driven simulators developed in academia are Rsim at Rice University by Hughes et al. [44], SimOS at Stanford University by Rosenblum et al. [94], fMW at Carnegie Mellon University by Bechem et al. [6], TFsim at the University of Wisconsin–Madison by Mauer et al. [73], M5 at the University of Michigan at Ann Arbor by Binkert et al. [9], Liberty at Princeton University by Vachharajani et al. [102], MicroLib at INRIA by Perez et al. [89] and PTLsim at the State University of New York at Binghamton by Yourst [120]. Companies have similar tools, for example, Asim described by Reilly and Edmondson [90] and Emer et al. [35] and used by DEC, Compaq and Intel design teams, and MET used by IBM and described by Moudgill [74] and Moudgill et al. [75]. It should be noted that due to the fact that these simulators do model a microarchitecture at a high abstraction level, discrepancies might occur when their performance results are compared to those of real hardware; see for example Black and Shen [10], Gibson et al. [38] and Desikan et al. [23].

*Full-system simulation* refers to the simulation of the entire computer system, not just the processor and the memory subsystem. Full-system simulation also models input/output (I/O) activity and operating system (OS) activity and enables booting and running of full-blown commercial operating systems within the simulator. To achieve this, full-system simulation models processors, memory subsystems, interconnection buses, network connections, graphics controllers and devices, and peripheral devices such as disks, printers and SCSI/IDE/FC controllers. Not all workloads require the complete details of full-system simulation though; for example, compute-intensive applications such as the SPEC CPU benchmarks do not need full-system simulation support. For other applications such as database and commercial workloads, it is extremely important to consider I/O and OS activities. Well-known examples of full-system simulators are SimOS by Rosenblum et al. [94], SimICs by Magnusson et al. [71], SimNow by Bedichek [7] and Mambo by Bohrer et al. [11].

John and Eeckhout [48] and Yi and Lilja [119] sketch the broader context of simulation technology and describe how simulation technology relates to benchmarking, benchmark selection, experimental design, statistically rigorous data analysis, and performance analysis on real hardware.

## 3. Sampled Simulation

Figure 1 illustrates the basic idea of sampled simulation: only a limited number of *sampling units* from a complete benchmark execution are simulated in full detail. We collectively refer to the selected sampling units as the *sampled execution*. The instructions between two sampling units are part of the *pre-sampling unit*. Sampled simulation reports only the performance of the instructions in the sampling units and discards the instructions in the pre-sampling units, which is the source of the dramatic improvement in performance: only the sampling units, which constitute only a small

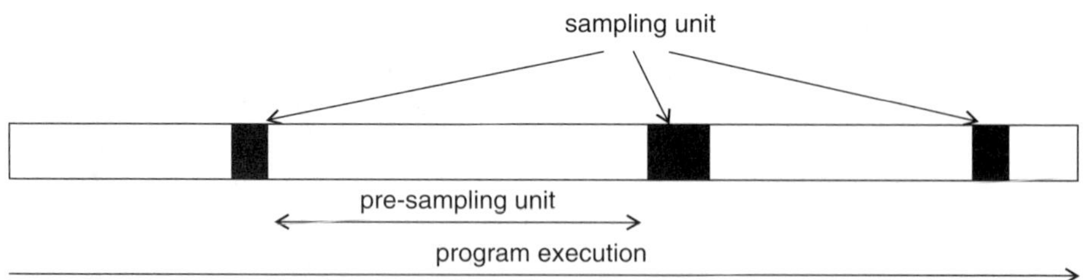


FIG. 1. Sampled processor simulation.

fraction of the total dynamic instruction count, are simulated in a cycle-by-cycle manner.

There are three major design issues with sampling:

(1) **What sampling units to select?** The problem is to select sampling units so that the sampled execution provides an accurate and representative picture of the complete execution of the program. As such, it is important that the selection of sampling units is not limited only to the initialization phase of the program execution. This is a manifestation of the more general observation that a program goes through various phases of execution. Sampling should reflect this, or, in other words, sampling units should be chosen in such a way that all major phases are represented in the sampled execution.

(2) **How to initialize the sampling units' architecture starting images?** The sampling unit's *Architecture Starting Image (ASI)* is the architecture state (register and memory content) needed to emulate accurately or simulate functionally the sampling unit's execution. This is not an issue for trace-driven simulation because trace-driven simulation separates functional simulation from timing simulation: there is no functional simulation involved when the timing simulation is executed. In other words, the instructions in the pre-sampling unit can simply be discarded from the trace, i.e., need not to be stored on disk. However, for execution-driven simulation, it is not trivial to obtain the correct ASI in an efficient manner.

(3) **How to estimate accurately the sampling units' microarchitecture starting images?** The sampling unit's *Microarchitecture Starting Image (MSI)* is the microarchitecture state at the beginning of the sampling unit. This is well known in the literature as the *cold-start* problem or the *microarchitecture state warmup* problem. At the beginning of a sampling unit, the correct microarchitecture state is unknown since the instructions preceding the sampling unit are not simulated through cycle-by-cycle simulation.

All three issues outlined above have an important impact on the sampling approach's **accuracy**: the sampling units collectively should be representative of the entire program execution; the ASIs should be correct to enable correct functional simulation; and the MSIs should be as accurate as possible to achieve accurate performance numbers per sampling unit. Also, all three issues have a substantial impact on the sampling approach's **speed**: selecting too many sampling units may not increase accuracy but may unnecessarily prolong the overall simulation time; to obtain the correct ASIs as well as to construct accurate MSIs under execution-driven simulation in an efficient manner is a challenging task.

This work surveys approaches proposed by researchers to address these three design issues. However, before doing so, we first discuss as to how the overall simulation time is affected in sampled simulation.

# 4. Simulation Speed

To get better insight into how these issues affect the speed of sampled simulation, we refer to Figure 2. Sampled simulation involves three basic steps. The first step is *cold simulation* in which the ASI is constructed. The traditional approach for constructing the ASI under execution-driven simulation is to fast-forward, i.e., functionally simulate updating architecture state without updating microarchitecture state. In case of trace-driven simulation, the instructions under cold simulation can be discarded from the trace, i.e., need not be stored on disk. The second step is *warm simulation* which, apart from maintaining the ASI, also estimates and establishes the MSI. This is typically done for large hardware structures such as caches, TLBs and branch predictors. The warm simulation phase can be very long since microarchitecture state can have an extremely long history. Under warm simulation, no performance metrics are calculated. The third step is *hot simulation* which involves the detailed processor simulation of the sampling unit while computing performance metrics, e.g., calculating cache and branch predictor miss rates and number of instructions retired per cycle. These three steps are repeated for each sampling unit.

Obviously, cold simulation is faster than warm simulation, and warm simulation is faster than hot simulation. Austin et al. [3] report simulation speeds for the various simulation tools in the SimpleScalar ToolSet. They report that the functional simulator sim-fast—to be used during cold simulation for building the ASI—attains a simulation speed of 7 million instructions per second (MIPS). Warm simulation which is a combination of functional simulation with specialized branch predictor and cache hierarchy simulation, sim-bpred and sim-cache, attains a speed of approximately 3 MIPS. Hot simulation is the slowest form of simulation with a speed of 0.3 MIPS

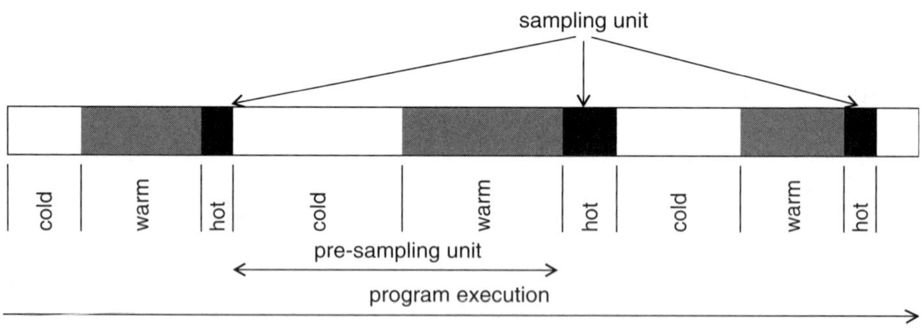


FIG. 2. Sampled processor simulation.

using sim-outorder. Bose [12] reports similar (relative) simulation speed numbers for the IBM design tools: functional simulation is at least one order of magnitude faster than timing simulation.

These simulation speed numbers give us some insight into how sampled simulation improves simulation speed compared with the simulation of entire benchmark executions. The sampling units collectively represent a very small fraction of the entire program execution, typically less than 1% or even around 0.1%. As such, only a very small fraction of the entire program execution is simulated in full detail, at the slowest simulation speed; the pre-sampling units are simulated at much faster speeds. This results in simulation time speedups of at least one order of magnitude compared with the detailed cycle-by-cycle processor simulation of entire benchmark executions.

Although sampled simulation as outlined above achieves a simulation speedup of one order of magnitude compared with entire benchmark simulation, this may still not be fast enough to be used during design space exploration where multiple design points of interest need to be simulated. For example, an entire benchmark simulation that takes multiple weeks, still takes hours under sampled simulation. Exploration of a huge design space for multiple benchmarks is still not feasible if a single simulation takes hours. As such, it is important to further reduce the simulation time under sampled simulation. This can be done by shortening the simulation time spent in the cold and warm simulation phases, because under sampled simulation, a considerable portion of the total simulation time is consumed in these simulation phases.

ASI and MSI techniques further reduce the simulation time by shortening the time spent during cold and warm simulations. The most efficient ASI and MSI techniques completely eliminate the cold and warm simulation phases between sampling units by replacing them with architecture and microarchitecture state checkpointing techniques. This results in dramatic simulation-time savings of two or three orders of magnitude.

Besides that, to further cut down on the overall simulation time, one could also employ parallel sampled simulation by distributing the sampling units across a cluster of machines for parallel simulation, as described by Lauterbach [64], Nguyen et al. [79], Girbal et al. [39], and Eeckhout and De Bosschere [28].

The end result is that these simulation time savings—made possible through sampled simulation, efficient ASI and MSI techniques and parallel simulation—lead to a simulation approach that estimates processor performance in the order of minutes with high accuracy. This simulation approach results in a dramatic reduction in simulation time compared with the detailed simulation of entire benchmark executions, which requires days to weeks. Simulation times in the order of minutes enable the exploration of the microprocessor design space both more thoroughly and more quickly. This leads to a shorter time-to-market as well as an improved overall design.

The following three sections discuss proposed solutions to the three major sampled processor simulation design issues in a detailed manner—selecting a representative sample and constructing the ASI and MSI efficiently.

## 5. Representative Sampling Units

In the literature, there are several approaches for finding representative sampling units. There are two major issues in finding representative sampling units. First, what's the appropriate size of the sampling units? And how many sampling units need to be considered? Second, how to find the representative sampling units? We discuss both the concerns in the following subsections.

### 5.1 Size and Number of Sampling Units

Different authors have used different sampling unit sizes as well as different numbers of sampling units per benchmark. Table I gives an overview of typical values observed in the literature for the sampling unit size and the number of sampling units. The table shows that the number of sampling units per benchmark varies from

TABLE I
TYPICAL VALUES AS OBSERVED IN THE LITERATURE FOR THE NUMBER OF SAMPLING UNITS PER BENCHMARK AND THE SAMPLING UNIT SIZE

| Paper | Number of sampling units | Sampling unit size $L$ |
|---|---|---|
| Skadron et al. [98] | 1 | 50,000,000 |
| Sherwood et al. [97] | 1 to 10 | 100,000,000 |
| Perelman et al. [86] | up to 300 | 1,000,000 |
| Wood et al. [114] | 19 to 35 | 10,000 to 5,000,000 |
| Laha et al. [58] | 35 | 60,000 |
| Conte et al. [19] | 40 | 100,000 |
| Haskins Jr. and Skadron [42] | 50 | 1,000,000 |
| Nguyen et al. [79] | 8 to 64 | 30,000 to 380,000 |
| Lauterbach [64] | at least 50 | 250,000 |
| Martonosi et al. [72] | 10 to 100 | 500,000 |
| Kessler et al. [52] | 20 to 200 | 100,000 to 1,000,000 |
| Crowley and Baer [21] | 20 to 300 | 500,000 |
| Conte et al. [20] | 2,000 | 1,000 to 10,000 |
| Wunderlich et al. [115] | 10,000 | 1,000 |

1 to 10000. The sampling unit size varies between 1000 instructions and 100 million instructions. It should be noted that in general a small number of sampling units coexists with a large sampling unit size and vice versa. For example, on the one hand, Sherwood et al. [97] use 1 to 10 sampling units of 100 million instructions each. Wunderlich et al. [115], on the other hand, use 10000 sampling units of 1000 instructions each. As will be obvious later, the number of sampling units and their sizes have an impact on the selection of representative sampling units, as well as ASI and MSI constructions.

## 5.2 Selecting Sampling Units

Sampling can be broadly categorized into two major types, namely (i) probability sampling or statistical sampling and (ii) non-probability sampling or representative sampling. We discuss both types in this study.

### *5.2.1 Statistical Sampling*

In statistical sampling, a number of sampling units is considered across the whole execution of the program. These sampling units are chosen randomly or periodically in an attempt to provide a representative cross-cut of the application being simulated.

*5.2.1.1 Statistical Foundation.* Statistical sampling has a rigorous mathematical foundation based on the central limit theorem, which enables the computation of confidence bounds, see Lilja [66]. In other words, it is possible to compute a confidence interval based on the sample which meaningfully extrapolates the sampled result to provide an estimate for the whole population. In particular, computation of a confidence interval requires that we have a number of measurements, $x_i, 1 \leq i \leq n$, from a population with mean $\mu$ and variance $\sigma^2$. These measurements are the metrics of interest for the various sampling units. The mean of these measurements $\overline{x}$ is computed as

$$\overline{x} = \frac{\sum_{i=1}^{n} x_i}{n}.$$

The actual true value $\mu$ is approximated by the mean of the measurements $\overline{x}$ and a range of values $[c_1, c_2]$ that defines the confidence interval at a given probability (called the confidence level) is computed around $\overline{x}$. The *confidence interval* $[c_1, c_2]$ is defined such that the probability of $\mu$ being between $c_1$ and $c_2$ equals $1 - \alpha$; $\alpha$ is called the *significance level* and $(1 - \alpha)$ is called the *confidence level*.

Computation of the confidence interval is based on the central limit theory. The central limit theory states that, for large values of $n$ (typically $n \geq 30$), the values of $\overline{x}$ shows an approximate Gaussian distribution, with mean $\mu$ and standard deviation $\sigma/\sqrt{n}$, provided that the samples $x_i$, $1 \leq i \leq n$, are (i) independent and (ii) are from the same population with mean $\mu$ and finite standard deviation $\sigma$ (the population does not need to show a Gaussian distribution).

Because the significance level $\alpha$ is chosen a priori, we need to determine $c_1$ and $c_2$ such that $Pr[c_1 \leq \mu \leq c_2] = 1 - \alpha$ holds. Typically, $c_1$ and $c_2$ are chosen to form a symmetric interval around $\overline{x}$, i.e., $Pr[\mu < c_1] = Pr[\mu > c_2] = \alpha/2$. Applying the central-limit theorem, we find that

$$c_1 = \overline{x} - z_{1-\alpha/2}\frac{s}{\sqrt{n}}$$

$$c_2 = \overline{x} + z_{1-\alpha/2}\frac{s}{\sqrt{n}},$$

where $\overline{x}$ is the sample mean, $n$ the number of measurements, and $s$ the sample standard deviation computed as follows:

$$s = \sqrt{\frac{\sum_{i=1}^{n}(x_i - \overline{x})^2}{n-1}}.$$

The value $z_{1-\alpha/2}$ is defined such that a random variable $Z$ that shows a Gaussian distribution with mean $\mu = 0$ and variance $\sigma^2 = 1$ obeys the following property:

$$Pr[Z \leq z_{1-\alpha/2}] = 1 - \alpha/2.$$

The value $z_{1-\alpha/2}$ is typically obtained from a precomputed table. For a 95% confidence level, $z_{1-\alpha/2}$ equals 1.96.

This statistics background can now be employed to compute a confidence interval and to determine the number of sampling units required to achieve a desired confidence interval at a given confidence level. To determine the amount of sampling units to be considered, the user determines a particular accuracy level (i.e., a confidence interval size) for estimating the metric of interest. The benchmark is then simulated and $n$ sampling units are collected, $n$ being an initial value for the number of sampling units. Error and confidence bounds are computed for the sample and, if they satisfy the accuracy limit, this estimate is good. Otherwise, more sampling units ($> n$) must be collected, and the error and confidence bounds must be recomputed for each collected sample until the accuracy threshold is satisfied. The SMARTS framework by Wunderlich et al. [115, 117] proposes an automated approach for applying this sampling technique.

#### 5.2.1.2 Example Statistical Sampling Approaches.

Laha et al. [58] propose *random sampling* for evaluating cache performance. They select multiple sampling units by randomly picking intervals of execution.

Conte et al. [20] pioneered the use of statistical sampling in processor simulation. They made a distinction between sampling bias and non-sampling bias. Non-sampling bias results from improperly constructing the MSI prior to each sampling unit, which will be discussed later. Sampling bias refers to the accuracy of the sample with respect to the overall average. Sampling bias is fundamental to the selection of sampling units and is affected by two primary factors for random sampling, namely, the number of sampling units and the sampling unit size.

The SMARTS (Sampling Microarchitecture Simulation) approach by Wunderlich et al. [115, 117] proposes *systematic sampling*, which selects sampling units periodically across the entire program execution: the pre-sampling unit size is fixed, as opposed to random sampling. The potential pitfall of systematic or periodic sampling compared with random sampling is that the sampling units may give a skewed view in case the periodicity of the program execution under measurement equals the sampling periodicity or its higher harmonics. However, this does not seem to be a concern in practice as SMARTS achieves highly accurate performance estimates compared with detailed entire-program simulation. We discuss the SMARTS sampling approach in more detail in Section 8.1.

*Stratified sampling* uses prior knowledge about the population that is to be sampled. The population is classified into groups, so-called strata, and each group is sampled. Stratified sampling is more efficient than random or systematic sampling because typically fewer sampling units are required to provide an overall accurate picture because of the lower variance within a strata. Wunderlich et al. [116] explore stratified sampling as an approach to sampled processor simulation and select fewer sampling units in low-variance program phases.

### 5.2.2 Representative Sampling

Representative sampling differs from statistical sampling in that it first analyses the program's execution to pick a representative sampling unit for each unique behavior in the program's execution. The key advantage of this approach is that the presence of fewer sampling units can further reduce simulation time.

Dubey and Nair [24] propose a profile-driven sampling technique that is based on basic block execution profiles. A basic block execution profile measures the number of times each basic block is executed during a program execution. They subsequently scale this basic block execution profile with the simulation speedup they want to attain through sampled simulation. For example, if a 10X simulation speedup is the goal, the basic block execution profile is scaled by a factor 10. Subsequently, a sampled trace is generated using this rescaled basic block execution profile, i.e., the occurrence of each basic block in the sampled trace is smaller by a factor 10 as it is in the original program execution. The scaling factor is chosen arbitrarily based on the simulation time reduction that researchers want to achieve. Although this approach is defendable from a simulation-time perspective, it may be not from the perspective of the representativeness of the sampled execution.

Lauterbach [64] evaluates the representativeness of a sampled program execution using the instruction mix, the function execution frequency and cache statistics. His approach works as follows: he starts by taking short sampling units and subsequently measures the program characteristics mentioned above to evaluate the quality of the sampled execution. If the sampled execution is not representative, sampling units are added to the sampled execution until the sampled execution is representative of the entire program execution.

Iyengar and Trevillyan [46] and Iyengar et al. [47] propose the R-metric to quantify the quality of a sampled execution. The R-metric is based on the notion of fully qualified instructions. A fully qualified instruction is an instruction that is given along with its context. The context of a fully qualified instruction consists of its $n$ preceding singly qualified instructions. A singly qualified instruction is an instruction along with its instruction type, I-cache behavior, TLB behavior, and if applicable, its branching behavior and D-cache behavior. The R-metric quantifies the similar/dissimilar dynamic code sequences, and makes a distinction between two fully qualified instructions that have the same history of preceding instructions; however, they differ in a single singly qualified instruction, which can be a cache miss in one case and a hit in another case. The R-metric for the sampled execution that is close to the R-metric of the entire program execution designates a representative sampled execution. Iyengar et al. also propose a heuristic algorithm to generate sampled executions based on this R-metric. However, a limitation of this method is the huge amount of memory that is required to keep track of all the fully-qualified basic blocks for large applications. The authors report that they were unable to keep track of all the fully-qualified basic blocks for gcc.

Skadron et al. [98] select a single representative sampling unit of 50 million instructions for their microarchitectural simulations. To this end, they first measure branch misprediction rates, data cache miss rates and instruction cache miss rates for each interval of 1 million instructions. By plotting these measurements as a function of the number of instructions simulated, they observe the time-varying program execution behavior, i.e., they can identify the initialization phase and/or periodic behavior in a program execution. On the basis of these plots, they manually select a contiguous sampling unit of 50 million instructions. Obviously, this sampling unit is chosen after the initialization phase. The validation of the 50 million instruction sampling unit is done by comparing the performance characteristics (obtained through detailed architectural simulations) of this sampling unit to 250 million instruction sampling units. The selection and validation of a representative sampling unit is done manually.

Lafage and Seznec [57] use cluster analysis to detect and select sampling units that exhibit similar behavior. In their approach, they first measure two microarchitecture-independent metrics for each instruction interval of 1 million instructions. These metrics quantify the temporal and spatial behaviors of the data reference stream in each instruction interval. Subsequently, they perform cluster analysis and group intervals that exhibit similar temporal and spatial behaviors into so-called clusters. For each cluster, the instruction interval that is closest to the center of the cluster is chosen as the representative sampling unit for that cluster. Only the representative sampling unit is simulated in detail under hot simulation. The performance characteristics per representative sampling unit are then weighted with the number of sampling units it represents, i.e., the weight is proportional to the number of intervals grouped in the cluster that the sampling unit represents. The microarchitecture-independent metrics proposed by Lafage and Seznec are limited to the quantification of data stream locality. Eeckhout et al. [32] extend this approach and consider a much broader set of microarchitecture-independent metrics, such as instruction mix, branch predictability, amount of ILP, register traffic characteristics, working set sizes and memory access patterns. They use this approach to find representative sampling units both within programs and across programs; in other words, rather than selecting representative sampling units per benchmark, they select representative sampling units across a set of benchmarks. They find that when this approach is applied to the SPEC CPU2000 benchmark suite, approximately one-third of all representative sampling units represent a single benchmark with a single input, approximately one-third represents a single benchmark with multiple inputs, and one-third represents multiple benchmarks.

SimPoint proposed by Sherwood et al. [97] is a very popular sampling approach that picks a small number of sampling units, which when simulated, accurately create a representation of the complete execution of the program. To do so, they break a program's execution into intervals, and for each interval they create a code signature. The code signature is a so-called Basic Block Vector (BBV), by Sherwood et al. [96], which counts the number of times each basic block is executed in the interval, weighted with the number of instructions per basic block. They then perform clustering on the code signatures, grouping intervals with similar code signatures into so-called phases. The notion is that intervals of execution with similar code signatures have similar architecture behavior, and this has been shown to be the case by Lau et al. [62]. Therefore, only one interval from each phase needs to be simulated in order to recreate a complete picture of the program's execution. They then choose a representative sampling unit from each phase and perform detailed simulation on that interval. Taken together, these sampling units (along with their respective weights) can represent the complete execution of a program. The sampling units are called *simulation points*, and each simulation point is an interval of the order of millions, or tens to hundreds of millions of instructions. The simulation points were found by examining only a profile of the code executed by a program. In other words, the profile is microarchitecture-independent and the selected simulation points can be used across microarchitectures. Several variations have been proposed on the SimPoint approach by the SimPoint research group, which we will discuss in Section 8.2, as well as by other researchers, such as Liu and Huang [67] and Perez et al. [88].

### 5.2.3 Matched-pair Comparisons

In research and development on computer architecture, comparison of design alternatives, i.e., the difference in relative performance between design alternatives, is often more important than the determination of absolute performance. Luo and John [68] and Ekman and Stenström [34] propose the use of the well-established matched-pair comparison for reducing the sample size when design alternatives are compared. Matched-pair comparison exploits the phenomenon that the difference in performance between two designs tends to be much smaller than the variability within a single design. In other words, the variability in performance between the sampling units for a given design is likely to be higher than the difference in performance between design alternatives for a given sampling unit. As a result, as the variability is smaller than the difference in performance, we need to evaluate fewer sampling units to get an accurate performance estimate for the relative difference in performance between design alternatives. Luo and John [68] and Ekman and Stenström [34] experimentally verify that matched-pair comparisons can reduce simulation time by an order of magnitude.

### 5.2.4 Multi-processor and Multi-threaded Processor Simulation

Simulation of multiprocessors and multithreaded processor systems poses a number of additional challenges to simulation technology. One particularly important challenge is the management of simulation time. Increasing the number of processors to be simulated, or increasing the number of hardware threads per processor, increases the simulation time dramatically: simulating a highly parallel machine on single-threaded hardware increases the simulation time by more than a factor $N$, with $N$ being the number of hardware threads being simulated. As such, simulation speedup techniques are even more important for multithreaded and multiprocessor hardware than for single processor systems. Given the recent trend toward multi-core and multi-threaded processor hardware, accurate and fast sampled simulation will be the key for research and development on computer architecture.

Ekman and Stenström [34] observed that overall system throughput variability when multiple independent threads are run concurrently is smaller than per-thread performance variability—there is a smoothening effect of different threads that execute high-IPC and low-IPC phases simultaneously. As such, if one is interested in the overall system throughput, a relatively small sample size will be enough to obtain accurate average performance estimates and performance bounds; on the other hand, if one is interested in per-thread performance, a larger sample size will be needed for achieving the same accuracy. The reduction in sample size is proportional to the number of hardware threads in the system. This smoothening effect assumes that the various threads are independent. This is the case, for example, in commercial transaction-based workloads where transactions, queries and requests arrive randomly, as demonstrated by Wenisch et al. [112]. This is also the case, for example, when independent threads, or different programs, are run concurrently on the parallel hardware. This assumes that the various threads do not interact through the microarchitecture, for example, through hardware resource sharing.

Addressing the latter assumption is a difficult problem. When two or more programs or threads share a processor's resource such as a shared L2 cache or bus—as is the case in many contemporary multi-core processors—or even issue queues and functional units—as is the case in Simultaneous Multithreading (SMT) processors—the performance of both threads becomes entangled. As such, co-executing programs affect each other's performance. And, changing a hardware parameter may result in a change in the parts of the program that are executed together, thereby changing overall system performance.

To address this problem, Van Biesbrouck et al. [107] proposed the co-phase matrix approach which enables modeling and estimation of the impact of resource sharing on per-thread and overall system performance when independent threads (multi-program workloads) are run on multithreaded hardware. The basic idea is to first use SimPoint to identify program phases in each of the co-executing threads and keep track of the performance data of previously executed co-phases in a so-called *co-phase matrix*; whenever a co-phase gets executed again, the performance data is easily picked from the co-phase matrix. By doing so, each unique co-phase gets simulated only once, which greatly reduces the overall simulation time. The co-phase matrix is an accurate and fast approach for estimating multithreaded processor performance both when the co-executing threads start at a given starting point, as well as when multiple starting points are considered for the co-executing threads, as demonstrated by Van Biesbrouck et al. [105]. Once the co-phase matrix is populated with performance numbers, the evaluation of the performance impact of multiple starting points is done in the order of minutes through analytical simulation. The multiple starting points approach provides a much more representative overall performance estimate than a single starting point. Whereas the original co-phase matrix work focuses on two or four independent programs co-executed on a multithreaded processor, Van Biesbrouck et al. [106] in their most recent work study how to select a limited number of representative co-phase combinations across multiple benchmarks within a benchmark suite.

Another important challenge is to overcome the *variability* that occurs when multithreaded workloads are simulated, as pointed out by Alameldeen and Wood [1]. Variability refers to the differences between multiple estimates of a workload's performance on a given system configuration. If not properly addressed, computer architects can draw incorrect conclusions from their simulation experiments. In real systems, the performance variability comes from a variety of sources such as the operating system making different scheduling decisions, or threads acquiring locks in a different order; and the cause for these variations may be small variations in timing. These divergent paths may result in different combinations and/or orders of threads being executed, which may substantially affect overall performance. Microarchitecture configuration changes, such as a more aggressive processor core, a larger cache or a better prefetching algorithm, can also introduce timing variations even during deterministic architectural simulation. Inclusion of system-level behavior when modeling multi-threaded workloads only broaden these effects. Small variations in timing (due to microarchitectural changes) can lead to different scheduling decisions, which by consequence can result in some thread(s) to spend more (or less) time executing idle-loop instructions, spin-lock wait instructions, or system-level privileged code, such as the TLB miss handler. To address the performance variability problem when simulating multithreaded workloads, Alameldeen and Wood [1] propose a simulation methodology that uses multiple simulations while adding small artificial perturbations to the memory subsystem timing and subsequently analyze the data from these multiple simulations using statistically rigorous data analysis techniques such as confidence intervals and hypothesis testing.

## 6. Architecture State

The second issue to be dealt with in sampled processor simulation is how to provide accurately a sampling unit's architecture starting image. The *Architecture Starting Image* (ASI) is the architecture state needed to functionally simulate the sampling unit's execution to achieve the correct output for that sampling unit. This means that the register state and memory state need to be established at the beginning of the sampling unit just as if all preceding instructions in the dynamic instruction stream would have been executed.

The two traditional approaches for providing the ASI are fast-forwarding and checkpointing. Fast-forwarding quickly emulates the program's execution from the start of execution or from the last sampling unit to the current sampling unit. The advantage of this approach is that this is trivial to implement. The disadvantage is that it serializes the simulation of all of the sampling units for a program, and it is non-trivial to have a low-overhead fast-forwarding implementation—most fast-forwarding implementations in current simulators are fairly slow.

Checkpointing is the process of storing the ASI right before the commencement of the sampling unit. This is similar to the storage of a core dump of a program so that it can be replayed at that point in execution. A checkpoint stores the register contents and the memory state prior to a sampling unit. The advantage of checkpointing is that it allows for efficient parallel simulation, i.e., checkpoints are independent of each other. The disadvantage is that if a full checkpoint is taken, it can be huge and consume too much disk space and take too long to load. To address the latter concern, recent work has proposed reduced checkpointing techniques, which reduce the overhead of storing and loading checkpoints.

We will now discuss all three ASI approaches; fast-forwarding, full checkpointing and reduced checkpointing.

## 6.1 Fast-Forwarding

As mentioned above, establishing the ASI of a sampling unit under fast-forwarding can be fairly time-consuming, especially when the sampling unit is located deep in the program's execution trace. Various researchers have proposed efficient fast-forwarding approaches.

Szwed et al. [101], for example, propose to fast-forward between sampling units through native hardware execution, called *direct execution*, and to use checkpointing to communicate the architecture state to the simulator. The simulator then runs the detailed processor simulation of the sampling unit using this checkpoint. When the end of the sampling unit is reached, native hardware execution comes into play again to fast-forward to the next simulation point, etc. Many ways to incorporate direct hardware execution into simulators for speeding up simulation and emulation systems have been proposed; see for example the approaches by Durbhakula et al. [25], Fujimoto and Campbel [36], Reinhardt et al. [91], Schnarr and Larus [95] and Krishnan and Torrellas [56].

One requirement for fast-forwarding through direct execution is that the simulation needs to be run on a machine with the same ISA as the program that is to be simulated—this may be a limitation when research is performed on ISA extensions. One possibility to overcome this limitation for cross-platform simulation would be to employ techniques from dynamic binary translation methods such as just-in-time

(JIT) compilation and caching of translated code, as is done in Embra by Witchell and Rosenblum [113], or through compiled instruction-set simulation as proposed by Nohl et al. [80], Reshadi et al. [92], and Burtscher and Ganusov [14]. Addition of a dynamic binary compiler to a simulator is a viable solution, but doing this is quite an endeavor, which is why most contemporary architecture simulators do not include such functionality. In addition, the introduction of JIT compilation into a simulator also makes the simulator less portable to host machines with different ISAs.

Related to this is the approach presented by Ringenberg et al. [93]. They present intrinsic checkpointing, which takes the ASI from the previous sampling unit and uses binary modification to bring the image up to state for the current sampling unit. The image is brought up to state for the current simulation interval by comparing the current ASI against the previous ASI and by providing fix-up checkpointing code for the loads in the simulation interval where different values are observed for the current ASI versus the previous ASI. The fix-up code for the current ASI then executes stores to put the correct data values in memory and executes instructions to put the correct data values in registers. Checkpointing as will be discussed subsequently is easier to implement as it does not require binary modification. In addition, when intrinsic checkpointing is implemented, one needs to be careful to ensure that the fix-up code is not simulated so that it does not affect the cache contents and branch predictor state for warmup.

## 6.2 Checkpointing

A checkpoint stores the architecture state, i.e., register and memory contents, prior to a sampling unit. There is one major disadvantage to checkpointing compared with fast-forwarding and direct execution, namely large checkpoint files need to be stored on disk. The use of many sampling units could be prohibitively costly in terms of disk space. In addition, the large checkpoint file size also affects total simulation time due to loading of the checkpoint file from disk when the simulation of a sampling unit is started and transferred over a network during parallel simulation.

## 6.3 Reduced Checkpointing

Reduced checkpointing addresses the large checkpoint concern by limiting the amount of information stored in the checkpoint. Particularly, the storage of memory state in an efficient way is challenging. We describe two efficient approaches for storing the ASI. One is a reduced checkpoint where we only store the words of memory that are to be accessed in the sampling unit we are going to simulate. The second approach is very similar, but is represented differently. For this approach, we store a sequence of executed load values for the sampling unit. Both of these approaches use approximately the same disk space, which is significantly smaller than that used in a full checkpoint. Since they are small, they also load instantaneously and are significantly faster than using fast-forwarding and full checkpoints.

Similar checkpointing techniques can also capture system interactions to provide application-level simulation without having to provide any emulation support for the system calls in the simulator. Narayanasamy et al. [78] present such an approach that creates a system effect log to capture automatically all system effects in a simulation. This approach automatically determines when a system effect has modified an application's memory location and uses techniques, similar to what is described below, to capture these changes due to external events such as system calls and interrupts. The important benefits of this approach are that (i) it enables deterministic re-executions of an application providing reproducible simulation results and (ii) there is no necessity for the simulation environment to support and maintain system call emulation.

### 6.3.1 Touched Memory Image

The *Touched Memory Image (TMI)* proposed by Van Biesbrouck et al. [103, 105] and the live-points approach used in TurboSMARTS by Wenisch et al. [110, 111] only store the blocks of memory that are accessed in the sampling unit that is to be simulated. The TMI is a collection of chunks of memory (touched during the sampling unit) with their corresponding memory addresses. The TMI contains only the chunks of memory that are read during the sampling unit. At simulation time, prior to simulating the given sampling unit, the TMI is loaded from disk and the chunks of memory in the TMI are written to their corresponding memory addresses. This guarantees a correct ASI when the simulation of the sampling unit is begun. A small file size is further achieved by using a sparse image representation, so regions of memory that consist of consecutive zeros are not stored in the TMI. In addition, large regions of non-zero sections of memory are combined and stored as one chunk. This saves storage space in terms of memory addresses in the TMI, since only one memory address needs to be stored for a large consecutive data region.

An optimization to the TMI approach, called the *Reduced Touched Memory Image* (*RTMI*), only contains chunks of memory for addresses that are read before they are written. There is no need to store a chunk of memory in the reduced checkpoint in case that chunk of memory is written prior to being read. A TMI, on the other hand, contains chunks of memory for all reads in the sampling unit.

### 6.3.2 Load Value Sequence

The *Load Value Sequence (LVS)*, also proposed by Van Biesbrouck et al. [105], involves the creation of a log of load values that are loaded into memory during the execution of the sampling unit. Collection of an LVS can be done with a functional simulator or binary instrumentation tool, which simply collects all data values loaded from memory during sampling unit execution (excluding those from instruction memory and speculative memory accesses). When the sampling unit is simulated, the load log sequence is read concurrently with the simulation to provide correct data values for non-speculative loads. The result of each load is written to memory so that, potentially, speculative loads accessing that memory location will find the correct value. The LVS is stored in a compressed format to minimize the required disk space. Unlike TMI, LVS does not require the storage of the addresses of load values. However, programs often contain many loads from the same memory addresses and loads with value 0, both of which increase the size of LVS without affecting TMI.

In order to further reduce the size of the LVS, Van Biesbrouck et al. [105] also propose the *Reduced Load Value Sequence (RLVS).* For each load from data memory, the RLVS contains one bit, indicating whether or not the data needs to be read from the RLVS. If necessary, the bit is followed by the data value, and the data value is written to the simulator's memory image at the load address so that it can be found by subsequent loads; otherwise, the value is not included in the RLVS and is read from the memory image. Thus the RLVS does not contain load values when a load is preceded by a load or store for the same address or when the value would be zero (the initial value for memory in the simulator). This yields a significant additional reduction in checkpoint file sizes.

### 6.3.3 Discussion

Van Biesbrouck et al. [103, 105] and Wenisch et al. [111] provide a comprehensive evaluation of the impact of reduced ASI checkpointing on simulation accuracy, storage requirements, and simulation time. These studies conclude that the impact on error is marginal (less than 0.2%)—the reason for the inaccuracy due to ASI checkpointing is that the data values for loads along mispredicted paths may be incorrect. Reduced ASI checkpointing reduces storage requirements by two orders of magnitude compared with full ASI checkpointing. For example, for SimPoint using one-million instruction sampling units, an average (compressed) full ASI checkpoint takes 49.3 MB, whereas a reduced ASI checkpoint takes only 365 KB. Finally, reduced ASI checkpointing reduces the simulation time by an order of magnitude (20X) compared with fast-forwarding and by a factor 4X compared with full checkpointing. Again, for SimPoint, the average simulation time per benchmark under reduced ASI checkpointing in combination with the MHS MSI approach (which will be discussed later) equals 14 minutes on a single processor, compared to 55 minutes under full checkpointing, compared to more than 5 hours under fast-forwarding.

# 7. Microarchitecture State

The third issue in sampled simulation is to establish an accurate microarchitecture starting image (MSI) for the sampling unit to be simulated. The MSI for the sampling unit should be as accurate as possible compared with the MSI that would be achieved in the case where all instructions preceding the sampling unit would have been simulated in full detail. It should be noted that there is a subtle but important difference between the MSI and the ASI. On the one hand, the ASI concerns the architecture state and should be 100% correct to enable the correct functional simulation of the sampling unit. The MSI, on the other hand, concerns the microarchitecture state and does not need to be 100% correct; however, the better the MSI under sampled simulation resembles the MSI under full benchmark simulation, the more accurate the sampled simulation will be.

The following subsections describe MSI approaches related to cache structures, branch predictors and processor core structures such as the reorder buffer, issue queues, store buffers and functional units.

## 7.1 Cache State Warmup

Cache state is probably the most critical aspect of the MSI since cache structures can be very large (up to several MBs) and can introduce a very long history. In this section, we use the term 'cache' to collectively refer to a cache, a Translation Lookaside Buffers (TLB) and a Branch Target Buffers (BTB) because all of these structures have a cache-like structure.

A number of cache state warmup strategies have been proposed over the past 15 years.

*No warmup.* The *cold* or *no warmup* scheme used by Crowley and Baer [21, 22] and Kessler et al. [52] assumes an empty cache at the beginning of each sampling unit. Obviously, this scheme will overestimate the cache miss rate. However, the bias can be small for large sampling unit sizes. Intel's PinPoint approach, for example, as described by Patil et al. [84], considers a fairly large sampling unit size, namely, 250 million instructions and does not employ any warmup approach because the bias due to an inaccurate MSI is small.

*Continuous warmup.* Continuous warmup, as the name indicates, continuously warms cache state between sampling units. In other words, there is no cold simulation; there is only warm simulation. This is a very accurate approach, but increases the time spent between sampling units. This approach is employed in the SMARTS approach by Wunderlich et al. [115, 117]: the tiny sampling units of 1000 instructions used in SMARTS require a very accurate MSI, which is achieved through continuous warmup called *functional warming* in the SMARTS approach.

*Stitch*. *Stitch* or *stale state* proposed by Kessler et al. [52] approximates the microarchitecture state at the beginning of a sampling unit with the hardware state at the end of the previous sampling unit. An important disadvantage of the stitch approach is that it cannot be employed for parallel sampled simulation.

*Prime*. The *prime-xx%* method proposed by Kessler et al. [52] assumes an empty hardware state at the beginning of each sampling unit and uses $xx\%$ of each sampling unit to warmup the cache. Actual simulation then starts after these $xx\%$ instructions. The warmup scheme *prime-50%* is also called *half* in the literature.

*Stitch/prime*. A combination of the two previous approaches was proposed by Conte et al. [20]: the hardware state at the beginning of each sampling is the state at the end of the previous sampling unit plus warming-up using a fraction of the sampling unit.

*Cache miss-rate estimation*. Another approach proposed by Kessler et al. [52] and Wood et al. [114] involves the assumption of an empty cache at the beginning of each sampling unit and the estimation of the cold-start misses that would have been missed if the cache state at the beginning of the sampling unit was known. This is a so-called cache miss rate estimator approach. A simple example of the cache miss estimation approach is hit-on-cold or assume-hit. Hit-on-cold assumes that the first access to a cache line is always a hit. This is an easy-to-implement technique which is fairly accurate for programs with a low cache miss rate.

*Warmup length estimation*. Nguyen et al. [79] use $W$ instructions to warmup the cache, which is calculated as follows:

$$W = \frac{C/L}{m \cdot r},$$

where $C$ is the cache capacity, $L$ the line size, $m$ the cache miss rate and $r$ the memory reference ratio. The idea is that $W$ instructions need to be simulated to warmup the cache, assuming that each cache miss refers to one cache line. The problem with this approach is that the cache miss rate $m$ is unknown—this is exactly what we are trying to approximate through sampling.

*Minimal subset evaluation*. Minimal Subset Evaluation (MSE) proposed by Haskins Jr. and Skadron [41, 43] determines the warmup length as follows. First, the user specifies the desired probability that the cache state at the beginning of the sample under warmup equals the cache state under perfect warmup. Second, the MSE formulas are used to determine the number of unique references required during warmup. Third, using a memory reference profile of the pre-sampling unit, the exact point in the pre-sampling unit where the warmup should get started is estimated in order to cover these unique references.

*Self-monitored adaptive (SMA) warmup*. Luo et al. [69, 70] propose a self-monitored adaptive cache warmup scheme in which the simulator monitors the warmup process of the caches and decides when the caches are warmed up. This warmup scheme is adaptive to the program being simulated as well as to the cache being simulated—the smaller the application's working set size, or the smaller the cache, the shorter the warmup phase. One limitation of SMA is that it is not known beforehand as to when the caches will be warmed up and thus when the full detail simulation should get started. This is not a problem for random statistical sampling, but it is a problem for periodic sampling and representative sampling.

We now discuss a number of warmup strategies in more detail, namely MRRL and BLRL, a number of hardware-state checkpointing techniques, as well as a hybrid warmup/checkpointing approach. And we subsequently evaluate the accuracy and efficacy of these MSI strategies.

### 7.1.1 Memory Reference Reuse Latency (MRRL)

Haskins Jr. and Skadron [42, 43] propose Memory Reference Reuse Latency (MRRL) for accurately warming up hardware state at the beginning of each sampling unit. As suggested, MRRL refers to the number of instructions between consecutive references to the same memory location, i.e., the number of instructions between a reference to address $A$ and the next reference to $A$. For their purpose, they divide the pre-sampling/sampling unit into $N_B$ non-overlapping buckets each containing $L_B$ contiguous instructions; in other words, a pre-sampling/sampling unit consists of $N_B \cdot L_B$ instructions; see also Figure 3. The buckets receive an index from 0 to $N_B - 1$, in which index 0 is the first bucket in the pre-sampling unit. The first $N_{B,P}$ buckets constitute the pre-sampling unit and the remaining $N_{B,S}$ buckets constitute the sampling unit; obviously, $N_B = N_{B,P} + N_{B,S}$.

The MRRL warmup strategy also maintains $N_B$ counters $c_i (0 \leq i < N_B)$. These counters $c_i$ will be used to build the histogram of MRRLs. Through profiling, the MRRL is calculated for each reference and the associated counter is updated accordingly. For example, for a bucket size $L_B = 10,000$ (as is used by Haskins Jr. and Skadron [42]) an MRRL of $124,534$ will increase counter $c_{12}$. When a pre-sampling/sampling unit is profiled, the MRRL histogram $p_i$, $0 \leq i < N_B$ is computed. This is done by dividing the bucket counters with the total number of references in

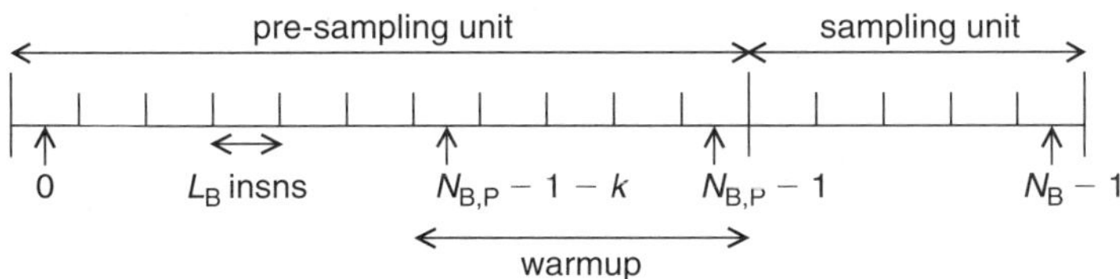


FIG. 3. Determination of warmup using MRRL.

the pre-sampling/sampling unit, i.e., $p_i = \frac{c_i}{\sum_{j=0}^{N_B-1} c_j}$. As such, $p_i = Prob\,[i \cdot L_B < MRRL \leq (i+1) \cdot L_B - 1]$. Not surprisingly, the largest $p_i$'s are observed for small values of $i$ due to the notion of temporal locality in computer program address streams. Using the histogram $p_i$, MMRL calculates the bucket corresponding to a given percentile $K\%$, i.e., bucket $k$ for which $\sum_{m=0}^{k-1} p_m < K\%$ and $\sum_{m=0}^{k} p_m \geq K\%$. This means that of all the references in the current pre-sampling/sampling unit, $K\%$ have a reuse latency that is smaller than $k \cdot L_B$. As such, MRRL defines these $k$ buckets as *warmup buckets*. In other words, warm simulation is started $k \cdot L_B$ instructions before the sampling unit.

An important disadvantage of MRRL is that a mismatch in the MRRL behavior in the pre-sampling unit versus the sampling unit may result in a suboptimal warmup strategy in which the warmup is either too short to be accurate, or too long for the attained level of accuracy. For example, if the reuse latencies are larger in the sampling unit than in the pre-sampling unit, the warmup will be too short and consequently, the accuracy might be poor. Whereas if the reuse latencies are shorter in the sampling unit than in the pre-sampling unit, the warmup will be too long for the attained level of accuracy. One way of solving this problem is to choose the percentile $K\%$ to be large enough. The result is that the warmup will be longer than needed for the attained level of accuracy.

### 7.1.2 Boundary Line Reuse Latency (BLRL)

Boundary Line Reuse Latency (BLRL) described by Eeckhout et al. [29] and Eeckhout et al. [30] is quite different from MRRL although it is also based on reuse latencies. In BLRL, the sample is scanned for reuse latencies that cross the pre-sampling/sampling unit boundary line, i.e., a memory location is referenced in the pre-sampling unit and the next reference to the same memory location is in the sampling unit. For each of these cross-boundary line reuse latencies, the *pre-sampling unit reuse latency* is calculated. This is done by subtracting the distance in the sampling unit from the memory reference reuse latency. For example, if instruction $i$ has a cross-boundary line reuse latency $x$, then the pre-sampling unit reuse latency is $x - (i - N_{B,P} \cdot L_B)$; see Figure 4. A histogram is built up using these pre-sampling unit reuse latencies. As is the case for MRRL, BLRL uses $N_{B,P}$ buckets of size $L_B$ to limit the size of the histogram. This histogram is then normalized to the number of reuse latencies crossing the pre-sampling/sampling unit boundary line. The required warmup length is computed to include a given percentile $K\%$ of all reuse latencies that cross the pre-sampling/sampling unit boundary line. There are three key differences between BLRL and MRRL. First, BLRL considers reuse latencies for memory references originating from instructions in the sampling unit only, whereas MRRL

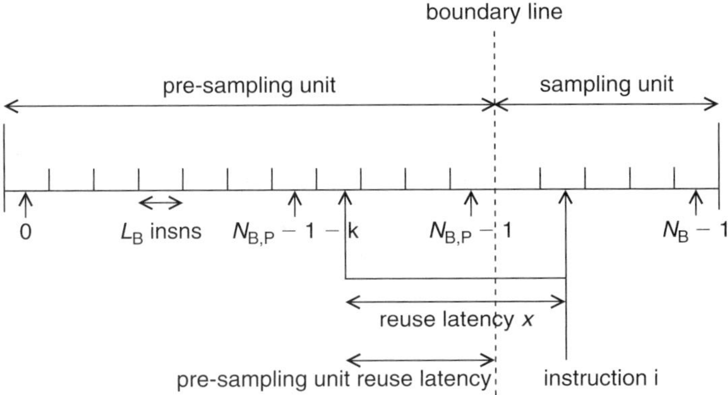


FIG. 4. Determination of warmup using BLRL.

considers reuse latencies for memory references originating from instructions in both the pre-sampling unit *and* the sampling unit. Second, BLRL only considers reuse latencies that cross the pre-sampling/sampling unit boundary line; MRRL considers all reuse latencies. Third, in contrast to MRRL which uses the reuse latency to update the histogram, BLRL uses the pre-sampling unit reuse latency.

### 7.1.3 MSI Checkpointing

Another approach to the cold-start problem is to *checkpoint* or to store the MSI at the beginning of each sampling unit and impose this state during sampled simulation. This approach yields perfectly warmed-up microarchitecture state. However, the storage needed to store these checkpoints can explode in case many sampling units need to be checkpointed. In addition, the MSI checkpoint needs to be stored for each specific hardware configuration. For example, a checkpoint needs to be made for each cache and for branch predictor configuration of interest. Obviously, the latter constraint implies that the complete program execution needs to be simulated for these various hardware structures.

Since this is practically infeasible, researchers have proposed more efficient approaches for MSI checkpointing. One example is the No-State-Loss (NSL) approach proposed by Conte et al. [19] and Lauterbach [64]. NSL scans the pre-sampling unit and records the latest reference to each unique memory location in the pre-sampling unit. This is the stream of unique memory references as they occur in the memory reference stream sorted by their least recent use. In fact, NSL keeps track of all the memory references in the pre-sampling unit and then retains the last occurrence of each unique memory reference. We will name the obtained stream the *least recently used (LRU) stream*. For example, the LRU stream of the following reference stream 'ABAACDABA' is 'CDBA'. The LRU stream can be computed by building the LRU stack for the given reference stream. An LRU stack operates as follows: when, on the one hand, address A is not present on the stack, it is pushed onto the stack. When, on the other hand, address A is present on the stack, it is removed from the stack and repushed onto the stack. As such, it is easily understandable that both reference streams, the original reference stream as well as the LRU stream, yield the same state when applied to an LRU stack. The no-state-loss warmup method exploits this property by computing the LRU stream of the pre-sampling unit and by applying this stream to the cache during the warm simulation phase. By consequence, the no-state-loss warmup strategy yields perfect warmup for caches with an LRU replacement policy.

Barr et al. [5] extended this approach for reconstructing the cache and directory state during sampled multiprocessor simulation using a so-called *Memory Timestamp Record (MTR)*. In order to do so, they keep track of a timestamp per unique memory location that is referenced. In addition, they keep track of whether the source of access of the memory location originates from a load or from a store operation. This information allows them to quickly build the cache and directory state at the beginning of each sampling unit, similar to reconstruction of the cache content using an LRU stream.

Van Biesbrouck et al. [104] proposed the *Memory Hierarchy State (MHS)* approach. Wenisch et al. [111] proposed a similar approach, called live-points, in TurboSMARTS. In MHS, the largest cache of interest is simulated once for the entire program execution. At the beginning of each sampling unit, the cache content is then stored on disk as a checkpoint. The content of smaller sized caches can then be derived from the MHS checkpoint. Reduction in the associativity of the cache is trivial to model using MHS—the most recently accessed cache lines need to be retained per set. Reduction in the number of sets in the cache is slightly more complicated: the new cache set retains the most recently used cache lines from the merging cache sets—this requires that access times to cache lines during MHS construction be kept track of. The disadvantage of the MHS approach compared with NSL is that MHS requires that the cache line size be fixed. Whenever a cache needs to be simulated with a different cache line size, the warmup info needs to be recomputed. NSL does not have this disadvantage. However, the advantage of MHS over NSL is that it is more efficient with respect to disk space, i.e., less disk space is required for storing the warmup info. The reason is that NSL stores all unique pre-sampling unit memory references; whereas MHS discards conflicting memory references from the warmup info for a given maximum cache size. A second advantage of MHS over NSL is that the computation of the MHS warmup is faster than that of the NSL warmup info; NSL does an LRU stack simulation, whereas MHS only simulates one particular cache configuration.

The major advantage of MSI checkpointing is that it is an extremely efficient warmup strategy, particularly in combination with ASI checkpointing. MSI checkpointing replaces the warm simulation phase by loading the MSI checkpoint, which is much more efficient in terms of simulation time. Use of ASI checkpointing in combination with MSI checkpointing leads to highly efficient sampled simulation approaches that can simulate entire benchmarks in minutes as demonstrated by Van Biesbrouck et al. [103, 104] and Wenisch et al. [110, 111]. In addition, MSI and ASI checkpointing is the preferred method for parallel sampled simulation where the simulation of sampling units is distributed across a cluster of machines.

### 7.1.4 NSL-BLRL: Combining NSL and BLRL

This section discusses a hybrid cache state warmup approach that combines MSI checkpointing through NSL with BLRL into NSL-BLRL, as presented by Van Ertvelde et al. [108, 109]. This is done by computing both the LRU stream as well as the BLRL warmup buckets corresponding to a given percentile $K\%$. Only the unique references (identified through NSL) that are within the warmup buckets (determined through BLRL) will be used to warm up the caches. This could be viewed of as pruning of the LRU stream with BLRL information. This method could also be viewed of as computing the LRU stream from the BLRL warmup buckets. Using NSL-BLRL as a warmup approach, the subsequent operation is as follows. The reduced LRU stream as it is obtained through NSL-BLRL is to be stored on disk as an MSI checkpoint. Upon simulation of a sampling unit, the reduced LRU stream is loaded from disk, the cache state is warmed up and finally, the simulation of the sampling unit commences.

The advantage over NSL is that NSL-BLRL requires less disk space to store the warmup memory references; in addition, the smaller size of the reduced LRU stream results in faster warmup processing. The advantage over BLRL is that loading of the reduced LRU stream from the disk is more efficient than the warm simulation needed for BLRL. According to the results reported by Van Ertvelde et al. [108], the warmup length for BLRL is at least two orders of magnitude longer than that for NSL-BLRL. As such, significant speedups are to be obtained compared with BLRL. It should be noted that NSL-BLRL inherits the limitation from NSL of only guaranteeing perfect warmup for caches with LRU replacement. Caches with other replacement policies such as random, first-in first-out (FIFO) and not-most-recently-used (NMRU) are not guaranteed to get a perfectly warmed-up cache state under NSL-BLRL (as is the case for NSL)—however, the difference in warmed up hardware state is very small, as experimentally verified by Van Ertvelde et al. [108]. On the other hand, NSL-BLRL is more broadly applicable during design space exploration than are MHS and the TurboSMARTS' live-points approaches because the NSL-BLRL warmup info is independent of the cache block size.

### 7.1.5 Discussion

We now compare the accuracy and efficacy of a number of cache-state warmup approaches, namely, MRRL, BLRL, NSL, and NSL-BLRL. We consider 9 SPEC CPU2000 integer benchmarks[1]. The binaries, which were compiled and optimized for the Alpha 21264 processor, were accessed from the SimpleScalar website[2]. All measurements presented in this paper are obtained using the modified MRRL software[3] which, in turn, is based on the SimpleScalar software by Burger and Austin [13]. The baseline processor simulation model is a contemporary 4-wide superscalar out-of-order processor with a 16-KB L1 I-cache, 32-KB L1 D-cache, and a unified 1MB L2 cache. We consider 50 sampling units (1M instructions each) and select a sampling unit for every 100M instructions. These sampling units were taken from the beginning of the program execution to limit the simulation time while evaluating the various warmup strategies. For a more detailed description of the methodology, we refer to Van Ertvelde et al. [108].

#### 7.1.5.1 Accuracy.

The first criterion to evaluate a warmup strategy is its accuracy. Figure 5 shows the IPC prediction error for MRRL, BLRL, NSL and NSL-BLRL for various benchmarks. (Note that NSL yields the same accuracy as NSL-BLRL 100%.) The IPC prediction error is the relative error compared with a full warmup run, i.e., all instructions prior to the sample are simulated in full detail. A positive error means an IPC overestimation of the warmup approach compared with the perfect warmup case. In the IPC prediction errors that we present here,

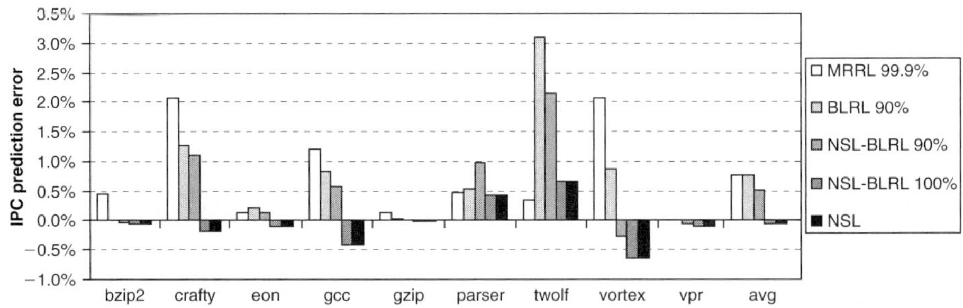


FIG. 5. Evaluation of the accuracy for the MRRL, BLRL, NSL-BLRL and NSL cache state warmup strategies: IPC prediction error is shown on the vertical axis compared with full warmup.

[1] http://www.spec.org

[2] http://www.simplescalar.com

[3] http://www.cs.virginia.edu/~jwh6q/mrrl-web/

we assume that there is no stale state (no stitch) when the hardware state is warmed up before simulating a sample. This is to stress the warmup techniques; in addition, this is also the error that one would observe under checkpointed parallel sampled simulation.

We observe that all warmup strategies are fairly accurate. The average IPC prediction error is less than 1%, with a maximum error of around 3%. (As a point of comparison, the cold or no warmup strategy, results in an average of 30% IPC prediction error.) The NSL and NSL-BLRL 100% are the most accurate strategies with an average IPC prediction error of less than 0.1%.

#### 7.1.5.2 *Warmup Length.*

We now compare the number of warm simulation instructions that need to be processed, see Figure 6 which shows the number of warm simulation instructions (for 50 1 M instruction sampling units). It should be noted that the vertical axis is on a logarithmic scale. The most striking observation from this graph is that the continuous warmup approaches, BLRL and MRRL, require a much longer warmup length than checkpoint-based MSI strategies. The number of warm simulation instructions is one to two orders of magnitude smaller for NSL-BLRL and NSL compared with MRRL and BLRL. Also, NSL-BLRL 100% results in around 46% shorter warmup lengths than NSL.

#### 7.1.5.3 *Simulation Time.*

The number of warm simulation instructions only gives a rough idea about the impact of the warmup strategies on overall simulation time. Figure 7 quantifies the overall simulation time for the various warmup strategies under checkpointed ASI. Checkpointed cache state warmup through NSL and NSL-BLRL reduces the overall simulation time by more than one order of magnitude (14X)

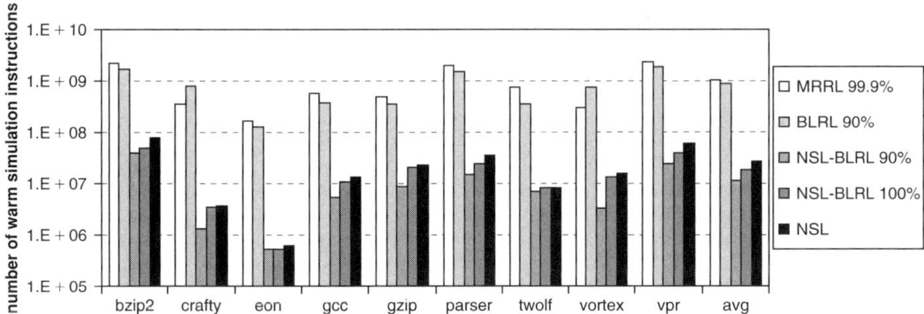


FIG. 6. Evaluation of the warmup length: the number of warm simulation instructions for MRRL, BLRL, NSL-BLRL and NSL.

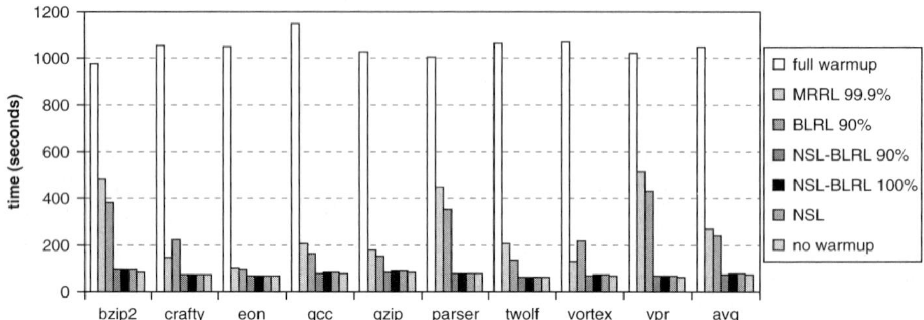


FIG. 7. Evaluation of the simulation time under sampled simulation considering various warmup strategies, assuming checkpointed ASI.

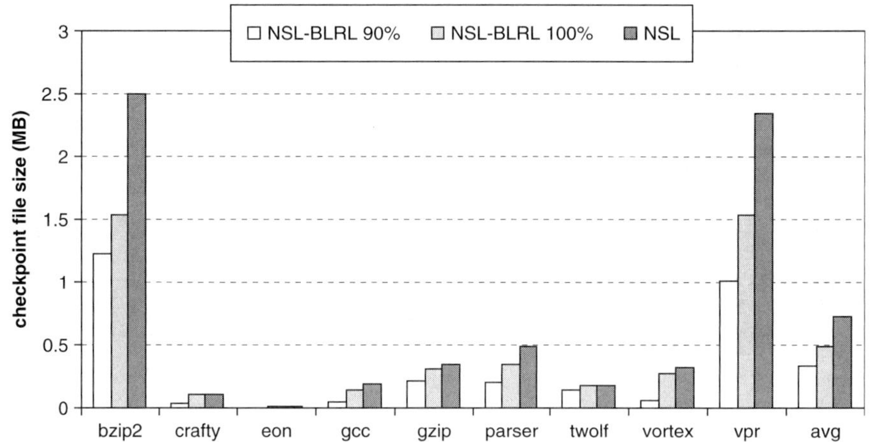


FIG. 8. Storage requirements for NSL-BLRL compared with NSL: average number of MBs of disk storage needed for storing one hardware state checkpoint in compressed format.

compared with full warmup, and by 3X to 4X compared with continuous warmup such as MRRL and BLRL, up to the point wherein the checkpointed warmup is nearly as fast as no warmup.

#### *7.1.5.4 Storage Requirements.*

We now quantify the storage requirements of checkpointed cache MSI approaches for storing the hardware state checkpoints on disk. Figure 8 shows the storage requirements for NSL-BLRL compared with NSL. (Note that MRRL and BLRL do not require any significant storage.) The numbers shown in Figure 8 represent the number of MBs of storage needed to store one hardware-state checkpoint in compressed format. For NSL, the average compressed storage requirement per sample is 810 KB; the maximum observed is for bzip2, 2.5 MB. For NSL-BLRL, the storage requirements are greatly reduced compared with NSL. For example, for $K = 100\%$, the average storage requirement is 553 KB (32% reduction); for $K = 90\%$, the average storage requirement is 370 KB (54% reduction). As such, we conclude that the real benefit of NSL-BLRL compared with NSL lies in reducing storage requirements by 30% while achieving the same accuracy and comparable simulation times.

## 7.2 Branch Predictor State Warmup

Compared to the amount of work done on cache state warmup, very little work has been done on branch predictor warmup. Before discussing existing branch predictor warmup approaches, we first illustrate the need for accurate branch predictor warmup during sampled simulation—which is often being overlooked.

### *7.2.1 The Need for Branch Predictor Warmup*

Branch predictors need to be warmed up during sampled simulation. This is illustrated in Figs. 9 and 10 where the number of branch mispredictions per thousand instructions (MPKI) is shown for gcc and mcf, respectively, for four sampling unit sizes: 10 K, 100 K, 1 M and 10 M instruction sampling unit sizes. Each graph shows the MPKI for four (fairly aggressive) branch predictors: a 128-Kbit gshare predictor, a 256-Kbit local predictor, a 128-Kbit bimodal predictor, and a 192-Kbit hybrid predictor—we refer to Kluyskens and Eeckhout [54, 55] for more details about the experimental setup. The various bars correspond to various branch predictor warmup strategies: no warmup, stale state and perfect warmup. The no-warmup approach assumes an initialized branch predictor at the beginning of a sampling unit, i.e., the branch predictor content is flushed at the beginning of the sampling unit—two-bit saturating counters in adjacent entries are initialized in alternate '01' and '10' states. The stale-state approach assumes that the branch predictor at the beginning of the sampling unit equals the branch predictor state at the end of the previous sampling unit. It should be noted that the stale-state approach assumes that sampling units are simulated sequentially—this excludes parallel sampled simulation. The perfect warmup approach is an idealized warmup scenario where the branch predictor is perfectly warmed up, i.e., the branch predictor state at the beginning of the sampling unit is the state in which it is assumed that all instructions prior to the sampling unit were simulated.

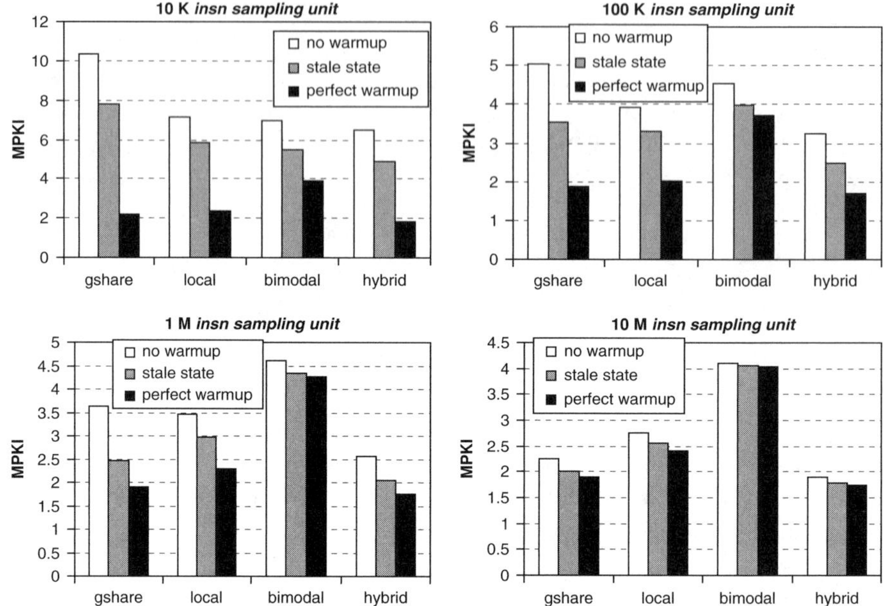


FIG. 9. No warmup, stale state and perfect warmup MPKI results for gcc and 4 branch predictors (gshare, local, bimodal and hybrid) and 4 sampling unit sizes (10 K, 100 K, 1 M and 10 M).

Figures 9 and 10 clearly show that the no-warmup and stale-state approaches are not accurate, particularly for small sampling unit sizes. For example for 10 K instruction sampling units, the $\Delta MPKI$ can be very high for both the no-warmup and stale-state approaches. Even for 1 M instruction sampling units, the error can be significant, more than 1.5 $\Delta MPKI$ for gcc and more than 3 $\Delta MPKI$ for mcf. It should be noted that the error varies across branch predictors. The error is typically higher for the gshare and local predictors than for the bimodal predictor, which is to be understood intuitively, the reason being that the hashing in the gshare and local predictor tables typically results in more entries being accessed in the branch predictor table than the bimodal predictor does.

As a result of the non-uniform warmup error across branch predictors, incorrect design decisions may be taken. For example, for gcc, using the no-warmup approach, a computer architect would conclude that the local predictor achieves a better accuracy (a lower MPKI) than the gshare predictor. This is the case for 10 K, 100 K and even 1 M instruction sampling units. For mcf, using the no-warmup approach, it would be concluded that the hybrid branch predictor outperforms all the other branch predictors;

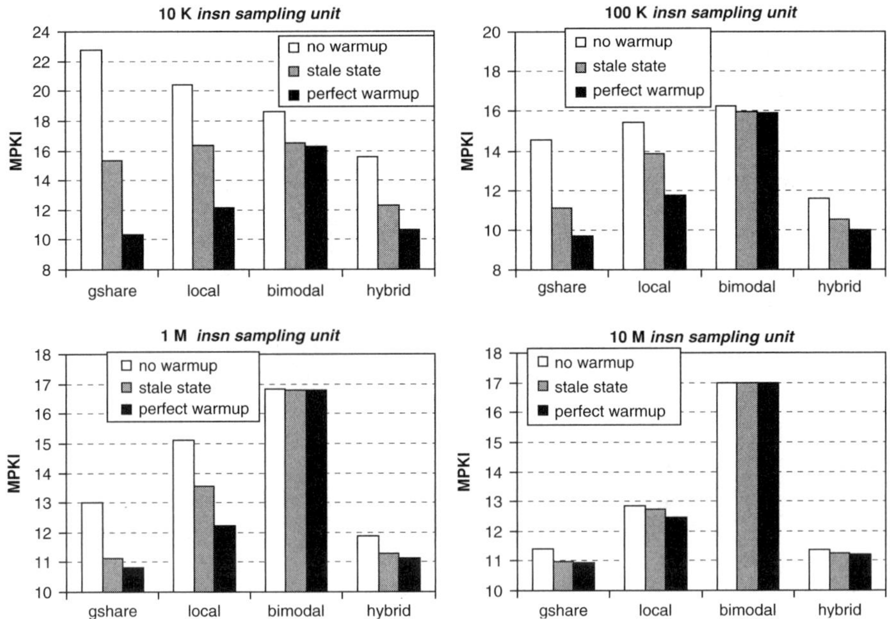


FIG. 10. No warmup, stale state and perfect warmup MPKI results for mcf and 4 branch predictors (gshare, local, bimodal and hybrid) and 4 sampling unit sizes (10 K, 100 K, 1 M and 10 M).

this is the case for all sampling unit sizes considered here (including the 10 M sampling unit size). However, these incorrect conclusions are just an artifact of the inadequate warmup approach. For gcc, perfect warmup shows that the gshare predictor outperforms the local predictor; for mcf, perfect warmup shows that the gshare predictor outperforms all other branch predictors. As a conclusion, no warmup may lead to incorrect design decisions for sampled branch predictor simulation. The stale-state warmup approach only solves this problem for the 1 M and 10 M instruction sampling unit sizes; however, it does not solve the problem for smaller sampling unit sizes and it cannot be used for parallel sampled simulation. As such, there is a need for accurate warmup strategies for sampled branch predictor simulation.

### *7.2.2 Branch Predictor Warmup Techniques*

Only a few branch predictor warmup techniques have been proposed so far, which we discuss in this section; a more accurate and most recently introduced approach, Branch History Matching, is discussed in the next section.

*Stale state and fixed-length warmup.* The paper by Conte et al. [20] was the first to deal with branch predictor warmup. They proposed two approaches to branch predictor warmup, namely, stale state and fixed-length warmup. Stale state (or stitch) means that the branch predictor state at the end of the previous sampling unit serves as an approximation for the branch predictor state at the beginning of the current sampling unit. An important disadvantage of stale state is that it serializes the simulation of the various sampling units, i.e., it is impossible to simulate the current sampling unit without having finalized the simulation of the previous sampling unit. Fixed-length warmup is a simple-to-implement method that achieves good accuracy if sufficiently long warmup lengths are chosen.

*Memory reference reuse latency.* The second paper that deals with branch predictor warmup is by Haskins Jr. and Skadron [42, 43], in which they propose memory reference reuse latency (MRRL). The idea of MRRL, as described in Section 7.1.1, is to look at the distribution of reuse distances between occurrences of the same static branch in the pre-sampling and in the sampling units. MRRL computes the reuse latency, i.e., the number of instructions between the branch instance in the pre-sampling unit and the one in the sampling unit, for all branch instances in the pre-sampling unit and in the sampling unit. For a given target cumulative probability, for example, 99.5%, it is then determined as to where warmup should start in the pre-sampling unit. During this warmup period, the branch predictor is warmed up, but no misprediction rates are computed.

*Checkpointed warming.* A number of papers have proposed MSI checkpointing to warm up cache state, as discussed above in Section 7.1.3. They suggest storing the branch predictor state as part of the microarchitecture state for the various branch predictors one may be interested in during design space exploration. This can be costly in terms of disk space in case multiple branch predictors need to be stored, and in addition, it prevents the simulation of a branch predictor that is not contained in the microarchitecture warmup.

*Branch trace compression.* For addressing this problem, Barr and Asanovic [4] propose branch trace compression. They store a compressed branch trace on disk and upon branch predictor warming, they simply decompress the compressed branch trace and use the decompressed trace for branch predictor warming. This approach is independent of branch predictor and can be used to warm any branch predictor during sampled simulation. However, the branch trace compression scheme by Barr and Asanovic [4] does not address the issue of how far one needs to go back in the pre-sampling unit. They assume that the entire branch trace from the beginning of the benchmark execution up to the current sampling unit needs to be compressed and decompressed. This can be time-consuming in practice, particularly for sampling units deep down the benchmark execution. BHM, as discussed in the following section, can be used to cut down the branch traces that need to be compressed. This saves both disk space and simulation time, while keeping the benefit of the warmup approach to be branch predictor independent.

### 7.2.3 Branch History Matching

Branch history matching (BHM) by Kluyskens and Eeckhout [54,55] is a recently proposed branch predictor warmup approach that computes the branch predictor warmup length in two steps. First, the BHM distribution is computed for all sampling units. Second, the warmup length is determined for each sampling unit for a given total warmup length budget using the BHM distributions for all sampling units.

#### 7.2.3.1 Computation of the BHM Distribution.

Computation of the BHM distribution for a given sampling unit is illustrated in Fig. 11. At the top of Fig. 11, a sampling unit along with its pre-sampling unit is shown. The bullets represent a single static branch that is being executed multiple times in the pre-sampling unit as well as in the sampling unit. Instructions with labels '1' thru '6' are part of the pre-sampling unit; instructions labeled '7', '8' and '9' are part of the sampling unit. A white bullet represents a non-taken branch; a black bullet shows a taken branch.

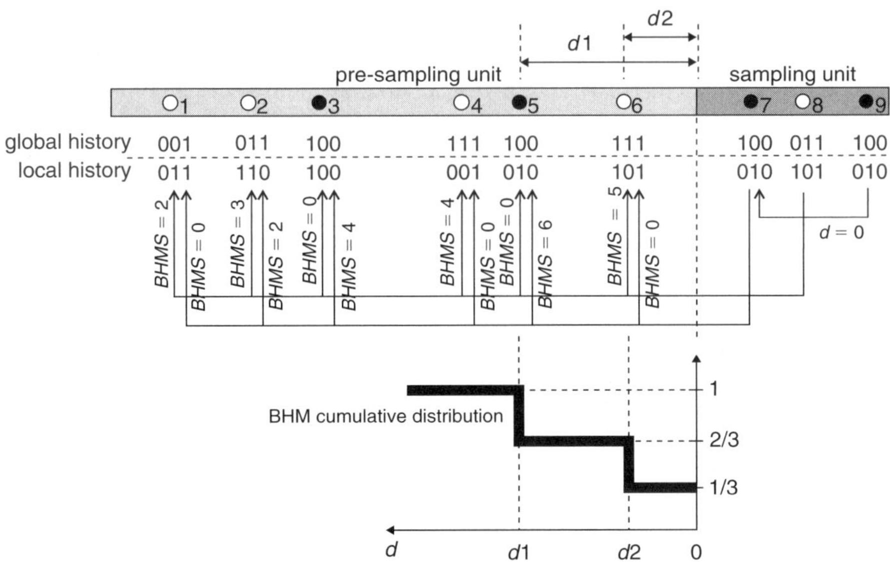


FIG. 11. An example illustrating as to how the cumulative BHM distribution is computed.

Figure 11 also shows the global and local history for each dynamic instance of the given static branch; the example assumes three global history bits and three local history bits. It should be noted that the most recent branch outcome is shifted in on the right-hand side of the history register; for example, a non-taken branch changes the local history from '011' to '110'.

The BHM histogram is computed by scanning all the branch instances in the sampling unit and proceeds as follows.

- *Searching the sampling unit.* It is first determined whether there is a perfect match for the local and global histories of the given branch instance in the sampling unit versus the local and global histories of all the preceding branch instances of the same static branch in the sampling unit. A perfect match means that both the local and global histories are identical for the two respective branch instances. For the example, as given in Fig. 11, the local and global histories of branch instance '9' in the sampling unit show a perfect match with the local and global histories of branch instance '7' in the sampling unit. This case increases the count for $d = 0$ in the BHM histogram.
- *Searching the pre-sampling unit.* In case there is no perfect match with a preceding branch instance in the sampling unit, the pre-sampling unit is searched for the most recent branch instance that shows the highest match with the local and global histories for the given branch instance. This is done by computing the Branch History Matching Score (BHMS) between the given branch instance in the sampling unit and all the branch instances of the same static branch in the pre-sampling unit. The BHMS between two branch instances is computed as the number of bit positions that are identical between the local and global histories of the respective branch instances. When the number of identical bit positions is computed, we count from the most recent bit to the least recent bit and stop counting as soon as there is disagreement for a given bit, i.e., we count the most matching recent history bits. This is done for both the global and local histories; the overall BHMS then is the sum of the global and local BHMSs. Computed BHMSs are shown in Fig. 11 for the first and second branch instances of the sampling unit. For example, the BHMS for branch instance '8' with relation to branch instance '4' equals 4, i.e., 2 (compare global histories '0$\underline{11}$' versus '1$\underline{11}$') plus 2 (compare local histories '1$\underline{01}$' versus '0$\underline{01}$').

  The first branch instance (with label '7') achieves a perfect match (BHMS equals 6) for the branch instance with label '5'. The idea is then to update the BHM histogram, reflecting the fact that in order to have an accurate warmup for instruction '7', we need to go back to instruction '5' in the pre-sampling unit. For this purpose, the BHM histogram is incremented at distance $d1$, with 'd1' being the number of instructions between the branch instance with label '5' and the beginning of the sampling unit—this is to say that branch predictor warmup should start at branch instruction ‘5’. For the second branch instance (with label ‘8’) in the sampling unit, the highest BHMS is obtained for the branch instance with label ‘6’; the number of instructions between that branch instance and the starting point of the sampling unit is denoted as $d2$ in Fig. 11. We then increase the BHM histogram at distance $d2$.

By dividing the BHM histogram with the number of branch instances in the sampling unit, we then obtain the BHM distribution. Figure 11 shows the cumulative BHM distribution for the given sampling unit: since there are three branch instances in our sampling unit that is given as an example, the cumulative distribution starts at $1/3$ for distance $d = 0$, reaches $2/3$ at distance $d = d2$, and finally reaches 1 at distance $d = d1$.

#### *7.2.3.2 Determination of Warmup Length.*

Once the BHM distribution is computed for each sampling unit, we determine the warmup length per sampling unit for a given total warmup length budget. The goal is to partition a given warmup length budget over a number of sampling units so that accuracy is maximized. In other words, sampling units that do not require much warmup are given a small warmup length; sampling units that require much more warmup are given a much larger warmup length.

The algorithm for determining the appropriate warmup length per sampling unit works as follows; see also Fig. 12 for the pseudocode of the algorithm. We start from $n$ BHM distributions, with $n$ being the number of sampling units. In each iteration, we determine the sampling unit $i$ out of the $n$ sampling units that faces the maximum slope in the BHM distribution. This means that the sampling unit $i$ (called max_i in the pseudocode in Fig. 12) that maximizes the slope $\frac{P_i(d_i+b)-P_i(d_i)}{b}$, is determined, with $P_i(d)$ being the probability for distance $d$ in the cumulative BHM distribution for sampling unit $i$ and $d_i$ being the warmup length given to sampling unit $i$ in the current state of the algorithm. For the sampling unit $i$ that maximizes the slope, we increase the granted warmup length $d_i$ to $d_i + b$. This algorithm is iterated until the total warmup length over all sampling units equals a user-defined maximum warmup length $L_w$, i.e., $\sum_{i=1}^{n} d_i = L_w$. By doing so, we effectively budget warmup to samples that benefit the most from the granted warmup.

It should be noted that this algorithm is only one possible design point in BHM warmup. In particular, this algorithm heuristically increases the warmup length for the sampling unit that faces the maximum slope in the BHM distribution. The algorithm does not take into account the distance over which this slope is observed; however, taking this distance into account for the determination of appropriate warmup lengths would be an interesting study in the future.

```
/* this function computes the current warmup
  length */
int current_warmup_length (int* d) {
  for (i = 0; i < n; i++)
    sum += d[i];
  return sum;
}

/* main algorithm */

/* initialize warmup length for each sampling
  unit */
for (i = 0; i < n; i++)
  d[i] = 0;


/* iterate as long as the user defined total
  warmup length L_w is not reached */ while
  (current_warmup_length (d) < L_w) {

  /* find the sampling unit max_j that
    faces the maximum slope */
  max_prob = 0.0;
  max_i = -1;
  for (i = 0; i < n; i++) {
    if ((P[i][d[i] + b] - P[i][d[i]])/b > max_prob){
      max_prob = (P[i][d[i] + b] - P[i][d[i]])/b;
      max_i = i;
    }
  }

/* update warmup length for sampling unit facing
  the maximum slope */ d[max_i] += d[max_i] + b;

}
```

FIG. 12. The algorithm in pseudocode for determining the warmup length per sampling unit using BHM distributions.

*7.2.3.3 Discussion.* We now demonstrate the accuracy of BHM compared with MRRL. In order to do so, we consider four fairly aggressive branch predictors: a gshare predictor, a local predictor, a bimodal predictor and a hybrid predictor; and we consider 50 sampling units of 10 K instructions each; see Kluyskens and Eeckhout [54, 55] for a detailed description on the experimental setup. Our primary metric for quantifying the accuracy of the branch predictor warmup approaches is

$\Delta MPKI$, which is defined as the absolute difference between the number of misses per thousand instructions under perfect warmup, $MPKI_{perfect}$, versus the number of misses per thousand instructions under the given branch predictor warmup approach, $MPKI_{warmup}$. In other words, $\Delta MPKI = \|MPKI_{warmup} - MPKI_{perfect}\|$ and thus the smaller the $\Delta MPKI$, the better will be the results obtained. Our second metric, next to accuracy, is warmup length which is defined as the number of instructions required by the given warmup technique. The smaller the warmup length and the smaller the total simulation time, the better will be the results obtained.

Figure 13 compares BHM against MRRL. As mentioned before, MRRL looks how far one needs to go back in the pre-sampling unit for encountering branch instances of the same static branch appearing in the sampling unit. The results in Fig. 13 show that BHM clearly outperforms MRRL. Across all four branch predictors, the average $\Delta MPKI$ decreases from 2.13 (under MRRL) to 0.29 (under BHM). The important difference between MRRL and BHM is that BHM, in contrast to MRRL, takes into account branch histories; this results in significantly more accurate branch predictor state warmup for BHM compared with MRRL. This is attributed to the fact that

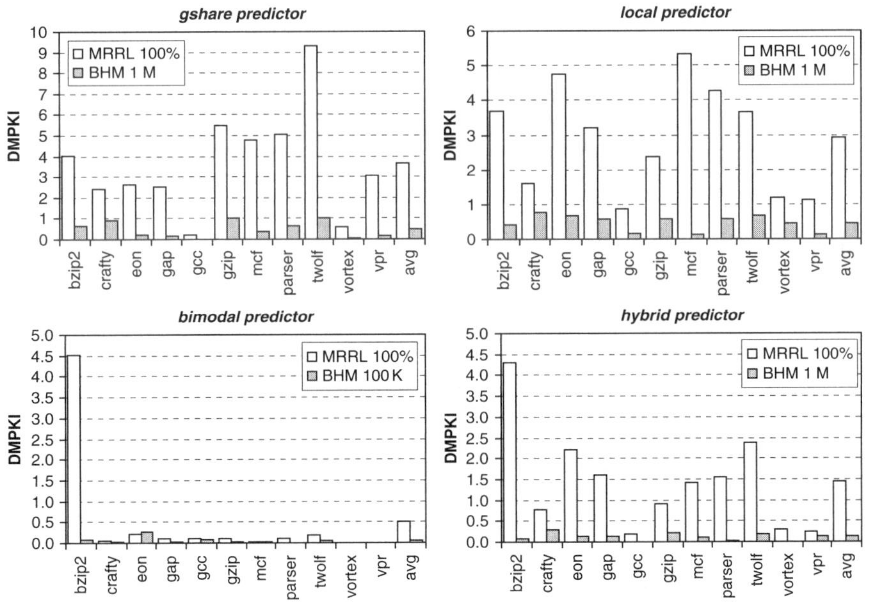


FIG. 13. $\Delta MPKI$ results for MRRL and BHM for the gshare, local, bimodal and hybrid branch predictors. For MRRL, we consider all branch instances in the sampling unit, hence the name 'MRRL 100%' labels.

MRRL does not take into account branch history and MRRL is unable to come up with warmup lengths that are long enough for accurately warming up the branch predictors. The average warmup length through MRRL is only 200 K instructions per sampling unit; whereas BHM achieves longer warmup lengths of 1 M instructions on average.

### 7.3 Processor Core State

So far, we discussed MSI techniques for cache and branch predictor structures. The processor core consists of a reorder buffer, issue queues, store buffers, functional units, etc., which also need to be warmed up. This is not a major concern for large sampling units because events in the processor core do not incur an as long history as that in the cache hierarchy and branch predictors. However, for small sampling units, it is crucial to warmup accurately the processor core. SMARTS as proposed by Wunderlich et al. [115, 117], which considers very small sampling units of 1000 instructions, involves fixed-length warming of the processor core prior to each sampling unit. The fixed-length warmup is limited to 2000 or 4000 instructions.

## 8. Case Studies

There are two well-known approaches to sampled processor simulation, namely, SMARTS and SimPoint, which we discuss in this section. Yi et al. [118] compared both approaches and conclude that SMARTS is slightly more accurate than SimPoint, whereas SimPoint provides a better speed versus accuracy trade-off.

### 8.1 SMARTS and TurboSMARTS

Wunderlich et al. [115, 117] propose SMARTS, or Sampling Microarchitecture Simulation, which uses systematic sampling. SMARTS selects sampling units periodically and considers around 10 000 sampling units per benchmark, with each sampling unit containing 1000 instructions each. And they use statistical sampling theory to compute confidence bounds on the performance estimate obtained from the sample. A critical issue when very tiny sampling units are employed is the establishment of an accurate hardware state at the beginning of each sampling unit. SMARTS builds the ASI and MSI through what they call *functional warming*, or by doing a functional simulation while warming the caches, TLBs and branch predictors; and they do a brief *detailed warming* prior to each sampling unit to warm the processor core state. They implemented the SMARTS approach in SimpleScalar and evaluated it with the SPEC CPU2000 benchmarks and reported a 0.64% CPI prediction error while simulating less than 50 million instructions in detail per benchmark. The SMARTS approach reduces the overall simulation time by a factor 35X to 60X.

A limitation of the SMARTS approach is that it requires functional simulation of the entire benchmark execution for building the ASI and MSI. To address this limitation, they developed TurboSMARTS as described by Wenisch et al. [110, 111]. They employ efficient ASI and MSI checkpointing techniques as described earlier in this survey: their ASI checkpointing technique is similar to TMI, and their cache MSI checkpointing technique is similar to MHS. They refer to an ASI/MSI checkpoint as a *live-point*. The end result is a 250X speedup for TurboSMARTS compared with SMARTS, while the same level of accuracy is maintained. This dramatic speedup results in very fast simulation turnaround times, 91 seconds on average per benchmark. Live-points for SPEC CPU2000 require 12 GBytes of storage.

Wenisch et al. [112] demonstrate that the SMARTS/TurboSMARTS is also feasible for multiprocessor throughput applications. They built an approach called SimFlex, which applies sampling to the full-system simulation of commercial applications run on multiprocessor hardware.

## 8.2 SimPoint

Sherwood et al. [97] propose SimPoint. SimPoint differs from SMARTS in a number of ways. SimPoint employs representative sampling using machine learning techniques to select sampling units and considers a relatively small number of fairly large sampling units. The sampling unit size varies between 1M instructions and hundreds of millions of instructions; the number of sampling units varies with their size: no more than 10 sampling units are selected for large sampling unit sizes of 100 M instructions, and a couple hundred sampling units are considered for small sampling unit sizes of 1M instructions.

SimPoint builds on the Basic Block Vector (BBV) concept proposed by Sherwood et al. [96] to identify a program's time-varying behavior. A basic block is a linear sequence of instructions with one entry and one exit point. A Basic Block Vector (BBV) is a one-dimensional array with one element per static basic block in the program binary. Each BBV element captures the number of times its corresponding basic block has been executed. This is done on an interval basis, i.e., one BBV is computed per (fixed-length) instruction interval in the dynamic instruction stream. Each BBV element is also multiplied with the number of instructions in the corresponding basic block. This gives a higher weight to basic blocks containing more instructions. A BBV thus provides a picture of what portions of code are executed and also how frequently those portions of code are executed. Lau et al. [62] have shown that there exists a strong correlation between the code being executed—this is what a BBV captures—and actual performance. The intuition is that if two instruction intervals execute roughly the same code and if the frequency of the portions of code executed is roughly the same, these two intervals should exhibit roughly the same performance. Once the BBVs are collected per interval, clustering groups these intervals into phases with similar code signatures. SimPoint then selects one interval from each phase to recreate a complete picture of the program's execution. The detailed simulation of these representatives, called *simulation points*, then represents the complete execution of a program.

The ASI and MSI techniques proposed for enhancing the overall simulation turnaround time for SimPoint are checkpointed ASI and MSI: Van Biesbrouck et al. [103, 104] proposed the ASI checkpointing techniques described in this survey (TMI, RTMI, LVS and RLVS), as well as MHS cache MSI checkpointing. The end result when these efficient ASI and MSI checkpointing techniques are applied to SimPoint is that a benchmark can be simulated in less than 14 minutes on average on a single processor. The storage requirements are limited to 52.6 MB per benchmark, assuming a 1 M instruction sampling unit size. A comparison of TurboSMARTS versus SimPoint provides some interesting insights in terms of speed versus storage trade-off as described by Van Biesbrouck et al. [104]. The storage requirements are smaller for SimPoint than for TurboSMARTS: the ASI/MSI checkpoints for TurboSMARTS are dominated by MSI checkpointing—ASI checkpointing is very efficient for TurboSMARTS because of the tiny sampling unit sizes, but MSI checkpointing is expensive because of the numerous sampling units. In terms of simulation time, TurboSMARTS is faster than SimPoint because of the tiny sampling units: the detailed simulation needs to be done for a small number of instructions only.

A fairly large body of work has been done on SimPoint over the recent years. The UCSD research group extended SimPoint in a number of ways. For example, Perelman et al. [86] extend the SimPoint clustering technique to find simulation points earlier in the dynamic instruction stream, thereby reducing the fast-forwarding time for building the ASI. Lau et al. [60, 63] propose and evaluate program characteristics such as loops and methods that could serve as an alternative for BBVs. Lau et al. [61] study variable-length simulation points instead of fixed-length simulation points and construct a hierarchy of phases at different time scales. Perelman et al. [87] build on the notions of variable-length intervals and software control flow such as loops and methods to identify phase behavior and propose cross-binary simulation points so that simulation points can be used by architects and compiler builders when studying ISA extensions and evaluating compiler and software optimizations. Hamerly et al. [40] improve the efficiency of the clustering algorithm in SimPoint through a number of optimizations which enable application of the clustering to very large data sets containing hundreds of thousands of intervals; the end result is that the SimPoint procedure for selecting representative simulation points can be applied, in on the order of minutes.

# 9. Summary

Sampled processor simulation is a practical solution to the simulation time problem in architectural processor simulation. It selects a limited number of sampling units and only simulates those sampling units in full detail instead of simulating the entire dynamic instruction stream. There are three major challenges in sampled processor simulation: (i) how to select a representative sample; (ii) how to establish the correct ASI efficiently; and (iii) how to establish an accurate MSI efficiently. Various researchers have proposed a variety of solutions to each of these challenges. The selection of representative sampling units can be done through statistical sampling or representative sampling. The establishment of the ASI can be done through fast-forwarding, full checkpointing and reduced checkpointing; reduced checkpointing is faster than both fast-forwarding and full checkpointing, and in addition, requires less storage than full checkpointing. And the establishment of an as accurate MSI as possible can be done through cache-state warmup, branch-predictor warmup and processor-core warmup approaches; MSI checkpointing and branch history matching are the most efficient and accurate approaches for cache-state and branch-predictor warmup, respectively. The end result is that sampled processor simulation can estimate performance of full benchmark executions in the order of minutes, with high accuracy, while requiring modest disk space for storing the (reduced) ASI and MSI checkpoints.

### Acknowledgments

Lieven Eeckhout thanks all of his past and current collaborators on the topics discussed in this paper: Koen De Bosschere, Stijn Eyerman, Bert Callens, Luk Van Ertvelde, Filip Hellebaut, from Ghent University; Brad Calder and Michael Van Biesbrouck, from the University of California, San Diego; and Lizy K. John and Yue Luo, from the University of Texas at Austin.

### References

[1] Alameldeen A., and Wood D., February 2003. Variability in architectural simulations of multi-threaded workloads. In *Proceedings of the Ninth International Symposium on High-Performance Computer Architecture (HPCA)*, pp. 7–18.

[2] Arvind, Asanovic K., Chiou D., Hoe J. C., Kozyrakis C., Lu S. -L., Oskin M., Patterson D., Rabaey J., and Wawrzynek J., 2005. RAMP: Research accelerator for multiple processors—a community vision for a shared experimental parallel HW/SW platform. Tech. rep., University of California, Berkeley.

[3] Austin T., Larson E., and Ernst D., February 2002. SimpleScalar: An infrastructure for computer system modeling. *IEEE Computer*, **35**(2):59–67.

[4] Barr K. C., and Asanovic K., March 2006. Branch trace compression for snapshot-based simulation. In *Proceedings of the International Symposium on Performance Analysis of Systems and Software (ISPASS)*, pp. 25–36.

[5] Barr K. C., Pan H., Zhang M., and Asanovic K., March 2005. Accelerating multiprocessor simulation with a memory timestamp record. In *Proceedings of the 2005 IEEE International Symposium on Performance Analysis of Systems and Software (ISPASS)*, pp. 66–77.

[6] Bechem C., Combs J., Utamaphetai N., Black B., Blanton R. D. S., and Shen J. P., May/June 1999. An integrated functional performance simulator. *IEEE Micro*, **19**(3):26–35.

[7] Bedichek R., August 2004. SimNow: Fast platform simulation purely in software. In *Proceedings of the Symposium on High Performance Chips (HOT CHIPS)*.

[8] Bell R. Jr., and John L. K., June 2005. Improved automatic testcase synthesis for performance model validation. In *Proceedings of the 19th ACM International Conference on Supercomputing (ICS)*, pp. 111–120.

[9] Binkert N. L., Dreslinski R. G., Hsu L. R., Lim K. T., Saidi A. G., and Reinhardt S. K., 2006. The M5 simulator: Modeling networked systems. *IEEE Micro*, **26**(4):52–60.

[10] Black B., and Shen J. P., May 1998. Calibration of microprocessor performance models. *IEEE Computer*, **31**(5):59–65.

[11] Bohrer P., Peterson J., Elnozahy M., Rajamony R., Gheith A., Rockhold R., Lefurgy C., Shafi H., Nakra T., Simpson R., Speight E., Sudeep K., Hensbergen and E. V., and Zhang L., March 2004. Mambo: A full system simulator for the PowerPC architecture. *ACM SIGMETRICS Performance Evaluation Review*, **31**(4):8–12.

[12] Bose P., May 1999. Performance evaluation and validation of microprocessors. In *Proceedings of the ACM SIGMETRICS International Conference on Measurement and Modeling of Computer Systems*, pp. 226–227.

[13] Burger D. C., and Austin T. M., 1997. The SimpleScalar Tool Set. Computer Architecture News, see also http://www.simplescalar.com for more information.

[14] Burtscher M., and Ganusov I., December 2004. Automatic synthesis of high-speed processor simulators. In *Proceedings of the 37th IEEE/ACM Symposium on Microarchitecture (MICRO)*, pp. 55–66.

[15] Burtscher M., Ganusov I., Jackson S. J., Ke J., Ratanaworabhan P., and Sam N. B., November 2005. The VPC trace-compression algorithms. *IEEE Transactions on Computers*, **54**(11):1329–1344.

[16] Chiou D., Sanjeliwala H., Sunwoo D., Xu Z., and Patil N., February 2006. FPGA-based fast, cycle-accurate, full-system simulators. In *Proceedings of the Second Workshop on Architectural Research using FPGA Platforms (WARFP), held in conjunction with HPCA*.

[17] Chiou D., Sunwoo D., Kim J., Patil N. A., Reinhart W., Johnson D. E., Keefe J., and Angepat H., December 2007. FPGA-accelerated simulation technologies (FAST): Fast, full-system, cycle-accurate simulators. In *Proceedings of the Annual IEEE/ACM International Symposium on Microarchitecture (MICRO)* (forthcoming).

[18] Cmelik B., and Keppel D., May 1994. SHADE: A fast instruction-set simulator for execution profiling. In *Proceedings of the 1994 ACM SIGMETRICS Conference on Measurement and Modeling of Computer Systems*, pp. 128–137.

[19] Conte T. M., Hirsch M. A., and Hwu W. W., June 1998. Combining trace sampling with single pass methods for efficient cache simulation. *IEEE Transactions on Computers*, **47**(6):714–720.

[20] Conte T. M., Hirsch M. A., and Menezes K. N., October 1996. Reducing state loss for effective trace sampling of superscalar processors. In *Proceedings of the 1996 International Conference on Computer Design (ICCD)*, pp. 468–477.

[21] Crowley P., and Baer J.-L., November 1998. Trace sampling for desktop applications on Windows NT. In *Proceedings of the First Workshop on Workload Characterization (WWC) held in conjunction with the 31st ACM/IEEE Annual International Symposium on Microarchitecture (MICRO).*

[22] Crowley P., and Baer J.-L., June 1999. On the use of trace sampling for architectural studies of desktop applications. In *Proceedings of the 1999 ACM SIGMETRICS International Conference on Measurement and Modeling of Computer Systems*, pp. 208–209.

[23] Desikan R., Burger D., and Keckler S. W., July 2001. Measuring experimental error in microprocessor simulation. In *Proceedings of the 28th Annual International Symposium on Computer Architecture (ISCA)*, pp. 266–277.

[24] Dubey P. K., and Nair R., April 1995. Profile-driven sampled trace generation. Tech. Rep. RC 20041, IBM Research Division, T. J. Watson Research Center. Yorktown Heights, NY.

[25] Durbhakula M., Pai V. S., and Adve S. V., January 1999. Improving the accuracy vs. speed tradeoff for simulating shared-memory multiprocessors with ILP processors. In *Proceedings of the Fifth International Symposium on High-Performance Computer Architecture (HPCA)*, pp. 23–32.

[26] Edler J., and Hill M. D., 1998. Dinero IV trace-driven uniprocessor cache simulator. Available at http://www.cs.wisc.edu/~markhill/DineroIV.

[27] Eeckhout L., Bell R. H. Jr., Stougie B., De Bosschere K., and John L. K., June 2004. Control flow modeling in statistical simulation for accurate and efficient processor design studies. In *Proceedings of the 31st Annual International Symposium on Computer Architecture (ISCA)*, pp. 350–361.

[28] Eeckhout L., and De Bosschere K., 2004. Efficient simulation of trace samples on parallel machines. *Parallel Computing*, **30**:317–335.

[29] Eeckhout L., Eyerman S., Callens B., and De Bosschere K., April 2003a. Accurately warmed-up trace samples for the evaluation of cache memories. In *Proceedings of the 2003 High Performance Computing Symposium (HPC)*, pp. 267–274.

[30] Eeckhout L., Luo Y., De Bosschere K., and John L. K., May 2005a. BLRL: Accurate and efficient warmup for sampled processor simulation. *The Computer Journal* **48**(4):451–459.

[31] Eeckhout L., Nussbaum S., Smith J. E., and De Bosschere K., Sept/Oct 2003b. Statistical simulation: Adding efficiency to the computer designer's toolbox. *IEEE Micro*, **23**(5):26–38.

[32] Eeckhout L., Sampson J., and Calder B., October 2005b. Exploiting program microarchitecture independent characteristics and phase behavior for reduced benchmark suite simulation. In *Proceedings of the 2005 IEEE International Symposium on Workload Characterization (IISWC)*, pp. 2–12.

[33] Eeckhout L., Vandierendonck H., and De Bosschere K., February 2003c. Designing workloads for computer architecture research. *IEEE Computer*, **36**(2):65–71.

[34] Ekman M., and Stenström P., March 2005. Enhancing multiprocessor architecture simulation speed using matched-pair comparison. In *Proceedings of the 2005 IEEE International Symposium on Performance Analysis of Systems and Software (ISPASS)*, pp. 89–99.

[35] Emer J., Ahuja P., Borch E., Klauser A., Luk C.-K., Manne S., Mukherjee S. S., Patil H., Wallace S., Binkert N., Espasa R., and Juan T., February 2002. Asim: A performance model framework. *IEEE Computer*, **35**(2):68–76.

[36] Fujimoto R. M., and Campbell W. B., December 1987. Direct execution models of processor behavior and performance. In *Proceedings of the 19th Winter Simulation Conference*, pp. 751–758.

[37] Genbrugge D., and Eeckhout L., 2007. Memory data flow modeling in statistical simulation for the efficient exploration of microprocessor design spaces. *IEEE Transactions on Computers (Accepted for publication).*

[38] Gibson J., Kunz R., Ofelt D., Horowitz M., Hennessy J., and Heinrich M., November 2000. FLASH vs. (simulated) FLASH: Closing the simulation loop. In *Proceedings of the 9th International Conference on Architectural Support for Programming Languages and Operating Systems (ASPLOS)*, pp. 49–58.

[39] Girbal S., Mouchard G., Cohen A., and Temam O., June 2003. DiST: A simple, reliable and scalable method to significantly reduce processor architecture simulation time. In *Proceedings of the 2003 ACM SIGMETRICS International Conference on Measurement and Modeling of Computer Systems*, pp. 1–12.

[40] Hamerly G., Perelman E., Lau J., and Calder B., September 2005. SimPoint 3.0: Faster and more flexible program analysis. *Journal of Instruction-Level Parallelism*, 7.

[41] Haskins J. W. Jr., and Skadron K., September 2001. Minimal subset evaluation: Rapid warm-up for simulated hardware state. In *Proceedings of the 2001 International Conference on Computer Design (ICCD)*, pp. 32–39.

[42] Haskins J. W. Jr., and Skadron K., March 2003. Memory reference reuse latency: accelerated warmup for sampled microarchitecture simulation. In *Proceedings of the 2003 IEEE International Symposium on Performance Analysis of Systems and Software (ISPASS)*, pp. 195–203.

[43] Haskins J. W. Jr., and Skadron K., March 2005. Accelerated warmup for sampled microarchitecture simulation. *ACM Transactions on Architecture and Code Optimization (TACO)*, **2**(1):78–108.

[44] Hughes C. J., Pai V. S., Ranganathan P., and Adve S. V., February 2002. Rsim: simulating shared-memory multiprocessors with ILP processors. *IEEE Computer*, **35**(2):40–49.

[45] Ipek E., McKee, S. A., de Supinski B. R., Schulz M., and Caruana R., October 2006. Efficiently exploring architectural design spaces via predictive modeling. In *Proceedings of the Twelfth International Conference on Architectural Support for Programming Languages and Operating Systems (ASPLOS)*, pp. 195–206.

[46] Iyengar V. S., and Trevillyan L. H., October 1996. Evaluation and generation of reduced traces for benchmarks. Tech. Rep. RC 20610, IBM Research Division, T. J. Watson Research Center. Yorktown Heights, NY.

[47] Iyengar V. S., Trevillyan L. H., and Bose P., February 1996. Representative traces for processor models with infinite cache. In *Proceedings of the Second International Symposium on High-Performance Computer Architecture (HPCA)*, pp. 62–73.

[48] John L. K., and Eeckhout L. (Eds.), 2006. Performance Evaluation and Benchmarking. CRC Press. Boca Rota, FL.

[49] Johnson E. E., Ha J., and Zaidi M. B., February 2001. Lossless trace compression. *IEEE Transactions on Computers*, **50**(2):158–173.

[50] Karkhanis T., and Smith J. E., June 2007. Automated design of application specific superscalar processors: An analytical approach. In *Proceedings of the 34th Annual International Symposium on Computer Architecture (ISCA)*, pp. 402–411.

[51] Karkhanis T. S., and Smith J. E., June 2004. A first-order superscalar processor model. In *Proceedings of the 31st Annual International Symposium on Computer Architecture (ISCA)*, pp. 338–349.

[52] Kessler R. E., Hill M. D., and Wood D. A., June 1994. A comparison of trace-sampling techniques for multi-megabyte caches. *IEEE Transactions on Computers*, **43**(6):664–675.

[53] KleinOsowski A. J., and Lilja D. J., June 2002. MinneSPEC: A new SPEC benchmark workload for simulation-based computer architecture research. *Computer Architecture Letters*, **1**(2):10–13.

[54] Kluyskens S., and Eeckhout L., January 2007a. Branch history matching: Branch predictor warmup for sampled simulation. In *Proceedings of the Second International Conference on High Performance Embedded Architectures and Compilation (HiPEAC)*, pp. 153–167.

[55] Kluyskens S., and Eeckhout L., January 2007b. Branch predictor warmup for sampled simulation through branch history matching. *Transactions on High-Performance Embedded Architectures and Compilers (HiPEAC)*, **2**(1):42–61.

[56] Krishnan V., and Torrellas J., October 1998. A direct-execution framework for fast and accurate simulation of superscalar processors. In *Proceedings of the 1998 International Conference on Parallel Architectures and Compilation Techniques (PACT)*, pp. 286–293.

[57] Lafage T., and Seznec A., September 2000. Choosing representative slices of program execution for microarchitecture simulations: A preliminary application to the data stream. In *IEEE 3rd Annual Workshop on Workload Characterization (WWC-2000) held in conjunction with the International Conference on Computer Design (ICCD)*.

[58] Laha S., Patel J. H., and Iyer R. K., November 1988. Accurate low-cost methods for performance evaluation of cache memory systems. *IEEE Transactions on Computers*, **37**(11):1325–1336.

[59] Larus J. R., May 1993. Efficient program tracing. *IEEE Computer*, **26**(5):52–61.

[60] Lau J., Perelman E., and Calder B., March 2006. Selecting software phase markers with code structure analysis. In *Proceedings of the International Symposium on Code Generation and Optimization (CGO)*, pp. 135–146.

[61] Lau J., Perelman E., Hamerly G., Sherwood T., and Calder B., March 2005a. Motivation for variable length intervals and hierarchical phase behavior. In *Proceedings of the International Symposium on Performance Analysis of Systems and Software (ISPASS)*, pp. 135–146.

[62] Lau J., Sampson J., Perelman E., Hamerly G., and Calder B., March 2005b. The strong correlation between code signatures and performance. In *Proceedings of the International Symposium on Performance Analysis of Systems and Software (ISPASS)*, pp. 236–247.

[63] Lau J., Schoenmackers S., and Calder B., March 2004. Structures for phase classification. In *Proceedings of the 2004 International Symposium on Performance Analysis of Systems and Software (ISPASS)*, pp. 57–67.

[64] Lauterbach G., December 1993. Accelerating architectural simulation by parallel execution of trace samples. Tech. Rep. SMLI TR-93-22, Sun Microsystems Laboratories Inc., Palo Alto.

[65] Lee B., and Brooks D., October 2006. Accurate and efficient regression modeling for microarchitectural performance and power prediction. In *Proceedings of the Twelfth International Conference on Architectural Support for Programming Languages and Operating Systems (ASPLOS)*, pp. 185–194.

[66] Lilja D. J., 2000. Measuring computer performance: A Practitioner's Guide. Cambridge University Press, Cambridge, UK, p. 278.

[67] Liu W., and Huang M. C., June 2004. EXPERT: Expedited simulation exploiting program behavior repetition. In *Proceedings of the 18th Annual International Conference on Supercomputing (ICS)*, pp. 126–135.

[68] Luo Y., and John L. K., January 2004. Efficiently evaluating speedup using sampled processor simulation. *Computer Architecture Letters*, **4**(1):6.

[69] Luo Y., John L. K., and Eeckhout L., October 2004. Self-monitored adaptive cache warm-up for microprocessor simulation. In *Proceedings of the 16th Symposium on Computer Architecture and High Performance Computing (SBAC-PAD)*, pp. 10–17.

[70] Luo Y., John L. K., and Eeckhout L., October 2005. SMA: A self-monitored adaptive warmup scheme for microprocessor simulation. *International Journal on Parallel Programming*, **33**(5):561–581.

[71] Magnusson P. S., Christensson M., Eskilson J., Forsgren D., Hallberg G., Hogberg J., Larsson F., Moestedt A., and Werner B., February 2002. Simics: A full system simulation platform. *IEEE Computer*, **35**(2):50–58.

[72] Martonosi M., Gupta A., and Anderson T., May 1993. Effectiveness of trace sampling for performance debugging tools. In *Proceedings of the 1993 ACM SIGMETRICS Conference on Measurement and Modeling of Computer Systems* pp. 248–259.

[73] Mauer C. J., Hill M. D., and Wood D. A., June 2002. Full-system timing-first simulation. In *Proceedings of the 2002 ACM SIGMETRICS Conference on Measurement and Modeling of Computer Systems*, pp. 108–116.

[74] Moudgill M., April 1998. Techniques for implementing fast processor simulators. In *Proceedings of the 31st Annual Simulation Symposium*, pp. 83–90.

[75] Moudgill M., Wellman J.-D., and Moreno J. H., May/June 1999. Environment for PowerPC microarchitecture exploration. *IEEE Micro*, **19**(3):15–25.

[76] Mukherjee S. S., Adve S. V., Austin T., Emer J., and Magnusson, P. S., February 2002. Performance simulation tools: Guest editors' introduction. *IEEE Computer, Special Issue on High Performance Simulators*, **35**(2):38–39.

[77] Mutlu O., Kim H., Armstrong D. N., and Patt Y. N., June 2005. Understanding the effects of wrong-path memory references on processor performance. In *Proceedings of the 3rd Workshop on Memory Performance Issues (WMPI) held in conjunction with the 31st International Symposium on Computer Architecture (ISCA)*, pp. 56–64.

[78] Narayanasamy S., Pereira C., Patil H., Cohn R., and Calder B., June 2006. Automatic logging of operating system effects to guide application level architecture simulation. In *Proceedings of the ACM Sigmetrics International Conference on Measurement and Modeling of Computer Systems (SIGMETRICS)*, pp. 216–227.

[79] Nguyen A.-T., Bose P., Ekanadham K., Nanda A., and Michael M., April 1997. Accuracy and speed-up of parallel trace-driven architectural simulation. In *Proceedings of the 11th International Parallel Processing Symposium (IPPS)*, pp. 39–44.

[80] Nohl A., Braun G., Schliebusch O., Leupers R., and Meyr H., June 2002. A universal technique for fast and flexible instruction-set architecture simulation. In *Proceedings of the 39th Design Automation Conference (DAC)*, pp. 22–27.

[81] Nussbaum S., and Smith J. E., September 2001. Modeling superscalar processors via statistical simulation. In *Proceedings of the 2001 International Conference on Parallel Architectures and Compilation Techniques (PACT)*, pp. 15–24.

[82] Nussbaum S., and Smith J. E., April 2002. Statistical simulation of symmetric multiprocessor systems. In *Proceedings of the 35th Annual Simulation Symposium 2002*, pp. 89–97.

[83] Oskin M., Chong F. T., and Farrens M., June 2000. HLS: Combining statistical and symbolic simulation to guide microprocessor design. In *Proceedings of the 27th Annual International Symposium on Computer Architecture (ISCA)*, pp. 71–82.

[84] Patil H., Cohn R., Charney M., Kapoor R., Sun A., and Karunanidhi A., December 2004. Pin-pointing representative portions of large Intel Itanium programs with dynamic instrumentation. In *Proceedings of the 37th Annual International Symposium on Microarchitecture (MICRO)*, pp. 81–93.

[85] Penry D. A., Fay D., Hodgdon D., Wells R., Schelle G., August D. I., and Connors D., February 2006. Exploiting parallelism and structure to accelerate the simulation of chip multi-processors. In *Proceedings of the Twelfth International Symposium on High Performance Computer Architecture (HPCA)*, pp. 27–38.

[86] Perelman E., Hamerly G., and Calder B., September 2003. Picking statistically valid and early simulation points. In *Proceedings of the 12th International Conference on Parallel Architectures and Compilation Techniques (PACT)*, pp. 244–256.

[87] Perelman E., Lau J., Patil H., Jaleel A., Hamerly G., and Calder B., March 2007. Cross binary simulation points. In *Proceedings of the Annual International Symposium on Performance Analysis of Systems and Software (ISPASS)*, pp. 179–189.

[88] Perez D. G., Berry H., and Temam O., December 2006. A sampling method focusing on practicality. *IEEE Micro*, **26**(6):14–28.

[89] Perez D. G., Mouchard G., and Temam O., December 2004. MicroLib: A case for the quantitative comparison of micro-architecture mechanisms. In *Proceedings of the 37th Annual International Symposium on Microarchitecture (MICRO)*, pp. 43–54.

[90] Reilly M., and Edmondson J., May 1998. Performance simulation of an alpha microprocessor. *IEEE Computer*, **31**(5):50–58.

[91] Reinhardt S. K., Hill M. D., Larus J. R., Lebeck A. R., Lewis, J. C., and Wood, D. A., May 1993. The wisconsin wind tunnel: Virtual prototyping of parallel computers. In *Proceedings of the ACM SIGMETRICS Conference on Measurement and Modeling of Computer Systems*, pp. 48–60.

[92] Reshadi M., Mishra P., and Dutt N. D., June 2003. Instruction set compiled simulation: A technique for fast and flexible instruction set simulation. In *Proceedings of the 40th Design Automation Conference (DAC)*, pp. 758–763.

[93] Ringenberg J., Pelosi C., Oehmke D., and Mudge T., March 2005. Intrinsic checkpointing: A methodology for decreasing simulation time through binary modification. In *Proceedings of the IEEE International Symposium on Performance Analysis of Systems and Software (ISPASS)*, pp. 78–88.

[94] Rosenblum M., Bugnion E., Devine S., and Herrod S. A., January 1997. Using the SimOS machine simulator to study complex computer systems. *ACM Transactions on Modeling and Computer Simulation (TOMACS)*, **7**(1):78–103.

[95] Schnarr E., and Larus J. R., October 1998. Fast out-of-order processor simulation using memoization. In *Proceedings of the Eighth International Conference on Architectural Support for Programming Languages and Operating Systems (ASPLOS)*, pp. 283–294.

[96] Sherwood T., Perelman E., and Calder B., September 2001. Basic block distribution analysis to find periodic behavior and simulation points in applications. In *Proceedings of the 2001 International Conference on Parallel Architectures and Compilation Techniques (PACT)*, pp. 3–14.

[97] Sherwood T., Perelman E., Hamerly G., and Calder B., October 2002. Automatically characterizing large scale program behavior. In *Proceedings of the Tenth International Conference on Architectural Support for Programming Languages and Operating Systems (ASPLOS)*, pp. 45–57.

[98] Skadron K., Ahuja P. S., Martonosi M., and Clark D. W., November 1999. Branch prediction, instruction-window size, and cache size: Performance tradeoffs and simulation techniques. *IEEE Transactions on Computers*, **48**(11):1260–1281.

[99] Sorin D. J., Pai V. S., Adve S. V., Vernon M. K., and Wood D. A., June 1998. Analytic evaluation of shared-memory systems with ILP processors. In *Proceedings of the 25th Annual International Symposium on Computer Architecture (ISCA)*, pp. 380–391.

[100] Sugumar R. A., and Abraham S. G., 1993. Efficient simulation of caches under optimal replacement with applications to miss characterization. In *Proceedings of the 1993 ACM Conference on Measurement and Modeling of Computer Systems (SIGMETRICS)*, pp. 24–35.

[101] Szwed P. K., Marques D., Buels R. B., McKee S. A., and Schulz M., February 2004. SimSnap: Fast-forwarding via native execution and application-level checkpointing. In *Proceedings of the Workshop on the Interaction between Compilers and Computer Architectures (INTERACT), held in conjunction with HPCA*.

[102] Vachharajani M., Vachharajani N., Penry D. A., Blome J. A., and August D. I., November 2002. Microarchitectural exploration with Liberty. In *Proceedings of the 35th International Symposium on Microarchitecture (MICRO)*, pp. 271–282.

[103] Van Biesbrouck M., Calder B., and Eeckhout L., July 2006a. Efficient sampling startup for SimPoint. *IEEE Micro*, **26**(4):32–42.

[104] Van Biesbrouck M., Eeckhout L., and Calder B., November 2005. Efficient sampling startup for sampled processor simulation. In 2005 International Conference on High Performance Embedded Architectures and Compilation (HiPEAC), pp. 47–67.

[105] Van Biesbrouck M., Eeckhout L., and Calder B., March 2006b. Considering all starting points for simultaneous multithreading simulation. In *Proceedings of the International Symposium on Performance Analysis of Systems and Software (ISPASS)*, pp. 143–153.

[106] Van Biesbrouck M., Eeckhout L., and Calder B., October 2007. Representative multiprogram workloads for multithreaded processor simulation. In *Proceedings of the IEEE International Symposium on Workload Characterization (IISWC)*, pp. 193–203.

[107] Van Biesbrouck M., Sherwood T., and Calder B., March 2004. A co-phase matrix to guide simultaneous multithreading simulation. In *Proceedings of the International Symposium on Performance Analysis of Systems and Software (ISPASS)*, pp. 45–56.

[108] Van Ertvelde L., Hellebaut F., and Eeckhout L., 2007. Accurate and efficient cache warmup for sampled processor simulation through NSL-BLRL. *Computer Journal* (Accepted for publication).

[109] Van Ertvelde L., Hellebaut F., Eeckhout L., and De Bosschere, K., April 2006. NSL-BLRL: Efficient cache warmup for sampled processor simulation. In *Proceedings of the 29th Annual International Simulation Symposium (ANSS)*, pp. 168–175.

[110] Wenisch T., Wunderlich R., Falsafi B., and Hoe J., June 2005. TurboSMARTS: accurate microarchitecture simulation in minutes. In *Proceedings of the 2005 ACM SIGMETRICS International Conference on Measurement and Modeling of Computer Systems*, pp. 408–409.

[111] Wenisch T. F., Wunderlich R. E., Falsafi B., and Hoe J. C., March 2006a. Simulation sampling with live-points. In *Proceedings of the Annual International Symposium on Performance Analysis of Systems and Software (ISPASS)*, pp. 2–12.

[112] Wenisch T. F., Wunderlich R. E., Ferdman M., Ailamaki A., Falsafi B., and Hoe J. C., July 2006b. SimFlex: Statistical sampling of computer system simulation. *IEEE Micro*, **26**(4):18–31.

[113] Witchell E., and Rosenblum M., June 1996. Embra: Fast and flexible machine simulation. In *Proceedings of the ACM SIGMETRICS Conference on Measurement and Modeling of Computer Systems*, pp. 68–79.

[114] Wood D. A., Hill M. D., and Kessler R. E., May 1991. A model for estimating trace-sample miss ratios. In *Proceedings of the 1991 SIGMETRICS Conference on Measurement and Modeling of Computer Systems*, pp. 79–89.

[115] Wunderlich R. E., Wenisch T. F., Falsafi B., and Hoe J. C., June 2003. SMARTS: Accelerating microarchitecture simulation via rigorous statistical sampling. In *Proceedings of the 30th Annual International Symposium on Computer Architecture (ISCA)*, pp. 84–95.

[116] Wunderlich R. E., Wenisch T. F., Falsafi B., and Hoe J. C., June 2004. An evaluation of stratified sampling of microarchitecture simulations. In *Proceedings of the Third Annual Workshop on Duplicating, Deconstructing and Debunking (WDDD), held in conjunction with ISCA.*

[117] Wunderlich R. E., Wenisch T. F., Falsafi B., and Hoe J. C., July 2006. Statistical sampling of microarchitecture simulation. *ACM Transactions on Modeling and Computer Simulation*, **16**(3): 197–224.

[118] Yi J. J., Kodakara S. V., Sendag R., Lilja D. J., and Hawkins D. M., February 2005. Characterizing and comparing prevailing simulation techniques. In *Proceedings of the 11th International Symposium on High-Performance Computer Architecture (HPCA)*, pp. 266–277.

[119] Yi J. J., and Lilja D. J., March 2006. Simulation of computer architectures: Simulators, benchmarks, methodologies, and recommendations. *IEEE Transactions on Computers*, **55**(3):268–280.

[120] Yourst M. T., April 2007. PTLsim: A cycle accurate full system x86-64 microarchitectural simulator. In *Proceedings of the International Symposium on Performance Analysis of Systems and Software (ISPASS)*, pp. 23–34.

# Distributed Sparse Matrices for Very High Level Languages

JOHN R. GILBERT

*Department of Computer Science,*
*University of California, Santa Barbara, CA, USA*

STEVE REINHARDT

*Interactive Supercomputing*

VIRAL B. SHAH

*Department of Computer Science,*
*University of California, Santa Barbara, CA, USA*
*and*
*Interactive Supercomputing*

**Abstract**

Sparse matrices are first-class objects in many VHLLs (very high-level languages) that are used for scientific computing. They are a basic building block for various numerical and combinatorial algorithms. Parallel computing is becoming ubiquitous, specifically due to the advent of multi-core architectures. As existing VHLLs are adapted to emerging architectures, and new ones are conceived, one must rethink about trade-offs in language design. We describe the design and implementation of a sparse matrix infrastructure for STAR-P, a parallel implementation of the MATLAB® programming language. We demonstrate the versatility of our infrastructure by using it to implement a benchmark that creates and manipulates large graphs. Our design is by no means specific to STAR-P—we hope it will influence the design of sparse matrix infrastructures in other languages.



ADVANCES IN COMPUTERS, VOL. 72
ISSN: 0065-2458/DOI: 10.1016/S0065-2458(08)00005-3



Copyright © 2008 Elsevier Inc.
All rights reserved.

# 1. Introduction

Of late, two trends have emerged in scientific computing. The first one is the adoption of high-level interactive programming environments such as MATLAB® [28], R [23] and Python [34]. This is largely due to diverse communities in physical sciences, engineering and social sciences using simulations to supplement results from theory and experiments.

Computations on graphs combined with numerical simulation is the other trend in scientific computing. High-performance applications in data mining, computational biology, and multi-scale modeling, among others, combine numerics and combinatorics in several ways. Relationships between individual elements in complex systems are typically modeled as graphs. Links between webpages, chemical bonds in complex molecules, and connectivity in social networks are some examples of such relationships.

Scientific programmers want to combine numerical and combinatorial techniques in interactive VHLLs, while keeping up with the increasing ubiquity of parallel computing. A distributed sparse matrix infrastructure is one way to address these challenges. We describe the design and implementation of distributed sparse matrices in STAR-P, a parallel implementation of the MATLAB® programming language.

Sparse matrix computations allow for the structured representation of irregular data structures and access patterns in parallel applications. Sparse matrices are also a convenient way to represent graphs. Since sparse matrices are first-class citizens in modern programming languages for scientific computing, it is natural to take advantage of the duality between sparse matrices and graphs to develop a unified infrastructure for numerical and combinatorial computing.

The distributed sparse matrix implementation in STAR-P provides a set of well-tested primitives with which graph algorithms can be built. Parallelism is derived from operations on parallel sparse matrices. The efficiency of our graph algorithms depends upon the efficiency of the underlying sparse matrix infrastructure.

We restrict our discussion to the design and implementation of the sparse matrix infrastructure in STAR-P, trade-offs made, and lessons learnt. We also describe our implementation of a graph analysis benchmark, using Gilbert, Reinhardt and Shah's 'Graph and Pattern Discovery Toolbox (GAPDT)'. The graph toolbox is built on top of the sparse matrix infrastructure in STAR-P [16, 17, 32, 33].

## 2. Sparse Matrices: A User's View

The basic design of STAR-P and operations on dense matrices have been discussed in earlier work [8, 21, 22]. In addition to MATLAB®'s sparse and dense matrices, STAR-P provides support for distributed sparse (dsparse) and distributed dense (ddense) matrices.

The *p* operator provides for parallelism in STAR-P. For example, a random parallel dense matrix (ddense) distributed by rows across processors is created as follows:

```
>> A = rand (1e4*p, 1e4)
```

Similarly, a random parallel sparse matrix (dsparse) also distributed across processors by rows is created as follows (The third argument specifies the density of non-zeros.):

```
>> S = sprand (1e6*p, 1e6, 1/1e6)
```

We use the overloading facilities in MATLAB® to define a *dsparse* object. The STAR-P language requires that almost all (meaningful) operations that can be performed in MATLAB® are possible with STAR-P. Our implementation provides a working basis, but is not quite a drop-in replacement for existing MATLAB® programs.

STAR-P achieves parallelism through polymorphism. Operations on ddense matrices produce ddense matrices. But, once initiated, sparsity propagates. Operations on dsparse matrices produce dsparse matrices. An operation on a mixture of dsparse and ddense matrices produces a dsparse matrix unless the operator destroys sparsity. The user can explicitly convert a ddense matrix to a dsparse matrix using sparse(A). Similarly, a dsparse matrix can be converted to a ddense matrix using full(S). A dsparse matrix can also be converted into a front-end sparse matrix using ppfront(S).

## 3. Data Structures and Storage

It is true in MATLAB®, as well as in STAR-P, that many key operations are provided by public domain software (linear algebra, solvers, fft, etc.). Apart from simple operations such as array arithmetic, MATLAB® allows for matrix multiplication, array indexing, array assignment and concatenation of arrays, among other things. These operations form extremely powerful primitives upon which other functions, toolboxes, and libraries are built. The challenge in the implementation lies in selecting the right data structures and algorithms that implement all operations efficiently, allowing them to be combined in any number of ways.

Compressed row and column data structures have been shown to be efficient for sparse linear algebra [19]. MATLAB® stores sparse matrices on a single processor in a Compressed Sparse Column (CSC) data structure [15]. The STAR-P language allows for distribution of ddense matrices by block rows or block columns [8, 21]. Our implementation supports only the block-row distribution for dsparse matrices. This is a design of choice for preventing the combinatorial explosion of argument types. Block layout by rows makes the Compressed Sparse Row data structure a logical choice to store the sparse matrix slice on each processor. The choice to use a block-row layout was not arbitrary, but the reasoning was as follows:

- The iterative methods community largely uses row-based storage. Since we believe that iterative methods will be the methods of choice for large sparse matrices, we want to ensure maximum compatibility with existing libraries.
- A row-based data structure also allows for efficient implementation of 'matvec' (sparse matrix dense vector product), the workhorse of several iterative methods such as Conjugate Gradient and Generalized Minimal Residual.

For the expert user, storing sparse matrices by rows instead of by columns changes the programming model. For instance, high-performance sparse matrix codes in MATLAB® are often carefully written so that all accesses into sparse matrices are by columns. When run in STAR-P, such codes may display different performance characteristics, since dsparse matrices are stored by rows. This may be considered by some to be a negative impact of our decision to use compressed sparse rows instead of compressed sparse columns.

This boils down to a question of design goals. We set out to design a high-performance parallel sparse matrix infrastructure and concluded that row-based storage was the way to go. Had our goal been to ensure maximum performance on existing MATLAB® codes, we might have chosen a column-based storage. Given all that we have learnt from our implementation, we might reconsider this decision in the light of 1-D distributions. However, it is much more likely that for a redesign, a 2-D distribution will be considered, to allow for scaling to thousands of processors. We describe some of these issues in detail in the Section 6.

The CSR data structure stores whole rows contiguously in a single array on each processor. If a processor has $nnz$ non-zeros, CSR uses an array of length $nnz$ to store the non-zeros and another array of length $nnz$ to store column indices, as shown in Fig. 1. Row boundaries are specified by an array of length $m + 1$, where $m$ is the number of rows on that processor.

Using double-precision floating-point values for the non-zeros on 32-bit architectures, an $m \times n$ real sparse matrix with $nnz$ non-zeros uses $12nnz + 4(m + 1)$ bytes of memory. On 64-bit architectures, it uses $16nnz + 8(m + 1)$ bytes. STAR-P supports complex sparse matrices as well. In the 32-bit case, the storage required is $20nnz + 4(m + 1)$ bytes, whereas it is $24nnz + 8(m + 1)$ bytes on 64-bit architectures.

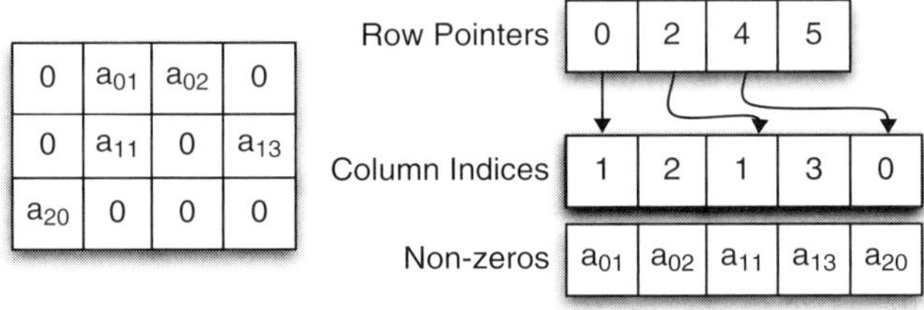


FIG. 1. The matrix is shown in its dense representation on the left, and its compressed sparse rows (CSR) representation is shown on the right. In the CSR data structure, non-zeros are stored in three vectors. Two vectors of length $nnz$ store the non-zero elements and their column indices. A vector of row pointers marks the beginning of each new row in the non-zero and column index vectors.

Consider the example described earlier: A sparse matrix with a million rows and columns, with a density of approximately one nonzero per row or column. The memory required for a dense representation would be $10^6 \times 10^6 \times 8$ bytes $= 8$ terabytes. The CSR data structure, on the other hand, would use $16 \times 10^6 + 8 \times 10^6$ bytes $=$ 24 megabytes.

# 4. Operations on Distributed Sparse Matrices

The design of sparse matrix algorithms in STAR-P follows the same design principles as in MATLAB® [15].

1. Storage required for a sparse matrix should be $O(nnz)$, proportional to the number of non-zero elements.
2. Running time for a sparse matrix algorithm should be $O(flops)$. It should be proportional to the number of floating-point operations required to obtain the result.

The data structure described in the previous section satisfies the requirement for storage. It is difficult to apply exactly the second principle in practice. Typically, most implementations achieve running time close to $O(flops)$ for commonly used sparse matrix operations. For example, accessing a single element of a sparse matrix should be a constant-time operation. With a CSR data structure, the time taken is proportional to the logarithm of the length of the row to access a single element. Similarly, insertion of single elements into a CSR data structure generates extensive data movement. Such operations can be performed efficiently with the sparse/find routines (described in the next section), which work with triples rather than individual elements.

## 4.1 Constructors

There are several ways to construct distributed sparse matrices in STAR-P:

1. ppback converts a sequential MATLAB® matrix to a distributed STAR-P matrix. If the input is a sparse matrix, the result is a dsparse matrix.
2. sparse creates a sparse matrix from dense vectors giving a list of non-zero values. A distributed sparse matrix is automatically created, if the dense vectors are distributed. find is the dual of sparse; it extracts the non-zeros from a sparse matrix.
3. speye creates a sparse identity matrix.
4. spdiags constructs a sparse matrix by specifying the values on diagonals.

5. sprand and sprandn construct random sparse matrices with specified density.
6. spones creates a sparse matrix with the same non-zero structure as a given sparse matrix, where all the non-zero values are 1.

## 4.2 Element-Wise Matrix Arithmetic

Sparse matrix arithmetic is implemented using a sparse accumulator (SPA). Gilbert, Moler and Schreiber [15] discuss the design of the SPA in detail. In brief, a SPA uses a dense vector as intermediate storage. The key to making a SPA work is to maintain auxiliary data structures that allow for direct ordered access to only the non-zero elements in the SPA. STAR-P uses a separate SPA for each processor.

## 4.3 Matrix Multiplication

### *4.3.1 Multiplication of Sparse Matrix with Dense Vector*

A sparse matrix can be multiplied by a dense vector, either on the right or on the left. The CSR data structure used in STAR-P is efficient for multiplying a sparse matrix by a dense vector: $y = A^*x$. It is efficient for communication and shows good cache behavior for the sequential part of the computation. Our choice of the CSR data structure was strongly influenced by our desire to have good matvec performance, since matvec forms the core computational kernel for many iterative methods.

The matrix $A$ and vector $x$ are distributed across processors by rows. The submatrix of $A$ on each processor will need some subset of $x$ depending upon its sparsity structure. When matvec is invoked for the first time on a dsparse matrix $A$, STAR-P computes a communication schedule for $A$ and caches it. Later, when matvecs are performed using the same $A$, this communication schedule does not need to be recomputed, which saves some computing and communication overhead, at the cost of extra space required to save the schedule. We experimented with overlapping computation and communication in matvec. It turns out in many cases that this is less efficient than simply performing the communication first, followed by the computation. As computer architectures evolve, this decision may need to be revisited.

Communication in matvec can be reduced by graph partitioning. Lesser communication is required during matvec, if fewer edges cross processor. STAR-P can use several of the available tools for graph partitioning [6, 18, 29]. However, STAR-P does not perform graph partitioning automatically during matvec. The philosophy behind this decision is similar to that in MATLAB®: user should be able to reorganize data to make later operations more efficient, but not automatic.

When multiplying from the left, $y = x' * A$, instead of communicating just the required parts of the source vector, each processor computes its own destination vector. All partial destination vectors are then summed up into the final destination vector. This require $O(n)$ communication. The choice of the CSR data structure which allows for efficient communication when multiplying from the right makes it more difficult to multiply on the left.

Multiplication of sparse matrix with dense-matrix in STAR-P is implemented as a series of matvecs. Such operations although not very common, do often show up in practice. It is tempting to simply convert the sparse matrix to a dense matrix and perform dense-matrix multiplication; the reasoning being that the result will be dense in any case. However, such action requires extra floating-point operations. Such a scheme may also be inefficient in storage if the resulting matrix is smaller in dimensions than the sparse argument.

### *4.3.2 Multiplication of Sparse Matrix with Sparse Matrix*

The multiplication of two sparse matrices is an important operation in STAR-P. It is a common operation for operation on large graphs. Its application to graph manipulation and numerical solvers is described by Shah [33]. Our implementation of multiplication of two sparse matrices is described by Robertson [30] and Shah [33].

The computation for matrix multiplication can be organized in several ways, leading to different formulations. One common formulation is the inner product formulation, as shown in code fragment 2. In this case, every element of the product $C_{ij}$ is computed as a dot product of a row $i$ in $A$ and a column $j$ in $B$.

```
01 function C = mult_inner_prod (A, B)
02 % Inner product formulation of matrix
           multiplication
03
04 for i = 1:n             % For each row of A
05    for j = 1:n          % For each col of B
06        C(i, j) = A(i, :) * B(:, j);
07    end
08 end
```

FIG. 2. Inner product formulation of matrix multiplication. Every element of $C$ is computed as a dot product of a row of $A$ and a column of $B$.

Another formulation of matrix multiplication is the outer product formulation (code fragment 3). The product is computed as a sum of $n$ rank-one matrices. Each rank-one matrix is computed as the outer product of column $k$ of $A$ and row $k$ of $B$.

MATLAB® stores its matrices in the CSC format. Clearly, computation of inner products (code fragment 2) is inefficient, since rows of $A$ cannot be efficiently accessed without searching. Similarly, in the case of computation of outer products (code fragment 3), rows of $B$ have to be extracted. The process of accumulating successive rank-one updates is also inefficient, as the structure of the result changes with each successive update.

The computation can be set up so that $A$ and $B$ are accessed by columns, computing one column of the product $C$ at a time. Code fragment 4 shows how column $j$ of $C$ is computed as a linear combination of the columns of $A$ as specified by the non-zeros in column $j$ of $B$. Figure 5 shows the same concept graphically.

STAR-P stores its matrices in CSR form. As a result, the computation is setup so that only rows of $A$ and $B$ are accessed, producing a row of $C$ at a time. Each row $i$ of $C$ is computed as a linear combination of the rows of $B$ specified by non-zeros in row $i$ of $A$ (code fragment 6).

```
01 function C = mult_outer_prod (A, B)
02 % Outer product formulation of matrix
           multiplication
03
04 for k = 1:n
05     C = C + A(:, k) * B(k, :);
06 end
```

FIG. 3. Outer product formulation of matrix multiplication. $C$ is computed as a sum of $n$ rank-one matrices.

```
01 function C = mult csc (A, B)
02 % Multiply matrices stored in compressed sparse
              column format
03
04 for j = 1:n
05     for k where B(k, j) ~= 0
06         C(:, j) = C(:, j) + A(:, k) * B(k, j);
07     end
08 end
```

FIG. 4. The column-wise formulation of matrix multiplication accesses all matrices $A$, $B$ and $C$ by columns only.

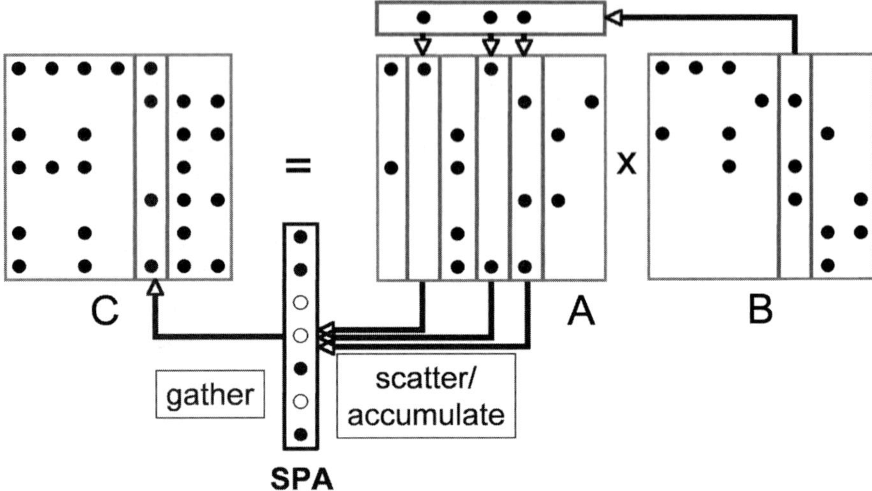


FIG. 5. Multiplication of sparse matrices stored by columns. Columns of $A$ are accumulated as specified by the non-zero entries in a column of $B$ using a SPA. The contents of the SPA are stored in a column of $C$ once all required columns are accumulated.

```
01 function C = mult csr (A, B)
02 % Multiply matrices stored in compressed sparse
               row format
03
04 for i = 1:n
05     for k where A(i, k) ~= 0
06         C(i, :) = C(i, :) + A(i, k) * B(k, :);
07     end
08 end
```

FIG. 6. The row-wise formulation of matrix multiplication accesses all matrices $A$, $B$ and $C$ by rows only.

The performance of sparse matrix multiplication in parallel depends upon the non-zero structures of $A$ and $B$. A well-tuned implementation may use a polyalgorithm. Such a polyalgorithm may use different communication schemes for different matrices. For example, it may be efficient to broadcast the local part of a matrix to all processors, but in other cases, it may be efficient to send only the required rows. On large clusters, it may be efficient to interleave communication and computation. On shared memory architectures, however, most of the time is spent in accumulating updates, rather than in communication. In such cases, it may be more efficient to schedule the communication before the computation. In the general case, the space required to store $C$ cannot be determined quickly, and Cohen's algorithm [9] may be used in such cases.

## 4.4 Sparse Matrix Indexing, Assignment and Concatenation

Several choices are available to the implementor to design primitives upon which a sparse matrix library is built. One has to decide early on in the design phase as to which operations will form the primitives and how other operations will be derived from them.

The syntax of matrix indexing in STAR-P is the same as that in MATLAB®. It is of the form $A(p, q)$, where $p$ and $q$ are vectors of indices.

```
>> B = A(p,q)
```

In this case, the indexing is done on the right side of '=', which specifies that $B$ is assigned a submatrix of $A$. This is the `subsref` operation in MATLAB®.

```
>> B(p,q) = A
```

On the other hand, indexing on the left side of '=' specifies that $A$ should be stored as a submatrix of $B$. This is the `subsasgn` operation in MATLAB®. Repeated indices in subsref cause replication of rows and columns. However, subsasgn with repeated indices is not well defined.

MATLAB® supports horizontal and vertical concatenation of matrices. The following code, for example, concatenates $A$ and $B$ horizontally, $C$ and $D$ horizontally, and finally concatenates the results of these two operations vertically.

```
>> S = [ A B; C D ]
```

All of these operations are widely used, and users often do not give second thought to the way they use indexing operations. The operations have to accept any sparse matrix and return a result in the same form with reasonable performance. Communication adds another dimension of complexity in a parallel implementation such as STAR-P. Performance of sparse-indexing operations depends upon the underlying data structure, the indexing scheme being used, the non-zero structure of the matrix, and the speed of the communication network.

Our implementation uses `sparse` and `find` as primitives to implement sparse indexing. The idea is actually quite simple. First, find all elements that match the selection criteria on each processor. Depending on the operation being performed, rows and columns may need to be renumbered. Once all processors have picked the non-zero tuples which will contribute to the result, call sparse will assemble the matrix.

Such a scheme is elegant because all the complexity of communication is hidden in the call to sparse. This simplifies the implementor's job, who can then focus on simply developing an efficient sparse routine.

## 4.5 Sparse Matrix Transpose

Matrix transpose exchanges the rows and columns of all elements of the matrix. Transpose is an important operation and has been widely studied in the dense case. In a sparse transpose, apart from communication, the communicated elements have to be re-inserted into the sparse data structure. The MATLAB® syntax for matrix transpose is as follows:

```
>> S = A'
```

Sparse matrix transpose can be easily implemented using the sparse and find primitives. First, find all non-zero elements in the sparse matrix with find. Then construct the transpose with sparse, exchanging the vectors for rows and columns.

```
[I, J, V] = find (S);
St = sparse (J, I, V);
```

## 4.6 Direct Solvers for Sparse Linear Systems

MATLAB® solves the linear system $Ax = b$ with the matrix division operator, $x = A\backslash b$. In sequential MATLAB®, $A\backslash b$ is implemented as a polyalgorithm [15], where every test in the polyalgorithm is cheaper than the next one.

1. If $A$ is not square, solve the least squares problem.
2. Otherwise, if $A$ is triangular, perform a triangular solve.
3. Otherwise, test whether $A$ is a permutation of a triangular matrix (a 'morally triangular' matrix), permute it, and solve it if so.
4. Otherwise, if $A$ is Hermitian and has positive real diagonal elements, find a symmetric approximate minimum degree ordering $p$ of $A$ and perform the Cholesky factorization of $A(p, p)$. If successful, finish with two sparse triangular solves.
5. Otherwise, find a column minimum degree order $p$ and perform the LU factorization of $A(:, p)$. Finish with two sparse triangular solves.

The current version of MATLAB® uses CHOLMOD [7] in step 4 and UMFPACK [10] in step 5. MATLAB® also uses LAPACK [2] band solvers for banded matrices in its current polyalgorithm.

Different issues arise in parallel polyalgorithms. For example, morally triangular matrices and symmetric matrices are harder to detect in parallel. In the next section, we present a probabilistic approach to test for matrix symmetry. Design of the best polyalgorithm for 'backslash' in parallel is an active research problem. For now, STAR-P offers the user a choice between two existing message-passing parallel sparse solvers: MUMPS [1] and SuperLU_Dist [25].

Sparse solvers are extremely complex pieces of software, often taking several years to develop. They use subtle techniques to extract locality and parallelism and have complex data structures. Most sparse solvers provide an interface only to solve linear systems, $x = A\backslash b$. They often do not provide an interface for the user to obtain the factors from the solution, $[L, U] = lu(A)$. MATLAB® uses UMFPACK only when backslash or the four output version of lu is used, $[L, U, P, Q] = lu(A)$. Many MATLAB® codes store the results of LU factorization for later use. Since STAR-P does not yet provide a sparse *lu* implementation, it may not be able to run certain MATLAB® codes in parallel.

## 4.7 Iterative Solvers for Sparse Linear Systems

Iterative solvers for sparse linear systems include a wide variety of algorithms that use successive approximations at each step. *Stationary* methods are older, simpler, but usually not very effective. These include methods such as Jacobi, Gauss–Seidel and successive over-relaxation. *Non-stationary* methods, also known as Krylov subspace methods, are relatively modern and are based on the idea of sequences of orthogonal vectors. Their convergence typically depends upon the condition number of the matrix. Often, a *preconditioner* is used to transform a given matrix into one with a more favorable spectrum, accelerating convergence.

Iterative methods are not used by default for solving linear systems in STAR-P. This is mainly due to the fact that efficient methods are not yet available for all classes of problems. *Conjugate Gradient* (CG) works well for matrices which are symmetric and positive definite (SPD). Methods such as *Generalized Minimal Residual* (GMRES) or *Biconjugate gradient* (BiCG, BiCGStab) are used for unsymmetric matrices. However, convergence may be irregular, and it is also possible that the methods may break.

Even when using CG, a preconditioner is required for fast convergence. Preconditioners are often problem specific; their construction often requires knowledge of the problem at hand. An exciting new area of research is that of combinatorial preconditioners. The graph toolbox in STAR-P provides tools for users to build such preconditioners [33].

Although STAR-P does not use iterative methods by default, it provides several tools for users to use them when suitable. Preconditioned iterative methods from software such as Aztec [31] and Hypre [14] may also be used in STAR-P through the STAR-P SDK [24].

## 4.8 Eigenvalues and Singular Values

STAR-P provides eigensolvers for sparse matrices through PARPACK [27]. PARPACK uses a reverse communication interface, in which it provides the essential routines for the Arnoldi factorization, and requires the user to provide routines for matvec and linear solutions. STAR-P implementations of matvec and linear solvers were discussed in earlier sections.

STAR-P retains the same calling sequence as the MATLAB® eigs function. STAR-P can also provide singular values in a similar fashion, and retains the same calling sequence for svds.

## 4.9 Visualization of Sparse Matrices

We have experimented with a few different methods to visualize sparse matrices in STAR-P. A MATLAB® spy plot of a sparse matrix shows the positions of all non-zeros. For extremely large sparse matrices, this approach does not work very well since each pixel on the screen represents a fairly large part of a matrix. Figure 7 shows a MATLAB® spy plot of a web-crawl matrix. It also shows a colored spy plot, with a different color for each processor. The row-wise distribution of the matrix is clearly observed in the

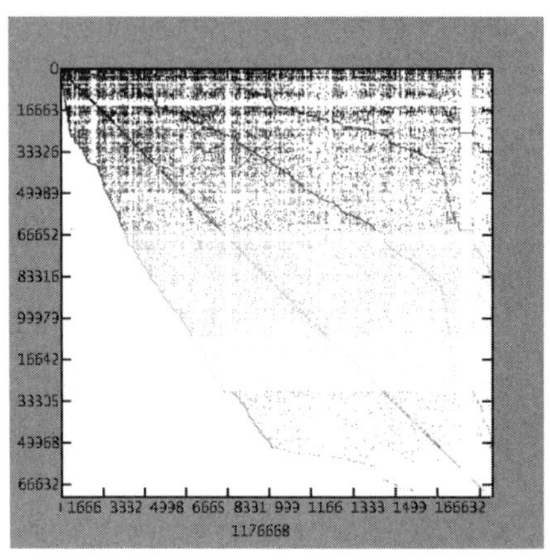


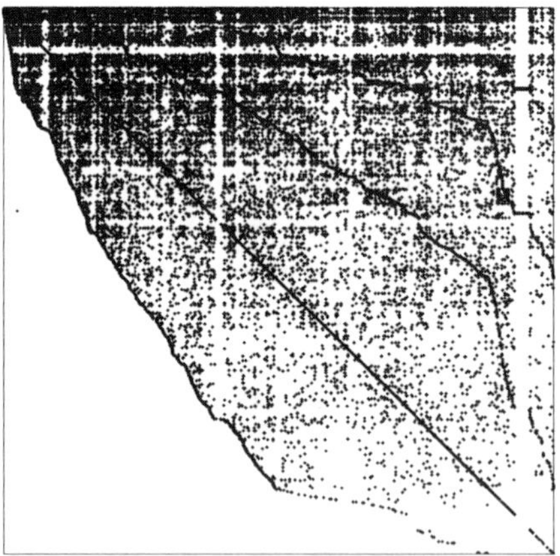

FIG. 7. MATLAB® and STAR-P spy plots of a web-crawl sparse matrix. The STAR-P plot also exposes the underlying block-row distribution of the sparse matrix. The matrix was constructed by running a breadth-first web crawl from www.mit.edu.

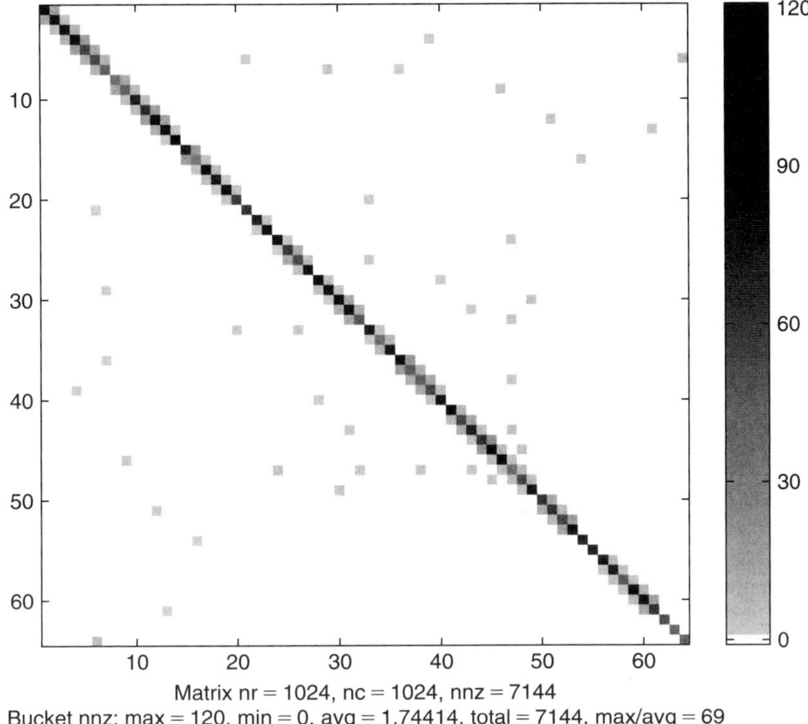


FIG. 8. A density spy plot. For large matrices, spy may not display the underlying structure. A density plot colors each pixel according to the density of the area of the sparse matrix it represents.

colored spy plot. Another approach is to use a 2-D histogram or a density spy plot, such as the one in Fig. 8, which uses different colors for different non-zero densities. spyy uses sparse matrix multiplication to produce density spy plots. It is similar to the cspy routine in CSparse [11], with the exception that cspy is implemented in *C* and cannot be used in STAR-P. spyy operates on large dsparse matrices on the backend, but the resulting images are small, which are easily communicated to the frontend.

## 5. SSCA #2 Graph Analysis Benchmark

We now describe our implementation of a graph analysis benchmark, which builds upon the sparse matrix infrastructure in STAR-P.

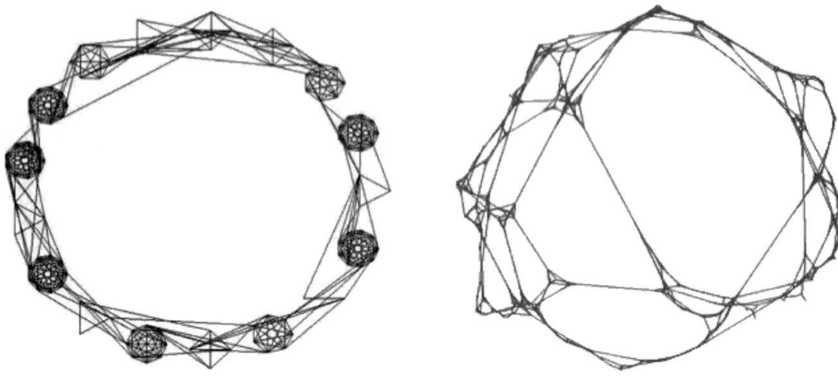

FIG. 9. The left image shows the conceptual SSCA #2 graph (Kepner). The image on the right is an SSCA #2 graph generated with scale 8 (256 nodes) and plotted with Fiedler co-ordinates.

The SSCAs (Scalable Synthetic Compact Applications) are a set of benchmarks designed to complement existing benchmarks such as the HPL [13] and the NAS parallel benchmarks [5]. Specifically, SSCA #2 [3] is a compact application that has multiple kernels accessing a single data structure (a directed multigraph with weighted edges). We describe our implementation of version 1.1 of the benchmark. Version 2.0 [4], which differs significantly from version 1.1, has since been released.

The data generator generates an edge list in random order for a multi-graph of sparsely connected cliques as shown in Fig. 9. The four kernels are as follows:

1. Kernel 1: Create a data structure for further kernels.
2. Kernel 2: Search graph for a maximum weight edge.
3. Kernel 3: Perform breadth-first searches from a set of start nodes.
4. Kernel 4: Recover the underlying clique structure from the undirected graph.

## 5.1 Scalable Data Generator

The data generator is the most complex part of our implementation. It generates edge tuples for subsequent kernels. No graph operations are performed at this stage. The input to the data generator is a scale parameter, which indicates the size of the graph being generated. The resulting graph has $2^{scale}$ nodes, with a maximum clique size of $\lfloor 2^{scale/3} \rfloor$, a maximum of 3 edges with the same endpoints, and a probability of 0.2 that an edge is uni-directional. Table I shows the statistics for graphs generated with this data generator at different scales.

TABLE I
STATISTICS FOR THE SSCA#2 GRAPH (VERSION 1.1). THE DIRECTED EDGES COLUMN COUNTS THE NUMBER OF EDGES IN THE DIRECTED MULTI-GRAPH. THE UNDIRECTED EDGES COLUMN COUNTS THE NUMBER OF EDGES IN THE UNDIRECTED GRAPH USED FOR KERNEL 4. THE STATISTICS ARE GENERATED BY SIMULATING THE DATA GENERATOR

| Scale | #Vertices | #Cliques | #Edges (directed) | #Edges (undirected) |
|---|---|---|---|---|
| 10 | 1024 | 186 | 13,212 | 3,670 |
| 15 | 32,768 | 2,020 | 1,238,815 | 344,116 |
| 20 | 1,048,576 | 20,643 | 126,188,649 | 35,052,403 |
| 25 | 33,554,432 | 207,082 | 12,951,350,000 | 3,597,598,000 |
| 30 | 1,073,741,824 | 2,096,264 | 1,317,613,000,000 | 366,003,600,000 |

The vertex numbers are randomized, and a randomized ordering of the edge tuples is presented to the subsequent kernels. Our implementation of the data generator closely follows the pseudocode published in the spec [3].

## 5.2 Kernel 1

Kernel 1 creates a read-only data structure that is used by subsequent kernels. We create a sparse matrix corresponding to each layer of the multi-graph. The multi-graph has three layers, since there is a maximum of three parallel edges between any two nodes in the graph. MATLAB® provides several ways of constructing sparse matrices, `sparse`, which takes as its input a list of three tuples: $(i, j, w_{ij})$. Its output is a sparse matrix with a non-zero $w_{ij}$ in every location $(i, j)$ specified in the input. Figure 10 shows a spy plot of one layer of the input graph.

## 5.3 Kernel 2

In kernel 2, we search the graph for edges with maximum weight. `find` is the inverse of `sparse`. It returns all non-zeros from a sparse matrix as a list of three tuples. We then use `max` to find the maximum weight edge.

## 5.4 Kernel 3

In kernel 3, we perform breadth-first searches from a given set of starting points. We use sparse matrix matrix multiplication to perform all breadth-first searches simultaneously from the given starting points. Let $G$ be the adjacency matrix representing the graph and $S$ be a matrix corresponding to the starting points. $S$ has one column for each starting point and one non-zero in each column. Breadth-first search is

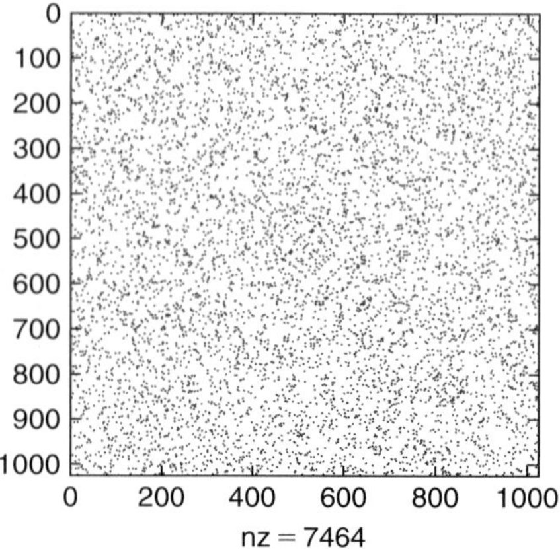


FIG. 10. MATLAB® spy plot of the input graph. The input graph is randomized, as evidenced by no observed patterns in the spy plot.

performed by repeatedly multiplying $G$ by $S$: $Y = G * S$. We perform several breadth-first searches simultaneously by using sparse matrix matrix multiplication. STAR-P stores sparse matrices by rows, and parallelism is achieved computation of some rows in the product [30, 32] by each processor.

## 5.5 Kernel 4

Kernel 4 is the most interesting part of the benchmark. It can be considered to be a partitioning problem or a clustering problem. We have several implementations of kernel 4 based on spectral partitioning (Fig. 9), 'seed growing' (Fig. 11) and 'peer pressure' algorithms. The peer pressure and seed-growing implementations scale better than the spectral methods, as expected. We now demonstrate how we use the infrastructure described above to implement kernel 4 in a few lines of MATLAB® or STAR-P. Figure 11 shows a spy plot of the undirected graph after clustering. The clusters show up as dense blocks along the diagonal.

Our seed-growing algorithm (Fig. 12) starts by picking a small set of seeds (about 2% of the total number of nodes) randomly. The seeds are then grown so that each seed claims that all nodes are reachable by at least $k$ paths of length 1 or 2, where $k$ is the size of the largest clique. This may cause some ambiguity, since some nodes might be claimed by multiple seeds. We tried picking an independent set of nodes from the graph by performing one round of Luby's algorithm [26] to keep the number of such ambiguities as low as possible. However, the quality of clustering

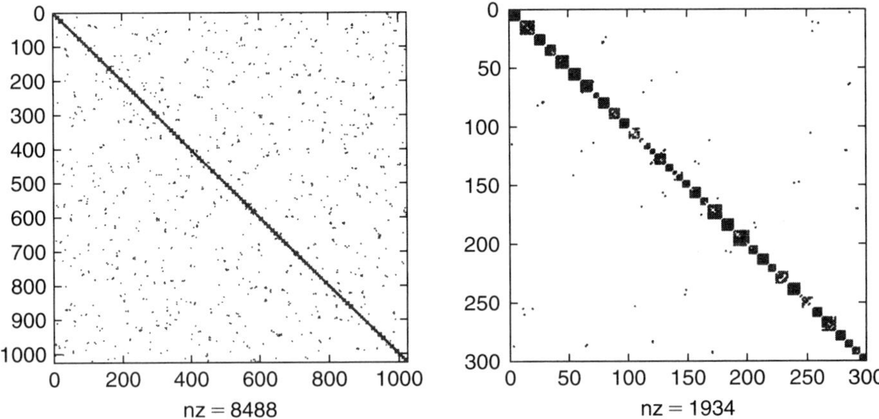


FIG. 11. The image on the left is a spy plot of the graph, reordered after clustering. The image on the right magnifies a portion around the diagonal. Cliques are revealed as dense blocks on the diagonal.

```
01 function J = seedgrow (seeds)
02 % Clustering by breadth first searches
03
04 % J is a sparse matrix with one seed per column.
05 J = sparse (seeds, 1:nseeds, 1, n, nseeds);
06
07 % Vertices reachable with 1 hop.
08 J = G * J;
09 % Vertices reachable with 1 or 2 hops.
10 J = J + G*J;
11 % Vertices reachable with at least k
                 paths of 1 or 2 hops.
12 J = J >= k;
```

FIG. 12. Breadth-first parallel clustering by seed growing.

remains unchanged when we use random sampling. We use a simple approach for disambiguation: the lowest numbered cluster claiming a vertex claims it. We also experimented by attaching singleton nodes to nearby clusters to improve the quality of clustering.

Our peer pressure algorithm (Fig. 13) starts with a subset of nodes designated as leaders. There has to be at least one leader neighboring every vertex in the graph. This is followed by a round of voting where every vertex in the graph selects a

```
01 function cluster = peerpressure (G)
02 % Clustering by peer pressure
03
04 % Use maximal independent set routine from GAPDT
05 IS = mis (G);
06
07 % Find all neighbors in the independent set.
08 neighbors = G * sparse(IS, IS, 1, length(G),
        length(G));
09
10 % Each vertex chooses a random neighbor in the
        independent set.
11 R = sprand (neighbors);
12 [ignore, vote] = max (R, [], 2);
13
14 % Collect neighbor votes and join the most
        popular cluster.
15 [I, J] = find (G);
16 S = sparse (I, vote(J), 1, n, n);
17 [ignore, cluster] = max (S, [], 2);
```

FIG. 13. Parallel clustering by peer pressure.

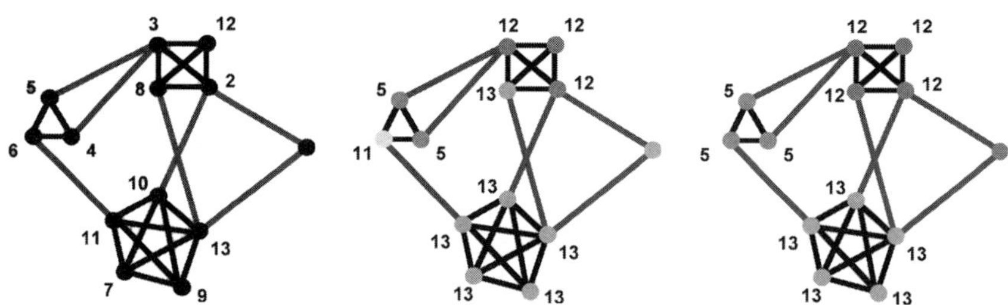


FIG. 14. The first graph is the input to the peer pressure algorithm. Every node then picks its largest numbered neighbor as a leader, as shown in the second graph. Finally, all nodes change their votes to the most popular vote amongst their neighbors, as shown in the third graph.

leader, selecting a cluster to join. This does not yet yield good clustering. Each vertex now looks at its neighbors and switches its vote to the most popular leader in its neighborhood. This last step is crucial, and in this case, it recovers more than 95% of the original clique structure of the graph. Figure 14 shows the different stages of the peer pressure algorithm on an example graph.

We experimented with different approaches to select leaders. At first, it seemed that a maximal independent set of nodes from the graph was a natural way to pick leaders. In practice, it turns out that simple heuristics (such as the highest numbered neighbor) gave equally good clustering. We also experimented with more than one round of voting. The marginal improvement in the quality of clustering was not worth the additional computation time.

## 5.6 Visualization of Large Graphs

Graphics and visualization are a key part of an interactive system such as MATLAB®. The question of how to effectively visualize large datasets in general, especially large graphs, is still unsolved. We successfully applied methods from numerical computing to come up with meaningful visualizations of the SSCA #2 graph.

One way to compute geometric co-ordinates for the nodes of a connected graph is to use Fiedler co-ordinates [20] for the graph. Figure 9 shows the Fiedler embedding of the SSCA #2 graph. In the 2-D case, we use the eigenvectors (Fiedler vectors) corresponding to the first two non-zero eigenvalues of the Laplacian matrix of the graph as co-ordinates for nodes of the graph in a plane.

For 3-D visualization of the SSCA #2 graph, we start with 3-D Fiedler co-ordinates projected onto the surface of a sphere. We model nodes of the graph as particles on the surface of a sphere. There is a repulsive force between all particles, inversely proportional to the distance between them. Since these particles repel each other on the surface of a sphere, we expect them to spread around and occupy the entire surface of the sphere. Since there are cliques in the original graph, we expect clusters of particles to form on the surface of the sphere. At each timestep, we compute a force vector between all pairs of particles. Each particle is then displaced by some distance based on its force vector. All displaced particles are projected back onto the sphere at the end of each time step.

This algorithm was used to generate Fig. 15. In this case, we simulated 256 particles and the system was evolved for 20 time steps. It is important to first calculate the Fiedler co-ordinates. Beginning with random co-ordinates results in a meaningless picture. We used PyMOL [12] to render the graph.

## 5.7 Experimental Results

We ran our implementation of SSCA #2 (ver 1.1, integer only) in STAR-P. The MATLAB® client was run on a generic PC. The STAR-P server was run on an SGI Altix with 128 Itanium II processors with 128G RAM (total, non-uniform memory access). We used a graph generated with scale 21. This graph has 2 million nodes.

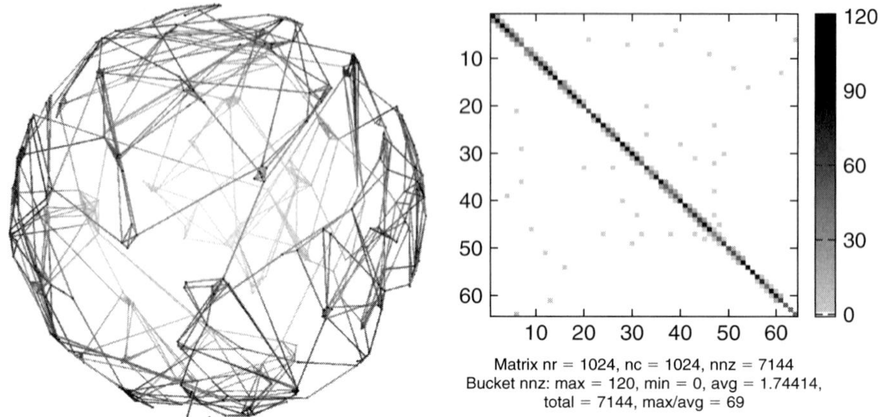


FIG. 15. The 3-D visualization of the SSCA #2 graph on the left is produced by relaxing the Fiedler co-ordinates projected onto the surface of a sphere. The right figure shows a density spy plot of the SSCA #2 graph.

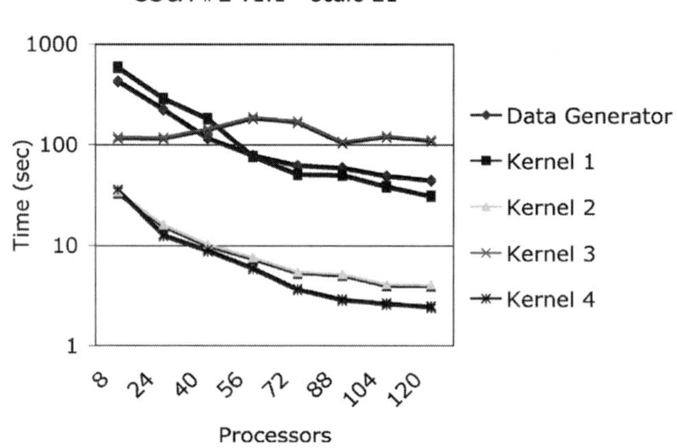


FIG. 16. SSCA #2 version 1.1 execution times (STAR-P, Scale = 21).

The multi-graph has 321 million directed edges; the undirected graph corresponding to the multi-graph has 89 million edges. There are 32 thousand cliques in the graph, the largest having 128 nodes. There are 89 million undirected edges within cliques, and 212 thousand undirected edges between cliques in the input graph for kernel 4. The results are presented in Fig. 16.

Our data generator scales well; the benchmark specification does not require the data generator to be timed. A considerable amount of time is spent in kernel 1, where data structures for the subsequent kernels are created. The majority of this time is spent in searching the input triples for duplicates, since the input graph is a multi-graph. Kernel 1 creates several sparse matrices using `sparse`, each corresponding to a layer in the multi-graph. Time spent in kernel 1 also scales very well with the number of processors. Time spent in Kernel 2 also scales as expected.

Kernel 3 does not show speedups at all. Although all the breadth-first searches are performed in parallel, the process of subgraph extraction for each starting point creates a lot of traffic between the STAR-P client and the STAR-P server, which are physically in different states. This client-server communication time dominates the computation time. This overhead can be minimized by vectorizing kernel 3 more aggressively.

Kernel 4, the non-trivial part of the benchmark, actually scales very well. We show results for our best performing implementation of kernel 4, which uses the seed-growing algorithm.

The evaluation criteria for the SSCAs also include software engineering metrics such as code size, readability and maintainability. Our implementation is extremely concise. We show the source lines of code (SLOC) for our implementation in Table II. We also show absolute line counts, which include blank lines and comments, as we believe these to be crucial for code readability and maintainability. Our implementation runs without modification in sequential MATLAB®, making it easy to develop and debug on the desktop before deploying on a parallel platform.

We have run the full SSCA #2 benchmark (version 0.9, integer only) on graphs with $2^{27} = 134$ million nodes on the SGI Altix. Scaling results for the full benchmark (version 1.1, integer only) are presented in Fig. 16. We have also generated and

TABLE II
LINE COUNTS FOR STAR-P IMPLEMENTATION OF SSCA #2. THE 'SOURCE LOC' COLUMN COUNTS ONLY EXECUTABLE LINES OF CODE, WHEREAS THE 'TOTAL LINE COUNTS' COLUMN COUNTS THE TOTAL NUMBER OF LINES INCLUDING COMMENTS AND WHITE SPACE

| Operation | Source LOC | Total Line Counts |
|---|---|---|
| Data generator | 176 | 348 |
| Kernel 1 | 25 | 63 |
| Kernel 2 | 11 | 34 |
| Kernel 3 | 23 | 48 |
| Kernel 4 (spectral) | 22 | 70 |
| Kernel 4 (seed growing) | 55 | 108 |
| Kernel 4 (peer pressure) | 6 | 29 |

manipulated extremely large graphs (1 billion nodes and 8 billion edges) on an SGI Altix with 256 processors using STAR-P.

This demonstrates that the sparse matrix representation is a scalable and efficient way to manipulate large graphs. It should be noted that the codes in Fig. 12 and Fig. 13 are not pseudocodes, but actual code excerpts from our implementation. Although the code fragments look very simple and structured, the computation manipulates sparse matrices, resulting in highly irregular communication patterns on irregular data structures.

## 6. Looking Forward: A Next-Generation Parallel Sparse Library

We now discuss the design goals of a next-generation parallel sparse library, based on our current experience.

Our initial goal was to develop a parallel sparse library for STAR-P similar to the one in MATLAB®. We wanted it to be robust, scalable, efficient and simple. Hence, all the design decisions we made always favored robustness and simplicity. For instance, we decided early on to support only the CSR data structure to store sparse matrices and to use a 1-D block layout by rows. A 2-D layout may be more efficient, and it would definitely be nice to support other data structures for storage. However, these would complicate the implementation to a point where it may not be possible to implement all the operations we currently support for all combinations of data structures and layouts.

There are some crucial differences between MATLAB® and STAR-P's sparse libraries. First, MATLAB®'s focus is solely on numerical computing. However, sparse matrices are increasingly lending themselves to more than just numerical computing. Second, parallel computing is still not as easy as sequential computing. Parallel sparse matrices provide an elegant way for a user to represent large sparse datasets as matrices without using complex data structures to store and query them. Operations on such large datasets often require irregular communication and irregular data access. Sparse matrix computations allow this to be done in a concise and systematic way, without worrying about low-level details. The use of distributed sparse matrices to represent graphs for combinatorial computing is one such example [33].

We have learnt some lessons from our experience with the STAR-P sparse matrix library, which might be helpful for the development of a next-generation parallel sparse library.

Although the CSR data structure has served us well, it does cause some problems. MATLAB® codes written to specifically take advantage of the column storage of sparse matrices must be rewritten to use row storage. Although it is not yet clear as to how much may be the performance difference for a real-life application, it is inconvenient for a user writing highly tuned codes using sparse matrices. Such a code will also have different performance characteristics in MATLAB® and STAR-P.

We propose adding a third design principle to the two stated in Section 4. The difference in performance between accessing a sparse matrix by rows or columns must be minimal. Users writing sparse matrix codes should not have to worry about organizing their sparse matrix accesses by rows or columns, just as they do not worry about how dense matrices are stored.

For an example of the third principle, consider the operation below. It is much simpler to extract the submatrix specified by $p$ from a matrix stored in the CSR format than from a matrix stored in the CSC format. In the latter case, a binary search is required for every column, making the operation slower.

```
>> A = S(p, :)     % p is a vector
```

A parallel sparse library that needs to scale to hundreds or thousands of processors will not work well with a one-dimensional block layout. A two-dimensional block layout is essential for scalability of several sparse matrix operations. The benefits of 2-D layouts are well known at this point, and we will not reiterate them. It is important to note that compressed row/column data structures are not efficient for storing sparse matrices in a 2-D layout.

Another point of departure is a different primitive for indexing operations. Currently, we use the 'sparse-find' method to perform all the indexing operations such as submatrix indexing, assignment, concatenation and transpose. We used the concept of the `sparse` function as a primitive, using which we built the rest of the operations. We propose that a next-generation sparse matrix library should use sparse matrix multiplication as the basic primitive in the library.

We illustrate the case of submatrix indexing using matrix multiplication. Suppose $A$ is a matrix, and we wish to extract the submatrix $B = A(I, J)$. Multiplying from the left picks out the rows, whereas multiplying from the right picks out the columns, as shown in code fragment 17.

We believe that it will be possible to implement sparse matrix multiplication more efficiently with a 2-D block distribution than with a 1-D block distribution for large numbers of processors. Indexing operations may then be implemented using sparse matrix multiplication as a primitive. An efficient sparse matrix multiplication implementation might actually use a polyalgorithm to simplify the implementation for special cases when more information is available about the structure of matrices being multiplied, as is the case for indexing operations.

The choice of a suitable data structure to store sparse matrices in a 2-D block layout and to allow for efficient matrix multiplication still remains an open question

```
01 function B = index_by_mult (A, I, J)
02 % Index a matrix with matrix multiplication
03
04 [nrows, nccols] = size(A);
05 nI = length(I);
06 nJ = length(J);
07
08 % Multiply on the left to pick the required rows
09 row_select = sparse(1:nI, I, 1, nI, nr);
10
11 % Multiply on the right to pick the required
      columns
12 col_select = sparse(J, 1:nJ, 1, nc, nJ);
13
14 % Compute B with sparse matrix multiplication
15 B = row_select * A * col_select;
```

FIG. 17. Matrix indexing and concatenation can be implemented using sparse matrix–matrix multiplication as a primitive. Multiplication from the left picks the necessary rows, whereas multiplication from the right picks the necessary columns.

for future research. We believe that once the right data structure is selected, there will not be a large difference in performance when multiplying from the left or the right. This directly translates into symmetric performance for all indexing operations when accessing a matrix either by rows or by columns. We believe that this will lead to higher programmer productivity, freeing users from tuning their codes in specific ways that depend on knowledge of the underlying implementation of indexing operations.

## 7. Conclusion

We described the design and implementation of a distributed sparse matrix infrastructure in STAR-P. This infrastructure was used to build the 'Graph Algorithms and Pattern Discovery Toolbox (GAPDT)'. We demonstrated the effectiveness of our tools by implementing a graph analysis benchmark in STAR-P, which scales to large problem sizes on large processor counts.

We conclude that distributed sparse matrices provide a powerful set of primitives for numerical and combinatorial computing. We hope that our experiences will shape the design of future parallel sparse matrix infrastructures in other languages.

## REFERENCES


[1] Amestoy P., Duff I. S., and L'Excellent J.-Y., 1998. Multifrontal solvers within the PARASOL environment. In *PARA*, pp. 7–11.

[2] Anderson E., Bai Z., Bischof C., Blackford S., Demmel J., Dongarra J., Du Croz J., Greenbaum A., Hammarling S., McKenney A., and Sorensen D., 1999. *LAPACK Users' Guide,* third edition Society for Industrial and Applied Mathematics, Philadelphia, PA.

[3] Bader D., Feo J., Gilbert J., Kepner J., Koester D., Loh E., Madduri K., Mann B., and Meuse T., HPCS scalable synthetic compact applications #2. Version 1.1.

[4] Bader D. A., Madduri K., Gilbert J. R., Shah V., Kepner J., Meuse T., and Krishnamurthy A., November 2006. Designing scalable synthetic compact applications for benchmarking high productivity computing systems. *Cyberinfrastructure Technology Watch.*

[5] Bailey D. H., Barszcz E., Barton J. T., Browning D. S., Carter R. L., Dagum D., Fatoohi R. A., Frederickson P. O., Lasinski T. A., Schreiber R. S., Simon H. D., Venkatakrishnan V., and Weeratunga S. K., Fall 1991. The NAS parallel benchmarks. *The International Journal of Supercomputer Applications*, **5**(3):63–73.

[6] Chan T. F., Gilbert J. R., and Teng S.-H., 1994. Geometric spectral partitioning. Technical Report CSL-94-15, Palo Alto Research Center, Xerox Corporation.

[7] Chen Y., Davis T. A., Hager W. W., and Rajamanickam S., 2006. Algorithm 8xx: Cholmod, supernodal sparse cholesky factorization and update/downdate. Technical Report TR-2006-005, University of Florida. Submitted to ACM Transactions on Mathematical Software.

[8] Choy R., and Edelman A., February 2005. Parallel MATLAB: doing it right. *Proceedings of the IEEE*, **93**:331–341.

[9] Cohen E., 1998. Structure prediction and computation of sparse matrix products. *Journal of Combinatorial Optimization*, **2**(4):307–332.

[10] Davis T. A., 2004. Algorithm 832: Umfpack v4.3—an unsymmetric-pattern multifrontal method. *ACM Transactions on Mathematical Software*, **30**(2):196–199.

[11] Davis T. A., 2006. *Direct Methods for Sparse Linear Systems (Fundamentals of Algorithms 2)*. Society for Industrial and Applied Mathematics, Philadelphia, PA, USA.

[12] DeLano W. L., and Bromberg S., 2004. *The PyMOL User's Manual*. DeLano Scientific LLC, San Carlos, CA, USA.

[13] Dongarra J. J., 1998. Performance of various computers using standard linear equations software in a FORTRAN environment. *SIGARCH Computer Architecture News*, **16**(1):47–69.

[14] Falgout R. D., Jones J. E., and Yang U. M., The design and implementation of hypre, a library of parallel high performance preconditioners. Design document from the hypre homepage.

[15] Gilbert J. R., Moler C., and Schreiber R., 1992. Sparse matrices in MATLAB: design and implementation. *SIAM Journal on Matrix Analysis and Applications*, **13**(1):333–356.

[16] Gilbert J. R., Reinhardt S., and Shah V., April 2007. An interactive environment to manipulate large graphs. In *Proceedings of the 2007 IEEE International Conference on Acoustics, Speech, and Signal Processing.*

[17] Gilbert J. R., Reinhardt S., and Shah V. B., 2006. High performance graph algorithms from parallel sparse matrices. In *Proceedings of the Workshop on state of the art in scientific and parallel computing.*

[18] Gilbert J. R., and Teng S.-H., 2002. Matlab mesh partitioning and graph separator toolbox. http://www.cerfacs.fr/algor/Softs/MESHPART/index.html.

[19] Gustavson F. G., 1978. Two fast algorithms for sparse matrices: multiplication and permuted transposition. *ACM Transactions on Mathematical Software*, **4**(3):250–269.

[20] Hall K., November 1970. An r-dimensional quadratic placement algorithm. *Management Science*, **17**(3):219–229.

[21] Husbands P., 1999. *Interactive Supercomputing*. PhD thesis, Massachussetts Institute of Technology.

[22] Husbands P., Isbell C., and Edelman A., 1999. MITMatlab: A tool for interactive supercomputing. In *SIAM Conference on Parallel Processing for Scientific Computing*.

[23] Ihaka R., and Gentleman R., 1996. R: a language for data analysis and graphics. *Journal of Computational and Graphical Statistics*, **5**(3):299–314.

[24] Interactive Supercomputing LLC. 2007. *Star-P Software Development Kit (SDK): Tutorial and Reference Guide*. Version 2.5.

[25] Li X. S., and Demmel J. W., 2003. SuperLU_DIST: a scalable distributed memory sparse direct solver for unsymmetric linear systems. *ACM Transactions on Mathematical Software*, **29**(2):110–140.

[26] Luby M., 1985. A simple parallel algorithm for the maximal independent set problem. In: *STOC '85: Proceedings of the seventeenth annual ACM symposium on Theory of computing*, pp. 1–10, ACM Press, New York, NY, USA.

[27] Maschhoff K., and Sorensen D., April 1996. A portable implementation of ARPACK for distributed memory parallel architectures. *Proceedings of Copper Mountain Conference on Iterative Methods*.

[28] Mathworks Inc. 2007. *MATLAB User's Guide*. Version 2007a.

[29] Pothen A., Simon H. D., and Liou K.-P., 1990. Partitioning sparse matrices with eigenvectors of graphs. *SIAM Journal of Matrix Analysis and Applications*, **11**(3):430–452.

[30] Robertson C., 2005. Sparse parallel matrix multiplication. Master's thesis, University of California, Santa Barbara, CA, USA.

[31] Shadid J. N., and Tuminaro R. S., 1992. Sparse iterative algorithm software for large-scale MIMD machines: an initial discussion and implementation. *Concurrency: Practice and Experience*, **4**(6):481–497.

[32] Shah V., and Gilbert J. R., 2004. Sparse matrices in Matlab*P: design and implementation. In L. Bougé and V. K. Prasanna, editors, *HiPC*, volume 3296 of *Lecture Notes in Computer Science*, pp. 144–155. Springer.

[33] Shah V. B., June 2007. *An Interactive System for Combinatorial Scientific Computing with an Emphasis on Programmer Productivity*. PhD thesis, University of California, Santa Barbara.

[34] van Rossum G., 2006. *Python Reference Manual*. Python Software Foundation. Version 2.5.

# Bibliographic Snapshots of High-Performance/High-Productivity Computing

MYRON GINSBERG

*HPC Research & Education,*
*Farmington Hills, MI,*
*USA*
*m.ginsberg@ieee.org*

**Abstract**

This chapter is intended to acquaint the reader with some of the important topics in high performance, or what is now being referred to as, 'high productivity computing' (HPC). The target audience is technical professionals who are not specialist in HPC. Some of the topics covered include: HPC benchmarking concerns and sample results in government research labs, private industry and academia; HPC environments in private industry vs. government labs/research sectors; emerging acceleration techniques to speed up scientific and engineering applications; the move to petaflop class hardware and software by 2010–2011; computational science programs to train future computer support staffs to exploit effectively and efficiently the emerging class of petaflop supercomputers; lists of some available HPC videos; studies by the U.S. Council on Competitiveness and others to improve U.S. global competitiveness. The emphasis is to provide mostly easily accessible internet references to these topics and at a level that enables the reader to discern possible relationships between his or her own specialty and the potential impact of HPC.



ADVANCES IN COMPUTERS, VOL. 72
ISSN: 0065-2458/DOI: 10.1016/S0065-2458(08)00006-5



Copyright © 2008 Elsevier Inc.
All rights reserved.

## 1. Introduction

The motivation for writing this chapter came from my desire to keep undergraduate and graduate students aware of HPC activities which could have direct or indirect influence on their academic studies and career objectives in a wide variety of computer-related disciplines. HPC issues are usually at the leading technological edge, but gradually filter down to impact larger and larger groups of people with very diverse computer interests. Unfortunately, the textbooks and faculty do not always provide early student awareness of such topics. Often exposure to such developments occurs after graduation and/or via emerging summer jobs or technical workshops. In my own case I started at the end of my junior year as a math major and continued throughout graduate school to spend many summers working in government research labs where I acquired significant insight into HPC. In college, I maintained a 'forbidden desk draw', which included technical articles which aroused my curiosity but which I sadly realized were very unlikely to ever be discussed in any of my formal courses. Thus, when I became a full-time faculty member I vowed that I would start exposing my students to some of those topics and attempt to relate them to various aspects of their formal computer science studies.

When I left full-time academia to work in private industry, I still maintained my desire to stimulate students with the excitement of HPC. For over 35 years I have continued to introduce HPC to students, faculty and a myriad of technical professionals while serving as a national and international HPC lecturer for ACM, SIAM, IEEE, ASME, SAE and Sigma Xi. I started to evolve what I euphemistically referred to as 'Bedtime Readings' in various HPC areas and distributed these guides whenever and wherever I gave lectures to both academic and city chapters of the aforementioned professional organizations. Since HPC tends to change very rapidly, so did the contents of my Bedtime Reading Lists, which also served as a means for me to keep up to date. This chapter has evolved from such reading lists. I hope it will be helpful to many of you who are not yet acquainted with numerous aspects of HPC.

My intent is NOT to provide an exhaustive compendium of all HPC references but rather to offer you snapshots of some interesting issues and concerns in the hope that many of you will be stimulated to explore these topics even if some of them are not explicitly mentioned in formal academic studies and/or textbooks. I have attempted to select recent (often very brief) references, most of which are available on the Internet with the URLs provided; for convenience, the references for each subsection are listed at the end of that subsection rather than at the end of the entire chapter. Content wise, these articles should be easily comprehendible and accessible to non-HPC scientific and engineering specialists in government labs, academia and private industry. No attempt is made to review in-depth details of advanced HPC issues or to review the computer science academic literature. Rather than paraphrase the content of the numerous references that I have compiled, I have tried to provide some brief commentary about the topics in each section and make a few remarks about what issues readers should keep in mind as they peruse many of the given articles. The natural bias in some of my remarks reflects my thoughts about many of these issues primarily from the viewpoint of an HPC person in private industry but also from the perspective of any scientist/engineer in private industry, a government research facility and/or in academia across a broad spectrum of computer-related disciplines. Most of the references come from vendor press releases, government and university research reports, abstracting services from ACM, SIAM, IEEE, HPCWIRE, EETimes, reports from U.S. Council on Competitiveness, etc. as well as from some of my own HPC papers.

Warning: The views expressed in this chapter are those of the author and do NOT necessarily reflect the perspective of any of the author's previous employers. I welcome any comments or suggestions from the readers about the content of this chapter; please send such remarks to m.ginsberg@ieee.org.

# 2. Computational Environments in Government, Academia and Industry

## 2.1 Overview of Computational Environments

There are some very distinct differences between the computational environments that exist in government research/academic centers and those in private industry. For example, the former tends to have large multidisciplinary support staffs to assist scientists and engineers with the details of their computational applications so that users can focus on details of their specific application. The support staff concentrates on fine-tuning the system's software and hardware as well as determining the optimal algorithms needed for high-speed performance on the given problem. Such centers also tend to have the very latest state-of-the-art HPC hardware and software technologies to support a myriad of applications. It is important to note that most government research/academic centers are using primarily in-house developed and/or open-source application softwares rather than commercial codes.

In sharp contrast, the industrial sector tends to have very small support staffs, often with little or no in-house in-depth multidisciplinary application expertise. Furthermore, the priority in most industrial facilities favors a very stable production environment which often excludes extensive access to leading-edge HPC hardware and software. The use of the latest research techniques is sometimes viewed by management as a risk to stability of their production environment.

In the typical industrial facility, most applications are solved using commercial independent software-based (ISVs) products which unfortunately often results in the accumulated use of lots of legacy code, which in turn makes it increasingly difficult to port industrial applications to the latest HPC environments. When a faster, more efficient HPC hardware/software solution exists, it may not be readily embraced unless it is already included in the ISV code in use in that specific industrial location. According to comments in several U.S. Counsel on Competitiveness supported studies (see [13–16]), most ISVs derive only a small percentage of their total revenue from HPC usage and thus tend to lack sufficient incentives to promote HPC, especially for larger industrial applications.

Fortunately, this situation is beginning to improve with widespread introduction of Windows-based HPC via MS CCS2003 [11]. Products such as MATLAB [10] and Star-P [12] combined with CCS2003 now empower users to generate from the desktop parallel application solutions interfaced with commodity cluster support.

It is very rare indeed for the technical people who would directly use HPC technology to also control the corporate resources to finance such equipment. At present, it is very rare indeed to find an industrial site which has successfully performed a return on investment (ROI) [18, 19] analysis for new HPC technology. This process is absolutely essential in order to cost justify rapidly to upper industrial management that a new and better approach for important applications is a financial benefit to corporate earnings. Even if upper management is convinced of the better solution, the financial resources may not be available within the company to expedite the use of the new HPC technology in a timely manner.

I personally witnessed an interesting example of this while working at a U.S. auto company during the 1980s. At that time, it took almost four years to convince upper management to obtain an in-house supercomputer because no other auto company had one, and management was not convinced of its immediate need. It then took another 7 years for auto companies in the rest of the world to acquire supercomputers. In contrast to this situation at a U.S. auto manufacturer, it only required about six months at a Japanese car company to accomplish this task after lower level technical people reached consensus on the need for an internal supercomputer. Then, upper management gave final corporate approval. The main difference is that in Japanese auto companies, technical professionals often attain high-level corporate positions and then mentor the low-level technical people; this promotes very good communications with those who control the corporate purse strings. In contrast, in U.S. auto companies, it is very rare for a technical professional to attain a very high-level corporate position; consequently dialogue with upper management does not tend to be as effective as with their Japanese counterpart.

The gap between the use of HPC in government/research sectors and private industry is still growing and is measured in as many as four to five years in some application areas. Action is being taken through a few government programs to narrow this chasm. Considerably more massive action must be taken to improve U.S. global competitiveness in the private sector; see [5–7] for more details. The issues in Fig. 1 summarize the major reasons why faster industrial HPC adoption has not yet occurred. Some current improvements in HPC in the industrial sector are given in Section 10.

Reference [20] based on Congressional testimony in 2003 by a Ford engineer, Vince Scarafino, indicates that since the mid 1990s, the use of commodity-based supercomputers as opposed to custom vector supercomputers (such as those made by Cray and NEC) have not really been as productive as possible with respect to a significant segment of the large automotive modeling applications.

**Government vs. Industrial HPC Environments**

| | |
|---|---|
| ➢ Leading-edge hardware | ➢ Stable commercial hardware |
| ➢ In-house applications software | ➢ Commercial ISV-based application software |
| ➢ Large, diverse in-house support | ➢ Small in-house support staff |
| ➢ Research mindset | ➢ Production mindset |

Dr. Myron Ginsberg • HPC Research & Education •

FIG. 1. Government vs. industrial HPC environments.

## REFERENCES


[1] The Council on Competitiveness, 2004 HPC Users Conference: Supercharging U.S. Innovation & Competitiveness, Report and DVD available, The Council on Competitiveness, http://www.compete.org/hpc/hpc_conf_report.asp, 2005.

[2] Council on Competitiveness, *High Performance Computing Software Workshop Report: Accelerating Innovation for Competitive Advantage: The Need for HPC Application Software Solutions*, July 13, 2005, Council on Competitiveness, Washington, D.C. 20005, January 2006.

[3] Council on Competitiveness, *Second Annual High Performance Computing Users Conference Report*, Report and DVD available, Council on Competitiveness, Washington, D.C. 20005, March 2006.

[4] Curns T., June 17, 2005. Improving ISV Applications to Advance HPC, *HPCWIRE*, Vol. **14**, No. 24, http://www.hpcwire.com/hpc/397415.html.

[5] Ginsberg M., 2001. Influences on the Solution Process for Large, Numeric-Intensive Automotive Simulations, *Lecture Notes in Computer Science Series*, Vol. **2073**, Springer, pp. 1189–1198.

[6] Ginsberg M., May 2005. Impediments to Future Use of Petaflop Class Computers for Large-Scale Scientific/Engineering Applications in U.S. Private Industry, Proc., International Conference on Computational Science (ICCS 2005) *Lecture Notes in Computer Science Series*, Vol. **3514**, Springer-Verlag, Berlin, pp. 1059–1066.

[7] Ginsberg M., June 2007. Challenges and Opportunities for U.S. Private Industry Utilization of HPC Technology, Proc., International Conference on Scientific Computing, World Congress in Computer Science, Computer Engineering, and Applied Computing, WORLDCOMP07, Monte Carlo Hotel and Resort, Las Vegas, NV, 25–28.

[8] Graham S. L., Snir M., and Patterson C. A. (eds.), 2004. Getting Up to Speed: The Future of Supercomputing, U.S. National Academy of Sciences CSTB Report, see http://www.cstb.org/project_supercomputing.html prepublication on-line version at http://books.nap.edu/catalog/11148.html executive summary, http://www.nap.edu/catalog/11148.html.

[9] HECRTF, Federal Plan for High-End Computing: Report of the High-End Computing Revitalization Task Force (HECRTF), Executive Office of the President, Office of Science and Technology Policy, Washington, D.C., May 10, 2004 (second printing – July 2004), available at http://www.ostp.gov/nstc/html/HECRTF-FINAL_051004.pdf.

[10] HPCWIRE, The MathWorks Announces Support for Microsoft CCS, *HPCWIRE*, Vol. **15**, No. 24, http://www.hpcwire.com/hpc/687944.html, June 16, 2006.
[11] HPCWIRE, Microsoft Releases Windows Compute Cluster Server 2003, *HPCWIRE*, Vol. **15**, No. 24, http://www.hpcwire.com/hpc/692814.html, June 16, 2006.
[12] ISC, The Star-P Platform: Delivering Interactive Parallel Computing Power to the Desktop, White paper, ISC, Waltham, MA, 2006, http://www.interactivesupercomputing.com/downloads/ISCwhitepaper.pdf.
[13] Joseph E., Snell A., and Willard C. G., July 2004. *Council on Competitiveness Study of U.S. Industrial HPC Users*, White paper, IDC, Framingham, MA, paper available at http://www.compete.org/pdf/HPC_Users_Survey.pdf.
[14] Joseph E., et al., July 2005. Study of ISVs Serving the High Performance Computing Market: The Need for Better Application Software, Council on Competitiveness Initiative, White paper, IDC, Framingham, MA, http://www.compete.org/pdf/HPC_Software_Survey.pdf.
[15] Joseph E., et al., May 2006. Council on Competitiveness Study of Industrial Partnerships with the National Science Foundation (NSF) IDC White Paper on Council of Competitiveness Study of Industrial Partnerships with The National Science Foundation (NSF), Council of Competitiveness, Washington, D.C., http://www.compete.org/pdf/Council_NSF_Partnership_Study.pdf.
[16] Joseph E., et al., June 2006. Industrial Partnerships through the NNSA Academic Strategic Alliance Program IDC White paper on Council on Competitiveness Study of Industrial Partnerships with the U.S. Department of Energy NNSA, Council on Competitiveness, Washington, D.C. http://www.compete.org/pdf/Council_NNSA_Partnership_Study.pdf.
[17] President's Information Technology Advisory Committee, Computational Science: Ensuring America's Competitiveness, PITAC, Office of the President, Washington, D.C., http://www.nitrd.gov/pitac/reports/20050609_computational/computational.pdf, June 2005.
[18] Reuther A., and Tichenor S., November 2006. Making the Business Case for High Performance Computing: A Benefit-Cost Analysis Methodology, *CTWatch Quarterly*, Vol. **2**, No. 4A, pp. 2–8, http://www.ctwatch.org/quarterly/articles/2006/11/making-the-business-case-for-high-performance-computing-a-benefit-cost-analysis-methodology.
[19] Tichenor S., November 2006. Application Software for High Performance Computers: A Soft Spot for U.S. Business Competitiveness, *CTWatch Quarterly*, Vol. **2**, No. 4A, pp. 39–45, http://www.ctwatch.org/quarterly/articles/2006/11/application-software-for-high-performance-computers-a-soft-spot-for-us-business-competitiveness.
[20] Scarafino V., July 16, 2003. The National Needs for Advanced Scientific Computing and Industrial Applications, Statement of The Ford Motor Company, Committee on Science, U.S. House of Representatives, http://www.house.gov/science/hearings/full03/jul16/scarafino.htm, see http://www.techlawjournal.com/home/newsbriefs/2003/07d.asp under 7/16. The House Science Committee Holds Hearing on Supercomputing titled Supercomputing: Is the U.S. on the Right Path?, paragraphs 4–7 inclusive.

# 3. Computational Science Education (CSE)

## 3.1 The Academic Origins of CSE

The early computer science departments started in the late 1960s. Initially, many had origins in mathematical science departments. In attempts to gain academic legitimacy, many such departments strongly believed that they must focus on a very theoretical foundation which is indeed a necessity for a new academic discipline. Several early computer science departments had strong roots in numerical analysis, which had a long and distinguished history in math departments. Soon other areas developed to enhance the theoretical landscape. This was great for producing academic faculty members, but was not so effective for producing graduates who desired to be 'users' of computing technology. At the other extreme, some computer science departments thought that the focus should be on learning multiple programming languages or systems programming and still others thought the emphasis should be on computer hardware. What tended to evolve are computer science departments that were very good at creating people for academic positions but tended to neglect the training of those who wanted to be users of computers in industry. Eventually, electrical engineering departments started developing computer science programs. The people who ended up working in computing in industry tended to learn what they needed via on-the-job training; for example even now (in 2007), few computer science program graduates have any exposure to use of commercial computer applications software such as those used in industry. As the industrial problems became more complex, some visionary computer science people realized that applied computer science needed to focus in a new direction. This recognition has now led to the creation of upwards of over 50 computational science programs (CSE) in the U.S. and abroad.

## 3.2 A Sampling of CSE Programs in the U.S.

Figure 2 lists some of the current U.S. educational institutions which have an undergraduate and/or graduate program in Computational Science. I am not aware of any comprehensive, up-to-date list of all such programs in the U.S. and elsewhere in the world. The references [11–14] offer some details about these initiatives and other such Computational Science programs. Such academic offerings can be centered in math, computer science, electrical engineering, or physics departments or even in a nuclear engineering program. Some newer programs are going one step further and establishing systems or informational science programs.

## 3.3 Impediments to the Growth of CSE Programs

Unfortunately, a prominent barrier to further expansion of CSE programs is the 'academic turf wars', which often seem to be overly concerned about which academic department should be the recipient of the semester credit hours for CSE courses!! CSE is inherently multidisciplinary in nature, involving theory, experimentation, and computer simulations. Graduates of CSE programs must have exposure to a variety of physical problems, mathematics that can be used as tools to analyze such problems, combined with insight from computer simulations in order to determine an optimal solution to the problem.

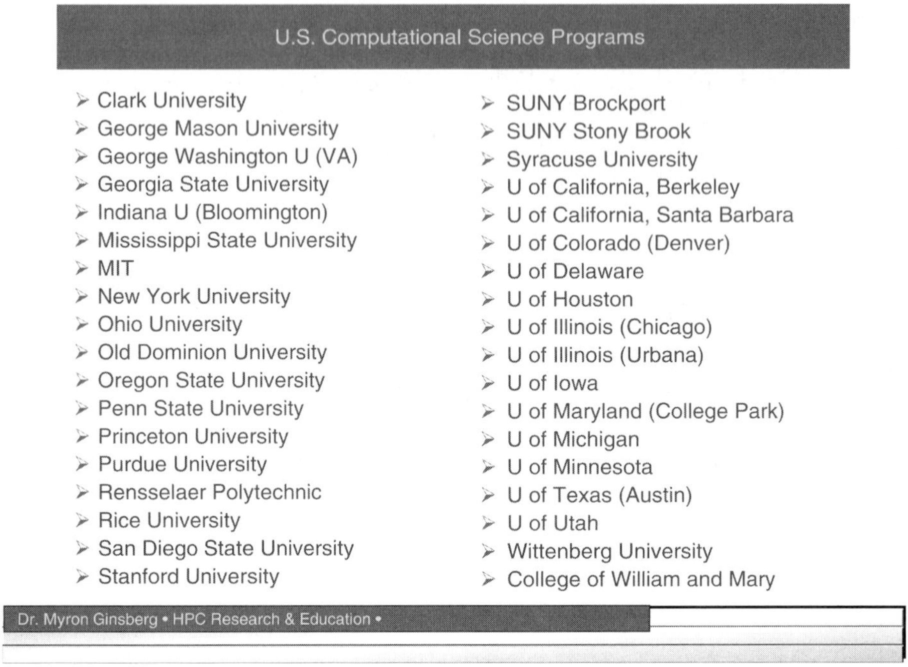

FIG. 2. U.S. computational science programs.

I have visited many of the existing CSE programs in the U.S. and Canada as well as institutions considering the creation of such a program. A simple litmus test to estimate if such a program is likely to succeed is to ask the existing faculty members the following three questions: 1. Do you frequently eat and/or socialize with other members of your own department regardless of their area of specialization? 2. Do you frequently eat and/or socialize with other faculty members in other departments of the same college in the university? 3. Do you frequently eat and/or socialize with faculty members in other departments in other colleges of the university? If the responses are generally affirmative, then there is a likely chance that a CSE program will be successful. Warning: This is not a foolproof test.

## 3.4 Content Needs in CSE Programs

It is very difficult to provide adequate exposure to all aspects of computational science in an undergraduate program because of the existing number of required courses already contained in such programs. Any attempt to do so must include one or more large student projects within the program and/or supplemented by apprenticeships offered in government labs and/or private industry. In most current industrial situations, the personnel working on a specific application usually could be characterized as having expertise in the problem discipline or in the computer science area. A crucial ingredient for success of a CSE program is the inclusion of a large variety of techniques which can be readily applied to a vast spectrum of problems across a vast expanse of disciplines.

For industrial success, at present and in the future, U.S. private industry must recruit a large number of trained personnel in computational science to fill in all the gaps between the discipline specialists and the computer science support people, especially as the HPC hardware and software demands grow with the introduction of petaflop class machines by 2010–2011. Most current computational scientists are working in government labs or in federally funded academic research centers. There is thus a severe scarcity of such people in U.S. private industry. The net effect is impeding of the growth of industrial HPC usage.

## 3.5 Comments on Section References

The references in this section fall into several categories: representative examples of a few recent CSE textbooks [6, 10, 16], examples of undergraduate and graduate CSE curricula including some vignettes about participating students [11–14], loss of computer science students and how to attract more students into CSE [2, 7–9, 17], leadership training [15].

I also want to direct your attention to an evolving course on 'HPC Concepts, Methods, and Means' created under the direction of Dr. Thomas Sterling at LSU; by the time you read this, the second iteration of the course should be in progress on the Internet at several colleges during the 2008 Spring semester. A textbook and several support documents should be available on the LSU web site by then. For more information, contact Dr. Sterling (mailto: tron@cct.lsu.edu) or look at http://www.cct.lsu.edu/csc7600/index.html. This web site has a recorded message from Dr. Sterling that briefly describes the HPC course and contains a complete class syllabus, a history of HPC, course info and a list of people involved including affiliates. I strongly encourage you to check out this course if you have any interest in learning more about HPC.

### References

[1] HPCWIRE, Economic Benefits of HPC Discussed at LSU, *HPCWIRE*, Vol. **16**, No. 23, http://www.hpcwire.com/hpc/1601590.html, June 8, 2007.

[2] HPCWIRE, Encouraging More Women in Science & Technology, *HPCWIRE*, Article 461928, http://news.taborcommunications.com/msgget.jsp?mid=461928&xsl, August 26, 2005.
[3] HPCWIRE, George Mason Announces New Type of IT Degree, *HPCWIRE*, Vol. **16**, No. 23, http://www.hpcwire.com/hpc/1601630.html, June 8, 2007.
[4] HPCWIRE, IBM, SHARE to Build Network of Mainframe Experts, *HPCWIRE*. Article 461061, http://news.taborcommunications.com/msgget.jsp?mid=461061&xsl=story.xsl., August 26, 2005.
[5] HPCWIRE, LSU Offers Distance Learning Course in HPC, *HPCWIRE*, Vol. **16**, No. 4, http://www.hpcwire.com/hpc/1225496.html, January 26, 2007.
[6] Landau R. H., 2005. A First Course in Scientific Computing: Symbolic, Graphic, and Numeric Modeling Using Maple, Java, Mathematica, and Fortran 90, Princeton University Press, Princeton, NJ.
[7] Madhavan K. P. C., Goasguen S., and Bertoline G. R., September 16, 2005. Talk Xanga: Capturing Gen-Zs Computational Imagination, HPCWIRE, http://news.taborcommunications.com/msgget.jsp?mid=471717&xsl=story.xsl.
[8] Murphy T., Gray P., Peck C., and Joiner D., August 26, 2005. New Directions for Computational Science Education, *HPCWIRE*, http://news.taborcommunications.com/msgget.jsp?mid=461139&xsl=story.xsl.
[9] Oblinger D. G., and Oblinger J. L. (eds.), 2005. Educating the Net Generation, educause.edu, http://www.educause.edu/ir/library/pdf/pub7101.pdf.
[10] Scott L. R., Clark T., and Bagheri B., 2005. Scientific Parallel Computing, Princeton University Press, Princeton, NJ.
[11] SIAM Working Group on CSE Education, Graduate Education in Computational Science and Engineering, March 2001. *SIAM Rev.*, Vol. **43**, No. 1, pp. 163–177.
[12] SIAM Working Group on CSE Education, Graduate Education for Computational Science and Engineering, http://www.siam.org/students/resources/report.php, 2007.
[13] SIAM Working Group on CSE Undergraduate Education, Undergraduate Computational Science and Engineering Education, SIAM, Philadelphia, http://www.siam.org/about/pdf/CSE_Report.pdf, September 2006.
[14] Swanson C. D., November 2003. Computational Science Education, Krell Institute, http://www.krellinst.org/services/technology/CSE_survey/index.html.
[15] West J. E., September 15, 2006. Leading for the Trenches *HPCWIRE*, http://www.hpcwire.com/hpc/890169.html, http://www.onlytraitofaleader.com.
[16] Shiflet A. B., and Shiflet G. W., 2006. Introduction to Computational: Modeling and Simulation for the Sciences, Princeton University Press, Princeton, NJ.
[17] Committee on Science, Engineering, and Public Policy (COSEPUP). *Rising Above the Gathering Storm: Energizing and Employing America for a Brighter Economic Future*, National Academy Press, http://www.nap.edu/catalog/11463.html, 2007.

# 4. Supercomputing Architecture

## 4.1 Distinguishing Differences Among the Content of Sections 4 through 8 Inclusive

Sections 4 through 8 inclusive overlap somewhat, but the focus is different in each of these: Section 4 spotlights specific architecture, while Section 5 presents HPC issues across these diverse architectures. Section 6 examines specific scientific and engineering application performance on many of the computers discussed in previous sections. Section 7 concentrates on specific heterogeneous components to enhance speed on one or more of the aforementioned architectures. Section 8 spotlights the initial attempts to create several petaflop systems developed within and external to the U.S. and to do so by the end of the first decade of the $21^{st}$ century. For those readers with little or no computer architecture background, I have intentionally avoided the inclusion of detailed hardware discussions and have provided mostly general layman-level articles in all these sections. For those desiring more information about the evolution of these machines, I recommend perusing a few recent publications of Hennessy and Patterson including in this section, [56, 89, 90], as well as several overviews provided in [86, 106] as well as in the two videos [20, 100].

## 4.2 Differentiating References for Specific Architectures

For specific architectures, see the following: for IBM Blue Gene/L, see the entire special issue [102] as well as [3–6, 10–12, 41, 48, 54, 64, 77, 102]; for the new BlueGene/P, see [5, 47, 69]; for the Sony PS3 as a potential supercomputer using the IBM Cell architecture, see [15, 16, 85A]; for the Cray Red Storm and its descendents XT3, XT4, see [2A, 2B, 14, 17, 32–36, 79, 82, 102A]; for the Cray X1 and X1E, see [26–30, 72, 84, 88, 92] for Cray XMT, see [38A, 38B]; for vector computers, see the Cray X1 and Cray X1E references above as well as NEC [59,73,78]. For instructional-level parallelism, see Chapters 2 and 3 in [56]; for multi-processor parallelism, see chapter 4 of [56] and for vector processors, see appendix F of [56]. For new low-energy computer, see [47B]. See [106] for more details of recent supercomputers not explicitly mentioned in this section.

### References

[1] Abts D., November 2004. Achieving a Balanced System Design, http://www.cray.com/downloads/sc2004/sc2004_dabts_balance.pdf SC2004, Pittsburgh, PA.

[2] Abts D., November 2004. Why Scalability and Reliability Are Inseparable, http://www.cray.com/downloads/sc2004/SC2004_dabts_ras2.pdf SC2004, Pittsburgh, PA.

[2A] Abts D., November 2004. The Cray BlackWidow: A Highly Scalable Vector Multiprocessor, http://sc07.supercomputing.org/schedule/pdf/pap392.pdf, SC07, Reno, NV.

[2B] Alam S. R., et al., November 2007. Cray XT4: An Early Evaluation for Petascale Scientific Simulation, http://sc07.supercomputing.org/schedule/pdf/pap201.pdf, SC07, Reno, NV.

[3] Almasi G., et al., August 2003. An Overview of the BlueGene/L System Software Organization, Proc., Euro-Par 2003 Conference, *Lecture Notes in Computer Science*, Springer-Verlag, http://www.llnl.gov/asci/platforms/bluegenel/pdf/software.pdf.

[4] Almasi G., et al., November 2004. Unlocking the Performance of the BlueGene/L Supercomputer, *Preliminary version* submitted to SC2004: High Performance Computing, Networking and Storage Conference, 6–12.

[5] Argonne National Laboratory, First IBM BlueGene/P Supercomputer Will Go to Argonne. *HPCWIRE*, Vol. **16**, No. 26, http://www.hpcwire.com/hpc/1633752.html, June 29, 2007.

[6] ASCII BlueGene/L Computing Platform, http://www.llnl.gov/asc/computing_resources/bluegenel/.

[7] ASCI Red Homepage, http://www.sandia.gov/ASCI/Red/.

[8] ASCI Purple Benchmark Page, http://www.llnl.gov/asc/computing_resources/purple/.

[9] ASCI White Homepage, http://www.llnl.gov/asci/platforms/white.

[9A] Banks M., September 4, 2007. Get Ready for HPC in the Mainstream, ITPRO, http://www.itpro.co.uk/features/123256/ get-ready-for-hpc-in-the-mainstream.html.

[10] The BlueGene/L Team, An Overview of the BlueGene/L Supercomputer, SC2002, paper available at http://sc-2002.org/paperpdfs/pap.pap207.pdf, November 2002.

[11] BlueGene/L: Applications, Architecture and Software Workshop Papers, Reno, NV, http://www.llnl.gov/asci/platforms/bluegene/agenda.html#links, October 2003.

[12] BlueGene/L Resources, http://www.llnl.gov/asc/computing_resources/bluegenel/.

[13] Brown D. H., October 2004. Associates, Inc., Cray XD1 Brings High-Bandwidth Supercomputing to the Mid-Market, White paper, Brown D. H., Associates, Inc., paper available at http://www.cray.com/downloads/dhbrown_crayxd1_oct2004.pdf.

[14] Brown D. H., January 19, 2005. Associates, Inc., *Cray XT3 MPP Delivers Scalable Performance*, White paper, Brown D. H., Associates, Inc., http://www.cray.com/downloads/05.01.19.CrayXT3.pdf.

[15] Buttari A., et al., May 2007. Limitations of the Playstation 3 for High Performance Cluster Computing, UTK Knoxville, TN, Computer Science Technical Report CS-07-594, http://www.netlib.org/utk/people/JackDongarra/PAPERS/ps3-summa-2007.pdf.

[16] Buttari A., et al., April 17, 2007. SCOP3: A Rough Guide to Scientific Computing on the Playstation 3, UTK, Knoxville, TN, Computer Science Technical Report UT-CS-07-595, http://www.netlib.org/utk/people/JackDongarra/PAPERS/scop3.pdf.

[17] Camp W. J., and Tomkins J. L., 2003. *The Design Specification and Initial Implementation of the Red Storm Architecture – in partnership with Cray Inc.*, CCIM, Sandia National Laboratories, Albuquerque, NM.

[18] Chamberlain B., September 14, 2005. An Introduction to Chapel – Cray Cascade's High-Productivity Language, AHPCRC/DARPA PGAS Conference, http://chapel.cs.washington.edu/ChapelForAHPCRC.pdf.

[18A] Chamberlain R. D., et al., November 2007. Application Development on Hybrid Systems, http://sc07.supercomputing.org/schedule/pdf/pap442.pdf, SC07, Reno, NV.

[19] A collection of FPGA references, http://www.openfpga.org/web_resource.shtml.

[20] Computer Museum, The Cray-1 Supercomputer: 30$^{th}$ Anniversary Event-Celebrating the Man and the Machine, September 21, 2006, http://www.computerhistory.org/events/index.php?id=1157047505 or http://archive.computerhistory.org/lectures/the_Cray_1_supercomputer_celebrating_the_man_and_the_machine.lecture.2006.09.21.wmv available for purchase from the Computer History Museum, 1401 N. Shoreline Blvd., Mountain View, CA 94043.

[21] Cray, Inc., Chapel – The Cascade High-Productivity Language, Chapel Programming Language Homepage, http://chapel.cs.washington.edu/.

[22] Cray, Inc., July 9, 2003. DARPA HPCS Cray Cascade Project, http://www.cray.com/cascade/.

[23] Cray, Inc., CAE Strategy: The XD1 Supercomputer, http://www.cray.com/downloads/sc2004/SC2004-CAE_nov4_pp.pdf.

[24] Cray, Inc., Technical Specifications, http://www.cray.com/products/xt3/specifications.html.
[25] Cray, Inc., 2004. The Cray XD1 High Performance Computer: Closing the gap between peak and achievable performance in high performance computing, White paper, WP-0020404, Cray Inc., Seattle, WA, paper available at http://www.cray.com/downloads/whitepaper_closing_the_gap.pdf.
[26] Cray, Inc., Cray X1E Datasheet, http://www.cray.com/downloads/X1E_datasheet.pdf.
[27] Cray, Inc., Cray X1E Technical Specifications, http://www.cray.com/products/x1e/specifications.html.
[28] Cray, Inc., Cray X1E Supercomputer Sample Configurations, http://www.cray.com/products/x1e/configurations.html.
[29] Cray, Inc., Cray X1E Supercomputer, http://www.cray.com/products/x1e/index.html.
[30] Cray, Inc., Cray X1E System Architecture, http://www.cray.com/products/x1e/architecture.html.
[31] Cray, Inc., Cray XT3 Scalability, http://www.cray.com/products/xt3/scalability.html.
[32] Cray, Inc., 2004. Cray XT3 Datasheet, http://www.cray.com/downloads/Cray_XT3_Datasheet.pdf.
[32A] Cray, Inc., September 14, 2007. Cray to Deliver Quad-Core Opteron Supers by the End of Year, *HPCWIRE*, Vol. **16**, No. 37, http://www.hpcwire.com/hpc/1771434.html.
[33] Cray, Inc., Cray Inc. Begins Shipping Cray XT3 Massively Parallel Supercomputer Based on Sandia 'Red Storm' Design, http://investors.cray.com/phoenix.zhtml?c=98390&p=irol-newsArticle&ID=634922&highlight=.
[34] Cray, Inc., Cray XT3 Supercomputer Overview, http://www.cray.com/products/xt3/index.html.
[35] Cray, Inc., Cray XT3 System Sample Configurations, http://www.cray.com/products/xt3/configurations.html.
[36] Cray, Inc., Cray XT3 3D Torus Direct Connected Processor Architecture, http://www.cray.com/products/xt3/architecture.html.
[37] Cray, Inc., System Balance – an HPC Performance Metric, http://www.cray.com/products/xd1/balance.html.
[38] Cray, Inc., February 26–28, 2007. Cray Technical Workshop, Gaylord Opryland Hotel, Nashville, TN, http://nccs.gov/news/workshops/cray/cray_agenda.pdf.
[38A] Cray, Inc., September 21, 2007. Pacific Northwest National Lab Acquires Cray XMT Super, *HPCWIRE*, Vol. **16**, No. 38, http://www.hpcwire.com/hpc/1789165.html.
[38B] Cray, Inc., Cray XMT Datasheet, http://www.cray.com/downloads/Cray_XMT_Datasheet.pdf.
[39] Curns T., June 3, 2005. Japan: Poised for a Supercomputings Comeback? HPCWIRE, http://news.taborcommunications.com/msgget.jsp?mid=391555&xsl=story.xsl.
[40] DARPA, DARPA Selects Three High Productivity Computing Systems (HPCS) Projects, http://www.darpa.mil/body/NewsItems/pdf/hpcs_phii_4.pdf, July 8, 2003.
[41] Davis K., et al., November 2004. A Performance and Scalability Analysis of the BlueGene/L Architecture, SC2004, Pittsburgh, PA, http://www.sc-conference.org/sc2004/schedule/pdfs/pap302.pdf.
[42] Deitz S., October 21, 2005. Chapel: Compiler Challenges, LCPC, http://chapel.cs.washington.edu/ChapelForLCPC.pdf.
[43] DeRose L., November 2004. Performance Analysis and Visualization with Cray Apprentice2, http://www.cray.com/downloads/sc2004/SC04-Apprentice2.pdf SC2004, Pittsburgh, PA.
[44] Elnozahy M., April 7, 2006. IBM Has Its PERCS, *HPCWIRE*, http://www.hpcwire.com/hpc/614724.html.
[45] Earth Simulator Homepage, http://www.es.jamstec.go.jp/esc/eng/index.html.
[46] Feldman M., November 24, 2006. DARPA Selects Cray and IBM for Final Phase of HPCS, Vol. **15**, No. 4, http://www.hpcwire.com/hpc/1119092.html.

[47] Feldman M., June 29, 2007. IBM Enters Petascale Era with Blue Gene/P, *HPCWIRE*, Vol. **16**, No. 26, http://www.hpcwire.com/hpc/1636039.html.

[47A] Feldman M., September 14, 2007. New Opterons Headed for Supercomputing Stardom, *HPCWIRE*, Vol. **16**, No. 37, http://www.hpcwire.com/hpc/1778857.html.

[47B] Feldman M., October 19, 2007. SiCortex Machine Gets Warm Reception at Argonne, *HPCWIRE*, Vol. **16**, No. 42, http://www.hpcwire.com/hpc/1842713.html.

[48] Gara A., et al., March/May 2005. Overview of the BlueGene/L System Architecture, IBM J. Res. & Dev., Vol. **49**, No. 2/3, http://www.research.ibm.com/journal/rd/492/gara.pdf.

[49] Goedecker S., and Hoisie A., 2001. Performance Optimization of Numerically Intensive Codes, SIAM, Philadelphia.

[50] Goh E. L., July 2004. SGI Project Ultraviolet: Our Next Generation HEC Architecture: Multi-ParadigmComputing, http://www.sgi.com/features/2004/july/project_ultraviolet/.

[51] Gokhale M. B., and Graham P. S., 2005. Reconfigurable Computing: Accelerating Computation with Field-Programmable Gate Arrays, Springer-Verlag.

[52] Gustafson J. L., August 7, 2003. DARPA HPCS Sun Hero Project, http://www.ncsc.org/casc/meetings/CASC2.pdf.

[53] Gustafson J. L., November 14, 2006. Understanding the Different Acceleration Technologies, *HPCWIRE*, Vol. **13**, No. 2, http://www.hpcwire.com/hpc/1091512.html.

[54] Haff G., August 22, 2005. Blue Gene's Teraflop Attack, Illuminata, Inc., Nashua, NH, http://www-03.ibm.com/servers/deepcomputing/pdf/teraflopattackilluminata.pdf.

[55] Harbaugh L. G., June 2004. *Building High-Performance Linux Clusters* (Sponsored by Appro), White paper, paper available at http://www.appro.com/whitepaper/whitepaper.pdf.

[56] Hennessy J., and Patterson D. A., October 2006. Computer Architecture: A Quantitative Approach, 4$^{th}$ Edition, Morgan Kauffman, San Francisco, CA.

[57] Hester P., June 29, 2007. Peta-Scale x86: Heterogeneous Processing Comes of Age, Hot Seat Session, Part 1, International Supercomputing Conference, Dresden, Germany. For additional information, please contact mailto: Rob.Keosheyan@amd.com.

[58] High-End Crusader, Petascale Computer Architecture: HEC Interviews Sterling, *HPCWIRE*, Vol. **14**, No. 18. http://news.taborcommunications.com/msgget.jsp?mid=377690&xsl=story.xsl., May 6, 2005.

[59] HPCWIRE, NEC Unveils New Fastest Supercomputer – 65 TFLOPS, *HPCWIRE*, Vol. **13**, No. 42, http://www.taborcommunications.com/hpcwire/hpcwireWWW/04/1022/108601.html, October 21, 2004.

[60] HPCWIRE, Research Labs Tap Star-P, *HPCWIRE*, Vol. **15**, No. 43, http://www.hpcwire.com/hpc/1017010.html, October 27, 2006.

[61] HPCWIRE, Cluster Computing: MSC. Software Delivers MD Nastran for Windows CCS, *HPCWIRE*, Vol. **15**, No. 44, http://www.hpcwire.com/hpc/1045404.html, November 3, 2006.

[62] HPCWIRE, Vendor Spotlight: Interactive Supercomputing Awarded NSF Grant, *HPCWIRE*, Vol. **15**, No. 47, http://www.hpcwire.com/hpc/1131808.html, December 1, 2006.

[63] HPCWIRE, Researchers Unveil New Parallel Processing Technology, *HPCWIRE*, Vol. **16**, No. 26, http://www.hpcwire.com/hpc/1630525.html and see http://www.umiacs.umd.edu/users/vishkin/XMT/spaa07paper.pdf and http://www.umiacs.umd.edu/users/vishkin/XMT/spaa07talk.pdf, June 29, 2007.

[64] IBM's Web Site on BlueGene, http://www.research.ibm.com/bluegene/ and http://www-03.ibm.com/servers/deepcomputing/bluegenel.html.

[65] IBM, Inc., DARPA HPCS IBM PERCS Project, http://www.research.ibm.com/resources/news/20030710_darpa.shtml, July 10, 2003.

[66] IBM, Inc., IBM to Build Cell-Based Supercomputer for Los Alamos, *HPCWIRE*, Vol. **15**, No. 36, http://www.hpcwire.com/hpc/872363.html, September 8, 2006.

[67] IBM, Inc., The X10 Programming Language, http://domino.research.ibm.com/comm/research_projects.nsf/pages/x10.index.html, March 17, 2006.

[68] IBM, Inc., Report on the Experimental Language X10, Draft v 0.41, http://domino.research.ibm.com/comm/research_projects.nsf/pages/x10.index.html/$FILE/ ATTH4YZ5.pdf, February 7, 2006.

[69] IBM, Inc., June 26, 2007. IBM Triples Performance of World's Fastest, Most Energy-Efficient Supercomputer: New BlueGene/P Designed to Break the 'Quadrillion' Barrier, see the following three references about BlueGene/P: http://www-03.ibm.com/press/us/en/pressrelease/21791. wss, http://www-03.ibm.com/servers/deepcomputing/bluegene.html, and http://www-03.ibm.com/servers/deepcomputing/bluegene/bgpfaq.html.

[70] Japan / Asia HPC Digest, High Performance Computing in Japan & Asia, *Japan / Asia HPC Digest*, http://www.atip.org/NEWS/182.pdf, October 2004.

[71] Joseph E., Conway S., and Wu J., June 2007. Improving HPC Performance, Scalability, and Availability with Blades: Introducing SGI Altix ICE, White paper # 207401, IDC, 5 Speen Street, Framingham, MA, http://www.sgi.com/pdfs/4015.pdf.

[72] Joseph E., II et al., November 2002. *A New High Bandwidth Supercomputer: The Cray X1*, Technology Assessment, IDC, Framingham, MA, paper available at http://www.cray.com/downloads/crayx1_idc.pdf.

[73] Joseph E., Snell A., and Willard C. G., October 2004. NEC Launches Next-Generation Vector Supercomputer: The SX-8, IDC White paper #4290, IDC, Framingham, MA 01701.

[74] Kindratenko V., and Pointer D., A Case Study in Porting a Production Scientific Supercomputing Application to a Reconfigurable Computer, submitted to IEEE Symposium on Field-Programmable Custom Computing Machines (FCCM'06).

[75] Kindratenko V., Pointer D., and Caliga D., January 10, 2006. High-Performance Reconfigurable Computing Application Programming in C, https://netfiles.uiuc.edu/dpointer/www/whitepapers/hprc_v1_0.pdf.

[76] Kindratenko V., Pointer D., Raila D., and Steffen C., February 21, 2006. Comparing CPU and FPGA Application Performance, NCSA, U of Illinois, Urbana-Champaign, IL, https://netfiles.uiuc.edu/dpointer/www/whitepapers/perf.pdf.

[77] Kissel L., Nowak D. A., Seager M., and Yates K., November 18, 2002. BlueGene/L: the next generation of scalable supercomputer, SC2002, paper available at http://www.llnl.gov/asci/platforms/bluegenel/images/BGL.pdf.

[78] Lazou C., June 18, 2004. Watanabe Discusses NEC's Position in HPC Industry, *HPCWIRE*, Vol. **13**, No. 24, http://www.taborcommunications.com/hpcwire/hpcwireWWW/04/0618/107850.html.

[79] Lazou C., July 8, 2005. Cray: '100 Percent Focused on HPC', *HPCWIRE*, Vol. **14**, No. 27, http://www.hpcwire.com/hpc/414962.html.

[80] Lazou C., July 6, 2007. A European's View on ISC2007, *HPCWIRE*, Vol. **16**, No. 27, 2007, http://www.hpcwire.com/hpc/1648193.html.

[81] Lazou C., February 24, 2006. Are FPGAs a Disruptive Technology for HPC? *HPCWIRE*, Vol. **15**, No. 8, http://www.hpcwire.com/hpc/570738.html.

[82] Leland R., June 16–18 2004. Red Storm Architecture and Applications, *Proceedings, Cray Advanced Technical Workshop*, Bologna, Italy.

[82A] Makino J., et al., November 2007. GRAPE-DR: 2 Pflops Massively Parallel Computer with 512 Core, 512 Gflops Processor Chips for Scientific Computing, http://sc07.supercomputing.org/schedule/pdf/pap247.pdf SC07, Reno, NV.

[83] Moore S. K., Winner: Multimedia Monster, http://www.spectrum.ieee.org/jan06/2609.

[84] Network Computing Services, *The AHPCRC Cray X1 Primer*, Network Computing Services, available at http://www.ahpcrc.org/publications/Primer.pdf, 2003.

[85] New Scientist News Service, NEC Strikes Blow in Supercomputer Battle, http://www.newscientist.com/news/news.jsp?id=ns99996562, October 21, 2004.

[85A] North Carolina State University, March 20, 2007. Engineer Creates First Academic Playstation3 Computer Cluster, *ScienceDaily*, http://www.sciencedaily.com/releases/2007/03/070319205733.htm.

[86] Owens J. D., et al., August 29–September 2, 2005. A Survey of General-Purpose Computation on Graphics Hardware, Proceedings, Eurographics 2005, Dublin, Ireland, pp. 21–51, http://graphics.idav.ucdavis.edu/graphics/publications/func/return_pdf?pub_id=844.

[87] Parsons M., November 14, 2006. Programming FPGAs for Real Applications: Understanding the Challenges, *HPCWIRE*, http://www.hpcwire.com/hpc/1091371.html.

[88] Partridge R., November 14, 2002. *Cray Launches X1 for Extreme Super computing*, D. H., Brown Associates, Inc., Port Chester, NY, paper available at http://www.cray.com/downloads/crayx1_dhbrown.pdf.

[89] Patterson D. A., and Hennessy J., 2004. Computer Organization and Design: The Hardware/Software Interface, Morgan Kauffman, San Francisco, CA.

[90] Patterson D. A., October 2004. Latency Lags Bandwidth, *Comm. ACM*, Vol. **47**, No. 10, pp. 71–75.

[91] Resch M., May 2004. Vector Computing: The Key to Sustained Performance? NEC User Group, NUG-25, available at mail to: resch@hlrs.de.

[92] Schwarzmeier L., November 2002. Cray X1 Architecture and Hardware Overview, Oak Ridge National Lab Cray X1 Tutorial, Oak Ridge, TN, available at mail to: jads@cray.com.

[93] Scott S., April 7, 2006. In Cray's 'Cascade' The Computer Will Adapt to the Codes, *HPCWIRE*, http://www.hpcwire.com/hpc/614695.html.

[94] Scott S., June 28, 2007. Cray's Cascade System and the Roadmap to Sustained Petascale Computing, Exhibitor Forum, International Supercomputing Conference (ISC07), Dresden, Germany, For additional information, please contact Kathy Kurtz, mail to: ksk@cray.com.

[95] Seminerio J., and Terry P., 2004. The XD1, *Proceedings, Cray Advanced Technical Workshop*, Bologna, Italy, June 16–18.

[96] SGI, Inc., November 17, 2003. SGI Unveils Plans for the Supercomputer of the Future, http://www.sgi.com/company_info/newsroom/press_releases/2003/november/sc_future.html.

[97] SGI, Inc., July 13, 2007. SGI Altix Cluster Tapped for Sikorsky Airflow Simulations, *HPCWIRE*, Vol. **16**, No. 28, http://www.hpcwire.com/hpc/1653015.html.

[98] Shan A., November 2004. Cray XD1-FPGA, http://www.cray.com/downloads/sc2004/SC-FPGABoothTheatre_pp_nov4.pdf SC2004, Pittsburgh, PA.

[99] Shankland S., October 25, 2004. IBM Supercomputing Goes Retro, CNET News.com, http://news.com.com/IBM+supercomputing+goes+retro/2100-1010_3-5425551.html.

[100] Simon H., June 22, 2005. Progress in Supercomputing: The Top Three Breakthroughs of the Last Twenty Years and the Top Three Challenges for the Next Twenty Years, ISC 2005, Heidelberg, video at mms://netshow01.eecs.berkeley.edu/Horst_Simon.

[101] Snell A., and Willard C. G., March 2006. Bridging the Capability Gap: Cray Pursues 'Adaptive Supercomputing' Vision, White paper No. 200808, IDC, Framingham, MA. http://www.cray.com/downloads/IDC-AdaptiveSC.pdf.

[102] Special Issue on BlueGene/L, *IBM J. of Res. & Dev*, Vol. **49**, No. 2/3, 2005, http://www.research.ibm.com/journal/rd49-23.html.

[102A] Swiss National Supercomputer Centre, New Cray XT Supercomputer Inaugurated at CSCS, *HPCWIRE*, Vol. **16**, No. 38, http://www.hpcwire.com/hpc/1783938.html, September 21, 2007.

[103] Steele Jr. G. L., Programming Language Research: Exploration of programming languages constructs and principles, http://research.sun.com/projects/plrg/.
[104] Tom's Hardware Guide Business Reports, Dueling Multicores: Intel and AMD Fight for the Future, Part 1 – Update, http://www.tomshardware.com/business/20050330/index.html, 2005.
[105] Underwood K., FPGAs vs. CPUs: Trends in Peak Floating-Point Performance. February 22–24, 2004. *Proc., ACM/SIGDA 12th International symposium on Field Programmable Gate Arrays*, Monterey, CA, pp. 171–180.
[106] van der Steen A. J., and Dongarra J. J., Overview of Recent Supercomputers, http://www.netlib.org/utk/papers/advanced-computers/.
[107] Vildibill M., April 7, 2006. Sun's Hero Program: Changing the Productivity Game, *HPCWIRE*, http://www.hpcwire.com/hpc/614805.html.

# 5. Some HPC Issues

## 5.1 Actual HPC Performance

When using HPC technology, it is extremely important to verify the accuracy of your computer results and explicitly indicate the conditions under which the performance tests were conducted. Unfortunately, that does not always happen. It can be caused by deceptive practices used during the performance tests and/or over zealousness by a vendor marketing person or even by ignorance of the persons conducting the performance tests. The Bailey references [1–3] reveal many such misleading practices and I strongly recommend that you scrutinize those papers. Sometimes vendor personnel with a strong desire not to reveal any bad attributes of their company's computer product may suffer from a disease I prefer to politely refer to as 'selective amnesia'; in such cases no major poor results will be reported or will be explained only by the use of marketing HYPE. This practice was obviously learned by observing the behavior patterns of many politicians. The best way to avoid such practices is to have several experts present before, during, and after the performance tests to try to verify that there is a very accurate written record which discloses all significant factors which could impact the reported performance outcomes.

## 5.2 Software Needs with Current and Future Supercomputers

For many years, there has been considerably more effort to develop HPC hardware rather than focus on expansion of HPC software needs. Now we are directly headed for a crisis in the latter area because of growing heat and energy concerns in the development of faster HPC performance. More and improved forms of software parallelism must be created to solve this problem if petaflop computing is to be successful between now and 2011. Solutions will involve the creation of new performance-enhancing techniques. See references [8A, 9, 10, 12, 21, 26, 26A, 27, 35, 36A, 38, 41, 42, 43, 44, 45].

## 5.3 U.S. Government Roadmaps

The federal government so far has failed to provide long-term implemented solutions to meet HPC needs, especially in industry. This has been the case despite many government initiatives that have been inadequate in meeting long-term HPC needs. The current software HPC crisis is an example of ineffective long-term plans. There have been several federal initiatives but few long-term implemented initiatives. See [14–16, 19, 22–26, 28, 30, 34–36].

## References

[1] Bailey D. H., 1998. Challenges of Future High-End Computers, in High Performance Computer Systems and Applications, edited by Schaeffer J., Kluwer Academic Press, Boston, MA; http://crd.lbl.gov/~dhbailey/dhbpapers/future.pdf.

[2] Bailey D. H., Misleading Performance Reporting in the Supercomputing Field, Scientific Programming, Vol. **1**, No. 2 (Winter 1992), pp. 141–151, http://crd.lbl.gov/~dhbailey/dhbpapers/mislead.pdf.

[3] Bailey D. H., June 23–25, 2004. Twelve Ways to Fool the Masses: Scientific Malpractice in High-Performance Computing, paper, International Supercomputing Conference (ISC04), Heidelberg, Germany, http://crd.lbl.gov/~dhbailey/dhbtalks/dhb-12ways.pdf.

[4] Bartling B., Increasing the Expert 'Bandwidth', http://www.sgi.com/features/2004/oct/landmark/.

[5] The Council on Competitiveness, 2004 HPC Users Conference: Supercharging U.S. Innovation & Competitiveness, Report and DVD available, The Council on Competitiveness, 2005, http://www.compete.org/hpc/hpc_conf_report.asp.

[6] Council on Competitiveness, *High Performance Computing Software Workshop Report: Accelerating Innovation for Competitive Advantage: The Need for HPC Application Software Solutions*, July 13, 2005, Council on Competitiveness, Washington, D.C.20005, January 2006.

[7] Council on Competitiveness, *Second Annual High Performance Computing Users Conference Report*, Report and DVD available, Council on Competitiveness,Washington D.C.20005, March 2006.

[8] Curns T., ed., January 13, 2005. Sun's Gustafson on Envisioning HPC Roadmaps for the Future, *HPCWIRE*, Vol. **14**, No. 2, http://www.hpcwire.com/hpc/324428.html.

[8A] Daniilidi C., September 28, 2007. Virginia Tech Explores Thermal-Aware Computing, *HPCWIRE*, Vol. **16**, No. 39, http://www.hpcwire.com/hpc/1802228.html.

[9] Dongarra J., February 2007. (Guest Editor), The Promise and Perils of the Coming Multicore Revolution and Its Impact, *CTWatch Quarterly*, Vol. **3**, No. 1, http://www.ctwatch.org/quarterly/pdf/ctwatchquarterly-10.pdf.

[10] Dongarra J., Gannon D., Fox G., and Kennedy K., February 2007. The Impact of Multicore on Computational Science Software, *CTWatch Quarterly*, Vol. **3**, No. 1, http://www.ctwatch.org/quarterly/articles/2007/02/the-impact-of-multicore-on-computational-science-software/.

[11] Ebisuzaki T., Germain R., and Taiji M., November 2004. PetaFLOPS Computing, *Comm. ACM*, Vol. **47**, No. 11, pp. 42–45.

[12] Feldman M., August 3, 2007. Parallel Vision, *HPCWIRE*, Vol. **16**, No. 31, http://www.hpcwire.com/hpc/1703560.html.

[13] Ginsberg M., 2001. Influences on the Solution Process for Large, Numeric-Intensive Automotive Simulations, *Lecture Notes in Computer Science Series*, Vol. **2073**, Springer, pp. 1189–1198.

[14] Ginsberg M., May 2005. Impediments to Future Use of Petaflop Class Computers for Large-Scale Scientific/Engineering Applications in U.S. Private Industry, Proc. of International Conference on Computational Science (ICCS 2005) *Lecture Notes in Computer Science Series*, Vol. **3514**, Springer-Verlag, Berlin, pp. 1059–1066.

[15] Ginsberg M., June 25–28, 2007. Challenges and Opportunities for U.S. Private Industry Utilization of HPC Technology, *Proceedings, International Conference on Scientific Computing*, CSREA Press, Las Vegas, NV, pp. 17–23.

[16] Graham S. L., Snir M., and Patterson C. A. (eds.), 2004. Getting Up to Speed: The Future of Supercomputing, U.S. National Academy of Sciences CSTB Report, see http://www.cstb.org/project_supercomputing.html prepublication on-line version at http://books.nap.edu/catalog/11148.html executive summary, http://www.nap.edu/catalog/11148.html.

[17] Gustafson J. L., April 6, 2007. Algorithm Leadership, *HPCWIRE*, Vol. **16**, No. 14, http://www.hpcwire.com/hpc/1347145.html.

[18] Gustafson J. L., 2006. Understanding the Different Acceleration Technologies, *HPCWIRE*, Vol. **13**, No. 2, November 14, http://www.hpcwire.com/hpc/1091512.html.

[19] HECRTF, Federal Plan for High-End Computing: Report of the High-End Computing Revitalization Task Force (HECRTF), Executive Office of the President, Office of Science and Technology Policy, Washington, D.C., May 10, 2004 (second printing – July 2004); available at http://www.ostp.gov/nstc/html/HECRTF-FINAL_051004.pdf.

[20] HPC User Forum, IDC Analyst Briefing, Technical Computing Market Update, Supercomputing 2004, Pittsburgh, PA, http://www.hpcwire.com/sponsors/idc/IDC_at_SC04.pdf, November 10, 2004.

[21] Joseph E., Conway S., and Wu J., June 2007. Improving HPC Performance, Scalability, and Availability with Blades: Introducing SGI Altix ICE, White paper # 207401, IDC, 5 Speen Street, Framingham, MA, http://www.sgi.com/pdfs/4015.pdf.

[22] Joseph E., Snell A., and Willard C. G., July 2004. *Council on Competitiveness Study of U. S. Industrial HPC Users*, White Paper, IDC, Framingham, MA, paper available at http://www.compete.org/pdf/HPC_Users_Survey.pdf.

[23] Joseph E., et al., July 2005. Study of ISVs Serving the High Performance Computing Market: The Need for Better Application Software, Council on Competitiveness Initiative, White Paper, IDC, Framingham, MA, http://www.compete.org/pdf/HPC_Software_Survey.pdf.

[24] Joseph E., et al., May 2006. Council on Competitiveness Study of Industrial Partnerships with the National Science Foundation (NSF) IDC White Paper on Council of Competitiveness Study of Industrial Partnerships with The National Science Foundation (NSF), May 2006, Council of Competitiveness, Washington, D.C., http://www.compete.org/pdf/Council_NSF_Partnership_Study.pdf.

[25] Joseph E., et al., June 2006. Industrial Partnerships through the NNSA Academic Strategic Alliance Program IDC White Paper on Council on Competitiveness Study of Industrial Partnerships with the U.S. Department of Energy NNSA, Council on Competitiveness, Washington, D.C. http://www.compete.org/pdf/Council_NNSA_Partnership_Study.pdf.

[26] Jeremy Kepner, (Guest Editor), High Productivity Computing Systems and the Path Towards Usable Petascale Computing, Part A: User Productivity Challenges, *CTWatch Quarterly*, Vol. **2**, No. 4A, November 2006, http://www.ctwatch.org/quarterly/pdf/ctwatchquarterly-8.pdf.

[26A] Lazou C., September 21, 2007. A Global Climate of Change, *HPCWIRE*, Vol. **16**, No. 38, http://www.hpcwire.com/hpc/1792077.html.

[27] Manferdelli J., February 2007. The Many-Core Inflection Point for Mass Market Computer Systems, *CTWatch Quarterly*, Vol. **3**, No. 1, http://www.ctwatch.org/quarterly/articles/2007/02/the-many-core-inflection-point-for-mass-market-computer-systems.

[28] Mark R., November 18, 2004. Congress OKs Funding U.S. Supercomputers, *Internet News*, http://www.internetnews.com/bus-news/article.php/3438081.

[29] McCalpin J., February 2007. The Role of Multicore Processors in the Evolution of General-Purpose Computing, *CTWatch Quarterly*, Vol. **3**, No. 1, http://www.ctwatch.org/quarterly/articles/2007/02/the-role-of-multicore-processors-in-the-evolution-of-general-purpose-computing.

[30] Merritt R., July 14, 2003. DARPA Seeds a Petaflops Push, *EE Times*, http://www.eet.com/article/showArticle.jhtml?articleId=18308889.

[31] Merritt R., and Mokhoff N., November 15, 2004. High and Dry at High End, *EE Times*, http://www.eet.com/article/showArticle.jhtml?articleId=52601292.

[32] National Coordination Office for Information Technology and Development (NITRD); http://www.itrd.gov.

[33] Patt Y. N., June 23–25, 2004. The Processor in 2014: What are the challenges? How do we meet them? Presentation, ISC2004, Heidelberg, Germany, paper available from patt@ece.utexas.edu.

[34] President's Information Technology Advisory Committee, Computational Science: Ensuring America's Competitiveness, PITAC, Office of the President, Washington D.C., http://www.nitrd.gov/pitac/reports/20050609_computational/computational.pdf, June 2005.

[35] Ricadela A., June 21, 2004. Petaflop Imperative, *Information Week*,http://www.information week.com/story/ showArticle.jhtml?articleID=22100641.

[36] Scarafino V., July 16, 2003. The National Needs for Advanced Scientific Computing and Industrial Applications, Statement of The Ford Motor Company, Committee on Science, U.S. House of Representatives, http://www.house.gov/science/hearings/full03/jul16/scarafino.html.

[36A] Sceales T., October 5, 2007. Talking the Green Talk, but Not Walking the Green Walk, *HPCWIRE*, Vol. **16**, No. 40, http://www.hpcwire.com/hpc/1815340.html.

[37] Scott S., June 28, 2007. Effective Scalable Computing, Hot Seat Session, Part II, International Supercomputing Conference (ISC07), Dresden, Germany, For additional information, please contact Kathy Kurtz, ksk@cray.com.

[37A] SiCortex, SiCortex Demos Human-Powered Supercomputer, *HPCWIRE*, Vol. **16**, No. 38, http://www.hpcwire.com/hpc/1789175.html, September 21, 2007.

[37B] SiCortex, SiCortex Marches to a Different Drummer, *HPCWIRE*, Vol. **15**, No. 49, http://www.hpcwire.com/hpc/1158993.html, December 15, 2006.

[38] Simon Management Group (SMG), The Development of Custom Parallel Computing Applications, Interactive Supercomputing, Corporation, Cambridge, MA, http://www.interactivesupercomputing.com/downloads/developcustompar2006.pdf, September 2006.

[39] Sterling T., June 27, 2007. HPC Achievement and Impact – 2007: A Personal Perspective International Supercomputing Conference (ISC07), Dresden, Germany. For additional information, please contact Terrie Bordelon, tbordelon@cct.lsu.edu.

[40] Sterling T., June 28, 2007. Multicore – The Next Moore's Law, International Supercomputing Conference (ISC07), Dresden, Germany. For additional information, please contact Terrie Bordelon, tbordelon@cct.lsu.edu.

[41] Tally S., May 25, 2007. Not So Fast, Supercomputers, Say Software Programmers, *HPCWIRE*, Vol. **16**, No. 21, http://www.hpcwire.com/hpc/1579050.html.

[42] Turek D., February 2007. High Performance Computing and the Implications of Multi-core Architectures, Vol. **3**, No. 1, http://www.ctwatch.org/quarterly/articles/2007/02/high-performance-computing-and-the-implications-of-multi-core-architectures.

[43] Ulfelder S., March 6, 2006. Supercomputer Architectures Battle for Hearts and Minds of Users, *Computerworld*, http://computerworld.com/hardwaretopics/hardware/story/0,10801,109177,00.html.
[44] U.S. Department of Energy-Office of Science, Overture Plays on Methods for Faster, More Accurate Models, http://ascr-discovery.science.doe.gov/kernels/henshaw_print.html, July 16, 2007.
[45] Wallach S., June 23, 2004. Searching for the SOFTRON: Will We Be Able to Develop Software for Petaflop Computing? Keynote Talk, International Supercomputing Conference (ISC2004), Heidelberg, Germany, paper available at wallach@cpventures.com.

# 6. Benchmarking Issues and Concerns

## 6.1 HPC Pitfalls and Difficulty in Testing

It is an extremely difficult task to create a comprehensive, unbiased, and relevant set of benchmark tests to assess accurately the performance of a particular user application. Scrutinizing the issues in Fig. 3 should convince the reader of the daunting nature of this task. It is very easy to be deceived when attempting to discern just exactly what a particular benchmark reveals about the inherent nature of a user

**High Performance Computing Pitfalls**

- Best performance often achieved in cases with minimal dependencies and/or strong locality of reference
- Large numbers of processors does NOT necessarily guarantee highest speed (Amdahl's Law) especially if interconnection network cannot move data sufficiently fast
- For high speed, must maintain a very high ratio of computations to communications, i.e., balance should be > 1
- Program with highest mflop/s does NOT necessarily have shortest wallclock time
- Do NOT be impressed by raw peak speed because sustained speed is often much less than peak for real industrial applications
- Amount of parallelism and/ or speedup may be impressive but wallclock time may be greater than for a machine with less parallelism
- Mflop/$ is a deceptive metric and can vary considerably

Dr. Myron Ginsberg • HPC Research & Education •

FIG. 3. High-performance computing pitfalls.

application. Just exactly what hardware, software, and/or algorithmic features significantly impacted the observed performance of a user application? Examine [5, 6] for examples of performance deceptions.

### 6.2 Benchmarking Approaches in Government/Academic Research vs. Industry

The differences in these two environments were discussed in Section 2. Those same factors affect the means by which benchmarking is performed in these two very different surroundings. For example, it is usually more difficult to benchmark industrial ISV-based codes on a new architecture because of dependencies in the ISV-based codes and because the ISV-based codes may have not been ported to the new environment. Even though some of the same applications are run in a government lab and in industry, it is difficult to compare performance because again the ISV-based code may produce different results than the in-house code even though both codes solve the same problem. The ISV problem makes it more difficult for an industrial person to assess if the government lab code would perform better than his ISV code.

In most academic research centers as well as in most government labs, relatively few, if any, commercial ISV-based codes are in extensive use. This helps contribute to the continuing lag between government and industrial uses of leading-edge HPC architectures. For example, the Cray X1 vector computer entered the marketplace in late 2002, yet by 2006 only one such machine was in use in U.S. industry. The commercial ISVs considered porting their codes to that machine but concluded that it would not be cost-effective even though extensive benchmark tests at Oak Ridge National Lab (ORNL) demonstrated superior performance on the Cray X1 for vector-oriented applications.

### 6.3 The One Number Syndrome for Industrial Benchmarking

Because benchmarking is so difficult, some industrial managers have jumped to the pragmatic conclusion that an effective shortcut is to find a single number that would totally characterize application performance and thereby avoid extensive and costly performance testing. From the factors discussed in this section so far, it should be obvious to the reader that such a single number might only be found in the mind of a computer vendor marketing person. Many such people look to the Top500 List [56] for such one number 'guidance'. Perhaps some of those individuals should read [22] and also reflect on the fact that the Top500 list is solely based upon the speed of solving a dense linear system which is not necessarily indicative of the overall performance for most scientific/engineering applications.

## 6.4 My Personal View of Industrial Benchmarking

I do not have the panacea for perfect application performance testing, but I do have a few ideas on how to improve industrial benchmarking. Even though most companies do not have large computer support staffs, benchmarking should not be left totally in the hands of a computer vendor; there is too much danger of undue marketing influence on any 'objective testing'.

The company should form an internal committee which includes those computer users whose programs are to be benchmarked as well as some financial people of the company who can assess the necessary costs of acquiring the HPC equipment being benchmarked vs. leasing the machine as well as estimate return on investment to the company. This latter exercise could produce useful information to provide to upper management to justify acquisition of the HPC equipment. If there are no sufficient people within the company to perform the evaluation, then certainly a reputable external consultant should be considered as well as some feedback can be obtained from computer vendor organizations. It is the responsibility of the evaluation committee to ensure that they do not accept unsubstantiated vendor claims and that all benchmark procedures are properly documented in written documents given to the internal company evaluation committee. This committee should also have good and complete performance data for the benchmarked user application run on current company computers for comparison with the benchmarked results.

Ideally, companies should seriously consider establishing a small full-time internal computer evaluation team that could continuously monitor application performance and maintain internal data, which could assist in evaluating new architectures as the organization contemplates future HPC acquisitions. Such an internal evaluation group exists in many government labs in order to collect their own independent performance data from both internal and external sources. Such activity helps to monitor closely vendor claims and recommendations.

The benchmarked tests should reflect both current and immediate future application use (say within the following 18 months). Also, in this connection it could be very helpful to perform some parameterized tests to observe any possible performance degradation as problem size of the application increases.

I tend to favor government lab benchmarking of new HPC architectures rather than rely solely on vendor tests. I have been particularly impressed with the objectivity and thoroughness of such tests performed at Oak Ridge National Lab (ORNL) as well as at Los Alamos National Lab (LANL). The only downside of those tests as far as industry is concerned is the lack of performance data on ISV-based codes which tend to be ubiquitous in U.S. private industry. What I greatly appreciate is that ORNL tends to report the Good, Bad, and the Ugly aspects of new HPC architecture benchmarks and displays many of the resulting unclassified reports on their web site. This has been contrary to my experience with some computer vendors who tend to have a case of selective amnesia when it comes to reporting any negative aspects of their computer products.

I have listed many benchmark results in the references for Section 6. Take a look at ORNL benchmark reports [2, 9–11, 15–20, 24, 41, 43, 47, 55, 58–62, 65]. Also, examine some of the benchmarks performed at LANL [25, 33, 34]. Other interesting benchmarks have been performed by personnel at Lawrence Berkeley Lab (LBL) [49–51] and by the Army High Performance Research Center (AHPCRC) [31, 42, 44, 45].

## 6.5 Pros and Cons of Various Types of Benchmarking

Figure 4 indicates certain categories of benchmark tests. Note that the first two types can often lead to deception. Peak speed is meaningless if your application (or for that matter anyone's application) cannot even approach that peak. The $/mflop is deceptive because if there are two or more flop rates, which one should be used to measure that ratio? The speedup ratios could seem to be high when the processors in use are slow. The standard benchmarks listed in this figure tend to be too specialized for general use. The Bait and switch approach tends to look at fast performance for a small-sized problem and then just extrapolate it to a larger problem, even though in reality such increase in speed might not happen. The HPC Challenge benchmark will

HPC Benchmarks

- Peak speed
- $/mflop
- Standard benchmarks (Linpack, NAS, PARKBENCH, SPEC, PmaC, IDC Balanced, etc.)
- % of parallelism and/or speedup
- Bait and switch (used car salesman approach)
- HPC Challenge Benchmark
- IDC Balanced Rating
- ORNL benchmarks
- Actual performance

Dr. Myron Ginsberg • HPC Research & Education •

FIG. 4. HPC benchmarks.

be discussed in the following Section (6.6). The ORNL benchmarks were discussed in Section 6.4. The private industry preference is for actual wall clock time.

A few industrial managers 'reason' that maximum performance on any HPC machine is within 15% of the best performance of any other supercomputer, so why 'waste time' benchmarking? Some computer vendors try to convince unsuspecting potential customers that machine selection should be based on the maximum number of processors that can be acquired for X$, but such a metric ignores the possibility that a few expensive processors may produce far better overall results than a very large number of less expensive processors; this is a good reason why a user should be aware of the attributes of his/her application and know if certain types of processors can produce better results for his/her problem.

Another important consideration is how important is it to solve a specific application fast and is the customer willing to pay a premium for such performance? I hope my comments in this subsection are helpful in assessing benchmarking concerns. Unfortunately, there are some predatory vendors in the HPC marketplace. Remember, Caveat Emptor-let the buyer beware. This is a wise advice in HPC acquisition as well as in other facets of life.

## 6.6 The HPC Challenge Benchmarks (HPCC)

The HPC Challenge Benchmarks (HPCC) (see Fig. 5 and [14, 26–28, 37–40]) are worthy of your attention even if you are not specializing in the HPC area. I suggest you look at least a few of the aforementioned references. HPCC is an attempt to create a canonical set of benchmarks that can effectively be used to characterize the supercomputer attributes, which most likely have significant impact on total performance of a user's application. The current tests in HPCC are listed in Fig. 5. These tests are in progress, so some of the current tests may be eventually modified or removed and new tests could be possibly added. The introduction of petaflop-class machine architecture may stimulate some changes in HPCC content, but the goal mentioned above shall remain. Please note that the criterion that is the basis for the Top 500 List [56] is also included in HPCC along with the other tests in Fig. 5. The complete current results for machines tested with HPCC are given in [28]. This will be constantly updated as new machines are tested.

One tool used to characterize results from HPCC is a Kiviat diagram. It is 'similar to radar plots in Excel'. A Kiviat diagram (see Fig. 6) is a two-dimensional graph of radially extending lines in which each line corresponds to a test. To create such a diagram, each score is first transformed into a per processor metric. Scores are then normalized with respect to the highest score in each category. An enclosed geometric region is then generated by connecting all the points for a given supercomputer. The shape of the enclosed region can provide the user with an intuitive assessment of how balanced a

HPC Challenge Benchmark

- HPL : the LINPACK TPP benchmark which measures the floating-point rate of execution (tflops/s) for solving a dense linear system of equations
- DGEMM : measures the floating-point rate of execution of double precision real matrix-matrix multiplication
- STREAM : a simple synthetic benchmark program that measures sustainable memory bandwidth (in GB/s) and the corresponding computation rate for simple vector kernel
- PTRANS (parallel matrix transpose) : exercises the communications where pairs of processors communicate with each other simultaneously. It is a useful test of the total communications capacity of the network (GB/s); is rate of transfer for large arrays of data from multiprocessor's memory
- RandomAccessMPI (per CPU) : measures the rate of integer random updates of memory (Gup/s)
- FFTE : measures the floating-point rate of execution of double precision complex one-dimensional Discrete Fourier Transform (DFT)
- B_eff(effective bandwidth benchmark) : a set of tests to measure latency (per CPU) (in microsecs) and bandwidth (per CPU) of a number of simultaneous communication patterns (GB/s)

Dr. Myron Ginsberg • HPC Research & Education •

FIG. 5. HPC challenge benchmarks.

Using Kiviat Diagrams

- HPCC website allows each computer to be plotted on a Kiviat diagram
- A Kiviat diagram is a two dimensional graph of radially extending lines where each line corresponds to an HPCC test
- To create such a diagram, each score is first turned into a per processor metric
- Scores are then normalized to the best score in each category
- A perimeter is then drawn connecting all the points for a given machine

Dr. Myron Ginsberg • HPC Research & Education •

FIG. 6. Using Kiviat diagrams.

given machine is with respect to all the plotted machine attributes, i.e., out-of-balanced machines will not produce a symmetrical enclosed region. A single Kiviat diagram can be automatically created for up to six supercomputers currently tested with HPCC. This information is located at http://icl.cs.utk.edu/hpcc/hpcc_results_kiviat.cgi. For additional information about Kiviat diagrams, see [21A] that includes a Kiviat diagram (Figure 1) which can be enlarged by the reader if he goes to the website reference and clicks on that Figure 1. The Kiviat diagram is not necessarily unique for a given computer. For example, variations in a specific configuration could result in the production of different Kiviat diagrams for the same machine. Thus, it is wise to consider a Kiviat diagram as an intuitive estimate for each computer tested with HPCC.

## 6.7 Predictive Benchmarks

It would be extremely helpful to HPC users (especially in industry) if benchmark tests could accurately predict performance on a new HPC architecture even before the new machine is benchmarked. Two such approaches are emerging from Los Alamos National Lab (LANL) and University of California at San Diego (UCSD). At LANL, Adolfy Hoisie is the leader of the Performance and Architecture Group (PAL). His team has access to a wide variety of HPC hardware both at government labs and from the hardware vendors. Hoisie and his people create models of many such machines and then refine those models with actual tests on the machine that was the subject for their benchmark. With such information, they continue to create new machines, utilizing what they have learned from previous machines. For additional information about PAL, see [21, 25, 33, 34].

Allan Snavely of UCSD has been involved with another predictive benchmark effort in the Performance Modeling and Characterization Group (PMaC) (see. http://www.sdsc.edu/PMaC/ ). The process proceeds as follows: (1) a Machine Profile is created; (2) an Application Profile is created based upon 'detailed summaries of the fundamental operations carried out by the application independent of any particular machine.' [52] Then 'algebraic mappings' (via 'convolution methods') map the Application Profile onto the Machine Profile 'to arrive at a performance prediction.' (See http://www.sdsc.edu/PMaC/projects/index.html and [52] for details.) For additional information about the methodology, see [7].

## References

[1] Agarwal P. A., et al., January 29, 2004. Cray X1 Status Report, ORNL TM-2004/13, http://www.csm.ornl.gov/evaluation/PHOENIX/PDF/CRAYEvaluationTM2004-15.pdf.

[2] Agarwal P. A., et al., May 17–21, 2004. Cray X1 Evaluation Status Report, *Proc., 46th Cray User Group Conference*, Oak Ridge, TN, http://www.csm.ornl.gov/~worley/papers/CUG04_X1eval.pdf.

[3] Akkerman A., and Strenski D., May 12–16, 2003. Porting FCRASH to the Cray X1 Architecture, *Proc., 45th Cray User Group Conference*, Columbus, OH, presentation available at aakkerma@ford.com.

[4] Akkerman A., et al., May 17–21, 2004. Performance Evaluation of Radioss-CFD on the Cray X1, *Proc., 46th Cray User Group Conference*, Oak Ridge, TN, paper available at aakkerma@ford.com.

[4A] Alam S. R., et al., November 10–16, 2007. Cray XT4: An Early Evaluation for Petascale Scientific Simulation, SC07, http://www.csm.ornl.gov/~worley/papers/SC07_XT4.pdf.

[4B] Alam S. R., et al., 2007. An Evaluation of the ORNL Cray XT3, IJHPCA07, http://www.csm.ornl.gov/~worley/papers/ornl_xt3_ijhpca07.pdf.

[5] Bailey D. H., Winter 1992. Misleading Performance Reporting in the Supercomputing Field, *Scientific Programming*, Vol. **1**, No. 2, pp. 141–151, http://crd.lbl.gov/~dhbailey/dhbpapers/mislead.pdf.

[6] Bailey D. H., June 23–25, 2004. Twelve Ways to Fool the Masses: Scientific Malpractice in High-Performance Computing, *Proc. of ISC*, Heidelberg, Germany, http://crd.lbl.gov/~dhbailey/dhbtalks/dhb-12ways.pdf.

[7] Bailey D. H., and Snavely A., August 30–September 2, 2005. Performance Modeling: Understanding the Present and Predicting the Future, *Proceedings of Euro-Par*, Lisbon, Portugal, http://www.sdsc.edu/PMaC/publications/pubs/bailey05modeling.pdf.

[8] Baring T. J., May 17–21, 2004. X1 Porting, *Proceedings, 46th Cray User Group Conference*, Oak Ridge, TN, paper available at baring@arsc.edu.

[9] Bland A. S., et al., March 2003. *Cray X1 Evaluation*, Oak Ridge Technical Report, ORNL/TM-2003/67, http://www.csm.ornl.gov/evaluation/PHOENIX/PDF/CrayX1-Evaluation-Plan.pdf.

[10] Bland A. S., Alexander R., Carter S. M., and Matney K. D., Sr., May 12–16, 2003. Early Operations Experience with the Cray X1 at the Oak Ridge National Laboratory Center for Computational Sciences, *Proc., 45th Cray User Group Conference*, Columbus, OH, http://www.csm.ornl.gov/evaluation/PHOENIX/PDF/CUG2003-Paper-Bland-pdf.

[11] Candy J., and Fahey M., May 16–19, 2005. GYRO Performance on a Variety of MPP Systems, *Proc., 47th Cray User Group Conference*, Albuquerque, NM, paper available at http://web.gat.com/comp/parallel/physics_results.html.

[12] Carrington L. C., et al., November 12–18, 2005. How Well Can Simple Metrics Represent the Performance of HPC Applications? SC05, Seattle, WA, http://www.sdsc.edu/PMaC/publications/pubs/carrington05metrics.pdf.

[13] Carter J., Oliker L., and Shalf J., July 10–13, 2006. Performance Evaluation of Scientific Applications on Modern Parallel Vector Systems, VECPAR, 7th International Meeting on High Performance Computing for Computational Science, Rio de Janeiro, Brazil, http://www.crd.lbl.gov/~oliker/papers/vecpar-2006.pdf.

[14] Dongarra J., June 23–26, 2006. The HPC Challenge Benchmark: A Candidate for Replacing LINPACK in the TOP500? ISC06, Dresden, Germany, http://www.netlib.org/utk/people/JackDongarra/SLIDES/isc-talk-2006.pdf.

[14A] Drake J. B., 2007. Software Design for Petascale Climate Science, Chapter 16, Software Design for Petascale Climate Science, CRC Press, http://www.csm.ornl.gov/~worley/papers/petaflop_climate.pdf.

[15] Drake J. B., et al., May 17–21, 2004. Experience with the Full CCSM, *Proc., 46th Cray User Group Conference*, Oak Ridge, TN, http://www.csm.ornl.gov/~worley/papers/CUG04_CCSM.pdf.

[16] Dunigan Jr. T. H., Fahey M. R., White J. B., III, and Worley P. H., November 15–21, 2003. Early Evaluation of the Cray X1, *Proc. of the ACM/IEEE Conference on High Performance Networking and Computing (SC03)*, Phoenix, AZ, http://www.csm.ornl.gov/~worley/papers/SC2003.Worley.CrayX1.pdf.

[17] Dunigan Jr. T. H., Vetter J. S., and Worley P. H., 2005. Performance Evaluation of the SGI Altix 3700, *Proc., 2005 Intl. Conference on Parallel Processing*, http://www.csm.ornl.gov/~worley/papers/2005-06-16_icpp_sgi-altix-evaluation.pdf.

[18] Fahey M. R., and White J. B., III, May 12–16, 2003. DOE Ultrascale Evaluation Plan of the Cray X1, *Proc., 45$^{th}$ Cray User Group Conference*, Columbus, OH, http://www.csm.ornl.gov/evaluation/PHOENIX/PDF/CUG2003-Paper-Fahey.pdf.

[19] Fahey M. R., and Candy J., May 17–21, 2004, GYRO: Analyzing New Physics in Record Time, *Proc., 46$^{th}$ Cray User Group Conference*, Oak Ridge, TN, paper available at http://www.csm.ornl.gov/evaluation/PHOENIX/PDF/fahey-CUG04-paper.pdf talk at http://www.csm.ornl.gov/evaluation/PHOENIX/PDF/fahey-CUG04-slides.pdf.

[20] Fahey M. R., et al., May 16–19, 2005. Early Evaluation of the Cray XD1, *Proc., 47$^{th}$ Cray User Group Conference*, Albuquerque, NM, contact mail to: faheymr@ornl.gov to get a copy of the paper.

[21A] Farber R., HPC Balance and Common Sense, 2007, http://www.scientificcomputing.com/ShowPR_Print~PUBCODE~030~ACCT~3000000100~ISSUE~0702~RELTYPE~PR~ORIGRELTYPE~HPCC~PRODCODE~00000000~PRODLETT~E~CommonCount~0~CompName~Scientific%20Computing.html.

[21] Feldman M., March 17, 2006. Beyond Benchmarking *HPCWIRE*, Vol. **15**, No. 11, http://www.hpcwire.com/hpc/593744.html.

[22] Feldman M., July 13, 2007. What the Top500 Doesn't Tell Us, *HPCWIRE*, Vol. **16**, No. 28, http://www.hpcwire.com/hpc/1660478.html.

[23] Garrick S. C. and Settumba N., May 12–16, 2003. Implementing Finite Difference Codes on the Cray X1, *Proc., 45$^{th}$ Cray User Group Conference*, Columbus, OH, presentation available at http://www.ahpcrc.org/publications/X1CaseStudies/Finite_Diff_Codes.pdf.

[24] Hoffman F. M., et al., May 17–21, 2004. Adventures in Vectorizing the Community Land Model, *Proc., 46$^{th}$ Cray User Group Conference*, Oak Ridge, TN, http://www.csm.ornl.gov/~worley/papers/CUG04_CLM.pdf.

[25] Hoisie A., et al., November 2006. A Performance Comparison through Benchmarking and Modeling of Three Leading Supercomputers: BlueGene/L, Red Storm, and Purple, SC06, Tampa, FL, http://sc06.supercomp.org/schedule/pdf/pap240.pdf.

[26] HPC Challenge Award Competition, http://www.hpcchallenge.org.

[27] ICL, *HPC Challenge Benchmark Tests*, The Innovative Computing Laboratory, Center for Information Technology Research, University of Tennessee, Knoxville, TN; available at http://icl.cs.utk.edu/hpcc/index.html.

[28] ICL, HPCC Challenge Benchmark Results, http://icl.cs.utk.edu/hpcc/hpcc_results.cgi M-C Sawley, CSCS Benefits from HPC Challenge Benchmarks, *HPCWIRE*, October 7, 2005, http://news.taborcommunications.com/msgget.jsp?mid=464623&xs A complete listing of the environment for each HPCC benchmark run can be found at http://icl.cs.utk.edu/hpcc/export/hpcc.xls.

[29] IDC Balanced HPC Benchmark Ratings, http://www.hpcuserforum.com/benchmark/.

[30] Joseph E., Williard C. G., and Kaufmann N. J., June 2003. Market Analysis: A Look at the HPC Server Market: A New Approach to the IDC HPC Balanced Rating, IDC #29617, Vol. **1**.

[31] Johnson A., May 12–16, 2003. Computational Fluid Dynamics Applications on the Cray X1 Architecture: Experiences, Algorithms, and Performance Analysis, *Proc., 45$^{th}$ Cray User Group*

*Conference*, Columbus, OH, paper available at http://www.ahpcrc.org/publications/X1CaseStudies/CFD_Paper_05152003.pdf Presentation at http://www.ahpcrc.org/publications/X1CaseStudies/CFD_Presentation_05152003.pdf.

[32] Kahney L., October 26, 2004. System X Faster, but Falls Behind, *Wired Magazine*, http://www.wired.com/news/mac/0,2125,65476,00.html.

[33] Kerbyson D. J., Hoisie A., and Wasserman H. J., 2003. Verifying Large-Scale System Performance during Installation Using Modeling, http://www.c3.lanl.gov/pal/publications/papers/kerbyson03:Qinstallation.pdf.

[34] Kerbyson D. J., Wasserman H. J., and Hoisie A., September 2002. Exploring Advanced Architectures Using Performance Prediction, in *Innovative Architecture for Future Generation High-Performance Processors and Systems*, IEEE Computer Society Press, http://www.c3.lanl.gov/pal/publications/papers/kerbyson02:AdvancedArchitectures.pdf.

[35] Kiefer D., 2004. Cray Product Roadmap: Hardware and Software (including X1E), *Proc., 46th Cray User Group Conference*, Oak Ridge, TN, May 17–21.

[36] Krishnan M., Nieplocha J., and Tipparaju V., May 17–21, 2004. Exploiting Architectural Support for Shared Memory Communication on the Cray X1 to Optimize Bandwidth-Intensive Computations, *Proceedings, 46th Cray User Group Conference*, Oak Ridge, TN, available from mail to: jarek.nieplocha@pnl.gov.

[37] Lazou C., January 20, 2005. Benchmarks: Going for Gold in a Computer Olympiad? HPCWIRE, Article 109098.

[38] Lazou C., September 2, 2005. Sending out an SOS: HPCC Rescue Coming HPCWIRE, Article 464623, http://news.taborcommunications.com/msgget.jsp?mid=464623&xsl.

[39] Luszczek P., et al., March 2005. Introduction to the HPC Challenge Benchmark Suite, SC05, http://www.netlib.org/utk/people/JackDongarra/PAPERS/hpcc-sc05.pdf.

[40] Luszczek P., Dongarra J., and Kepner J., November 2006. Design and Implementation of the HPC Challenge Benchmark Suite, *CTWatch Quarterly*, A, http://www.ctwatch.org/quarterly/print.php?p=48.

[41] G. (Kumar) Mahinthakumar et al., 2004. Performance Evaluation and Modeling of a Parallel Astrophysics Application, *Proceedings of the High Performance Computing Symposium*, pp. 27–33, Ed. Meyer J., The Society for Modeling and Symulation International, ISBN 1-56555-278-4, Arlington, VA, http://www.csm.ornl.gov/~worley/papers/hpc2004_kumar.pdf.

[42] Mays T., May 12–16, 2003. Modeling the Weather on a Cray X1, *Proc., 45th Cray User Group Conference*, Columbus, OH, paper available at http://www.ahpcrc.org/publications/X1CaseStudies/MM5_Paper_05152003.pdf, presentation at http://www.ahpcrc.org/publications/X1CaseStudies/MM5_Presentation_05152003.pdf.

[43] Mills R. T., D'Azevedo E., and Fahey M., May 16–19, 2005. Progress Towards Optimizing the PETSC Numerical Toolkit on the Cray X-1, *Proc., 47th Cray User Group Conference*, Albuquerque, NM, paper available at http://www.ccs.ornl.gov/~rmills/pubs/cug2005.pdf, slides at http://www.ccs.ornl.gov/~rmills/pubs/cug2005_slides.pdf.

[44] Muzio P., and Johnson A., June 2003. Early Cray X1 Experience at the Army High Performance Computing Research Center, presentation available at http://www.ahpcrc.org/publications/X1CaseStudies/X1_Overview_06092003.pdf.

[45] Muzio P., and Walsh R., May 12–16, 2003. Total Life Cycle Cost Comparison: Cray X1 and Pentium 4 Cluster, *Proc., 45th Cray User Group Conference*, Columbus, OH, paper available at http://www.ahpcrc.org/publications/X1CaseStudies/Cluster_CrayX1_Comparison_Paper.pdf, presentation available at http://www.ahpcrc.org/publications/X1CaseStudies/Cluster_CrayX1_Comparison_Presentation.pdf.

[46] NAS Parallel Benchmarks, http://www.nas.nasa.gov/Software/NPB/.

[47] Oak Ridge National Laboratory, Papers and Presentations on Cray X1 Evaluation, http://www.csm.ornl.gov/evaluation/PHOENIX/index.html.

[48] PMaC HPC Benchmark Suite, http://www.sdsc.edu/PMaC/Benchmark/.

[49] Oliker L., et al., 2004. A Performance Evaluation of the Cray X1 for Scientific Applications, *Proc., VECPAR: 6th International Meeting on High Performance Computing for Computational Science*, http://www.crd.lbl.gov/~oliker/papers/vecpar_2004.pdf.

[50] Oliker L., et al., November 6–12, 2004. Scientific Computations on Modern Parallel Vector Systems, SC2004: High Performance Computing, Networking and Storage Conference, http://www.crd.lbl.gov/~oliker/papers/SC04.pdf.

[51] Oliker L., et al., November 12–18, 2005. Leading Computational Methods on Scalar and Vector HEC Platforms, SC05, http://www.csm.ornl.gov/~worley/papers/SC05_Oliker_Etal.pdf.

[51A] Oliker L., et al., March 24–30, 2007. Scientific Application Performance on Candidate PetaScale Platforms, IPDPS, http://crd.lbl.gov/~oliker/papers/ipdps07.pdf.

[52] SDSC, PMaC Prediction Framework, http://www.sdsc.edu/PMaC/projects/index.html.

[53] Shan H., Strohmaier E., and Oliker L., May 17–21, 2004. Optimizing Performance of Superscalar Codes for a Single Cray X1 MSP Processor, *Proc., 46th Cray User Group Conference*, Oak Ridge, TN, available from estrohmaier@lbl.gov.

[54] Standard Performance Evaluation Corporation, SPEC Benchmark, http://www.specbench.org/.

[55] Studham R. S., et al., May 16–19, 2005. Leadership Computing at Oak Ridge National Laboratory, *Proc., 47th Cray User Group Conference*, Albuquerque, NM, http://www.studham.com/scott/files/Leadership_CUG.pdf.

[56] Top500 Supercomputer Sites; http://www.top500.org.

[57] van der Steen A. A., June 2004. Benchmarking for Architectural Knowledge: How to Get to Know a Machine, 19th International Supercomputer Conference, ISC2004, Heidelberg, Germany, slides available from mail to: steen@phys.uu.nl.

[58] Vetter J. S., May 18, 2004. A Progress Report on the Cray X1 Evaluation by CCS at ORNL, *Proc., 46th Cray User Group Conference*, Oak Ridge, TN, http://www.csm.ornl.gov/evaluation/PHOENIX/PDF/CUG04-Vetter-talk.pdf.

[59] Vetter J. S., et al., May 16–19, 2005. Early Evaluation of the Cray XT3 at ORNL, *Proc., 47th Cray User Group Conference*, Albuquerque, NM, paper available at http://www.csm.ornl.gov/~worley/papers/2005-05-17_cug-ornl-xt3-eval.pdf.

[60] Wayland V., May 17–21, 2004, Porting and Performance of PCM on the Cray X1, *Proc., 46th Cray User Group Conference*, Oak Ridge, TN, available from wayland@ucar.edu.

[61] White J. B., III, May 12–16, 2003. An Optimization Experiment with the Community Land Model on the Cray X1, *Proc., 45th Cray User Group Conference*, Columbus, OH, http://www.csm.ornl.gov/evaluation/PHOENIX/PDF/CUG2003-Presentation-White.pdf.

[62] White J. B., III, May 17–21, 2004. Dangerously Clever X1 Application Tricks, *Proc., 46th Cray User Group Conference*, Oak Ridge, TN, available from mail to: trey@ornl.gov.

[63] Wichmann N., May 16–18, 2005. Cray and HPCC: Benchmark Developments and Results from the Past Year, *Proc., 47th Cray User Group Conference*, Albuquerque, NM, paper available from wichmann@cray.com.

[64] Wichmann N., May 17–21, 2004. HPCC Performance on the Cray X1, *Proc., 46th Cray User Group Conference*, Oak Ridge, TN, available from mail to: wichmann@cray.com.

[65] Worley P. H., May 7–10, 2007. Comparison of Cray XT3 and XT4 Scalability, *Proc., 49th Cray Users Group Conference*, Seattle, WA, http://www.csm.ornl.gov/~worley/papers/CUG2007_Worley.pdf.

[66] Worley P. H., February 26, 2004. Cray X1 Evaluation: Overview and Scalability Analysis, SIAM Conference on Parallel Processing for Scientific Computing, San Francisco, CA, http://www.csm.ornl.gov/~worley/talks/SIAMPP2004/SIAMPP04.Worley.htm.
[67] Worley P. H., May 17–21, 2004. Cray X1 Optimization: A Customer's Perspective, *Proc., 46th Cray User Group Conference*, Oak Ridge, TN, http://www.csm.ornl.gov/~worley/talks/CUG2004.OPT/CUG2004.OPT.Worley.htm.
[67A] Worley P. H., 2007. Comparison of Cray XT3 and XT4 Scalability, Proc., Cray Users Group, http://www.csm.ornl.gov/~worley/papers/CUG2007_Worley.pdf.
[68] Worley P. H., and Dunigan T. H., May 12–16, 2003. Early Evaluation of the Cray X1 at Oak Ridge National laboratory, *Proc., 45th Cray User Group Conference*, Columbus, OH, http://www.csm.ornl.gov/~worley/papers/CUG03.WorleyDunigan.X1.pdf.
[69] Worley P. H., and Foster I. T., 1994. PSTSWM: A Parallel Algorithm Testbed and Benchmark Code for Spectral General Circulation Models, Tech Report, TM-12393, Oak Ridge, TN.
[70] Worley P. H., and Levesque J., May 17–21, 2004. The Performance Evaluation of the Parallel Ocean Program on the Cray X1, *Proc., 46th Cray User Group Conference*, Oak Ridge, TN, paper available at http://www.csm.ornl.gov/~worley/papers/CUG04_Worley_POP.pdf, presentation available at http://www.csm.ornl.gov/~worley/talks/CUG2004.POP/CUG2004.POP.pdf.

# 7. Acceleration Techniques for HPC Applications

## 7.1 There is no "One Size/type Fits all" Mentality for Selecting the Ideal Accelerator

In the past, computer acceleration was most often achieved by speeding up the clock and/or increasing the number of computer processors, but this simplistic approach is no longer a panacea because of increasing heat and energy concerns, which impact the entire range of computers from laptop to supercomputers. There are several approaches to deal with this dilemma: use of field programmable gate arrays (FPGAs); use of graphics processors; use of combined cpus and gpus (gpcpus); special accelerator boards; and heterogeneous processors such as Cell BE, multicore processors and several combinations of the aforementioned approaches. None of these options are without negative repercussions. Often times, improved performance is achieved for a specific class or classes of applications, while at the same time these options have deleterious effects on other application problem types. Unfortunately, in wild pursuit of increased market share, many vendors are willing to make unsubstantiated performance claims. Although some dramatic performance improvements can be achieved with one or more of these approaches, the warning 'Caveat Emptor' should be heeded by all potential users; check out performance claims vs. your specific application type and problem size. Some of the options will only work well for certain problem sizes and may not easily scale up or down with the same positive or negative effects.

Performance improvements on application kernels may not be extrapolated upward when applied to the entire problem. Some articles on various aspects of acceleration approaches employed in HPC are described here.

## 7.2 Categories of Accelerators in this Section

FPGAs: 4, 6, 8B, 11, 11A, 12, 14A, 18, 22, 31B, 33, 34, 40, 45, 46, 50, 62, 64, 65, 66, 72

GPGPUs: 13, 15, 23, 28

Multicore: 2, 2A, 5, 9, 10, 13A, 17, 19, 29, 41, 41A, 42, 43, 44, 49, 51, 52, 55, 61, 67, 71

GPU: 15A, 20, 24, 26A, 30, 30A, 36, 51A, 56, 57, 58, 62, 62A

CELL BE: 21, 26A, 37, 41A, 53, 54, 61A, 61B, 70 and see references [15, 16] in Section 4

Software Considerations: references 8D, 60, 63, 68, 74,74A, 75

Convergence of CPUs and GPUs: reference 59

Heterogenous processors: reference 27

Vector processors: reference 48

Algorithms and trade-offs among accelerators: references 25 and 26

Threads issues: reference 47

Accelerators for financial analysis: references 2A, 8A,15B,18, 31A, 41B and 50

Accelerator boards: references 8C,70A

### References

[1] AMD, AMD to Ship Quad-Core Processors in August, *HPCWIRE*, Vol. **16**, No. 27, http://www.hpcwire.com/hpc/1642830.html, July 6, 2007.

[2] AMD, AMD Spec to Enable Real-Time Performance Optimization, GRID today, http://www.gridtoday.com/grid/1725696.html, August 14, 2007.

[2A] AMD, AMD Highlights Expansion of Torrenza Solutions, HPCWIRE, Vol. **16**, No. 38, http://www.hpcwire.com/hpc/1786269.html, September 21, 2007.

[3] Arizona Daily Star, New Generation of Processors Presents Big Problems, Potential Payoffs for Software Industry, Arizona Daily Star, http://www.azstarnet.com/news/192914, July 23, 2007.

[4] Baxter R., et al., July 18–20, 2007. Maxwell – A 64 FPGA Supercomputer, http://rssi.ncsa.uiuc.edu/docs/academic/Baxter_presentation.pdf, reconfigurable Systems Summer Institute, RSSI, NCSA, University of Illinois, Urbana, IL.

[5] Buttari A., et al., The Impact of Multicore on Math Software, Para 2006, Umea Sweden, June 2006, http://www.netlib.org/utk/people/JackDongarra/PAPERS/para-multicore-2006.pdf.

[6] D'Amour M., July 13, 2007. Standards-based Reconfigurable Computing for HPC, *HPCWIRE*, Vol. **16**, No. 28, http://www.hpcwire.com/hpc/1653583.html.

[7] Baetke F., June 29, 2007. Addressing New Trends and Challenges in High Performance Computing, Hot Seat Session, Part 1, International Supercomputing Conference (ISC07), Dresden, Germany, For additional information, please contact mail to: frank.baetke@hp.com.

[8] Baetke F., July 2, 2007. Towards Peta-scale Computing: Trends and Challenges for Designers and Vendors, Third Erlangen High-End Computing Symposium, University of Erlangen, Erlangen, Germany, see http://www10.informatik.uni-erlangen.de/Misc/EIHECS3/Baetke.pdf.

[8A] Blake B., September 14, 2007. Credit Modeling with Supercomputing, *HPCWIRE*, Vol. **16**, No. 37, http://www.hpcwire.com/hpc/1768656.html.

[8B] Cantle A., July 17–20, 2007. Why FPGAs Will Win the Accelerator Battle: Building Computers That Minimize Date Movement, http://rssi.ncsa.uiuc.edu/docs/industry/Nallatech_presentation.pdf reconfigurable Systems Summer Institute, University of Illinois, Urbana, IL.

[8C] ClearSpeed Technology, ClearSpeed Demos Ultra-Dense Computing at IDF, *HPCWIRE*, Vol. **16**, No. 38, September 21, 2007, http://hpcwire.com/hpc/1789146.html.

[8D] Dabiilidi C., September 28, 2007. Virginia Tech Explores Thermal-Aware Computing, *HPCWIRE*, Vol. **16**, No. 39, http://www.hpcwire.com/hpc/1802228.html.

[9] Dongarra J., (Guest Editor), February 2007. The Promise and Perils of the Coming Multicore Revolution and Its Impact, *CTWatch Quarterly*, Vol. **3**, No. 1, http://www.ctwatch.org/quarterly/pdf/ctwatchquarterly-10.pdf.

[10] Dongarra J., Gannon D., Fox G., and Kennedy K., February 2007. The Impact of Multicore on Computational Science Software, *CTWatch Quarterly*, Vol. **3**, No. 1, pp. 3–10, http://www.ctwatch.org/quarterly/articles/2007/02/the-impact-of-multicore-on-computational-science-software/

[11] DRC Computer Corp., DRC Computer Ships Reconfigurable Processor Unit, *HPCWIRE*. Vol. **16**, No. 28, July 13, 2007, http://www.hpcwire.com/hpc/1652992.html.

[11A] E. El-Araby et al., July 18–20, 2007. Portable Library Development for Reconfigurable Computing Systems, http://rssi.ncsa.uiuc.edu/docs/academic//El-Araby_presentation.pdf, Reconfigurable Systems Summer Institute, RSSI, NCSA, University of Illinois, Urbana, IL.

[12] T. El-Ghazawi et al., November 2006. Is High-Performance Reconfigurable Computing the Next Supercomputing Paradigm, sc06, Tampa, FL, http://sc06.supercomp.org/schedule/pdf/pan102.pdf.

[13] Feldman M., April 13, 2007. Another Look at GPGPU, *HPCWIRE*, Vol. **16**, Issue 15, http://www.hpcwire.com/hpc/1385786.html.

[13A] Feldman M., September 7, 2007. As the Chip Turns, *HPCWIRE*, Vol. **16**, No. 36, http://www.hpcwire.com/hpc/1766373.html.

[14] Feldman M., July 20, 2007. Because It's There?, *HPCWIRE*, Vol. **16**, No. 29, http://www.hpcwire.com/hpc/1673201.html.

[14A] Feldman M., September 21, 2007. FPGA Acceleration Gets a Boost from HP, Intel *HPCWIRE*, Vol. **16**, No. 38, http://www.hpcwire.com/hpc/1791479.html.

[15] Feldman M., May 25, 2007. GPGPU Looks for Respect, *HPCWIRE*, Vol. **16**, No. 21, http://www.hpcwire.com/hpc/1582455.html.

[15A] Feldman M., September 28, 2007. Supercharging Seismic Processing with GPUs *HPCWIRE*, Vol. **16**, No. 39, http://www.hpcwire.com/hpc/1803161.html.

[15B] Feldman M., September 21, 2007. Wall Street-HPC Lovefest; Intel's Fall Classic, *HPCWIRE*, Vol. **16**, No. 38, http://www.hpcwire.com/hpc/1791855.html.

[16] Feldman M., July 20, 2007. HP Looks to Bring HPC Applications Up to Speed, *HPCWIRE*, Vol. **16**, No. 29, http://www.hpcwire.com/hpc/1673152.html.

[17] Feldman M., May 11, 2007. RapidMind Looks to Tame the Multicore Beast, *HPCWIRE*, Vol. **16**, Issue 19, http://www.hpcwire.com/hpc/1560982.html.

[18] Feldman M., June 8, 2007. High Frequency Traders Get Boost from FPGA Acceleration, *HPCWIRE*, Vol. **16**, No. 23, http://www.hpcwire.com/hpc/1600113.html.

[19] Feldman M., July 27, 2007. Intel Opens Up Multicore Development Library, *HPCWIRE*, Vol. **16**, No. 30, http://www.hpcwire.com/hpc/1688555.html.

[20] Feldman M., June 22, 2007. NVIDIA Takes Direct Aim at High Performance Computing, *HPCWIRE*, Vol. **16**, No. 25, http://www.hpcwire.com/hpc/1625213.html.

[21] Georgia Tech, Georgia Tech 'CellBuzz' Cluster in Production Use, *HPCWIRE*, Vol. **16**, No. 28, July 13, 2007, http://www.hpcwire.com/hpc/1657876.html.

[22] Gokhale M. B. and Graham P. S., 2005. ***Reconfigurable Computing: Accelerating Computation with Field-Programmable Gate Arrays***, Springer-Verlag.

[23] GPGPU: General-Purpose Computation Using Graphics Hardware, http://www.gpgpu.org/.

[24] GPUBench: a benchmark suite for assessing the performance of programmable graphics processors in areas of particular importance to general-purpose computations, http://graphics.stanford.edu/projects/gpubench/.

[25] Gustafson J. L., November 14, 2006. Understanding the Different Acceleration Technologies, *HPCWIRE*, Vol. **13**, No.14, http://www.hpcwire.com/hpc/1091512.html.

[26] Gustafson J. L., April 6, 2007. Algorithm Leadership, *HPCWIRE*, Vol. **16**, No. 14, http://www.hpcwire.com/hpc/1347145.html.

[26A] Hall S. G., April 27, 2007. Using Gaming Technology to Save Lives, with Medical Imaging, medic-exchange.com, http://www.medicexchange.com/mall/departmentpage.cfm/MedicExchangeUSA/_81675/1378/departments-contentview.

[27] Hester P., June 29, 2007. Peta-Scale x86: Heterogeneous Processing Comes of Age, Hot Seat Session, Part 1, International Supercomputing Conference (ISC07), Dresden, Germany. For additional information, please contact Rob.Keosheyan@amd.com.

[28] Houston M., 2005. General Purpose Computation on Graphics Processors (GPGPU), Stanford University Graphics Lab, http://graphics.stanford.edu/~mhouston/public_talks/R520-mhouston.pdf.

[29] HP, HP Announces Multi-core Optimization Program for HPC, *HPCWIRE*, Vol. **16**, No. 26, http://www.hpcwire.com/hpc/1635207.html, June 29, 2007.

[30] HPCWIRE, Acceleware Intros Four-GPU System for Technical Computing, *HPCWIRE*, Vol. **16**, No. 23, http://hpcwire.com/hpc/1597780.html, June 8, 2007.

[30A] HPCWIRE, Acceleware to Demo Pre-Stack Time Migration Software at SEG, *HPCWIRE*, Vol. **16**, No. 38, http://hpcwire.com/hpc/1792141.html, September 21, 2007.

[31] HPCWIRE, CEES, Maxeler to explore Seismic Processing Acceleration, *HPCWIRE*, Vol. **16**, No. 23, http://www.hpcwire.com/hpc/1599684.html, June 8, 2007.

[31A] HPCWIRE, Cisco, Reuters, Sun Create Low-Latency Trading Solution, *HPCWIRE*, Vol. **16**, No. 38, http://www.hpcwire.com/hpc/1789804.html, September 21, 2007.

[31B] HPCWIRE, DRC Stakes Claim in Reconfigurable Computing, *HPCWIRE*, Vol. **16**, No. 36, http://www.hpcwire.com/hpc/1763516.html, September 7, 2007,

[32] HPCWIRE, Europe Unites to Foster HP Technologies with the Launch of ParMA, *HPCWIRE*, Vol. **16**, No. 26, http://www.hpcwire.com/hpc/1635828.html, June 29, 2007.

[33] HPCWIRE, FPGAs in HPC Mark 'Beginning of a New Era, *HPCWIRE*, Vol. **15**, No. 26, http://www.hpcwire.com/hpc/709193.html, June 29, 2006.

[34] HPCWIRE, FPGA Video Imaging Acceleration Spotlighted at IFSEC, *HPCWIRE*, Vol. **16**, No. 21, http://www.hpcwire.com/hpc/1577633.html, May 25, 2007.

[35] HPCWIRE, Google Acquires PeakStream, *HPCWIRE*, Vol. **16**, No. 23, http://www.hpcwire.com/hpc/1599723.html, June 8, 2007.

[36] HPCWIRE, GPU-Tech Delivers GPU Technical Computing Libraries, *HPCWIRE*, Vol. **16**, No. 24, http://www.hpcwire.com/hpc/1611290.html, June 15, 2007.

[37] HPCWIRE, IBM to Build Cell-Based Supercomputer for Los Alamos, *HPCWIRE*, Vol. **15**, No. 36, http://www.hpcwire.com/hpc/872363.html, September 6, 2006.

[38] HPCWIRE, PeakStream Dissolution Shines Spotlight on Stream Computing, *HPCWIRE*, Vol. **16**, No. 24, http://www.hpcwire.com/hpc/1613242.html, June 15, 2007.

[39] HPCWIRE, PeakStream Unveils HPC Software Platform, *HPCWIRE*, Vol. **15**, No. 38, http://www.hpcwire.com/hpc/905530.html, September 22, 2006.

[40] HPCWIRE, Shanghai Scientists Use SGI, Mitrionics HPC Technology, *HPCWIRE*, Vol. **16**, No. 30, http://www.hpcwire.com/hpc/1682211.html, July 27, 2007.

[41] HPCWIRE, Quad-Core Opteron Servers Previewed at Computex Taipei, *HPCWIRE*, Vol. **16**, No. 23, http://www.hpcwire.com/hpc/1597784.html, June 8, 2007.

[41A] IBM, IBM Claims Power6 Dominance Across Range of Applications, *HPCWIRE*, Vol. **16**, No. 36, http://www.hpcwire.com/hpc/1763261.html, September 7, 2007.

[41B] IBM, IBM, Red Hat Deliver Financial Trading Platform, *HPCWIRE*, Vol. **16**, No. 38, http://www.hpcwire.com/hpc/1783890.html, September 21, 2007.

[42] Intel Corp., New Intel Software Products Target Multicore Environments, *HPCWIRE*, Vol. **16**, No. 23, http://www.hpcwire.com/hpc/1597779.html, June 8, 2007.

[43] Intel Corp., Intel Introduces Multi-core Software Training Curriculum, *HPCWIRE,* Vol. **16**, No. 26, http://www.hpcwire.com/hpc/1635685.html, June 29, 2007.

[44] Kale L., June 22–23, 2007. PetaScale and Multicore Programming Models: What Is Needed, Petascale Applications Symposium, Pittsburgh Supercomputer Center, Pittsburgh, PA, http://www.psc.edu/seminars/PAS/Kale.pdf.

[45] Koehler S., et al., July 18–20, 2007. Challenges for Performance Analysis in High-Performance Reconfigurable Computing, http://rssi.ncsa.uiuc.edu/docs/academic/Koehler_presentation.pdf, Reconfigurable Systems Summer Institute, RSSI, NCSA, University of Illinois, Urbana, IL.

[46] Lazou C., June 15, 2007. Mitrionics CEO Details Company Vision, *HPCWIRE*, Vol. **16**, No. 24, http://www.hpcwire.com/hpc/1606919.html.

[47] Lee E. A., May 2006. The Problem with Threads, IEEE Computer, Vol. **39**, No. 5, pp. 33–42, http://www.eecs.berkeley.edu/Pubs/TechRpts/2006/EECS-2006-1.pdf.

[48] Lemuet C., et al., November 2006. The Potential Energy Efficiency of Vector Acceleration, sc06, Tampa, FL, http://sc06.supercomp.org/schedule/pdf/pap247.pdf.

[49] Lowney G., June 22–23, 2007. Software for Multi-core Processors, Petascale Applications Symposium, Pittsburgh Supercomputer Center, Pittsburgh, PA, http://www.psc.edu/seminars/PAS/Lowney.pdf.

[50] Mackin B., May 25, 2007. A New Engine for Financial Analysis, *HPCWIRE*, Vol. **16**, No. 21, http://www.hpcwire.com/hpc/1578042.html.

[51] Manferdelli J., February 2007. The Many-Core Inflection Point for Mass Market Computer Systems, *CTWatch Quarterly*, Vol. **3**, No. 1, pp. 11–17, http://www.ctwatch.org/quarterly/articles/2007/02/the-many-core-inflection-point-for-mass-market-computer-systems.

[51A] Mason C., November 21, 2007. Minding the Gap: Learn How Hardware Acceleration Can Outperform Your Existing PC Architecture, Acceleware, register to access archived version at http://acceleware.webex.com/acceleware/onstage/g.php?t=a&d=921610329.

[52] McCalpin J., Moore C., and Hester P., February 2007. The Role of Multicore Processors in the Evolution of General-Purpose Computing, *CTWatch Quarterly*, Vol. **3**, No. 1, pp. 18–30, http://www.ctwatch.org/quarterly/articles/2007/02/the-role-of-multicore-processors-in-the-evolution-of-general-purpose-computing.

[53] Mercury Computer Systems, Inc., Algorithm Performance on the Cell Broadband Processor, Mercury Computer Systems, Inc., Chelmsford, MA, Revision 1.1.2, http://www.mc.com/uploadedFiles/Cell-Perf-Simple.pdf, June 28, 2006.

[54] Mercury Computer Systems, Inc., Cell Architecture Advantages for Computationally Intensive Applications, Mercury White Paper, Mercury Computer Systems, Inc., Chelmsford, MA, 2005, http://www.mc.com/uploadedFiles/Cell-WP.pdf.

[55] MIT Lincoln Laboratory, Lincoln Lab Releases PVTOL Multicore Software, *HPCWIRE*, Vol. **16**, No. 26, http://www.hpcwire.com/hpc/1630587.html, June 29, 2007.

[56] NVIDIA Corp., NVIDIA Releases CUDA 1.0 for GPU Computing, *HPCWIRE*, Vol. **16**, No. 28, http://www.hpcwire.com/hpc/1660214.html, July 13, 2007.

[57] NVIDIA Corp., NVIDIA CUDA Slashes Compute Times for MATLAB Users, *HPCWIRE*, Vol. **16**, No. 29, http://www.hpcwire.com/hpc/1667977.html, July 20, 2007.

[58] Owens J. D., et al., August 29–September 2, 2005. A Survey of General-Purpose Computation on Graphics Hardware, *Proc., Eurographics 2005*, Dublin, Ireland, pp. 21–51, http://graphics.idav.ucdavis.edu/graphics/publications/func/return_pdf?pub_id=844.

[59] Papakipos M., January 19, 2007. Converging Features in CPUs and GPUs, *HPCWIRE*, Vol. **16**, No. 3, http://www.hpcwire.com/hpc/1209133.html.

[60] Patterson D. A., et al., December 18, 2006. The Landscape of Parallel Computing Research: A View from Berkeley, Tech Report No. UCB/EECS-2006-183, http://www.eecs.berkeley.edu/Pubs/TechRpts/2006/EECS-2006-183.pdf.

[61] Patterson D. A., et al., November 24, 2006. RAMP: A Research Accelerator for Multiple Processors, UCB, EECS, http://www.eecs.berkeley.edu/Pubs/TechRpts/2006/EECS-2006-158.pdf.

[61A] Perez J. M., et al., September 2007. Cells: Making It Easier to Program the Cell Broadband Engine Processor, *IBM J Res & Dev*, Vol. **51**, No. 5, pp. 593–604.

[61B] RapidMind, Inc., Cell BE Porting and Tuning with RapidMind: A Case Study, White paper http://www.rapidmind.net/case-cell.php.

[62] Schneider R., May 15, 2007. How GPU Computing Can Benefit Your High Performance Computing Tasks, Acceleware, register to see archived event at http://events.onlinebroadcasting.com/acceleware/051507/index.php?page=launch.

[62A] Schneider R., October 31, 2007. Accelerators Unveiled: Your Guide to Accelerators Available in the Market and How They Compare, Acceleware, register for archived event at http://acceleware.webex.com/acceleware/onstage/g.php?t=a&d=923377828.

[63] Schoenauer W., July 27, 2007. A Remark About Petascale Computing, *HPCWIRE*, Vol. **16**, No. 30, http://www.hpcwire.com/hpc/1688404.html.

[64] Steffen C. P., July 18–20, 2007. Parametrization of Algorithms and FPGA Accelerators to Predict Performance, http://rssi.ncsa.uiuc.edu/docs/academic/Steffen_presentation.pdf Reconfigurable Systems Summer Institute, RSSI, NCSA, University of Illinois, Urbana, IL.

[65] Storaasli O. O., et al., May 2007. Performance Evaluation of FPGA-Based Biological Applications, Proceedings, Cray User's Group, Seattle, WA, http://ft.ornl.gov/~olaf/pubs/CUG07Olaf17M07.pdf.

[66] Strenski D., July 18–20, 2007. Accelerators in Cray's Adaptive Supercomputing, http://rssi.ncsa.uiuc.edu/docs/industry/Cray_presentation.pdf, Reconfigurable Systems Summer Institute, RSSI, NCSA, University of Illinois, Urbana, IL.

[67] Sun Microsystems, Sun Adds Multicore Enhancements to Solaris Development Suite, *HPCWIRE*, Vol. **16**, No. 24, http://www.hpcwire.com/hpc/1611110.html, June 15, 2007.

[68] Tally S., May 25, 2007. 'Not So Fast, Supercomputers,' Say Software Programmers, *HPCWIRE*, Vol. **16**, No. 21, http://www.hpcwire.com/hpc/1579050.html.

[69] Tan L., July 10, 2007. Will Supercomputer Speed Hit a Plateau? *ZDNETASIA*, http://www.zdnetasia.com/news/hardware/0,39042972,62028027,00.htm.

[70] TotalView Technologies, Totalview Adds Debugger Support for Cell Broadband Engine, *HPCWIRE*, Vol. **16**, No. 26, http://www.hpcwire.com/hpc/1633105.html, June 29, 2007.

[70A] Trader T., September 7, 2007. ClearSpeed Technology Takes Flight, *HPCWIRE*, Vol. **16**, No. 36, http://www.hpcwire.com/hpc/1766576.html.

[71] Turek D., February 2007. High Performance Computing and the Implications of Multi-core Architectures, *CTWatch Quarterly*, Vol. **3**, No. 1, pp. 31–33, http://www.ctwatch.org/quarterly/articles/2007/02/high-performance-computing-and-the-implications-of-multi-core-architectures.

[72] Underwood K. D., Hemmert H. S., and Ulmer C., November 2006. Architectures and APIs: Assessing Requirements for Delivering FPGA Performance to Applications, SC06, Tampa, FL, http://sc06.supercomp.org/schedule/pdf/pap213.pdf.

[73] Wheat S. R., June 28, 2007. High Performance Intel Clusters Made Easy, Hot Seat Session 2, International Supercomputing Conference (ISC'07), Dresden, Germany. For details or questions, please contact stephan.gillich@intel.com.

[74] Wolfe M., July 27, 2007. Compilers and More: Productivity and Compilers, *HPCWIRE*, Vol. **16**, No. 30, http://www.hpcwire.com/hpc/1679143.html.

[74A] Wolfe M., October 19, 2007. Compilers and More: Are Optimizing Compilers Important? *HPCWIRE*, Vol. **16**, No. 42, http://www.hpcwire.com/hpc/1838764.html.

[75] Yelick K., November 10, 2006. The Software Challenges of Petascale, *HPCWIRE*, Vol. **15**, No. 45, http://www.hpcwire.com/hpc/1071362.html.

# 8. The Race for Petaflop Computing

The current U.S. government's concerted effort for petaflop computing is focused on the U.S. Defense Advanced Research Projects Agency (DARPA) activity discussed below.

## 8.1 DARPA's Competition for a Petaflop Class Supercomputer

DARPA decided to initiate a long-term, multiple-year project to create one or more petaflop class machines. Phase 1 in 2002 was a one-year concept study for a trans petaflop machine. The selected vendors were IBM, Cray, Sun, SGI and HP. Each of these vendors was awarded 3 million dollars; Phase 2 selection was in mid 2003 and funding was provided for three years to IBM (53.3 million dollars), Cray (43.1 million dollars) and Sun (49.7 million dollars). Phase 3 winners were announced in late 2006 to create one or more prototype petaflop systems. The winners of Phase 3 were IBM and Cray, which are each supposed to produce a petaflop class machine by 2010–2011. Both vendors are also partnering with several government labs and academic institutions and are also expected to cost share the total project with their DARPA stipends. Both IBM and Cray are likely to introduce several intermediate machines on their way to producing a petaflop class machine.

## 8.2 Petaflop Programming Language Concerns

Both IBM and Cray as well as Sun (from Phase 2 DARPA competition) are proposing new computer languages for these petaflop class machines; IBM has proposed

X10 [23, 24], Cray has proposed Chapel [3, 6, 13], and Sun has proposed Fortress [41]. More information about all three of these languages is given in the references in this section. Some readers may be old enough to remember a failed international artificial language effort called 'Esperanto' If X10, Chapel, and/or Fortress are to avoid similar extinction, then more than use on petaflop class machines is needed. What is most likely to happen is that the best attributes of all three language proposals (as well as others) will form the basis of one of more software libraries which will be ported to multiple vendor machines and made compatible with current programming languages such as FORTRAN, C and C++. Once such libraries are widely used in the HPC community, it may then be an easier task to gain acceptance for a new HPC language incorporating those extensions. For more discussion of this issue, see reference [27A].

## 8.3 Speed Nomenclature

Figure 7 defines the nomenclature used to define supercomputer speed classes and usually refers to floating-point operations. Current top-end supercomputers (circa 2007) are in the teraflop range so that the petaflop machines could be up to three orders of magnitude faster than current supercomputers. Please closely distinguish between peak speed defined for each such machine and sustained speed. In most cases, computer vendors prefer to quote a peak speed for their computer even when in reality such a performance is rarely, if ever, approached on real, complete industrial applications or may only be approached on small segments of a large problem. Also

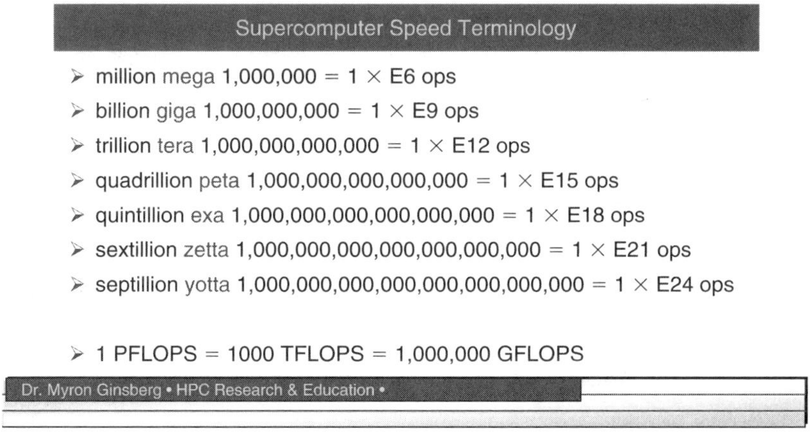

Supercomputer Speed Terminology

- million mega 1,000,000 = 1 × E6 ops
- billion giga 1,000,000,000 = 1 × E9 ops
- trillion tera 1,000,000,000,000 = 1 × E12 ops
- quadrillion peta 1,000,000,000,000,000 = 1 × E15 ops
- quintillion exa 1,000,000,000,000,000,000 = 1 × E18 ops
- sextillion zetta 1,000,000,000,000,000,000,000 = 1 × E21 ops
- septillion yotta 1,000,000,000,000,000,000,000,000 = 1 × E24 ops

- 1 PFLOPS = 1000 TFLOPS = 1,000,000 GFLOPS

Dr. Myron Ginsberg • HPC Research & Education •

FIG. 7. Supercomputer speed terminology.

keep in mind that the number of floating-point operations just defines one of several metrics for characterizing supercomputer performance; please see Section 6 for more details about assessing actual supercomputer performance.

## 8.4 Some Candidate Petaflop Class Applications

The reader may wonder if there are existing applications that could benefit from use of petaflop class machines. The answer is an emphatic yes. Many physical modeling problems that currently require lots of computing time even on large, fast machines today would be candidates for use on the petaflop class machines mentioned above. Figure 8 lists several petaflop class applications that may be the beneficiaries of such machines that may offer one or more orders of magnitude speed up over performance on current computers.

**Applications for Petaflops Computers**

- Weather forecasting
- Business data mining
- DNA sequence analysis
- Protein folding simulations
- Inter-species DNA analyses
- Medical imaging and analysis such as virtual surgery planning
- Nuclear weapons stewardship
- Multi-user immersive virtual reality
- National-scale economic modeling
- Climate and environmental modeling including rapid detection of wildfires
- Molecular nanotechnology design tools
- Cryptography and digital signal processing
- Complete simulation of an automotive design including interactions of all subsystems and biological human occupant models, I.e., full-fidelity automotive crash testing as well as advanced aircraft and spacecraft design
- Combating pandemics and bioterrorism
- Improving electrical power generation and distribution

Dr. Myron Ginsberg • HPC Research & Education •

FIG. 8. Applications for petaflops computers.

## 8.5 Some Foreign Petaflop Chasers

Other countries also recognize potential advantages for producing a petaflop class machine in the 2010–2011 time frame. For example, in Japan, NEC, Fujitsu, and Hitachi [10, 32, 40] are involved in a national plan to build such a machine; the director of the project is Tadashi Watanabe who led the development of the Earth Simulator (ES) built by NEC and was also honored with the Seymour Cray Award in 2006 at SC06. The ES project really stimulated increased U.S. efforts to produce a faster supercomputer. At the time of introduction of the Earth Simulator, the fastest U.S. supercomputer had a peak speed of about 7 teraflops but the Earth Simulator had a peak speed of about 40 teraflops. Ironically, the ES is a vector machine, whereas the U.S. had more or less abandoned vector machines (with the exception of Cray) as their construction was very expensive and had opted for use of commodity scalar processors as the basis of supercomputers for both business and scientific/engineering computations.

Also, China joined the petaflop race [31] with three companies hoping to build a 1, 2 or possibly 3 petaflop machine by 2010. The three Chinese companies are Lenovo (who took over IBM's personnel computer business a few years ago), Dawning and Galactic Computing. The latter company was established by Steve Chen who earlier worked for Cray Research under Seymour Cray.

Most recently, France has joined the petaflop computing race [2B, 27D, 34A]. SYSTEM@TIC Paris-Region global competitiveness cluster and POPS (PetaOperations Per Second) (December 2007) are being led by computer hardware company, Bull, working with 260 major French science and industry organizations focusing on hardware as well as systems and applications software issues to build a petaflop class supercomputer by 2013.

## 8.6 Adaptive Supercomputing: the Good, the Bad, and the Ugly Reality

Cray (and IBM to a lesser extent) has been advocating the idea of 'adaptive supercomputing' [37, 41A] (see Fig. 9) in which supposedly user-application optimization would be performed primarily by smart compiler technology, delegating individual heterogeneous computer components to focus on those parts of the user problem that it can best improve. It is a great idea because most users do not want to become amateur computer scientists in order to maximize the performance of their application. Figure 10 indicates the initial heterogeneous components from previous Cray machines; in Section 7 we discussed some of the types of accelerators which could be used to create heterogeneous components.

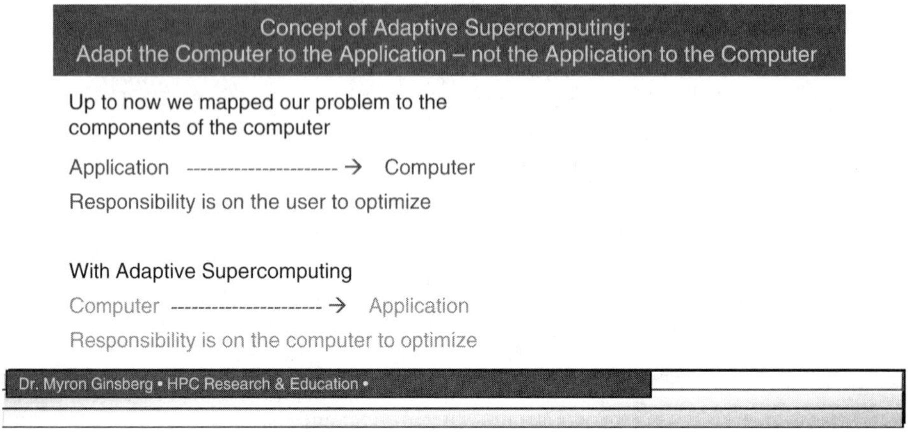

FIG. 9. Concept of adaptive supercomputing.

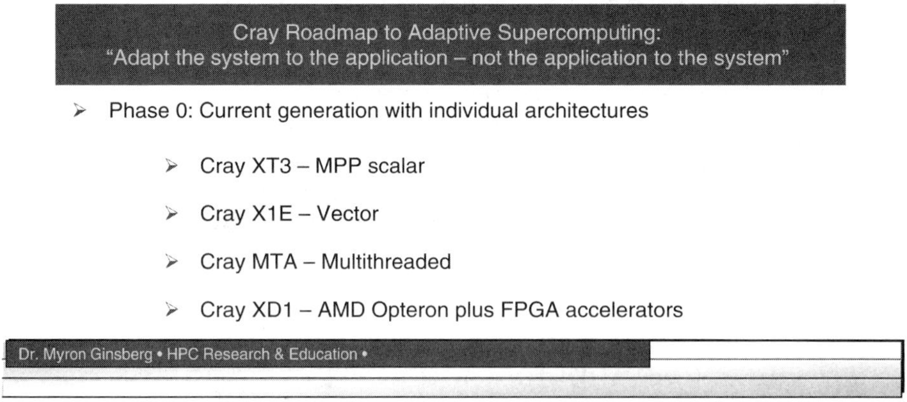

FIG. 10. Cray roadmap to adaptive supercomputing.

The real challenge to the degree of effectiveness of an adaptive supercomputing strategy is to create the 'smart' compiler technology (and support software) to orchestrate this process efficiently and at the same time produce the best possible optimal performance for the user's problem. Another challenge is to make this process easily transportable to other supercomputers. Considering that the supercomputer application may be defined by several hundred thousand lines of code, then adaptive supercomputing could be an extremely daunting task. Unless the necessary software is developed in that time frame, I would suspect that initial adaptive supercomputing efforts will be somewhat modest, working best on applications which are essentially embarrassingly parallel. See [41A] for some interesting thoughts expressed by a compiler expert.

## 8.7 Influence of Optimizing Compiler

In the past, HPC users shouldered most of the burden to optimize their application code. In large government/academic research labs, this responsibility has been shared with a multidisciplinary support staff. In most of the private industries, especially where such diversified support personnel are often not readily available on site, commercial software vendors take on this task. On the leading edge of HPC, the early software is often inadequate to optimize effectively user-application code. For example, with the introduction of vector supercomputers in the 1970s, it was very difficult to achieve optimal performance from applications code written strictly in a high-level language such as Fortran or C; compiler directives, software libraries and assembly language code were used to improve performance. Often early optimizing compilers could not achieve significantly better performance than that obtained by an experienced hand coder working with assembly language. Eventually, the optimizing compilers produced much better performance and thereby trained users how to achieve improved performance by emulating the compiler patterns that tended to produce high-speed results. The same exercise will have to be repeated with new languages and application codes on petaflop class machines. Given this situation, of course, HPC users would prefer to use an adaptive supercomputing approach as briefly described above. Initially, the complexity of petaflop class computers with heterogeneous processing elements on multicore chips is unlikely to achieve the desired adaptive supercomputing for complex application code.

Intelligent optimizing compiler decisions sometimes can only be made at run-time because the critical information to make the best selection may not be available at compilation time. The example in Fig. 11 is a simple illustration of this. Suppose you have the simple Do loop shown in that figure and each iteration is totally independent of all other iterations. With vector hardware, the elements of a participating vector are moved from main memory to fast pipelined vector registers from which the vector elements are directly sent to vector processing functional units via a strip-mining strategy. If the vector length is expressed as N and that value is not known at compilation time, how can the compiler determine if the vector length is too short to benefit from vector processing? If hardware vector facilities are non-existent on the machine, then the user, compiler and /or the operating system have to take on this responsibility, if indeed, hardware vectors are 'dead'. Such a decision has to take into account the actual vector length at run-time and whether the vector elements

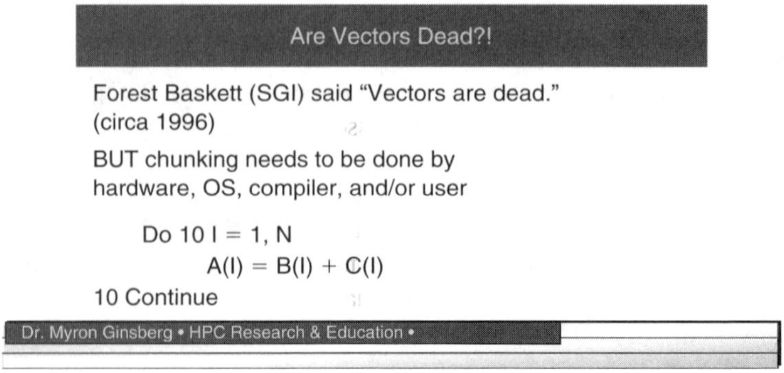

FIG. 11. Are vectors dead?

are in contiguous or non-contiguous storage locations in memory. Given the number of available functional units for the vector operation, some entity (hardware, software, or user) must determine the best distribution of vector elements among the available processors. Of course, an optimizing compiler can handle such a situation if the user has available vector directives and can use them to provide the necessary information to the compiler at run-time; however, in a long complex program, a user may not actually readily know the necessary information to alert the compiler. This is just the situation for a simple loop with no iteration dependencies. So I hope you can envisage in the initial era of petaflop class machines that the use of an adaptive supercomputing strategy could easily produce disappointing performance results.

## 8.8 Cray vs. IBM Supercomputing Philosophy

Cray and IBM have been selected by DARPA to produce viable petaflop class machines. Readers should note some of the distinguishing attributes of these two companies. IBM is a huge corporate monolith compared to Cray Inc. which has well under a thousand employees. Computers at IBM are essentially designed by a committee approach, i.e., a very large number of people are involved with the necessary hardware and software for each machine and these people are present at IBM locations all over the world. Cray currently has facilities in Washington State and in Minnesota. Most of the early Cray machines were designed by Seymour Cray with a very small support staff. These days at Cray, Inc, Steve Scott has inherited the Seymour Cray designer position. Upper level IBM executives have never understood as to how effective supercomputers could be created by such a small staff as that at Cray.

IBM has a very large marketing staff whose presence is felt throughout the entire corporation. IBM dominates the supercomputer market with slightly less than 50% of the total machines. When IBM creates a large supercomputer such as IBM Blue Gene/L (with approximately 131072 processors and located at Lawrence Livermore National Laboratory), it very wisely offers many smaller versions (such as a one-cabinet version) to satisfy needs at lower price points. IBM is very adept in covering all price points in its target markets and usually prefers to use its own computer chips although it does make computers with other non-IBM chips. It also offers on demand services to those companies that have fluctuating needs.

In contrast, Cray tends to target a relatively small segment of the total supercomputer market, mainly at the very high end where many of the customers are government labs or large research organizations. It makes no attempt (so far) to produce smaller versions of its high-end products and does not offer on-demand services such as those offered by IBM. Cray at present has little representation in most of U.S. industries. Cray tends not to make its own computer chips and has to depend on other companies such as IBM or Texas Instruments for fabricating application-specific integrated circuits. Current Cray computers are using AMD Opteron chips and Cray has made a long-term commitment to AMD for future chips for its upcoming products.

Cray and IBM seem to prefer different metrics for measuring supercomputer performance. IBM marketing likes to point out the number of IBM machines that are on the Top 500 List (http://www.top500.org) even though the metric for ranking on that list is based solely upon speed of solving a dense linear system of equations and does not directly reflect total performance on a real industrial strength application. Cray prefers to look at the HPC Challenge Benchmark Tests (.... http://icl.cs.utk.edu/hpcc/index.html) which measures many other attributes of total computer performance in addition to the Peak LINPACK numbers used in the Top 500 list. For supercomputers IBM prefers to state peak performance rather than sustained performance for a real application even when actual sustained performance is significantly below peak performance and cannot be even closely approached in real industrial applications. Cray prefers to look at sustained problem performance. Given these differences, it will be interesting to observe how performance on the Cray and IBM DARPA petaflop machines is measured.

## 8.9 Discussion of Algorithms

With the introduction of the petaflop era, users should be reminded that they can sometimes be misled about performance. For example, it will be easy to be enchanted about flop rates for applications on a petaflop machine. Consider two algorithms to solve the same problem and one has a higher flop rate than the other one. Does this imply that the algorithm with the higher flop rate is to be preferred? The answer is not necessarily because it is possible that the algorithm with the higher flop rate could actually require more wall-clock time for execution and/or have more accumulated roundoff error. In an industrial environment, wall-clock time to execute is far more important than flop rate. An algorithm could have very good flop rates but more time may be consumed in the solution process and thus may require more wall-clock time than that for the algorithm with the lesser flop rate.

Furthermore, the overall performance could be hindered by using certain types of operations on one architecture which are not necessarily efficient on that machine. Some interesting ideas about this situation can be found in [18A]. Gustafson makes some observations which may seem counter-intuitive to those working with dense and sparse algorithm solvers. It is very rewarding for users to be aware of the hardware and software effects, which can contribute to algorithm error propagation and/or performance inefficiency [2A].

## References


[1] Bailey D. H., 1998. Challenges of Future High-End Computers, in *High Performance Computer Systems and Applications*, edited by Schaeffer J., Kluwer Academic Press, Boston, MA, http://crd.lbl.gov/~dhbailey/dhbpapers/future.pdf.

[2] Bailey D. H., et al., 1989. Floating Point Arithmetic in Future Supercomputers, *Int'l J. of Supercomputing Applications*, Vol. **3**, No. 3, pp. 86–90, http://crd.lbl.gov/~dhbailey/dhbpapers/fpafs.pdf.

[2A] Bader D., ed., 2008. Petascale Computing: Algorithms and Applications, CRC Press, Atlanta, GA.

[2B] Bull, March 7, 2008. Bull Highlights Commitment to HPC, *HPCWIRE*, Vol. 17, No. 10, http://www.hpcwire.com/hpc/2190661.html.

[3] Chamberlain B., September 14, 2005. An Introduction to Chapel – Cray Cascade's High-Productivity Language, AHPCRC/DARPA PGAS Conference, http://chapel.cs.washington.edu/ChapelForAHPCRC.pdf.

[4] Council on Competitiveness, *High Performance Computing Software Workshop Report: Accelerating Innovation for Competitive Advantage: The Need for HPC Application Software Solutions*, July 13, 2005, Council on Competitiveness, Washington, D.C.20005, January 2006.

[5] Council on Competitiveness, *Second Annual High Performance Computing Users Conference Report*, Report and DVD available, Council on Competitiveness,Washington D.C.20005, March 2006.

[6] Cray, Inc., Chapel – The Cascade High-Productivity Language, Chapel Programming Language Homepage, http://chapel.cs.washington.edu/.

[7] Cray, Inc., July 9, 2003. DARPA HPCS Cray Cascade Project, http://www.cray.com/cascade/.

[8] Cray, Inc., July 13, 2007. Two Cray Supercomputers Surpass 100 Teraflops Mark, *HPCWIRE*, Vol. **16**, No. 28, http://www.hpcwire.com/hpc/1655656.html.

[9] Curns T., ed., Sun's Gustafson on Envisioning HPC Roadmaps for the Future, *HPCWIRE*, Vol. **14**, No. 2, http://www.hpcwire.com/hpc/324428.html.

[10] Curns T., ed., June 3, 2005. Japan: Poised for a Supercomputings Comeback? *HPCWIRE*, Vol. **14**, No. 22, http://news.taborcommunications.com/msgget.jsp?mid=391555&xsl=story.xsl.

[11] Curns T., ed., January 13, 2005. Sun's Gustafson on Envisioning HPC Roadmap for the Future, *HPCWIRE*, Vol. **14**, No. 2, http://www.hpcwire.com/hpc/324428.html.

[12] DARPA, DARPA Selects Three High Productivity Computing Systems (HPCS) Projects, http://www.darpa.mil/body/NewsItems/pdf/hpcs_phii_4.pdf, July 8, 2003.

[13] Deitz S., October 21, 2005. Chapel: Compiler Challenges, LCPC, http://chapel.cs.washington.edu/ChapelForLCPC.pdf.

[14] Ebisuzaki T., Germain R., and Taiji M., November 2004. PetaFLOPS Computing, *Comm. ACM*, Vol. **47**, No. 11, pp. 42–45.

[15] Elnozahy M., April 7, 2006. IBM Has Its PERCS, *HPCWIRE*, Vol. **15**, No. 14, http://www.hpcwire.com/hpc/614724.html.

[16] Feldman M., November 24, 2006. DARPA Selects Cray and IBM for Final Phase of HPCS, *HPCWIRE*, Vol. **15**, No. 4, http://www.hpcwire.com/hpc/1119092.html.

[16A] Feldman M., September 28, 2007. Parallel Thoughts, *HPCWIRE*, Vol. **16**, No. 39, http://www.hpcwire.com/hpc/1805039.html.

[16B] Fragalla J., September 13, 2007. Sun Constellation System: The Open Petascale Computing Architecture, *8^th Biennial Session of Computing in Atmospheric Sciences* (CAS2K7), NCAR Workshop, Annecy, France, http://www.cisl.ucar.edu/dir/CAS2K7/Presentations/ThuAM/fragalla.pdf.

[17] Ginsberg M., May 2005. Impediments to Future Use of Petaflop Class Computers for Large-Scale Scientific/Engineering Applications in U.S. Private Industry, *Proceedings of International Conference on Computational Science* (ICCS 2005) *Lecture Notes in Computer Science Series*, Vol. **3514**, Springer-Verlag, Berlin, pp. 1059–1066.

[18] Ginsberg M., June 25–28, 2007. Challenges and Opportunities for U.S. Private Industry Utilization of HPC Technology, *Proc., International Conference on Scientific Computing*, World Congress in Computer Science, Computer Engineering, and Applied Computing, WORLDCOMP07, Monte Carlo Hotel and Resort, Las Vegas, NV.

[18A] Gustafson J., April 6, 2007. Algorithm Leadership, *HPCWIRE*, Vol. **16**, No. 14, http://www.hpcwire.com/hpc/1347145.html.

[19] HECRTF, Federal Plan for High-End Computing: Report of the High-End Computing Revitalization Task Force (HECRTF), Executive Office of the President, Office of Science and Technology Policy, Washington, D.C., May 10, 2004 (second printing – July 2004), available at http://www.ostp.gov/nstc/html/HECRTF-FINAL_051004.pdf.

[19A] Heinzel S., September 10, 2007. Towards Petascale Computing: A Challenge for the Application Developers and the Hardware Vendors, *8^th Biennial Session of Computing in Atmospheric Sciences* (CAS2K7), NCAR Workshop, Annecy, France, http://www.cisl.ucar.edu/dir/CAS2K7/Presentations/MonAM/heinzel.pdf.

[20] Henkel M., July 13, 2007. Computers Keep Pace with Climate Change, *HPCWIRE*, Vol. **16**, No. 28, http://www.hpcwire.com/hpc/1655890.html.

[21] HPCWIRE, ORNL Closes in on Petascale Computing, *HPCWIRE*, Vol. **16**, No. 28, http://www.hpcwire.com/hpc/1660201.html, July 13, 2007.

[22] IBM, Inc., DARPA HPCS IBM PERCS Project, http://www.research.ibm.com/resources/news/20030710_darpa.html, July 10, 2003.

[23] IBM, Inc., Report on the Experimental Language X10, *Draft v 0.41*, http://domino.research.ibm.com/comm/research_projects.nsf/pages/x10.index.html/$FILE/ATTH4YZ5. pdf, February 7, 2006.

[24] IBM, Inc., The X10 Programming Language, http://domino.research.ibm.com/comm/research_projects.nsf/pages/x10.index.html, March 17, 2006.

[25] Joseph E., et al., May 2006. Council on Competitiveness Study of Industrial Partnerships with the National Science Foundation (NSF), *IDC White Paper on Council of Competitiveness Study of*

*Industrial Partnerships with The National Science Foundation (NSF)*, Council of Competitiveness, Washington, D.C., May 2006, http://www.compete.org/pdf/Council_NSF_Partnership_Study.pdf.

[26] Joseph E., et al., June 2006. Industrial Partnerships through the NNSA Academic Strategic Alliance Program, *IDC White Paper on Council on Competitiveness Study of Industrial Partnerships with the U.S. Department of Energy NNSA*, Council on Competitiveness, Washington D.C., http://www.compete.org/pdf/Council_NNSA_Partnership_Study.pdf.

[27] Joseph E., et al., July 2005. Study of ISVs Serving the High Performance Computing Market: The Need for Better Application Software, Council on Competitiveness Initiative, White paper, IDC, Framingham, MA, http://www.compete.org/pdf/HPC_Software_Survey.pdf.

[27A] Kepner J., (Guest Editor), November 2006. High Productivity Computing Systems and the Path Towards Usable Petascale Computing, Part A: User Productivity Challenges, *CTWatch Quarterly*, Vol. **2**, No. 4A, http://www.ctwatch.org/quarterly/pdf/ctwatchquarterly-8.pdf.

[27B] Leite T., September 28, 2007. Avoiding Application Porting Pitfalls, *HPCWIRE*, Vol. **16**, No. 39, http://www.hpcwire.com/hpc/1800677.html.

[27C] Lurie R., September 28, 2007. Language Design for an Uncertain Hardware Future, *HPCWIRE*, Vol. **16**, No. 39, http://www.hpcwire.com/hpc/1796964.html.

[27D] Markoff, J., August 19, 2005. A New Arms Race to Build the World's Mightiest Computer, http://www.mindfully.org/Technology/2005/Computer-Arms-Race19aug05.htm.

[27E] McCool M. D., September 28, 2007. Programming Models for Scalable Multicore Programming, *HPCWIRE*, Vol. **16**, No. 39, http://www.hpcwire.com/hpc/1798054.html.

[28] Merritt R., July 14, 2003. DARPA Seeds a Petaflops Push, *EE Times*, http://www.eet.com/article/showArticle.jhtml?articleId=18308889.

[29] Merritt R., and Mokhoff N., November 15, 2004. High and Dry at High End, *EE Times*, http://www.eet.com/article/showArticle.jhtml?articleId=52601292.

[30] National Coordination Office for Information Technology and Development (NITRD), http://www.itrd.gov.

[31] Novakovic N., April 24, 2007. China Gunning for Three Petaflop Systems,*inquirerinside.com*, http://www.inquirerinside.com/Default.aspx?article=39142.

[32] Nozawa T., June 14, 2007. Next-Generation Supercomputer to be Scalar/Vector Multi-System Developed by Hitachi, NEC, and Fujitsu, *Tech-On*, http://techon.nikkeibp.co.jp/english/NEWS_EN/20070614/134244/?ST=english_PRINT.

[33] Patt Y. N., June 23–25, 2004. The Processor in 2014: What are the challenges? How do we meet them? *Presentation, ISC2004, Heidelberg, Germany, paper available from* patt@ece.utexas.edu.

[34] President's Information Technology Advisory Committee, Computational Science: Ensuring America's Competitiveness, *PITAC, Office of the President, Washington D.C.,* http://www.nitrd.gov/pitac/reports/20050609_computational/computational.pdf, June 2005.

[34A] Primeur Monthly, December 6, 2007. Bull and Partners from SYSTEM@TIC Paris-Region Global Competitiveness Cluster Announces Launch of the POPS Project, http://enterthegrid.com/primeur/08/articles/monthly/AE-PR-01-08-46.html.

[35] Probst D., September 22, 2006. Another Perspective on Petascale, *HPCWIRE*, Vol. **15**, No. 38, http://www.hpcwire.com/hpc/906848.html.

[36] Ricadela A., June 21, 2004. Petaflop Imperative, *Information Week*, http://www.informationweek.com/story/showArticle.jhtml?articleID=22100641.

[37] Scott S., April 7, 2006. In Cray's 'Cascade' The Computer Will Adapt to the Codes, *HPCWIRE*, http://www.hpcwire.com/hpc/614695.html.

[38] Sexton J., July 20, 2007. Petascale Era Will Force Software Rethink, *HPCWIRE,* Vol. **16**, No. 29, http://www.hpcwire.com/hpc/1670733.html.

[39] Snell A., and Willard C. G., March 2006. Bridging the Capability Gap: Cray Pursues 'Adaptive Supercomputing' Vision, White paper No. 200808, IDC, Framingham, MA, http://www.cray.com/downloads/IDC-AdaptiveSC.pdf.

[40] Springboard Research, Japan's Next-Generation Supercomputer Project *Springboard Research*, http://www.springboardresearch.com/content/sampleresearch/hpc_focuspoint.pdf, May 15, 2007.

[41] Steele Jr. G. L., Programming Language Research: Exploration of programming languages constructs and principles, http://research.sun.com/projects/plrg/.

[41A] Strenski D., July 17–20, 2007. Accelerators in Cray's Adaptive Supercomputing, http://rssi.ncsa.uiuc.edu/docs/industry/Cray_presentation.pdf, Reconfigurable Systems Summer Institute, University of Illinois, Urbana, IL.

[42] Vildibill M., April 7, 2006. Sun's Hero Program: Changing the Productivity Game, *HPCWIRE*, http://www.hpcwire.com/hpc/614805.html.

[43] Wallach S., June 23, 2004. Searching for the SOFTRON: Will We Be Able to Develop Software for PetaFlop Computing? *Keynote Talk, ISC2004, Heidelberg, Germany*, paper available from wallach@cpventures.com.

# 9. Influences of Floating-Point Arithmetic on Computational Results

## 9.1 The Need for Creating a Floating-Point Standard

This section is included because floating-point computations could face some additional challenges with respect to accuracy with the introduction of petaflop class supercomputers. In the 1970s, there was a move to standardize floating-point arithmetic for all computers performing extensive non-integer arithmetic. Until that time, users could experience significant variations in their numerical results from one computer platform to another.

For those readers not familiar with such problems, I remind you that the real-line is continuous but the representation of the real line in a computer is not and is instead represented by a finite number of discrete data points. Thus, some points on the real line will not necessarily be exactly representable in a computer. Furthermore, the internal representation may differ from one computer to another with respect to total accumulated roundoff error encountered in solving a problem. This is due to algorithm, hardware, and software influences on the host machine. IEEE Floating-Point standard 754 [4] was created to improve the situation by introducing more accuracy in computing intermediate results so that the results of the final problem will have the best possible internal representation. Comprehending all the details of the standard can be difficult, but the intent of the standard is to protect the average user from encountering serious inaccuracies. The standard has generally worked very well, but of course it cannot prevent all possible discrepancies.

## 9.2 Coping with Accuracy Problems on Petaflop Computers

Now with the impending introduction of petaflop machines, there is renewed concern that increased precision will be necessary. This brings up several issues. How much more precision is needed? Should it be accomplished by hardware, software or both? How will the user reliably and efficiently assess the accuracy of final computed results?

Many petaflop class machines are likely to have 100,000 or more processors. Although with the exception of the very largest models run on such machines, some applications will use far fewer processors, but it should be remembered that a petaflop processor performing floating-point arithmetic could be as much as three orders of magnitude faster than teraflop class units and thus the total application accumulated roundoff error could overwhelm the accuracy of 64 bit floating-point arithmetic. Such difficulties are discussed in several articles by Bailey [1–3] and Kahan [13–18]. There are several additional available floating-point discussions in Hennessy and Patterson [11] in Appendix I written by D. Goldberg as well as given in [6, 7, 10, 19–21, 23]. A very interesting interview with W. Kahan ('Father of the IEEE Floating-Point Standards') is given in [22] and reveals many of the difficulties in defining those standards and gaining industrial compliance from hardware and software vendors.

It is interesting to note that of all the U.S. hardware vendors competing in the DARPA Program to produce one or more Petaflop machines by 2010 (see discussion in Section 8), only one vendor (Sun) seems to have considered the potential floating-point inadequacy of 64-bit floating-point arithmetic for the target machines [5].

## References

[1] Bailey D. H., June 23–25, 2004, Twelve Ways to Fool the Masses: 10 Years Later, *paper, ISC2004, Heidelberg, Germany*, paper available at http://crd.lbl.gov/~dhbailey/dhbtalks/dhb-12ways.pdf.

[2] Bailey D. H., 1998. *Performance of Future High-End Computers, in High Performance Computer Systems and Applications*, edited by Schaeffer, J., Kluwer Academic Press, Boston, MA, http://crd.lbl.gov/~dhbailey/dhbpapers/future.pdf.

[3] Bailey D. H. et al., 1989. Floating Point Arithmetic in Future Supercomputers, *Int'l J of Supercomputer Applications*, Vol. **3**, No. 3, pp. 86–90, http://crd.lbl.gov/~dhbailey/dhbpapers/fpafs.pdf.

[4] Cody W. J. et al., August 1984. IEEE Standards 754 and 854 for Floating-Point Arithmetic, *IEEE Micro Magazine*, pp. 84–100.

[5] Curns T., ed., 2005. Sun's Gustafson on Envisioning HPC Roadmap for the Future, *HPCWIRE*, Vol. **14**, No. 2, January 13, http://www.hpcwire.com/hpc/324428.html

[6] Demmel J. W., December 1984. The Effects of Underflow on Numerical Computation, *SIAM Jl. Scientific & Statistical Computing*, Vol. **5**, No. 4, pp. 887–919.

[7] Einarsson B. (ed.), 2005. *Accuracy and Reliability in Scientific Computing*, SIAM, Philadelphia, PA.

[8] Goedecker S. and Hoisie A., 2001. *Performance Optimization of Numerically Intensive Codes*, SIAM, Philadelphia, PA.
[9] Goldberg D., 2007. Computer Arithmetic, in Appendix I of **Computer Architecture: A Quantitative Approach,** 4th Edition, Morgan Kaufmann Publishers, San Francisco, CA.
[10] Hauser J. R., March 1996. Handling Floating-Point Exceptions in Numeric Programs, *ACM Trans. On Prog. Lang and Syst*, Vol. **8**, No. 2.
[11] Hennessy J. L., and Patterson D. A., 2007. Computer *Architecture: A Quantitative Approach, 4th Edition*, Morgan Kaufmann Publishers, San Francisco, CA.
[12] Higham N. J., 2002. *Accuracy and Stability of Numerical Algorithms,* 2nd edition.
[13] Kahan W., October 1, 1997. Lecture Notes on the Status of IEEE Standard 754 for Binary Floating-Point Arithmetic, http://www.cs.berkeley.edu/~wkahan/ieee754status/IEEE754.PDF.
[14] Kahan W., August 15, 2000. Marketing versus Mathematics and Other Ruminations on the Design of Floating-Point Arithmetic, Presentation upon receiving the IEEE's Emanuel R. Piore Award, http://www.cs.berkeley.edu/~wkahan/MktgMath.pdf.
[15] Kahan W., July 31, 2004. Matlab's Loss Is Nobody's Gain, August. 1998 with revision, http://www.cs.berkeley.edu/~wkahan/MxMulEps.pdf.
[16] Kahan W., September 5, 2002. *The Numerical Analyst as Computer Science Curmudgeon, Presentation to the EE & CS Dept. Research Fair, University of California at Berkeley*, http://www.cs.berkeley.edu/~wkahan/Curmudge.pdf.
[17] Kahan W., November 20, 2004. On the Cost of Floating-Point Computation Without Extra-Precise Arithmetic, *Work in Progress*, http://www.cs.berkeley.edu/~wkahan/Qdrtcs.pdf.
[18] Kahan W., and Darcy J. D., How Java's Floating-Point Hurts Everyone Everywhere, *ACM 1998 Workshop on Java for High-Performance Network Computing*, Stanford University, Palo Alto, CA, http://www.cs.berkeley.edu/~wkahan/JAVAhurt.pdf.
[19] Langou J. et al., April 2006. Exploiting the Performance of 32 bit Floating Point Arithmetic in Obtaining 64 bit Accuracy, Utk CS Tech Report CS-06-574, LAPACK Working Note #175, http://www.netlib.org/utk/people/JackDongarra/PAPERS/iter-refine-2006.pdf.
[20] Overton M. L., 2001. *Numerical Computing with IEEE Floating-Point Arithmetic*, SIAM, Philadelphia, PA.
[21] Patterson D. A., and Hennessy, J., 2004. *Computer Organization and Design: The Hardware/Software Interface*, Morgan Kauffman, San Francisco, CA.
[22] Severance C., February 20, 1998. An Interview with the Old Man of Floating-Point *Reminiscences elicited from William Kahan*, http://www.cs.berkeley.edu/~wkahan/ieee754status/754story.html.
[23] Sterbenz P. H., 1974. **Floating-Point Computation**, Prentice-Hall, Englewood Cliffs, NJ.

# 10. Industrial HPC Progress

## 10.1 HPC in the U.S. Automotive Industry

Until the early 1980s all automotive design and prototyping was performed exclusively via the construction of a series of physical prototype vehicles. The lead time from design of a new vehicle to the beginning of actual production was on the order of 60 months or approximately five years. With such a long time interval, it was very difficult to make significant design changes and/or rapidly respond to competitive action from both foreign and domestic car makers once the process was initiated.

To reduce this lead time, in the early 1980s some of the physical prototyping was replaced by math-based modeling using computer simulation. Initially such math modeling and computer simulation were only performed on small sub-assemblies of the total vehicle, still relying on physical prototyping for the bulk of the design process. The math modeling was executed primarily on large mainframe computers because sophisticated desktop computers were not in existence at that time, were too slow, and/or the necessary application software was not readily available to most auto manufacturers. In a sense at that time, mainframe computers were the supercomputers of that era. As more time was required for processing math modeling on such mainframes, bottlenecks arose as such activity competed with other computational work, also vying for time on the same computers. As supercomputers became available in government labs in the 1970s and early 1980s, it seemed only natural to move the math modeling simulations to these much faster machines. Consequently, the amount of physical prototyping steadily decreased as more and more of the entire vehicle began to be created using math modeling and computer simulations. The net effect with respect to General Motors as well as that with respect to the automotive industries world wide has been a drastic decrease in new vehicle lead time from 60 months in the early 1980s to under 18 months in 2007, with cost savings of well over a billion dollars or more with respect to General Motors alone [24]. For additional information about HPC at GM, please examine [16–21].

GM acquired the first in-house supercomputer in the world auto industry in late 1983 [16, 17], but the same vintage supercomputer had been installed at LANL in 1976. Within seven years following the GM supercomputer acquisition, most of the rest of the world automotive industry also obtained supercomputers. The main reasons for this major time lag are as follows: (1) lack of sufficient and diverse in-house computational science support staffs; (2) failure of automotive company personnel to convince upper management of the immediate need of innovative HPC hardware and software technology to improve global competitiveness via the production of more cost-effective, superior quality vehicles; (3) The burden of dependence on a number of ISV-based commercial legacy codes which made it very difficult if not impossible for quick and effective transition to newer HPC technology; (4) lack of in-house definitive application benchmarks and predictive benchmarking techniques to provide the necessary insight to guarantee accurately that any new HPC technology would necessarily improve product quality and further reduce lead time; (5) lack of sufficient in-house access to the latest HPC technology to even run meaningful tests to determine benefits of using the new HPC technology; (6) inability to define larger accurate math models and HPC-optimized algorithms that are needed to assess properly the creation of near-future product needs; (7) too much dependence upon computer vendor marketing hype of unverified claims of actual computer performance on total realistic industrial-sized applications; (8) lack of sufficient financial resources, appropriate personnel, visionary management, and insufficient interaction with the government and academic research communities to compensate for the inherent industrial weaknesses. Clearly, it would be unfair to blame solely the industrial community because many of the underlying causes were beyond their control.

Now, most of the car designs rely on a diverse collection of HPC technologies. The sophistication of the math modeling has dramatically increased from the early 1980s when it was difficult to perform even simple 3-D car modeling on a supercomputer. Today much more realistic 3-D structural simulations can routinely be performed as well as a variety of interactions among automotive subsystems including increasing realistic modeling of human passengers beyond what had previously been achieved with sophisticated instrumented physical dummies. It is still estimated that it could require an increase of three orders of magnitude in current computer power in order to model completely all possible structural and human interactions with all automotive subsystems and to do so in real time or faster in order to make cars much safer. Unfortunately, at present (mid 2007) the poor financial condition of the U.S. auto industry makes it difficult at times to focus on the use of appropriate leading-edge HPC. Over the years, however, the U.S. car industry has been able to benefit from HPC-related activities in academia and at U.S. government research labs [4].

Despite several financial downturns throughout the U.S. auto industry, there has been sporadic activities that continue to help advance the U.S. automotive industry. Recently, for example, General Motors has won two DOE INCITE awards [26, 37]. GM partnering with one of its ISVs (Fluent) was awarded 166,000 hours to use the FLUENT off the shelf engine simulation product with DOE HPC resources at NERSC [37] 'for CAE simulation of full vehicle wind noise and other CFD phenomena.' In this DOE INCITE Project, HPC supercomputer resources will be utilized with the FLUENT CFD code to 'illustrate the competitive benefits of large scale engineering simulation early in the design phase of automotive production [37]'. The project will explore the use of FLUENT software to perform emerging CFD and thermal calculations on high-end parallel processing computers in order to determine the hardware resources and behavior of software systems required to deliver results in time frames that significantly impact GM's Global Vehicle Development Process (GVDP). Five specific application areas will be investigated: (1) Full vehicle open-sunroof wind buffeting calculations; (2) Full vehicle transient thermal calculations; (3) Simulations of semi-trucks passing stationary vehicles with raised hoods; (4) Vehicle underhood buoyancy convection airflow and thermal simulations; (5) Vehicle component and sub-assembly fluid immersion and drainage calculations.

Another GM Team is using the DOE ORNL Leadership Computing Facility's Jaguar supercomputer (Cray XT3) to 'perform first-principles calculations of thermoelectric materials capable of turning waste heat into electricity'. The goal of this project is to help GM and other automakers to capture the '60% of the energy generated by a car's engine that is currently lost through waste heat and to use it to boost fuel economy. These calculations would not have been possible if the scientists had not have access to the Leadership computing resources of DOE'. 'This is another example of how computational simulation can contribute to scientific advances and energy security [26]'.

At the International Supercomputing Conference (ISC07) in Dresden, Germany, it was apparent in their Automotive Day presentations, that German and European auto companies also embrace HPC usage; for example, see references [1, 3, 12, 39].

## 10.2 Formula 1 Auto Racing HPC Usage

Another automotive segment quickly learned the advantages of adopting HPC modeling techniques after observing developments in the commercial passenger car business. Several papers presented at ISC07 demonstrate very strong interest in using HPC modeling techniques to improve engine design as well as in employing racing car aerodynamics (computational fluid dynamics techniques, CFD) to even tune performance based on certain attributes of specific racing venues. Some examples of Formula 1 HPC usage are given in references [3, 12, 35, 39, 41].

## 10.3 Boeing Corporation is Beneficiary of HPC Technology

It is interesting to observe that often the same HPC applications are useful in different industries. The automotive companies discovered that substantial amounts of physical prototyping could be replaced by accurate computer simulations, i.e., math-based modeling could help shorten lead time for the design and production of new vehicles. Similar reductions have occurred in the aircraft industry. For example, Boeing physically tested 77 wing designs for the 767 aircraft, but for the new Dreamliner 787, only 11 wing designs had to be physically tested (a seven-fold reduction in the needed amount of physical prototyping), mainly because over 800,000 hours of computer simulations on Cray supercomputers had drastically reduced the amount of needed physical prototyping. Also, the computer simulations on the Crays very closely matched the wind tunnel results of the tests that Boeing performed in several of its facilities around the world [2, 11].

## 10.4 Stimulus for Future Expansion of Industrial HPC Usage

Supercomputer-based math modeling and simulation is far more efficient, cost-effective, and considerably more practical than physical prototyping for testing and verifying the effects of large numbers of design variables. While physical prototyping is still very important for final design validation, accurate supercomputer simulations enable automotive and aircraft industries as well as other manufacturing organizations to dramatically reduce lead time from design to implementation of a new product. In both the automotive and aerospace industries, fuel efficiency can be improved by paying more attention to aerodynamics via use of computational fluid dynamics (CFD) software; this approach also makes it possible to improve racing car and boat designs. The CFD modeling for Formula 1 racing cars is now being adopted by Speedo [15, 30] to produce innovative swimwear, which improves the speed of swimmers engaged in competitive meets such as in the Olympics. Even Ping, a golf manufacturer, uses a Cray XD1 to create better clubs [38]. HPC is used to design additional sport equipment [14A, 35A]. Bioinformatics-related activities are now using HPC to track infectious diseases as well as to enter a new era in which pharmaceutical companies will be able to create boutique medicines based upon individual attributes of a person's DNA. The videos shown at SC05 and SC06 illustrate some of the aforementioned uses of HPC and are available for viewing; see Section 12, references [2,6]. The U.S. Council on Competitiveness also stimulates uses of HPC in U.S. industry; see [6–10].

Only a small percentage of industry has yet to initiate HPC usage. The situation is improving as more companies become aware that an HPC mindset can strengthen bottom-line finances by increasing global competitiveness, reducing product lead time, and promoting product innovation. A major barrier to many companies using HPC is the lack of sufficient internal manpower with expertise in HPC and/or sufficient access to HPC physical resources. Several alternatives have arisen to cope with such problems: Blue Collar Computing program [34], on-demand HPC resources [see Section 11], government-subsidized training efforts [29], and cooperative activities on large and/or costly projects. The references in this section offer some examples of these alternatives to help industry utilize HPC.

## 10.5 Blue Collar Computing

A few large corporations such as General Motors and Boeing seem to have now discovered the benefits of using HPC technology in their manufacturing operations. Unfortunately, most small-to medium-sized U.S. companies have had little, if any, exposure to the direct benefits of utilizing HPC in their day-to-day operations. The initiatives of the Ohio Supercomputer Center (OSC) are now dramatically improving the situation; see [28, 29, 34]. A partnership between OSC and Edison Welding Institute (EWI) [28] involves 200 companies; most of those companies have no HPC expertise. The partnership will offer 'remote portal access of HPC systems' and also provide specific software tools for EWI welding applications. This action will result in significant cost savings while providing integrated numerical simulation tools accessible to engineers in EWI member companies. They in turn will have online access using the necessary software through which they can input product dimensions, welding process parameters, and other specs in order to run online simulations of their welding procedures. This capability will enable users to assess directly the strength and viability of their prototypes. It will reduce much trial and error with physical prototypes and allow engineers to investigate 'what if' scenario calculations that could directly lead to improvements in their welding procedures. This approach is analogous to how automotive and aerospace companies have been able to reduce lead time, cut production costs, and reduce physical prototyping via use of math-based HPC simulations. Other Blue Collar Computing initiatives will have similar objectives such as the new STAR initiative at the Texas Advanced Computing Center [41A].

## 10.6 U.S. Council on Competitive Case Studies

Several case studies of important industrial applications have been defined with the help of the U.S. Council on Competitiveness. These will be used as the focal points for further industrial actions. The four case studies deal with automotive crash analysis [6], ways to increase crude oil yields [7], vehicle design optimization [8], improvement of oil and gas recovery [9], and speeding up of the fiber spinning process to help U.S. textile manufacturing to increase global competitiveness [10]. Even if a few of these goal oriented projects are successful, then U.S. industrial profitability should significantly improve at the international level.

## 10.7 The Flavors of HPC

From the above discussion, it should be obvious to the reader that HPC requires various approaches depending upon the attributes of the user, the nature of the application to be solved, and the resources readily available. For large science and engineering applications, the user must have considerable HPC resources or must utilize a national grid or seek help from government program resources such as those offered by the DOE INCITE Program [5].

For more modest applications such as those targeted by the Blue Collar Computing Projects for small- and medium-sized companies, a good starting point involves the exploitation of the scientific/engineering HPC desktop tools such as those available with MATLAB [23,42] and many commercial ISVs. This is usually referred to as the 'desktop mainstream HPC approach' Many industrial people feel comfortable using such desktop tools. If the applications grow larger, there are now several emerging alternatives to link the desktop tools to the use of commodity clusters [23] accessed via use of MATLAB, MS CCS2003 server [42, 42A], Star-P [31, 32, 33, 33A] and/or Field Programmable Gate Arrays (FPGAs) (see Section 7).

## References


[1] Allrutz R., June 26, 2007. Challenges of Design and Operation of Heterogeneous Clusters in Automotive Engineering, *Automotive Day presentation, International Supercomputing Conferences (ISC'07)*, Dresden, Germany, for more details, please contact mail to: R.Allrutz@science-computing.de.

[2] Boeing, Boeing Dreamliner Fact Sheet, http://www.boeing.com/commercial/787family/programfacts.html and Cray Supercomputers Play Key Role in Designing Boeing 787 Dreamliner, http://www10.mcadcafe.com/nbc/articles/view_article.php?articleid=407552 details available at http://787premiere.newairplane.com.

[3] Bruder U., and Mayer S., June 26, 2007. Simulation Data and Process Management in HPC Environments, *Automotive Day presentation, International Supercomputing Conferences (ISC'07)*, Dresden, Germany, please contact stefan.mayer@mscsoftware.com.

[4] Coalition for Academic Scientific Computation, High Performance Computing Improves Automotive Products, Builds Competitive Edge for U.S. Auto Industry http://www.casc.org/papers/paper12.html.

[5] Conway S., February 9, 2007. INCITE Program Targets American Competitiveness, *HPCWIRE*, Vol. **16**, No. 6, http://www.hpcwire.com/hpc/1255558.html.

[6] Council on Competitiveness, Auto Crash Safety: It's Not Just for Dummies, *High Performance Computing and Competitiveness Grand Challenge Case Study*, U.S. Council on Competitiveness, 1500K Street, NW, Suite 850, Washington, DC 20005, http://www.compete.org/pdf/HPC_Auto_Safety.pdf, 2005.

[7] Council on Competitiveness, Customized Catalysts to Improve Crude Oil Yields: Getting More Bang from Each Barrel, *High Performance Computing and Competitiveness Grand Challenge Case Study*, U.S. Council on Competitiveness, 1500K Street, NW, Suite 850, Washington, DC 20005, http://www.compete.org/pdf/HPC_Customized_Catalysts.pdf, 2005.

[8] Council on Competitiveness, Full Vehicle Design Optimization for Global Market Dominance, *High Performance Computing and Competitiveness Grand Challenge Case Study*, U.S. Council on Competitiveness, 1500K Street, NW, Suite 850, Washington, DC 20005, http://www.compete.org/pdf/HPC_Full_Design.pdf, 2005.

[9] Council on Competitiveness, Keeping the Lifeblood Flowing: Boosting Oil and Gas Recovery from the Earth *High Performance Computing and Competitiveness Grand Challenge Case Study*, U.S. Council on Competitiveness, 1500K Street, NW, Suite 850, Washington, DC 20005, http://www.compete.org/pdf/HPC_Keeping_Lifeblood.pdf, 2005.

[10] Council on Competitiveness, Spin Fiber Faster to Gain a Competitive Edge for U.S. Textile Manufacturing, *High Performance Computing and Competitiveness Grand Challenge Case Study*, U.S. Council on Competitiveness, 1500K Street, NW, Suite 850, Washington, DC 20005, http://www.compete.org/pdf/HPC_Spin_Faster.pdf, 2005.

[11] Cray, Inc., July 6, 2007. Cray Supercomputers Play Key Role in Dreamliner Design, *HPCWIRE*, Vol. **16**, No. 27, http://www.hpcwire.com/hpc/1648048.html.

[12] Diethelm K., and Renner M., June 26, 2007. Numerical Forming Simulation on Cluster Systems in the Automotive Industry, Automotive Day presentation, International Supercomputing Conferences (ISC'07), Dresden, Germany, http://www.gns-systems.de/images/ISC07_Automotive.pdf.

[13] DreamWorks Animation SKG, DreamWorks: Pushing the Limits of HPC, *HPCWIRE*, Vol. **15**, No. 26, http://www.hpcwire.com/hpc/710286.html, June 29, 2006.

[14] DreamWorks Animation SKG, High Performance Computing: Accelerating Innovation to Enhance Everyday Life DreamWorks Animation SKG, DVD available for purchase from U.S. Council on Competitiveness, Washington D.C.; excerpt preview available at http://www.compete.org/hpc/WEB_TRAILER_8-30.mov.

[14A] EPSRC Computer Models Raise Bar for Sporting Achievement, HPCWIRE, Vol. **16**, No. 37, http://www.hpcwire.com/hpc/1779188.html, September 14, 2007.

[15] Fluent, Inc., March. 10, 2004. Speedo Brings Formula One Technology to the Pool, Fluent, Inc., http://www.fluent.com/news/pr/pr69.htm.

[16] Ginsberg M., 1994. An Overview of Supercomputing at General Motors Corporation, Frontiers of Supercomputing II: A National Reassessment, edited by Ames K. R., and Brenner A. G., volume in the Los Alamos Series in Basic and Applied Sciences, University of California Press, Berkeley, pp. 359–371.

[17] Ginsberg M., 1996. Streamlined Design: Supercomputers Help Auto Manufacturers Decrease Lead Time, High-Performance Computing Contributions to Society, Tabor Griffin Communications, San Diego, CA.

[18] Ginsberg M., 1997. AUTOBENCH: A 21st Century Vision for an Automotive Computing Benchmark Suite, High Performance Computing in Automotive Design, Engineering, and Manufacturing, edited by Sheh M., Cray Research, Inc., Eagan, MN, pp. 67–76.

[19] Ginsberg M., 1999. Current and Future Status of HPC in the World Automotive Industry, Object Oriented Methods for Inter-Operable Scientific and Engineering Computing, edited by Henderson, M. E. et al., SIAM, Philadelphia, PA, pp. 1–10.

[20] Ginsberg M., December. 1999. Influences, Challenges, and Strategies for Automotive HPC Benchmarking and Performance Improvement, *Parallel Computing J.*, Vol. **25**, No. 12, pp. 1459–1476.

[21] Ginsberg M., 2001. Influences on the Solution Process for Large, Numeric-Intensive Automotive Simulations, *Lecture Notes in Computer Science*, Vol. **2073**, Springer-Verlag, New York, NY, pp. 1189–1198.

[22] Ginsberg M., May 2005. Impediments to Future Use of Petaflop Class Computers for Large-Scale Scientific/Engineering Applications in U.S. Private Industry, *Lecture Notes in Computer Science*, Vol. **3514**, edited by Sunderam, S. V. et al., Springer-Verlag, Berlin, Germany, pp. 1059–1066.

[23] Ginsberg M., June 2007. Challenges and Opportunities for U.S. Private Industry Utilization of HPC Technology, *Proceedings of the International Conference on Scientific Computing*, CSC2007, CSREA Press, Las Vegas, NV, pp. 17–23.

[24] HPCWIRE, Government Expands HPC Giveway Program, *HPCWIRE*, Vol. **16**, No. 2, http://www.hpcwire.com/hpc/1198276.html, January 12, 2007.

[25] HPCWIRE, IDC's HPC User Forum Meets in Manchester, *HPCWIRE*, Vol. **15**, No. 44, http://www.hpcwire.com/hpc/1051123.html, November 3, 2006.

[26] HPCWIRE, ORNL Closes in on Petaflop Computing, *HPCWIRE*, Vol. **16**, No. 28, http://www.hpcwire.com/hpc/1660201.html, July 13, 2007.

[27] HPCWIRE, ORNL Supercomputer Rises to No. 2 Worldwide, *HPCWIRE*, Vol. **16**, No. 26, http://www.hpcwire.com/hpc/1635950.html, June 29, 2007.

[28] HPCWIRE, OSC Announces HPC Partnership with Edison Welding , *HPCWIRE*, Vol. **15**, No. 47, December 1, 2006, http://www.hpcwire.com/hpc/1129969.html and also see update, EWI Launches Welding Simulation Tool, *HPCWIRE*, Vol. **16**, No. 36, http://www.hpcwire.com/hpc/1763231.html, September 7, 2007.

[29] HPCWIRE, Merle Giles to Lead NCSA Private Sector Program, *HPCWIRE*, Vol. **16**, No. 23, http://www.hpcwire.com/hpc/1601935.html, June 8, 2007.

[30] HPCWIRE, Speedo Dives Into Supercomputing, *HPCWIRE*, http://www.hpcwire.com/hpc/671349.html, May 26, 2006.

[31] Interactive Supercomputing Corp., The Star-P Platform: Delivering Interactive Parallel Computing Power to the Desktop, Whitepaper, Interactive Supercomputing Corp., Waltham, MA 2006, http://www.interactivesupercomputing.com/downloads/ISCwhitepaper.pdf.

[32] Interactive Supercomputing Corp., New Star-P Software Targets Life Sciences, Interactive Supercomputing Corp., Waltham, MA, *HPCWIRE*, Vol. **16**, No. 23, http://www.hpcwire.com/hpc/1599717.html, June 8, 2007.

[33] Interactive Supercomputing Corp., Star-P Software Enables High-Definition Ultrasound, *HPCWIRE*, Vol. **16**, No. 28, http://www.hpcwire.com/hpc/1655648.html, July 13, 2007.

[33A] Interactive Supercomputing Corp., Reverse-Engineering the Brain for Better Computers, *HPCWIRE*, Vol. **16**, No 38, http://www.hpcwire.com/hpc/1786389.html, September 21, 2007.

[34] Krishnamurthy A., 2006. Blue Collar Computing Update, http://www.bluecollarcomputing.org/docs/BCC_master.pdf.

[35] Larsson T., January 16, 2007. Supercomputing in Formula One Auto Racing, Automotive Day presentation, International Supercomputing Conferences (ISC'07), Dresden, Germany. For additional details see the following five related references about this presentation: abstract of ISC07 presentation; http://www.supercomp.de/isc2007/index.php5?s=conference&s_nav=speaker&speaker_id=1261, June 26, 2007. F1 Supercomputing: Unlocking the Power of CFD, (brief written version) by Larsson T., Sato T., and Ullbrand B., Fluent News, Summer 2005, pp. s8–s9; http://www.fluent.com/about/news/newsletters/05v14i2/pdfs/s6.pdf, expanded paper version with the same title and written by the same authors, Proc., $2^{nd}$ European Automotive CFD Conference (EACC2005), Frankfurt, Germany, June 29–30, 2005, pp. 45–54, BMW Sauber Unveils New Supercomputer for Automotive Design, *HPCWIRE*, Vol. **15**, No. 49, http://www.hpcwire.com/hpc/1158325.html, December 15, 2006, and BMW Focuses Supercomputer on F1 Aerodynamics, gizmag.com, http://www.gizmag.com/go/6734/.

[35A] Loughborough University, Computer Models Help Raise the Bar for Sporting Achievement, PR Office, Loughborough University, http://www.lboro.ac.uk/service/publicity/news-releases/2007/117_festival.html, September 13, 2007.

[36] McLane B., October 6, 2006. Computer-on-Demand Drives Efficiencies in Oil and Gas, *HPCWIRE*, Vol. **15**, No. 40, http://www.hpcwire.com/hpc/948245.html.

[37] NERSC, CAE Simulation of Full Vehicle Wind Noise and Other CFD Phenomena NERSC, INCITE Award; http://www.nersc.gov/projects/incite/bemis_07.php, January 8, 2007.

[38] PING Inc., PING Shaves Strokes Off Its Golf Club Design Cycle with a Cray, http://www.wordcrft.com/LinkClick.aspx?link=samples%2FCRAY+Ping.pdf&tabid=136&mid=497, November 7, 2005.

[39] Resch M., June 26, 2007. The Impact of Virtual Reality and High Performance Computing in the Automotive Industry- A Showcase, Automotive Day presentation, International Supercomputing Conferences (ISC'07), Dresden, Germany, see resch@hlrs.de for details.

[40] Scarafino V., The National Needs for Advanced Scientific Computing and Industrial Applications, Statement of The Ford Motor Company, Committee on Science, U.S. House of Representatives, http://www.house.gov/science/hearings/full03/jul16/scarafino.htm, July 16, 2003.

see http://www.techlawjournal.com/home/newsbriefs/2003/07d.asp, under 7/16 The House Science Committee Holds Hearing on Supercomputing titled Supercomputing: Is the U.S. on the Right Path?, paragraphs 4–7 inclusive.

[41] SGI, Inc., SGI Solutions Underpin Winning Formula at Vodafone McLaren Mercedes, SGI, July 2007, http://www.sgi.com/company_info/newsroom/press_releases/2007/july/formula.html.

[41A] Texas Advanced Computing Center, TACC Initiates Science and Technology Affiliates Program, *HPCWIRE*, Vol. **16**, No. 42, http://www.hpcwire.com/hpc/1843062.html, October 19, 2007.

[42] West J. E., July 20, 2007. Windows CCS and the End of *nix in HPC, *HPCWIRE*, Vol. **16**, No. 29, http://www.hpcwire.com/hpc/1673371.html.

[42A] Milliman Inc., October 15, 2007. Milliman, Microsoft Offer CCS-Based Financial Solutions, *GRID Today*, http://www.gridtoday.com/grid/1835069.html.

# 11. Access to On-Demand HPC

## 11.1 Need for Industrial On-Demand HPC Services

As has been indicated in several previous sections, advances in use of HPC technology in industry have significantly lagged behind those in government labs and university research centers. One of the principle reasons for this situation has been the lack of significant access to the latest HPC hardware. Many industrial companies either do not have the internal financial resources to pay for such services and/or need some flexible arrangement with an external source to provide service as needed, which can vary extensively over time. This fluctuating demand is now being addressed via several available services.

The availability of external on-demand services offers an excellent opportunity for an industrial organization to verify actual need of HPC with relatively little risk, while at the same time it is able to justify to the top upper management for future HPC return on investment (ROI).

## 11.2 Sample of On-Demand HPC Services

Alternatives include sharing use of HPC resources with government labs [2,8], university research centers [7, 9, 9A, 10] and a growing number of hardware/software vendors and service facilities [1, 3, 5, 6, 11, 12, 14]. A representative number of these sources are listed in this section. Large multi-year HPC resources can be obtained on a competitive basis from several DOE labs under the INCITE [2] program referenced below. Event-driven science services [13] and computer bandwidth on-demand service [4] are also beginning to become available.

REFERENCES

[1] Altair Engineering, Altair Engineering Unveils New On-Demand Licensing Model, *HPCWIRE*, Vol. **16**, No. 22, http://www.hpcwire.com/hpc/1589462.html, June 1, 2007.
[2] Conway S., February. 9, 2007. INCITE Program Targets American Competitiveness, *HPCWIRE*, Vol. **16**, No. 6, http://www.hpcwire.com/hpc/1255558.html.
[3] Harris D., July 16, 2007. Data Solutions Provider Finds Utility-Based Business Model, *GRID today*, http://www.gridtoday.com/grid/1663866.html.
[4] HPCWIRE, European NRENs Establish 'Bandwidth-on-Demand' *HPCWIRE*, Vol. **16**, No. 28, http://www.hpcwire.com/hpc/1658441.html, July 13, 2007.
[5] HPCWIRE, Fluent to Showcase New Airflow Modeling Software, *HPCWIRE*, Vol. **15**, No. 44, http://www.hpcwire.com/hpc/1038004.html, November 3, 2006.
[6] HPCWIRE, IBM Offers Blue Gene On Demand, *HPCWIRE*, Vol. **14**, No. 10, http://www.hpcwire.com/hpc/350226.html, March 10, 2005.
[7] HPCWIRE, Merle Giles to Lead NCSA Private Sector Program, *HPCWIRE*, Vol. **16**, No. 23, http://www.hpcwire.com/hpc/1601935.html, June 8, 2007.
[8] HPCWIRE, ORNL Supercomputer Rises to No. 2 Worldwide, *HPCWIRE*, Vol. **16**, No. 26, http://hpcwire.com/hpc/1635950.html, June 29, 2007.
[9] HPCWIRE, OSC Announces HPC Partnership with Edison Welding , *HPCWIRE*, Vol. **15**, No. 47, http://www.hpcwire.com/hpc/1129969.html, December 1, 2006.
[9A] Interactive Supercomputing, Inc., SDSC Brings On-Demand Supercomputing to the Masses, *HPCWIRE*, Vol. **16**, No. 40, http://www.hpcwire.com/hpc/1817666.html, October 5, 2007.
[10] Krishnamurthy A., 2006. Blue Collar Computing Update, http://www.bluecollarcomputing.org/docs/BCC_master.pdf.
[11] McLane B., October 3, 2006. Computing-on-demand, *HPCWIRE*, http://www.hpcwire.com/hpc/948245.html. http://www.cyrusone.com and http://www.appro.com.
[12] Sun Microsystems, Inc., Sun Expands Utility Computing Offering, *HPCWIRE*, Vol. **16**, No. 11, http://www.hpcwire.com/hpc/1316215.html, March.16, 2007.
[13] Tooby P., July 13, 2007. Supercomputing On Demand: SDSC Enables Event-Driven Science, *HPCWIRE*, Vol. **16**, No. 28, http://www.hpcwire.com/hpc/1655918.html.
[14] Virtual Compute Corporation, vCompute Reduces Pricing on Supercomputing Services, *HPCWIRE*, Vol. **16**, No. 42, http://www.hpcwire.com/hpc/1840970.html, October 19, 2007.

# 12. A Few HPC Videos

## 12.1 A Brief History of HPC

In the late 1960s and throughout the 1970s and 1980s, one pragmatic definition of a supercomputer was whatever Seymour Cray was currently building for 10M$. This was in the golden era of custom vector processor systems. By the mid 1990s, the tide had turned in favor of commodity-based processors which were supposedly much more economical and showed high speed performance. The introduction of the Earth Simulator on the scene in 2002 claimed the title of the fastest supercomputer on the Top 500 list and demonstrated that vector processing machines had been resurrected from the dead, showing better performance than that of most commodity cluster systems for at least several important application areas. By 2006, heterogeneous systems consisting of vector processors, scalar processors, and a host of multicore-based systems with a variety of accelerators began to enter the market place. This was a direct consequence of energy and heat concerns, which prevented increase in processor speed-up improvements. The videos in this section chronicle many of the events in the aforementioned history of HPC.

## 12.2 Comments about the References in Section 12

There are many available webcasts on the Internet, but unfortunately many are marketing pitches to viewers for hardware, software and/or service products. I have attempted to select a more diverse sample which includes personal HPC historical perspectives [1,3,5,7,10], academic presentations [4,8,17], some balanced HPC product discussions [11–14], two brief HPC applications videos originally shown during the opening ceremonies at the ACM/IEEE Supercomputing Conferences (SC05 and SC06), [2,6], an interesting visualization simulation based on the 9/11 World Trade Center Towers destruction [9] and a Microsoft view of the future potential applications of multicore technology [7]. In addition, videos 6A and 6B describe attributes of IBM Blue Gene/L, and webinars in 6C provide details about the new IBM petaflop class Blue Gene/P. [18] gives an illustration of how desktop computing can interact with a computer cluster via the use of automated parallelism with Star-P. [19] directs you to some Intel webinars focusing on several aspects of multi-core technology.

Videos [15–17] contrast the costs to build three distinctive supercomputers at different price points: The Earth Simulator (a Japanese Government national project) is a vector processor machine designed and built by NEC with an estimated cost of the order of 400M$ [15]. In contrast, a PS3 [16] which costs about 600$ can be used to build a cluster with approximately 10,000 PS3 machines which would have the potential to create one of the fastest computers in the world with some limited constraints with respect to capability; in the middle between the latter two extreme price points, is a system with 1100 Power Mac G5s [17] at a cost of about 5M$ and which has been assembled at Virginia Tech and rated No. 3 on the Top 500 list in 2006. The events and thoughts depicted in all the videos in this section had and are still having significant impact as the HPC area continues to evolve.

## References

[1] Fran Allen, 2006 ACM Turing Award Lecture Video on the Challenges for Software Systems Designers to Develop New Tools, video released on July 31, 2007, http://beta.acm.org/news/featured/turing-2006-lecture-webstream.

[2] ACM/IEEE SC06 Opening video, Powerful beyond Imagination, Tampa, FL, http://sc06.supercomputing.org/video.php, November 2006.

[3] Computer Museum, The Cray-1 Supercomputer: 30th Anniversary Event- Celebrating the Man and the Machine, http://www.computerhistory.org/events/index.php?id=1157047505 or http://archive.computerhistory.org/lectures/the_Cray_1_supercomputer_celebrating_the_man_and_the_machine.lecture.2006.09.21.wmv available for purchase from the Computer History Museum, 1401 N. Shoreline Blvd., Mountain View, CA 94043, September 21, 2006.

[4] Distinguished Lecture Series in Petascale Simulation, Texas Advanced Computing Center (TACC), Austin, TX, the following webcasts are available, see http://petascale.theacesbuilding.com and http://webcast_plugin.theacesbuilding.com includes the following lectures:
David Keyes, Petaflops, Seriously, abstract at http://www.tacc.utexas.edu/petascale/keyes.php, May 23, 2006.
Clint Dawson, Modeling Coastal Hydrodynamics and Hurricanes Katrina and Rita June 22, 2006.
Dimitri Kusnezov, Discovery through Simulation: The Expectations of Frontier Computational Science October 3, 2006.
Omar Ghattas, Towards Forward and Inverse Earthquake Modeling on Petascale Computers October 31, 2006.
Chandrajit Bajaj, Computational Drug Diagnostics and Discovery: The Need for Petascale Computing in the Bio-Sciences November 30, 2006.
John Drake, High Performance Computing and Modeling in Climate Change Science April 12, 2007.
Klaus Schulten, The Computational Microscope May 10, 2007. For a complete list of future and archived lectures in this series, see the following URL: http://www.tacc.utexas.edu/petascale/.

[5] Jack Dongarra, Supercomputers & Clusters & Grids, Oh My, talk given and recorded at Ohio Supercomputer Center, Columbus, OH, January 11, 2007, for a copy contact Stan Ahalt, OSC Executive Director (sca@ee.eng.ohio-state.edu).

[6] DreamWorks Animation SKG, High Performance Computing: Accelerating Innovation to Enhance Everyday Life (shown at SC05) DreamWorks Animation SKG, DVD available for purchase from U.S. Council on Competitiveness, Washington D.C., excerpt preview at http://www.compete.org/hpc/WEB_TRAILER_8-30.mov.

[6A] IBM, Blue Gene: Unsurpassed Performance, Ultrascale Computing, IBM System Blue Gene Solution, http://www-03.ibm.com/servers/deepcomputing/bluegenel.html (click on first video, Blue Gene: Unsurpassed Performance, Ultrascale Computing.)

[6B] IBM, Blue Gene: Unsurpassed Performance, Ultrascale Computing, IBM System Blue Gene Solution, http://www-03.ibm.com/servers/deepcomputing/bluegenel.html (click on second video, IBM Blue Gene Enabling Breakthrough Science, Delivering Competitive Advantage. Full gas turbine burners simulation with AVBP – result of Cerfacs/Turbomeca/IBM collaboration.)

[6C] IBM, View any or all the following four IBM webinars about the new petaflop class IBM Blue Gene/P: Blue Gene/P Overview, Blue Gene/P Technical Deep Dive, Code Enablement on Blue Gene/P, and CFD Codes on Blue Gene/P; all presentation slides can be downloaded for each broadcast. Webinars are archived on line for six months after each live presentation. For more details and to register to view any of these, see http://www-03.ibm.com/servers/deepcomputing/pdf/bg_webcast.pdf.

[7] Mundie C., July 26, 2007. The Computing Pendulum, Microsoft Financial Analyst Meeting, http://www.microsoft.com/msft/speech/FY07/MundieFAM2007.mspx.

[8] Mark Parsons, March 23, 2007. FPGA High Performance Computing Alliance (FHPCA), Brief video of Uses of FPGAs and facilities at University of Edinburgh, video at http://www.fhpca.org/video.html, additional information in FPGA-based Supercomputer Launched in Edinburgh, *HPCWIRE*, Vol. **16**, No. 12, http://www.hpcwire.com/hpc/1325618.html.

[9] Purdue University, Purdue Creates Visual Simulation of 9/11 Attack, *HPCWIRE*, Vol. **16**, No. 24, http://www.hpcwire.com/hpc/1609571.html and simulation video at, http://www.cs.purdue.edu/cgvlab/papers/popescu/popescuWTCVIS07.mov, June 15, 2007.
[10] Horst Simon, June 22, 2005. Lawrence Berkeley National Lab (LBNL) Progress in Supercomputing: The Top Three Breakthroughs of the Last Twenty Years and the Top Three Challenges for the Next Twenty Years, ISC 2005, Heidelberg, video at mms://netshow01.eecs.berkeley.edu/Horst_Simon.
[11] Scientific Computing R & D Magazine, Crossing the Chasm with Microsoft Compute Cluster Edition – HPC Goes Mainstream, One hour panel On-Demand video webcast with Earl Joseph C. II (Vice President, IDC), Barbara Hutchings (ANSYS), Antonio Zurlo (Microsoft), Saifur Rahman (Advanced Research Institute, Virginia Tech) and Tim Studt (Scientific Computing R&D Magazine) serving as Moderator. Register for this free webcast at http://www.scientificcomputing.com/compute.
[12] Scientific Computing R & D Magazine, Emerging Trends in HPC: How HPC Is Joining the Computing Mainstream, One hour On-Demand video webcast with Earl Joseph C. II Vice President, IDC), Simon Cox (School of Engineering Sciences, U of Southampton), Tony Hey, Corporate Vice President for Technical Computing, Microsoft), and Suzanne Tracy (Editor-in-Chief, Scientific Computing Magazine) serving as Moderator. Register for this free webcast at http://www.ScientificComputing.com/mainstream.
[13] Scientific Computing R & D Magazine, Scale-Up Linux Goes Mainstream, One hour On-Demand video webcast with Karthik Prabhakar (HP), John Connolly (Center for Computational Sciences at U of Kentucky), and Gary Skouson (Pacific Northwest National Lab), and Suzanne Tracy (Editor-in-Chief, Scientific Computing R & D Magazine) serving as Moderator. Register for this free webcast at http://www.scientificComputing.com/linux.
[14] Tabor Communications and Microsoft, A Perspective on HPC - 2007 and beyond webcast recorded at SC06, Tampa FL, http://www.taborcommunications. com/hpcwire/webcasts/microsoft/sc06/index.html, November 2006.
[15] You Tube, Japan's Earth Simulator System, Video 31, http://www.youtube.com/watch?v=hrVS45nuIfs&NR=1&v3, June 18, 2007.
[16] You Tube, How a PS3 Can be Used as a Super Computer (hi res version), Video 88, March 19, 2007, http://www.youtube.com/watch?v=P1G6HP6bH1w&mode=related&search= and see The Potential of the Cell Processor for Scientific Computing by Williams S. et al., ACM Intl Conference on Computing Frontiers, available at http://www.cs.berkeley.edu/~samw/projects/cell/CF06.pdf, May 2–6, 2006 and see Engineer Creates Academic Playstation 3 Computing Cluster, http://www.physorg.com/news92674403.html, March 9, 2007.
[17] You Tube, Apple G5 supercomputer at Virginia Tech Amazing, Video 18, http://www.youtube.com/watch?v=vLujLtgBJC0&NR=1, June 14, 2006.
[18] Wilkins-Diehr, N., Parallel Computing with Star-P at San Diego Supercomputer Center, http://www.interactivesupercomputing.com/success/sdsc/
[19] Intel, Multi-Core is Mainstream: Are You Ready? Intel Software Developer Webinars are available online live and archived. For details and to register, visit http://event.on24.com/event/36/88/3/rt/1.

# Author Index

Numbers in *italics* indicate the pages on which complete references are given.

## Y



## Z

# Subject Index

**E**



**F**



**G**

## H



## I



## J



## K



## L

## M



## N



## O



## P

## R



## S

# Contents of Volumes in This Series

**Volume 52**

Eras of Business Computing
ALAN R. HEVNER AND DONALD J. BERNDT
Numerical Weather Prediction
FERDINAND BAER
Machine Translation
SERGEI NIRENBURG AND YORICK WILKS
The Games Computers (and People) Play
JONATHAN SCHAEFFER
From Single Word to Natural Dialogue
NEILS OLE BENSON AND LAILA DYBKJAER
Embedded Microprocessors: Evolution, Trends and Challenges
MANFRED SCHLETT

**Volume 53**

Shared-Memory Multiprocessing: Current State and Future Directions
PER STEUSTRÖM, ERIK HAGERSTEU, DAVID I. LITA, MARGARET MARTONOSI, AND MADAN VERNGOPAL
Shared Memory and Distributed Shared Memory Systems: A Survey
KRISHNA KAUI, HYONG-SHIK KIM, BEU LEE, AND A. R. HURSON
Resource-Aware Meta Computing
JEFFREY K. HOLLINGSWORTH, PETER J. KELCHER, AND KYUNG D. RYU
Knowledge Management
WILLIAM W. AGRESTI
A Methodology for Evaluating Predictive Metrics
JASRETT ROSENBERG
An Empirical Review of Software Process Assessments
KHALED EL EMAM AND DENNIS R. GOLDENSON
State of the Art in Electronic Payment Systems
N. ASOKAN, P. JANSON, M. STEIVES, AND M. WAIDNES
Defective Software: An Overview of Legal Remedies and Technical Measures Available to Consumers
COLLEEN KOTYK VOSSLER AND JEFFREY VOAS

**Volume 54**

An Overview of Components and Component-Based Development
ALAN W. BROWN
Working with UML: A Software Design Process Based on Inspections for the Unified Modeling Language
GUILHERME H. TRAVASSOS, FORREST SHULL, AND JEFFREY CARVER
Enterprise JavaBeans and Microsoft Transaction Server: Frameworks for Distributed Enterprise Components
AVRAHAM LEFF, JOHN PROKOPEK, JAMES T. RAYFIELD, AND IGNACIO SILVA-LEPE
Maintenance Process and Product Evaluation Using Reliability, Risk, and Test Metrics
NORMAN F. SCHNEIDEWIND
Computer Technology Changes and Purchasing Strategies
GERALD V. POST
Secure Outsourcing of Scientific Computations
MIKHAIL J. ATALLAH, K. N. PANTAZOPOULOS, JOHN R. RICE, AND EUGENE SPAFFORD

**Volume 61**



**Volume 62**



**Volume 63**